ST. THOMAS AQUINAS AND THE NATURAL LAW TRADITION

ST. THOMAS AQUINAS AND THE NATURAL LAW TRADITION

Contemporary Perspectives

EDITED BY
John Goyette, Mark S. Latkovic, and Richard S. Myers

The Catholic University of America Press
Washington, D.C.

Copyright © 2004
The Catholic University of America Press
All rights reserved
The paper used in this publication meets the minimum requirements of American
National Standards for Information Science—Permanence of Paper for Printed
Library materials, ANSI Z39.48-1984.

∞

Library of Congress Cataloging-in-Publication Data
St. Thomas Aquinas and the natural law tradition : contemporary perspectives /
edited by John
Goyette, Mark S. Latkovic, and Richard S. Myers.
p. cm.
Papers from a conference held in June 2000 in Michigan.
Includes bibliographical references (p.) and index.
ISBN 0-8132-1378-9 (alk. paper)
ISBN 978-0-8132-1399-1 (pbk. : alk. paper)
1. Thomas, Aquinas, Saint, 1225?–1274-Congresses. 2. Natural law-Congresses.
3. Natural law-Religious aspects-Catholic Church-Congresses. I. Title: Saint
Thomas Aquinas and the natural law tradition. II. Goyette, John, 1969–
III. Latkovic, Mark S., 1963–   IV. Myers, Richard S., 1955–   V. Title.
B765.T54S7 2005
171´.2-dc22
2003021546

CONTENTS

Acknowledgments vii
Introduction ix

PART I. PHILOSOPHICAL FOUNDATIONS OF THE NATURAL LAW

1. *Benedict M. Ashley, O.P.*, The Anthropological Foundations of the Natural Law: A Thomistic Engagement with Modern Science 3

   RESPONSE

   Janet E. Smith, Character as an Enabler of Moral Judgment 17

2. *Ralph McInerny*, Thomistic Natural Law and Aristotelian Philosophy 25

PART II. NATURAL LAW IN A THEOLOGICAL CONTEXT

3. *David Novak*, Maimonides and Aquinas on Natural Law 43

   RESPONSES

   Martin D. Yaffe, Natural Law in Maimonides? 66

   John Goyette, Natural Law and the Metaphysics of Creation 74

4. *Romanus Cessario, O.P.*, Why Aquinas Locates Natural Law within the *Sacra Doctrina* 79

   RESPONSES

   Robert Fastiggi, Natural Reason in the Service of Faith 94

   Earl Muller, S.J., The Christological Foundation of Natural Law 102

PART III. THE NEW NATURAL LAW THEORY

5. *William E. May,* Contemporary Perspectives on
   Thomistic Natural Law 113
   RESPONSE
   Mark S. Latkovic, Natural Law and Specific Moral Norms 157

6. *Steven A. Long,* Natural Law or Autonomous Practical Reason:
   Problems for the New Natural Law Theory 165

PART IV. LAW AND POLITICS

7. *Christopher Wolfe,* Thomistic Natural Law and the
   American Natural Law Tradition 197
   RESPONSE
   William Mathie, Aquinas, Locke, and Lincoln in the
   American Regime 229

8. *Robert P. George,* Kelsen and Aquinas on the
   Natural Law Doctrine 237

9. *Russell Hittinger,* Thomas Aquinas on Natural Law
   and the Competence to Judge 261

   Contributors 285
   Works Cited 295
   Index 309

ACKNOWLEDGMENTS

The editors want to note that a version of Russell Hittinger's paper appears as chapter 4 of his *The First Grace: Rediscovering the Natural Law in a Post-Christian World*. A version of the paper by Romanus Cesssario, O.P., forms part of chapter 2 of his *An Introduction to Moral Theology*. Permission from, respectively, ISI Books and The Catholic University of America Press to reprint these two papers is thankfully acknowledged. A version of Robert P. George's paper first appeared in *Notre Dame Law Review* and is reprinted here with permission of the author.

The editors also want to thank the Rev. John Bustamante and Mr. Albert A. Starkus III for providing invaluable assistance in the preparation of the manuscript, as well as Ave Maria School of Law for its financial support, and Sacred Heart Major Seminary for both its financial support and its hospitality in hosting the conference upon which the volume is based.

John Goyette
Mark S. Latkovic
Richard S. Myers

INTRODUCTION

We are in the midst of a great revival of interest in natural law. Much of this thinking is traced in one degree or another to the thought of St. Thomas Aquinas. In the area of moral philosophy and moral theology the works of Father Martin Rhonheimer and Servais Pinckaers, O.P., come to mind. In recent years, Aquinas has also influenced the works of leading political and legal philosophers. John Finnis's book—*Aquinas: Moral, Political, and Legal Theory*—is just one example, although there is much debate about whether Finnis's work can be said to follow the teaching of Aquinas. That St. Thomas's understanding of natural law is the subject of debate, however, testifies to the renewed interest in the Common Doctor. Indeed, the recent attention to Thomistic natural law has sparked a greater interest in other areas of Aquinas's thought. This is not surprising. His natural law doctrine is embedded in a larger philosophical and theological context. For instance, natural law theory requires a normative view of nature, one that implicitly rejects a purely mechanistic natural science in favor of a philosophy of nature that appeals to formal and final causality. An account of natural law also requires certain metaphysical and theological presuppositions since it presumes that nature is governed by divine providence. In many ways the recent interest in natural law resonates with Pope John Paul II's *Veritatis splendor* and confirms his comment in *Fides et ratio* about the enduring originality of the thought of St. Thomas Aquinas.

All but one of the papers in this volume were originally presented at a conference on "St. Thomas Aquinas and the Natural Law Tradition" in June 2000. The conference was cosponsored by Sacred Heart Major Seminary (Detroit, Michigan) and Ave Maria School of Law (Ann Arbor, Michigan). Not all of the responses presented at the conference are included in the collection. The volume is divided into four parts, beginning with a part discussing some of the philosophical foundations of natural law, especially the understanding of nature it presupposes. The second part is devoted to the theological context in which St. Thomas's natural law doctrine is situated. The papers in the third part discuss the new natural law theory espoused by Germain Grisez and John Finnis and the hotly debated question as to whether their theory is genuinely Thomistic. Finally, the papers in the fourth part turn to Aquinas's natural law doctrine in the context of contemporary legal and political issues.

Part I: Philosophical Foundations of the Natural Law

First, natural law presupposes an account of nature that makes human freedom possible. The problem, however, is that the mechanistic tendencies of modern natural science appear to call into question human freedom. Second, natural law presupposes a moral law rooted in nature. The difficulty here is twofold. Nature is usually distinguished from what is the product of human deliberation and design. How, then, can we reconcile human freedom with obedience to the moral law? The solution to this difficulty lies in the distinction between the ultimate end, which is fixed by nature, and the means to the end, which is subject to human deliberation and choice. The natural desire for the ultimate end, which is encapsulated in the first principle of the natural law ("do good and avoid evil"), is the starting point of all moral reasoning. But this raises a second difficulty, at least for Christian thinkers such as St. Thomas: If natural law is based upon our natural end, how can natural law be reconciled with a supernatural goal? If our ultimate end is eternal beatitude, isn't the natural law vitiated by grace? The solution to this problem, for St. Thomas, seems to rest upon a distinction between a formal account of man's ultimate end—one that is founded upon our natural desire for the good—and the concrete realization of this end which, as it turns out, is supernatural in character. The papers in this part explore these issues.

Benedict M. Ashley, O.P., defends the notion of human freedom and the natural moral law in the context of modern natural science. He takes up first the task of clearing away confusion with respect to the terms "nature," "chance," and "freedom." The natural moral law is so often rejected today, Ashley argues, precisely because in fact "these concepts are confused and their interrelationship misconstrued." He shows, for instance, that the universal determinism championed by early modern science presupposes a notion of nature that eliminates both chance and freedom. Determinism, however, is not supported by more recent scientific evidence that points to the role of chance and deliberate human design in the workings of the cosmos.

Second, Ashley finds that Aquinas's account of the human person "provides a more secure basis for psychology than the many warring theories in this field have been able to supply." Central to St. Thomas's theory of human nature is his account of the immateriality of the human soul, which Ashley defends against those who attempt to reduce human intelligence to the mechanisms of the brain. Immateriality is a necessary precondition for the moral law, Ashley notes, since "spiritual beings, because they transcend the determinism of natural law and of chance, have a *responsibility* for their own lives." But this implies the need for a science of ethics. Hence, Ashley turns to Aquinas's understanding of the natural moral law as the exemplification of this ethical theory.

For Aquinas, the natural law includes, first, "a concrete understanding of the supreme goal [of human life] and the subordinate goals that we must seek to be happy," and, second, a "true understanding of the various means to this supreme goal and its integrated subordinate goals," that is, the means we need to adopt if happiness is to be truly realized. Ashley concludes by articulating the three levels of natural law precepts or principles, along with examples of them, characteristic of Aquinas's approach to the natural moral law.

Janet E. Smith develops some points found in Ashley's paper. From the perspective of Aristotelian/Thomistic epistemology and anthropology, she shows how to defend, against ethical relativism, the objectivity of moral judgments. Smith also explains how a Thomist would understand the expression "the natural law is written on ours hearts," and defends the importance of moral virtue for natural law. Indeed, she argues that "virtue has primacy over moral norms in Thomistic natural law ethics."

Ralph McInerny argues that the fundamental structure of St. Thomas's moral thinking and his understanding of the first principles of the natural law are based upon the philosophy of Aristotle. While McInerny is opposed to those Thomists who seek to equate Thomism with Aristotelian philosophy, he seeks to counter a kind of anti-Aristotelianism that can be found among many Thomists. In the area of moral philosophy, this anti-Aristotelianism is exemplified by Jacques Maritain, who posits a split between Aristotle and St. Thomas regarding the nature of the human good. According to Maritain, since moral philosophy can only be practical if it guides us to our ultimate end, and since our ultimate end in the present order of divine providence is eternal beatitude, Aristotelian moral philosophy cannot serve as an adequate guide to the moral order. The problem here arises from Aristotle's account of man's ultimate end as a comprehensive good, one that leaves nothing to be desired. Since St. Thomas, guided by his Christian faith, gives an account of the comprehensive good that differs from Aristotle, it seems that we must choose between two rival accounts of the human good. McInerny avoids Maritain's conclusion by making a distinction between Aristotle's formal account of the ultimate end as a comprehensive good and his account of its concrete realization. McInerny notes that St. Thomas, based upon his reading of the *Nicomachean Ethics,* concluded that Aristotle did not believe that human happiness—the comprehensive human good that Aristotle articulates in his formal account—could be perfectly realized in this life. This paves the way for St. Thomas to subsume Aristotle's account of the ultimate end into the Christian vision of the ultimate end, one that overcomes the vicissitudes of this life.

The fundamental agreement between Aristotelian and Thomistic moral philosophy regarding man's ultimate end naturally leads to the subject of natural law, since natural law is a precept or command to do that which leads to the end. Hence, those who see an opposition between the moral part of the *Summa theologiae* (which emphasizes prudence and the moral virtues, in a manner reminiscent of Aristotle) and the treatment of law, have failed to attend to the fact that precepts of the natural law, no matter how mundane, are nonetheless ordered to the ultimate good. McInerny argues that the influence of Aristotle in St. Thomas's account of natural law is most obvious in the description of the first principles of the natural law as analogous to the starting points of speculative reasoning. The "precepts of the natural law are the last fallback position in moral argument" because such principles are so evident, so etched in the heart of man, that they can never be completely eradicated. Nowhere is this more evident than in the first precept of the natural law: to seek the good and to avoid evil. McInerny notes that no matter how much we may fail to grasp the particulars of the moral life, no one can fail to desire the ultimate good: "A remark of

Chesterton's has always seemed to me to capture the comprehensive nature of the good in Aristotle and Thomas: the young man knocking on the brothel door, Chesterton remarked, is looking for God." McInerny concludes by stressing Thomas's reliance upon Aristotle, his use of him as "an authority and ally," and cites the relationship between Aquinas and Aristotle as "a particular instance of the way the believer must engage in philosophy if he is to engage in theology."

Part II: Natural Law in a Theological Context

Although natural law theory is often thought to provide a strictly philosophical account of the human good, it inevitably raises theological questions. This is due in part to the fact that natural law presupposes a divine lawgiver. As St. Thomas notes, "[N]atural law is nothing other than the rational creature's participation in the eternal law." Questions abound, however, when we attempt to spell out the relation between natural law as a subject of moral philosophy and the theological context it presupposes. Can one articulate a natural law theory without some kind of theological foundation? Is it possible to supply this foundation by means of natural theology, that is, metaphysics, or does it require divine revelation? Not surprisingly, natural law has become the focus of questions concerning the relations between faith and reason and nature and grace. The papers in this section explore some of these questions.

David Novak aims to compare and contrast the relation between natural law and divine law in Maimonides and Aquinas as a way of exploring the broader question of the relation between nature and grace. He first tries to establish that Maimonides has a doctrine of natural law. Although Maimonides never uses the term "natural law," Novak argues that Maimonides's account of the Noahide laws ("the commandments of the children of Noah") in the Mishneh Torah is similar, if not equivalent, to a natural law teaching. The Noahide laws are moral norms that are binding on all human beings and can be understood from "the inclination of reason" apart from revelation. Novak's claim to find a natural law teaching in Maimonides is controversial: there are disputed texts from the Mishneh Torah suggesting that the man who accepts Noahide laws out of rational inclination rather than because they are commanded by God is neither wise nor pious. According to Novak, Maimonides's hesitation to treat Noahide law apart from the Mosaic Torah is not because he doubts that the Noahide law is known by rational inclination, but because the Noahide law needs to be completed by Mosaic law: "to see natural law apart from its metaphysical ground is to make human reason rather than divine wisdom the measure of all things." Natural/Noahide law is a necessary, but not a sufficient, condition for human happiness. For Maimonides, natural/Noahide law is the universal precondition for the acceptance of the divine law.

Novak goes on to show that Aquinas views the relation between the Old Law and the New Law in a way similar to Maimonides's view of the relation between Noahide law and Mosaic law. In both cases, the relation is construed as one of potency to act: the later law contains and completes the earlier one. For Aquinas, the continued validity of the Old Law lies in its superior constitution of natural law which, like Maimonides's Noahide law, is necessary but insufficient for human perfection. Novak notes that both Maimonides and Aquinas insist that the divine law contains a natural law doctrine because they both recognize the fundamental importance of combating fideism. Yet Maimonides and Aquinas differ regarding the broader question of nature and grace since Maimonides ultimately admits no real distinction between natural law and supernatural law. "In principle, all the laws of the Torah have universalizable reasons that can be rationally intended here and now. All of them are, thus, natural law in principle." The rationalism of Maimonides was opposed, of course, by those theologians who inclined toward the opposite extreme, the kabbalists, who tended to reduce all of the commandments to the work of grace, not nature. St. Thomas's natural law doctrine appears to be a mean between the rationalistic tendencies of Maimonides and the fideistic tendencies of the kabbalists.

Martin D. Yaffe raises some questions about Novak's attempt to find a natural law doctrine in Maimonides. Yaffe argues that the fact that Maimonides nowhere uses the term "natural law" ought to be taken as a sign that he does not have a natural law teaching. Indeed, he argues that the absence of the term is explained by the fact that Maimonides's view is finally much closer to Plato and Aristotle than to Aquinas, and Plato and Aristotle do not have a natural law teaching. In response to Novak's appeal to the Mishneh Torah as evidence of a natural law teaching in Maimonides, Yaffe argues for the theoretical superiority of the *Guide of the Perplexed* which, he claims, does not support a natural law doctrine. Finally, Yaffe expresses doubts about Novak's passing remark that "it might well be fantastic to attempt to engage in the type of Aristotelian metaphysics that occupied both

[Maimonides and Aquinas]." Yaffe suggests that we need to engage in some kind of metaphysical speculation if we are to accurately address such pressing moral issues as the natural bonds of the family and "the terra incognita of human cloning."

John Goyette also raises doubts about finding a natural law teaching in Maimonides, but he does so by examining the question from the perspective of St. Thomas. Given Maimonides's claim that one cannot rationally demonstrate the creation of the world, he questions whether one can make the case for a natural law doctrine in Maimonides. Natural law presupposes a divine lawgiver, and this in turn requires a creator and providential governor of the cosmos. Absent a metaphysics of creation, one cannot attain a rationally knowable moral law. Aquinas recognizes that for most men, however, the knowledge of God necessary to know the natural law is supplied by divine revelation rather than by rational demonstration. According to Goyette, this is not because such knowledge is naturally unknowable; rather, it is because original sin has so clouded man's reason that he is in need of divine revelation. Thus, Goyette concludes, "Aquinas differs from Maimonides to the extent that he defends the possibility of knowing, in principle, the content of the precepts of the natural law by means of unaided human reason."

Romanus Cessario, O.P., wants to show that the theologian can competently address the topic of natural law since St. Thomas himself locates it within sacred doctrine. First, he clarifies the relationship between the notions of divine wisdom, the eternal law, and Jesus Christ—Incarnate Son of God and Eternal Logos. In doing so, he articulates Vatican II's teaching that it is only Jesus Christ who fully reveals man to himself (cf. *Gaudium et spes,* 22). Because he is the divine "Logos-Son, Christ, 'the image of the invisible God, the first born of all creation' (Col 1:15), he embodies and displays," Cessario explains, "the definitive shape or form that the order of human existence should take in the world." In clarifying how "the eternal Word provides the pattern" for good moral action, Cessario shows that the "appropriation of eternal law to the Word of God, the eternal Son of the Father," goes beyond the idea of the God-man as a sort of external model of upright conduct for Christians to imitate. Rather, by taking on our human nature, Christ *divinizes* that same nature, thereby restoring "to the offspring of Adam the divine likeness that had been deformed since the first sin" (cf. *Gaudium et spes,* 22).

Second, Cessario turns his attention to why the moral realist would "describe eternal law as how God knows the world to be." Cessario rejects the voluntarism typical of late-fourteenth-century nominalism as "an appropriate context for understanding eternal law as an expression of the divine creative wisdom." He argues that acceptance of what he calls the "Logos pattern of the created order" does not imply that "Christian theology espouses [at the other extreme from nominalism's stress on God's absolute freedom] a form of determinism." In other words, eternal law and human freedom are ultimately compatible realities.

Finally, Cessario, in discussing eternal law and salvation, analyzes both human knowledge of this eternal law and the extent to which various creatures participate in it. His main point here is that theologically, "the eternal law undergirds the economy of salvation that is accomplished definitively by the promulgation of the new law of grace." This leads him to describe the harmony between law and grace. Furthermore, it leads Cessario to conclude that "[a] properly theological appreciation of natural law arises only within the context of the Trinitarian ordering of human existence that flows from what the tradition has identified as the eternal law." Aquinas understood this truth, and thus included natural law within the framework of the *sacra doctrina*.

Robert Fastiggi offers a friendly criticism of the views set forth by Cessario, noting five points that he believes could be better thought out. First, Fastiggi thinks that Cessario needs to specify more clearly what Aquinas means by *sacra doctrina*. He argues that there are good reasons for thinking that Aquinas uses *sacra doctrina* in a broader sense than the order of divine faith. Second, pace Cessario, he thinks that "the significance of Christ for the created moral order—even prior to the Incarnation—was not something foreign" to either Aquinas or the Catholic tradition. Third, although he agrees with Cessario on the dangers of extreme forms of voluntarism, Fastiggi wants to note "the importance of God's will in the establishment of the moral law in the created order." Fourth, Fastiggi argues that Cessario has mischaracterized the centuries-old debate between the Dominican Thomists and the Jesuit Molinists as one of freedom versus law. Finally, Fastiggi argues, contrary to Cessario, that "insight into the loving nature of God does not seem to have occurred only in the first century of our era."

The response of *Earl Muller*, S.J., begins with the affirmation—one he thinks might go too far for Cessario, despite his Christological and Trinitarian focus—that natural law must be understood "within a fundamentally ecclesial context, which is to say, within a fundamentally Christological context." To argue this point, Muller revisits the mid-twentieth-century debates between Chenu and Gilson, on the one hand, and Hayen and Rondet, on the other, over the structure of the *Summa theologiae*. Muller follows the view of Corbin, who held that the unity of the *Summa* "resides in Christ, the God-man." He then develops three indications for thinking that Aquinas "understands the humanity of the *secunda* in terms of Christ." Muller concludes by arguing that although Aquinas gives a role to apologetics, in practice, "[n]atural law theory can only be successfully pursued by someone who has been converted to Christ, by someone who is part of the ecclesial context that is the primary referent of Thomas's understanding of natural law."

Part III: The New Natural Law Theory

For the past four decades, Germain Grisez—often in collaboration with John Finnis, Joseph Boyle, William E. May, and others—has articulated a theory of natural law usually identified as the "new natural law theory" or the "theory of basic human goods." While the influence of this theory is no doubt partially responsible for the recent revival of natural law thinking, it has also sparked considerable debate. Notable for its emphasis on the inviolability of (eight) incommensurable basic human goods, this theory is rejected by proportionalist moral theologians for, among other reasons, its defense of moral absolutes. However, proportionalists are not the only ones who reject major tenets of the Grisez school. Many Thomist scholars, among them Ralph McInery, Russell Hittinger, and Benedict Ashley, who otherwise admire this school for its defense of moral absolutes, question whether the Grisezian approach is, in fact, a theory of natural law—or at least a theory that can claim Thomistic provenance. Indeed, the editors disagree among themselves about whether the Grisez school is truly Thomistic in character.

The authors in this part treat such contested areas as the following: the relationship between the theoretical and the practical order; the is/ought problem; the nature of the first principle or precept of the natural law; the question of whether the human goods are ordered in a hierarchy; the role that prudence plays in the derivation of specific moral norms; and the role of God and divine providence in ethical theory.

William E. May provides a comprehensive overview and critique of some recent natural law thinking among American philosophers and theologians. May's summary of the contemporary natural law thought of Pamela Hall, Benedict Ashley, Ralph McInerny, and the Grisez school focuses on, among other things, how these thinkers define the natural law, how they understand its first principle of practical reasoning, and how they understand the ordering of the needs and goods of the natural law (i.e., the question of hierarchy). His paper also addresses their views of how we come to know the precepts of the natural law and how we derive specific moral norms from the first principles of the natural law. After summarizing the thought of each thinker on these points, May offers various criticisms against the positions taken by the authors and does so on explicitly Thomistic grounds. Throughout the paper, May is concerned with two questions as he considers the disagreement between Hall, Ashley, and McInerny and the views of the Grisez school: (1) How faithful are the authors to Aquinas's own thought?; and (2) Are the ideas of these thinkers objectively true?

May also aims to defend the new natural law theory. May briefly summarizes its main tenets; responds to the criticisms of Hall, Ashley, and McInerny; and then offers two criticisms of his own that deal with the place of virtue and with the question of the "moral good" being a good of the person in Grisez et al. These latter criticisms are offered from the perspective of one who is in fundamental agreement with the Grisez school, but who is nonetheless puzzled by these aspects of their thought.

Mark S. Latkovic's sympathetic response to May's paper does two things. First, Latkovic summarizes May's overview of recent natural law thinkers, noting areas of agreement and disagreement among them. Second, Latkovic expands upon an issue raised by May: How does one derive specific moral norms from the first and general principles of the natural law? Against the views of Hall, Ashley, McInerny, and Rhonheimer, which emphasize the virtue of prudence, Latkovic defends a position rooted in the thought of Grisez et al.

Steven A. Long critically examines the new natural law theory with particular attention to the work of John Finnis. Long zeroes in on a tendency he finds in this theory that, he argues, is expressed in Kant's argument for an ethic founded solely on practical reason, in which law is understood not as subject to God's eternal law, but as merely the product of the rational agent's mind. Despite the fact that Grisez et al. believe in God, they do not hold, contrary to St. Thomas, either that God is first in our knowledge of the natural law or that God is even necessary to a natural law theory. They fail to see that natural law, according to Aquinas, is not merely the product of natural reason, "it is the normative theological and metaphysical order that undergirds, makes possible, and flows into our moral logic."

Long focuses on two areas that not only address the new natural law theory, but which indirectly address the more general distance of modern and postmodern thinkers from St. Thomas's approach, with their favoring of ethical *autonomy* in rationalist terms. First, Long shows the central importance Thomas accords to the priority of the speculative to the practical in matters of ethics. Second, he argues that a robust theonomic understanding of natural law, such as we find in St. Thomas, implies that the liberty of the rational moral agent is subject to God's causality and therefore also to his providence.

With respect to the first point, Long argues against the view of Finnis that the basic human goods are not derived from any principles of speculative reason. He argues that for St. Thomas speculative knowledge is prior to practical knowledge because practical knowledge must contain a prior adequation of the mind which is then further ordered toward operation. Long claims that the new natural law theorists "confuse the truth that certain propositions by their nature bear essentially upon action—and hence are practical—with the distinct character of the knowing that is *presupposed by* such propositions *in order that they may be able to bear upon action.*" He argues that the theory of basic human goods posited by the new natural law theorists is essentially "a category of truth with no speculative content," while for St. Thomas the grasp of "speculative content—even by the practical intellect—is required by the very nature of knowledge itself." Besides this formal element of the priority of the speculative to the practical, Long also argues that there is a material element betokened to us through the formal priority of the speculative in moral philosophy: the Thomistic notion of the "hierarchy of ends prior to choice," in contradistinction to the new natural law view that the basic goods are incommensurable, that is, "not normatively ordered prior to choice."

With respect to the second point, Long explores the practical implications of those who suppose, wrongly, that "moral responsibility requires a liberty of indifference" with respect to God's causality. This error explains the "antinomian disposition" concerning the normativity of the natural law that constitutes the major feature of moral reflection in both the previous and the current century. Indeed, Long argues, "it is a remote reflection of this error" that accounts for Grisez et al.'s reluctance to use the term "natural law" since it implies that "the human agent is naturally subject to the author and promulgator of the law," that is, God. But, he queries, if man's freedom "is indeed absolute with respect to divine causality as such, then in what sense can the rational creature be *naturally subject* to divine governance?" According to Long, one must in truth affirm with St. Thomas that acts of the rational will "are both free and caused by God." He argues that St. Thomas's definition of the natural law as the rational creature's participation in the eternal law "requires and implies that the liberty of the rational moral agent is subject to divine causality and therefore to divine providence." Long concludes his paper by arguing that those who, like Grisez et al., "do not center their account of moral law on the ordinance of God do not according to St. Thomas Aquinas so much as *possess* a doctrine of natural law." In sum, with their theory, as with Kant's, we have nothing (except, according to Long, for the basic goods) of "the ethical normativity of the metaphysical and teleological order" that in essence defines St. Thomas's natural law doctrine.

Part IV: Law and Politics

As noted earlier, Aquinas's thought is being explored with great fruitfulness in contemporary legal and political philosophy. The authors in this part consider such themes as the relationship between Thomistic natural law and the American natural law tradition, the critique of natural law theory from a leading positivist legal philosopher of the twentieth century, and the obligation of a judge with respect to natural law. This last theme—the role of a judge with respect to natural law—is one of the most contentious issues in modern American constitutional law, and it is worthy of note that even here the writings of Aquinas have much to contribute.

Christopher Wolfe focuses on the nature of the relationship between Thomistic natural law and the American natural law tradition. After briefly describing Thomistic natural law and the modern tradition of natural rights, Wolfe considers the use of natural law in American political history. Wolfe concludes that "[t]he fact of the matter is that the more influential forms of 'natural law' in America have been forms of modern natural rights theory, and the influence of more traditional or Thomistic natural law theory has been quite limited." Wolfe does note, however, that "it may be possible to find in the American natural law tradition important sources of support for principles central to the older natural law theory." The classical/medieval and American natural law traditions share a similar moral perspective.

Wolfe goes on to discuss the unraveling of this shared perspective in the twentieth century, especially since the 1960s. After reviewing more recent developments in contemporary America, Wolfe concludes that the influence of natural law is still "quite weak, and it remains, for the most part, at the margin of American intellectual and public life." His focus here is on the distance between natural law thought and the philosophy dominant in the academy and in the political and social institutions of America, particularly in decisions of the U. S. Supreme Court. Nevertheless, Wolfe sees several bright spots. He notes that "Americans as a whole continue to resist the more radical tendencies of intellectual elites," that "there is a limited, but growing respectability of certain forms of natural law in the academy and intellectual life," and that there is "growing interest in natural law outside Catholic intellectual circles." He concludes by outlining a program for "the emergence of a whole new cohort of young natural law scholars and of political writers and activists who respect and draw on natural law thought."

William Mathie's response to Wolfe's paper focuses on the difference between Locke ("the teacher of those who founded the American regime") and Thomistic natural law. Mathie points out that this difference is indeed stark, but that there is support for principles central to the older natural law theory "in the perceptions or misperceptions of that teaching entertained by an earlier generation of Americans." Mathie concludes his response by suggesting that the moral and political insufficiency of the Lockean and Jeffersonian understanding can be addressed by Abraham Lincoln's understanding of the nature of the American regime.

Robert P. George revisits Hans Kelsen's influential essay "The Natural-Law Doctrine before the Tribunal of Science." George considers the extent to which Kelsen's account of the natural law adequately describes Aquinas's natural law doctrine, and therefore whether Kelsen's critique undermines the teaching of Aquinas. George concludes that Kelsen's treatment of natural law "has virtually no points of contact with Aquinas's thought. Hence, Kelsen's critique . . . has little or no applicability to Thomistic natural law theory."

First, George establishes that Kelsen's understanding of natural law is at sharp variance with Aquinas's account of natural law. In particular, George explains that Aquinas is not guilty of committing the naturalistic fallacy, which Kelsen had attributed to "the natural law doctrine," and that natural law need not "collapse . . . into a form of ethical noncognitivism." George then critiques Kelsen's claim that natural law theory renders positive law superfluous. According to George, "Aquinas holds that positive law is necessary *both* because actual human beings sometimes need the threat of punishment to deter them from doing what the natural law already proscribes . . . as a matter of basic justice *and* because authoritative stipulations are frequently needed to coordinate action for sake of the common good." Finally, George takes up Kelsen's charge that natural law theory merges the categories of "moral" and "legal" and that this theory ends up "as an ideological apologetic for existing regimes. . . ." George argues that Kelsen has set up a strawman in an attempt to discredit all of natural law thinking. According to George, Aquinas "deploys the term 'law' in an appropriately flexible way to take into account the differences between the demands of (1) intrasystemic legal analysis or argumentation . . . ; (2) what we would call 'descriptive' social theory . . . ; and (3) fully critical (i.e., 'normative,' 'moral,' conscience-informing) discourse." Moreover, Aquinas "plainly does not embrace Kelsen's alleged 'dogma that under the law of nature there is no or only a restricted right of resistance.'" In the end, the curiosity in Kelsen's treatment of natural law is that the "tribunal of science" does not come to grips with "the thought of so central an exponent of the natural law tradition."

Russell Hittinger considers the obligation of a judge with respect to natural law. More specifically, he considers whether "a judge qua judge ha[s] the authority to ignore or change laws, or to remit sentences required by laws, on the basis of his judgment of what is required by natural law." Hittinger attempts to focus on what Aquinas says about judges and natural law and avoids, for the most part, speculating about what St. Thomas might have said about the judicial usurpation of politics by American courts.

Hittinger begins by making some general remarks about law and natural law. He asks "'What is law *in*'?" For Aquinas, law is essentially in the mind of the legislator, and this "is the ground for Thomas's doctrine of original intent, as well as his insistence that the judge must sometimes favor the intent rather than the written words of the legislator." Hittinger then discusses the nature of jurisprudence and the difference between the roles of legislators and judges. He explains the limited position of a judge who must obey both natural law (just as everyone must) and also the law made by the human legislator. The judge is a servant who enjoys delegated authority and must, in judging, appeal to the law that is in the mind of the legislator.

Finally, Hittinger turns to the question of what a judge should do if he has reason to think that the law of the legislator somehow falls short of, or is contrary to, the natural law? For contemporary purposes the most interesting portion of this discussion is Hittinger's estimation that "Thomas's understanding of equity does not permit the judge to prefer natural law to the law of the human legislator. The judge can bring natural law into the picture only on the assumption that this or that precept of natural law is what the legislator had in mind, and which is contained in a materially defective (but not morally defective) way in the written statute." Aquinas does not believe, however, that a judge can enforce a human law that requires some action contrary to the natural law. As Hittinger quotes, "'judgment should not be delivered according to'" such laws. But even here, St. Thomas "does not say that one is entitled to make a new rule and measure, for that would imply legislative authority. A corrupt law does not give the judge a license to legislate." As Hittinger notes, "Thomas, however, would not allow a freewheeling appeal to natural law, even for a constitutional court. . . ." In regard to the contemporary debates about the role of American courts, Hittinger's conclusion—based on his reading of Aquinas—is clear: "even in the extreme case of refusing to render judgment, the judge, insofar as he is a judge, is not entitled to plough ahead and substitute his own law for that of the legislator."

PART I

PHILOSOPHICAL FOUNDATIONS OF THE NATURAL LAW

I

THE ANTHROPOLOGICAL FOUNDATIONS OF THE NATURAL LAW

A Thomistic Engagement with Modern Science

Benedict M. Ashley, O.P.

The nature-nurture debate goes on acrimoniously today among experts in different fields. Thus E. O. Wilson, the sociobiologist, tries to explain human behavior by evolutionary genetics, while another expert, Richard C. Lewontin, denounces sociobiology as a pseudoscience.[1] The debate usually ends with the banal agreement that nature and nurture "interact" in such a complex way that no workable criteria can be found to determine their respective contributions to human behavior. This agreement, however, does not put an end to the controversy. Why this impasse? The term "nature" is inescapable in science since by "science" we mean *natural* science not the sciences of pure mathematics, ethics, theology, and so on. We also speak of *natural* laws and we distinguish *artificial* objects or *artifacts* made by humans from *natural* objects.

Moreover, reliable criteria are used by scientists to distinguish whether

---

1. For a history of the controversy, see Ullica Segerstrale, *Defenders of the Truth: The Battle for Science in the Sociobiology Debate and Beyond* (New York: Oxford University Press, 2000), esp. chap. 3, 35–52.

an observed phenomenon can or cannot be explained by natural law. Thus scientists measure Newton's natural law of gravitation by observing the mutual attraction of massive bodies. In practice this is quite difficult because gravity is a very weak force and the observations can be easily disturbed by *chance* influences. Yet no one doubts that it is possible with proper ingenuity to devise methods that will determine gravitational force to a high degree of accuracy. Thus all of scientific knowledge depends on observations, sometimes requiring elaborate techniques, by which "natural" events are distinguished from those that are by *chance* or due to *artificial* human intervention. Thus "nature" is that uniform or regular behavior that things are observed to exhibit when isolated from the interventions of chance or deliberate human design.

If we understand the term "nature" as does physics, there is, in principle, no difficulty in separating what is natural in human behavior from what is not. All that is necessary is to observe human behavior and then leave out all features of that behavior that are not universal, regular, and uniform. When this is attempted, of course, it becomes obvious that human behavior is so variable that much of it cannot be considered "natural" and therefore has to be ascribed to chance or artifice. But there is a verifiable residue of features common to all human beings. If there were not, it would be meaningless to speak of the species *Homo sapiens*.

Nor does the vast number of exceptions that can be cited to any such generalizations about human nature undermine their scientific validity. Even the law of gravitation appears to have many exceptions—for example, a leaf in the wind or a balloon rises not falls. But when we find an exception we look for some element of chance, for example, the current of air that strikes the leaf, or the human artifice that made the balloon and filled it with helium, that accounts for these exceptions; we do not abandon the law of falling bodies. Thus it would seem that the nature-nurture controversy is solvable in principle if not always in practice. The more and more precise observations we make of human behavior, the clearer and more certain it will become what is human nature as distinct from the results of "nurture" or, to use another term, "culture" and chance.

But how are to we to distinguish between "culture" and "chance"? The reality of "chance" was rejected by the deterministic science of the nineteenth century. It believed Laplace's claim that if he knew the exact condition of the universe at a given moment he could infallibly predict its whole future.² Today the quantum and chaos theories have made that mechanist claim absurd. The natural laws of quantum physics do not predict the exact future of a material entity but only provide a range of probabilities as to its behavior.³ Such laws give an appearance of determinism that increases with the average behavior of the entities involved, but it never rules out highly improbable events. Chaos theory states that very small variations in the initial conditions of natural processes, perhaps even ones so small as to be undetectable, can make a huge difference in the ultimate outcome of the process. It also reveals that what at first appear to be purely random processes, that is, ones determined by chance, when sufficiently repeated converge on certain definite results that manifest previously hidden natural determinisms.⁴ For example, the swing of a pendulum is actually quite random, yet if sustained for many swings it averages out sufficiently that it can serve as a regular measure of time and thus manifests Newton's law of gravity.

Hence chance cannot be eliminated from our explanations of what we observe in the natural world but is implied by the very fact of the reality of natural laws. Nature and chance are distinguishable but inextricably linked together. Thus Stephen Jay Gould can say that Darwinian biological evolution, the natural process that today is taken as the foundation of all biological science, is largely a matter of chance.⁵ We can reconstruct the history of the emergence of a species using various natural laws, but we cannot eliminate the element of chance. The reality of chance does not contradict natural law, since by chance we mean that one thing acting lawfully according to its nature interferes with the behavior of another thing acting lawfully according to *its* nature. Experiments used to measure the law of gravitational attraction between two massive bodies are never quite precise because they may be interfered with by slight convection currents in the air of the laboratory, a vibration from a passing truck outside the laboratory, or other factors.

---

2. Pierre Simon de Laplace (1749–1782), *Philosophical Essay on Probabilities,* trans. F. W. Truscott and F. L. Emory (New York: Dover, 1951), 4.

3. On this topic, see Murray Gell-Mann, *The Quark and the Jaguar: Adventures in the Simple and the Complex* (New York: W. H. Freeman, 1994).

4. On this, see James Gleick, *Chaos: Making a New Science* (New York: Penguin Books, 1988).

5. Not all Darwinians would agree with Gould, but see Niles Eldredge, *Reinventing Darwin: The Great Debate at the High Table of Evolutionary Theory* (New York: John Wiley & Sons, 1995).

Of course, it is possible that there may be still a third law that regulates the interference of the two other agencies in a uniform manner. If this is the case we have a complex system of causes. There is, however, no scientific evidence whatsoever that our universe is a system of a kind that is so tightly regulated by some single law that this eliminates all chance events. The only reason to suppose that it is would be to satisfy a determinist prejudice like that of Laplace. But not only is that concession to determinism unnecessary for the advance of science, but it has actually proved an obstacle to that advance, as Einstein's bias for determinism for a while blocked the acceptance of the Copenhagen interpretation of quantum phenomena.

The same goes for the concept of the "artificial," or free, man-made, element in explaining our observations of the world. Of course some have thought that if we knew human nature and the situations in which humans are placed well enough we could predict their future behavior. They have tried to find "laws of history." But now that chance has been shown to play a large part in the history of the universe, how can we suppose that human history is any more deterministic? In fact observation of human behavior in comparison with the behavior of those hominoid animals closest to us in evolutionary descent quickly reveals that besides deterministic laws and chance concurrences free choice enters human behavior. The very notion of "culture" implies that the human animal is highly inventive.

To be inventive means to be able to consider alternative possibilities and to choose among them to find the appropriate means to a given end. This is what is meant by the term "freedom."[6] Therefore, the debate between nature and nurture is precisely about the relative degree in which nature—and the element of chance in nature—contributes to explaining human behavior and the degree that human freedom contributes to it. This interlinking of freedom and nature, like the linking of nature and chance, does not contradict the deterministic or natural aspect of human behavior but complements it. For example, a characteristic feature of human culture is language, yet linguistics shows us how intertwined are psychological laws and human free invention in human speech. All normal human infants have a remarkable facility in learning the language of their parents and the language they learn is determined by the culture of their parents. But this language changes a bit every day by the invention of new words or new usages

---

6. *ST* I, q. 83.

of words. Thus the historic variety of human languages is immense; today it is about six thousand.

I have gone into all this at some length to show that to talk about a "natural law" requires the well-defined concept of "nature" and of "chance" and to talk about the "natural moral law" requires also the concept of "freedom." The reason that in today's culture the traditional concept of "natural moral law," so basic to the value systems out of which modern society grew, is today so often rejected, is that these concepts are confused and their interrelationships misconstrued.

Aquinas's Anthropology or Theory of Human Nature

St. Thomas Aquinas can be of help to us today in trying to recover the sense of the "natural moral law" because he so carefully analyzed the distinctions between and the relationships of nature, chance, and freedom neglected in much current ethical debates. Aquinas's anthropology is genuinely empirical, that is, based on an analysis of human behavior as we observe it. He lacked, of course, much of the vast store of information now available in biology, anthropology, psychology, and sociology. No doubt, if he had been faced with this knowledge explosion, he might have been as confused as we often are. But the very paucity of his data forced him to subject it to a foundational analysis. Today it is too often overlooked that when we use a telescope or a microscope we have to interpret and validate what we see through them by its broad conformity with what we see with our naked eye. The same goes for the kind of anthropological and psychological data that we can now gather by traveling around the globe or compiling clinical histories. An outside observer has special difficulties in accurately perceiving what is going on in a foreign culture. A clinician knows that the way people behave in his office may not reveal how they behave in their families.

Aquinas carefully analyzed for us the knowledge we can acquire in daily life prior to any special technique of observation. His results, therefore, have the special value of not being colored by current ideologies, but at the same time they must not be taken for anything but an extremely broad outline that must always be filled in with much more detail as our study of human nature advances.

Approaching human nature in this outlining and naïve way, we recognize that we are living things, animals, and very remarkable animals indeed, precisely in that we have an invented culture marked by social communication through a true language that contains abstract concepts. St. Thomas did not begin, as did Plato of old or most modern philosophers since Descartes, with introspection into our self-consciousness and then attempt to deduce the other marks of human nature and our relation to our environment from a *cogito ergo sum*. As an Aristotleian in his epistemology, Aquinas held that nothing is more mysterious and obscure than our self-consciousness, our inner life. Since we ought to always go from what is more knowable to what is less knowable, the right way to study human nature is to begin with the objects that form our environment, including in particular other human beings that we can touch, see, hear, and smell. From what we can observe about such sensed objects and their behaviors little by little we can come to understand something about our inner life in its obscure mystery.[7] Thus Aquinas would never have accepted Descartes's dualistic account of the human person. Although we are composed of a spiritual soul and a material body, these are correlative, like the organization of a system and its parts. We can only know the system if we know the parts, yet we cannot understand the parts except insofar as they function within the system as a whole.

Taking this approach to human nature, Aquinas concluded that there is a human species all members of which are essentially alike, although in secondary ways they can differ very much, for example, in gender and in maturity, while remaining essentially the same. The best view of human nature will be achieved only if we give special attention to normal and mature specimens. As regards gender, this means considering both man and woman in their complementary relation, and as regards maturation, it is necessary to consider human life from conception to death and on into eternity. Many variations in humanity, however, are irrelevant in exploring human nature, for example, that of skin color or education or of customary habits peculiar to this or that place or time. It is by looking to what is uni-

---

7. Authors who present Aquinas's philosophy from the *Summa theologiae* have often obscured his philosophical thought. In *ST* I, q. 75, Aquinas begins from the spiritual human soul and then descends to its material body in q. 76. This is because theology follows an order that descends from God's self-revelation to his work of creation, and hence from the angels to the spiritual soul to corporeal creation. But in St. Thomas's commentaries on Aristotle's works a strictly philosophical order is followed that begins with the body and only gradually ascends to the spiritual soul.

versal and specific that we will come closer to what is natural to human beings.

The fact of human language and the special form of family life and the larger social life that is characteristic of the human animal Aquinas finds as the clue to understanding what is most specific and unique to human nature and thus explanatory of the particular kind of animal body that we possess. This specific ability that marks out the human species is its power of abstract thought manifested in human language.[8] From this power also flows human freedom, the possibility of free choice and of morality, and therefore the power of human society to invent a culture and its artificial technology. Today careful study of animal behavior has shown that some apes have the capacity not only to learn new behaviors but to transmit them to future generations in a sort of culture, that they have a kind of language and can learn better communications, and that they can not only use but invent tools. Of course Aquinas probably knew that birds build nests, and bees hives, and that apes can wield a stick as a weapon. Today we are beginning to think that the Neanderthals had stone tools and used fire, yet may not yet have been able to speak, and were genetically not of our human species.[9]

Such findings, however, are not surprising once we have admitted with Pope John Paul II that humans came to be through biological evolution.[10] In an evolutionary process some lower form of life must very closely approximate the next higher form of life. Yet there is a critical point at which a new species originates, marked by some new specific trait that has previously had only analogous approximations, first sketches as it were. Again, what is specific to humans, according to Aquinas, is not just any kind of language, nor any kind of transmitted learning, nor any kind of use or invention of tools, but the capability of abstract thought and the power of free choice that it makes possible.[11] Nothing we know about past or living hominoids unequivocally manifests such an ability to think abstractly and choose freely, yet we can observe such activities emerge in every growing human child in normal health.

8. *SCG* IV, c. 41.

9. See Ian Tattersall, *Becoming Human: Evolution and Human Uniqueness* (New York: Harcourt Brace, 1998), 164–73.

10. Pope John Paul II, "Message to Pontifical Academy of Sciences on Evolution," *Origins* 26, no. 25 (5 December 1996): 414–16.

11. *ST* I, q. 79, a. 1; q. 80, a. 2; q. 83.

If Aquinas was right in concluding from these observations that what specifies human nature is intelligence and free will, the question arises of the relation of these abilities to the fact that we are also obviously animals, living by the powers of nutrition and reproduction possessed also by plants, and subject to the laws of physics that govern inanimate substances. Aquinas knew far less than we do about human anatomy, physiology, and genetics. He even followed Aristotle's erroneous opinion that seems today absurd, although it was based on Greek medical science, that the primary organ of the body is the heart rather than, as we know it to be, the brain.[12] Yet we can follow Aquinas's view that the special traits of the human body are appropriate to a kind of organism whose behavior is intelligent and free and able to control its environment. He notes that the human hand with its opposable thumb and ability to make very finely controlled movements is just the kind of instrument an intelligent animal needs.[13] Today we can explain the anatomy and physiology of the body and in particular the brain in vast detail in view of its evolutionary adaptation to serve intelligent life and that by developing modern science and technology can now exercise such remarkable control over its physical environment.

Nevertheless, the specific human ability for abstract thought that explains why we need so big a brain, and why the human child matures so slowly as this brain develops, and so on, raises the question of the relation of the power of intelligence to the brain. Many today believe that soon we will be able to make computers that think abstractly, perhaps even better than humans can think, and that hence the brain is simply a fine computer and the human intelligence merely the operation of that computer. If one explores modern literature on this subject,[14] however, one begins to see that even if Aquinas knew what we now know he still would never have drawn the conclusion that our intelligence is the operation of the brain. Instead he would reason that the primary organ of the body must be the or-

---

12. On why Aristotle made such scientific mistakes, see my articles in the *New Scholasticism*, "Aristotle's Sluggish Earth, Part 1: Problematics of the *De Caelo*," 32 (January 1958): 1–31; Part 2, "Media of Demonstration," 32 (April 1958): 202–34. The biological part was never published.

13. See Aquinas's commentary on Aristotle's *De anima* III, lect. 13, n. 789f.

14. For an introduction to this question in present science, see Roger Penrose, *The Emperor's New Mind: Concerning Computers, Minds, and the Laws of Physics* (New York: Viking-Penguin, 1990).

gan of internal sensation and that this organ must be the principal instrument of the intelligence, but only its instrument.[15]

The act of intelligence in knowing material objects abstractly transcends their materiality, and intelligent human beings in intelligently knowing these objects indirectly know their own transcendent acts and hence their own transcendence of matter. Thus we are not merely material, bodily beings, but rather material beings whose form is immaterial, that is, spiritual, and hence we can perform acts impossible to animals or any material substance. Many modern scientists who have thought deeply about what is called "the mind-body problem" recognize that no artificial intelligence machine can ever really think, but can only perform calculations that thinking persons have programmed it to calculate. As the mathematician Kurt Gödel demonstrated, the human mind can always think of a problem that cannot be solved by any computer program the human mind has so far constructed. Yet the human mind can probably invent a new program that will successfully solve this new problem. We can always keep one step ahead of our computers!

Aquinas gives a general account of what it means to say that our intelligence and free will are spiritual faculties and that we are persons who are not only animals, but also spiritual beings, *persons*. We can know this only by analogy to the material things that we can directly observe, and hence our account will always remain imperfect and capable of improvement. Yet Aquinas is able to analyze the human body-person in a way that provides a more secure basis for psychology than the many warring theories in this field seem able to supply. The most relevant feature of this analysis is that spiritual beings, because they transcend the determinism of natural law and of chance, have a *responsibility* for their own lives. To meet this responsibility a science of ethics is most helpful.

Aquinas's Theory of the Natural Moral Law

Since we have the responsibility to make intelligent free choices about what we are going to do or not, we are responsible for shaping not only our lives but our very selves. Persons who act intelligently and realistically make themselves ever more capable of intelligent and realistic decisions.

---

15. *ST* I, q. 76, aa. 4, 7.

This growth of character or ability to make good life decisions consistently and with a certain spontaneity is what Aquinas calls a *virtue,* and its contrary, a tendency to act unintelligently and compulsively, he calls a *vice*.[16] By our free decisions we grow virtuous or vicious, freer or more addictive, good or bad human persons.

But how do we determine what decisions will be constructive and what decisions will be destructive of the human nature with its great potentialities given us at conception? Aquinas answers that decisions are always about means not ends as such.[17] Granted that we want to attain a particular goal, our intelligence and freedom make it possible for us to determine whether a particular action will or will not help us move toward that goal or defeat our efforts to attain it and thus to choose or not choose a certain means freely. What, then, determines what my ends, my goals, are to be? Obviously people have different goals to which they are committed and in view of which they make decisions about the means to take to those goals. One person is committed to seek virtue; another has chosen to live a vicious life.

This is where nature and the natural moral law enter the picture. Aquinas maintains that human nature both in its materiality and in its spirituality is inherently directed toward the goal of *happiness*.[18] No one can really choose not to be happy. For human beings this happiness that our nature motivates us to seek is complex. It consists in the satisfaction of several different needs or goals fixed in our very nature. Yet these must be harmonized by some scale of values in which one value is supreme.

According to Aquinas,[19] these basic human needs are (1) for food, health, physical security, and the material goods required to achieve these needs; and (2) for a community with other humans in which we can attain and share what as individuals we cannot attain alone. This social need has two levels (a) for a family to be born and educated in, and for most people when mature a loving and fruitful sexual companionship that preserves our species; (b) for a larger community in which the variety of gifts and cooperative effectiveness will enable all to achieve both the primary needs of physical well-being and family security. (3) Our third great need is for truth, that is, to understand the world, ourselves, other persons, and, above all, the Creator who made us to become his friends.

16. *ST* I-II, qq. 49–56.
17. *ST* I-II, q. 13, a. 3.
18. *ST* I-II, q. 1.
19. *ST* I-II, q. 94, a. 2.

These three basic needs form a hierarchy. The first need is fundamental to the attainment of the others, yet we can sacrifice many physical goods, even health and life itself, to strengthen our family and larger society and to attain some wisdom. As for society, whether of the family or the larger community, its highest achievement is the advance of truth, both as it guides life to its goals, and as the supreme object of human life in friendship with others persons, human, angelic, and divine. To this last goal the others, although they are also true goals, are subordinate. Thus the achievement of truth makes wise decisions possible, because it shows us what are the means that are realistically available to achieve happiness and which of these are likely to be the more effective.

Yet, though by nature we all seek happiness because of the very freedom that makes it possible to choose the right means to these goals, it is possible also for us in our freedom to make wrong choices that make happiness impossible for ourselves and may make it more difficult for others to attain. How is this possible? Socrates and Plato thought that no one who knows what is good could possibly choose what is bad, since that would be to seek misery not happiness. That would be true if our creaturely intelligence, like that of our Creator, were omniscient. All intelligent creatures, however, have finite intelligences. What they see best is not the big picture but the little one of their own immediate interests, their own happiness rather than the happiness of all in which individual happiness can only be a part.

Satan was the most intelligent of all creatures, a pure spirit of vast knowledge and freedom, yet he blinded himself to his true happiness to be found only in a life conformable to God's plan for all his creatures. He and other angels committed the sin of pride by seeking their individual happiness without regard to the happiness of others. Because they are so intelligent they realistically knew this was a fatal self-destructive choice, yet they focused on their individual self-interests. Thus Socrates and Plato were right in saying that wrong choices are due to ignorance, but they missed Aquinas's point that we can abuse our freedom by deliberately ignoring the truth we know more abstractly and willfully seek a more immediate good.

Aquinas explains that it is possible for us but not for the fallen agents to repent our sinful choices.[20] The extremely intelligent angels, free of bodily

---

20. On this point in Aquinas, see Jacques Maritain, *The Sin of the Angels* (Westminister, Md.: Newman Press, 1959).

changes, knew exactly what they were doing and will never change their minds. We, however, see things differently at different times as our bodies change their moods and perceptions, and so we can, with God's help, repent. The man who at night drinks too much can repent the next morning when he is suffering a hangover. Yet he should not forget that by getting drunk that once, he has (possibly) begun an addiction that will incline him to again get drunk and each time repentance will be more difficult. On the other hand, if he resists temptation he will begin to build a virtue that will eventually make temperance easy.

What, then, in Aquinas's understanding, is the "natural moral law"?[21] It is first of all a true understanding of our human nature, our need for happiness, and the elements of a happy life and their relative importance, in brief, a concrete understanding of the supreme goal and the subordinate goals that we must seek to be happy. Second, it consists in a true understanding of the various means to this supreme goal and its integrated subordinate goals, that is, the means among which we must choose if we are to strive realistically for happiness. As regards such choices it should be obvious that the varying life circumstances in which each person finds himself sometimes exclude certain means as impractical and open up other means as available.

Hence in making choices we observe certain very general principles that are based on the innate goals of human nature. These general principles are said to be the primary precepts of the natural law and are very evident to any thinking and experienced person, such as our need to keep healthy and secure, to have friends, and to gain a realistic understanding of what is good and bad behavior. Then there are more specific principles that we gain from a mature experience of human life and the sources of ethical wisdom that are widely available. From these we learn more detailed rules of good living, such as the importance of developing self-control over our eating habits and our sexual appetites, of doing what we know to be right with courage in difficult situations, and of respecting the rights of others and our responsibilities to them in family and community.

At this level of moral understanding, it becomes clear that some actions that may seem attractive are nevertheless always and in all circumstances wrong. They are said to be "intrinsically evil" not because they have no

---

21. *ST* I-II, q. 94.

good aspects, but because they essentially block our way to our true goal in life and hence can never be an effective practical means to it.[22]

For example, sex with an unwilling partner (rape) is intrinsically evil, not because it may not in certain circumstances seem to have some advantages, but because our human nature as sexual beings can really be satisfied only when sex is used to express familial love. When sex is forced on another, that person's rights are violated and the rapist makes himself more of an animal than a real man. Similarly lying, although it seems sometimes a means to a good result, in fact always violates the relation of trust basic to community and isolates the liar from the community he needs. Note, however, that what would be a lie in some social contexts in others would be only a joke or conventional statement that anyone would recognize as such and hence as noncommunicative. Thus good moral decisions in some matters require nuanced and precise understanding of what we are really choosing to do or refusing to do and for what motives.

Finally, at the third level of moral judgment, there is the mature virtue of prudence by which we become skillful in thoughtfully making good decisions even in especially complicated and unusual circumstances.[23] The prudent person, in whom thoughtful decision making becomes, as it were, "second nature," also knows how to take counsel with others and to seek the guidance of those who are wiser. While we may be excused for making mistakes due to ignorance, we are not excused when we recognize our need for guidance and refuse to seek it or obey it. Thus acting in conformity with the natural law is more than simply following general rules. Rather, it requires a continuing search for a true understanding of what nature requires in any given situation.

Aquinas had no illusions that this kind of practical, prudent moral wisdom is easy to attain or obvious to all. The Bible vividly shows us how slowly the human race has acquired an adequate understanding of what is

---

22. John Paul II's encyclical *Veritatis splendor* defends the Church's traditional teaching that certain concrete negative precepts against certain human acts are always obligatory because they condemn these acts as *intrinsically evil,* i.e., in all circumstances and for whatever intentions performed these acts are contradictory to the true end of human life and therefore always objectively sinful. This declaration was made necessary by the theory of "proportionalism" that denied this doctrine but was advocated by some prominent Catholic moral theologians.

23. *ST* II-II, qq. 47–56.

for its own true good. Without God's guidance through revelation the human race would probably have destroyed itself long ago. In our own lifetime we have experienced the nuclear crisis when we came close to eliminating the human species altogether and it is highly probable that such crises will arise in the future.

The individual finds it especially difficult to understand the natural law in its finer points in a society where moral views are in such conflict. Even to follow the natural law as we know it at a given time is difficult because our culture, which should help us to do what is right, so often tempts us to do the opposite. For a woman to destroy her own child is obviously contrary to both her own nature as a woman and the child's nature, yet in our society of death we find ways to blind ourselves and others in the name of "free choice" and fail to do what we can to help her make a good choice in situations where she lacks good social support.

There is a profound saying, "God is always ready to forgive, but Nature never forgives." Natural law demands that we make free, reasonable, and realistic choices in view of what we know the natural consequences of our actions will be for ourselves and for others whose common life we need to share. If we do not obey the natural law or society does not reinforce this obedience by its own laws or social sanctions, the natural law enforces itself. Its price has to be paid even if we violated it in ignorance or repent our knowing violations of it. We cannot attain happiness if we do not take the practical road that leads to it.

❈ RESPONSE ❈

CHARACTER AS AN ENABLER OF MORAL JUDGMENT

Janet E. Smith

Father Ashley has done well to point out that a variance in moral judgments from culture to culture does not mean that there are no universal objectively true moral judgments. He makes the point well in the context of the difficulty in proving gravity and the gravitational pull between things; chance intervening forces may skew the reading of the data, but with careful enough observation and calibration one can substantiate one's claim about gravity. One needs the proper instruments or standards to make a correct judgment.

I have much appreciated a technique I once saw Steven Covey use. He asked a room full of individuals to point an arm in the direction north; the diversity in judgments was great. He then asked if just because people disagree where north is, does that mean there is no such direction as north or no way of knowing what it is?

I was making a similar point recently to students who wanted to know how to refute cultural relativism—how to decide, for instance, whether polygamy or monogamy is the right form of marriage or whether homosexual acts are morally permissible. I said that we do not employ across the board the principle that different judgments by different cultures indicate that there are no objective truths. For instance, because some cultures or ages may think that bloodletting is a cure for certain diseases, we do not allow that it is truly a cure for these diseases. Certainly there may be more than one way to cure diseases, such as herbal remedies or surgery for some cancers, but this does not mean that there are not ineffective ways as well. Since these students were in the midst of some European travel, I noted that they would readily observe great differences between bathroom facilities, say those in Austria or those in Italy, and that they would have no trouble making judgments of the superiority of one over the other.

Observing that health and continued life were standards by which we could judge medical cures and bathrooms, they next asked, of course, what standard would be used to judge the truth of moral claims. Now these are students who, of course, all think that rape is wrong and slavery is wrong, but they don't know how they have come to those conclusions and how they would prove their convictions. I tried to show them that the problems involved in proving moral claims are shared in proving other claims for which they think they are justified in having certainty. Let me hasten to say that my intention was not to extend the skepticism that they have about moral judgments to all judgments, but to extend the confidence they have about many matters to moral matters as well.

I flummoxed them a bit by asking them how they know that health and continued life are goods since they generally deem good what advances health and enhances life. One could, of course, say that it is obvious or self-evident or that it is natural for us to want health and continued life, but we moderns don't permit ourselves such assertions: we need studies or proof of some kind. The students' difficulty in answering this question reveals a deep need, the need to explain how it is that we can know anything.

Perhaps here would be a good place to say a little bit about Aristotelian/Thomistic epistemology. A passage not much noticed from *Metaphysics* 11.6 makes points I want to emphasize here:

> The saying of Protagoras is like the views we have mentioned; he said that man is the measure of all things, meaning simply that that which seems to each man also assuredly is. If this is so, it follows that the same thing both is and is not, and is bad and good, and that the contents of all other opposite statements are true, because often a particular thing appears beautiful to some and the contrary of beautiful to others, and that which appears to each man is the measure.

Here is exactly the point we are considering—because different cultures and different people see things differently, is there no way of adjudicating their claims or settling the dispute? Aristotle goes on to state:

> But to attend equally to the opinions and the fancies of disputing parties is childish; for clearly one of them must be mistaken. And this is evident from what happens in respect of sensation; for the same thing never appears sweet to some and the contrary of sweet to others, unless in the one case the sense-organ which discriminates

the aforesaid flavours has been perverted and injured. And if this is so the one party must be taken to be the measure, and the other must not. And I say the same of good and bad, and beautiful and ugly, and all other such qualities. For to maintain the view we are opposing is just like maintaining that the things that appear to people who put their finger under their eye and make the object appear two instead of one must be two (because they appear to be of that number) and again one (for to those who do not interfere with their eye the one object appears one).[1]

Why don't we all perform this little experiment? Poke your finger under your eye and you will find that you see multiple images. So does this mean that there are now twice as many people in the room as before, or does it just mean that you are misperceiving things? How do we know who is perceiving things correctly? We pick the one with his senses working properly. How do we know whose senses are working properly? We might find all kinds of tests useful—in some cases a vote might do, but in other cases we might need to test some sense perception against other sense perceptions or devise certain instruments to filter out distortion. Generally we believe we can find some way of determining whose sense perceptions are accurate—even though we often disagree initially.

Two points from this passage are of particular importance. One is that the condition of the perceiver determines to some extent what is being perceived, and the other is that when our organs of perception and faculties of judgment are operating properly, broadly speaking our perceptions about sense data and our aesthetic and moral judgments are correct.

Again, the example using vision is useful. Those who have distorted vision are not accurate guides to visible reality. Aristotle also holds that in moral judgments those who are perverse are not accurate guides to what is good or evil. I believe what Aristotle is saying in the passage from the *Metaphysics* is that just as our senses when working properly are reliable guides to reality, so too when our souls, that is, when our emotions and reason are working together correctly, our judgments are reliable guides to what is good and what is bad. Those who have properly ordered souls are the ones able to judge what is good and evil. When my students tell me that drug addicts think that cocaine rather than virtue is the key to happiness and that their views should be respected, I ask them why we should take the

---

1. Aristotle, *Metaphysics,* trans. W. D. Ross, in *The Basic Works of Aristotle* (New York: Random House, 1941).

views of those who make such bad judgments seriously. After all, we don't consult the blind about colors. We know their judgment to be skewed. And I believe Aristotle thinks it not much more difficult in general to distinguish the moral individual from the immoral one than it is to distinguish those who are blind from those who can see.

Let me refine this point somewhat. Fundamental to the ethical views of Aristotle and Aquinas is the belief that all men share a nature or essence and that by their essence they are able to perceive reality correctly. It is that essence or nature, not the laws of nature, that is truly the foundation for natural law. Certainly we have natural desires for what is good for us, and thus they are useful indicators for what is good for us, but they must be ordered by reason. As we saw in the passage cited from the *Metaphysics*, Aristotle draws a very strong parallel between man's physical, emotive, and rational appetites, a view that Aquinas shares. They hold that man's senses are capable of grasping certain material objects accurately; they also hold that man's appetites draw him to objects that are good for him.

Unless defective, the eye perceives colors correctly, taste perceives bitter and sweet correctly, touch perceives soft and hard correctly. Our desires for food, drink, sleep, sex, companionship, justice, and friendship are also natural and direct us to what is good for us. With little or no training, our emotive appetites can also perceive much of reality correctly; we easily take delight in gentleness and justice; we readily fear the threats of ferocious creatures such as bears and the cruelty of tyrants. After all, for Aristotle and Aquinas, the virtuous man takes delight in virtuous actions and feels pain at vicious ones; he is able, then, to take his experiences of what is pleasurable and what is painful as guides to what is right and what is wrong. Yet, because our appetites can be disordered, we must use our reason to order them.

Furthermore, although we are naturally able to delight in what is good, we need experience of nature to teach us what is good. The key to an Aristotelian/Thomistic ethics is the point made by Father Ashley that Aquinas's anthropology is "genuinely empirical," meaning that we know that man is a rational, social animal by observing his behavior and we know what is good for that nature by observing that nature in operation. Nor do the judgments made upon the basis of empirical observations constitute first principles from which all of morality can subsequently be deduced; rather, through further empirical observation we must judge which actions are in accord with the rational, social, and animal aspects of human nature.

Yet, while moral reasoning then is not a matter of deduction from analytic *a priori* premises, deduction certainly has a place in moral reasoning as it does in all reasoning. But we must keep in mind that deduction about contingent matters—and human matters are very contingent—requires data acquired through empirical observation and reflection. We make ethical deductions quite regularly: for instance, we may reason that innocent human life is not to be deliberately killed, that fetal life is innocent human life, and that we ought not therefore to take fetal life. Not all moral reasoning of a moral agent will proceed in such a strict syllogistic fashion but facts and values will be intertwined in all moral reasoning.

Now let me take up a related feature of natural law that has received attention but not much explanation, and that is the claim that in some respect the natural law is written on our hearts. Let me take a quick stab at an explanation.

Many make the erroneous judgment that since Aquinas makes the claim that natural law is imprinted upon man's soul this means that the two tables of the Decalogue are somehow already imprinted upon our consciousness and that everybody innately knows that murder, theft, and so on, are wrong. I think Aquinas is not making this claim. Rather, as was noted above, Aristotle and Aquinas believed that our beings are designed to grasp the truth about reality. Consistent with their views would be the claim that our minds have "imprinted" upon them the spectrum of colors; we need to have eyes that can see and some experience that will expose us to color and activate colors within us but we will be able to recognize various colors when we see them and the proper ordering of them will not be difficult for us to grasp. The more refined or nuanced shades of them will not be easily accessible to all—because of native talent or training some can discern all kinds of subtle distinctions. The same is true with moral judgments. We very easily understand that life is a good and that innocent life ought not to be taken. Little experience of life is necessary for us to grasp these truths. With some further experience and information—if we did not live in such corrupt times—we could also easily grasp that abortion is a violation of the good of life. That is, the principles and precepts of natural law are not innate but they are easily known to the human person raised well, for we are designed to grasp them. In that sense, like colors "written" on the optical nerves, natural laws are "written" on the "heart." And the most morally sensitive among us are the best judges of what is right and wrong.

Not only must a great deal be clarified about the process by which we come to know the natural law, but more must be said about the soul and its role in natural law ethics. Ashley's paper rightly emphasizes the necessity of recognizing the existence of spiritual and rational capacities for natural law morality. His paper gives a kind of a proof for the existence of these spiritual capacities by arguing that we can do more than the most intelligent machine and thus must have capacities that they do not have. But Ashley never uses the word "soul," and I wonder why he has not done so. Is it because he believes the word to have too much religious baggage? Or is there some other reason? The word "spirit" does much of the same work as the word "soul" but not all. I find it useful to retain the word with my students at least, because speaking of the soul as the principle of life and explaining that plants and animals have souls too (though not spiritual or immortal souls) helps them better to understand the hierarchy of being. Speaking of philosophical arguments for the existence of the soul and the immortality of the soul helps them better understand the human person and human happiness.

Recognizing the centrality of the soul to natural law ethics also makes it easier to emphasize the centrality of virtue to natural law, for virtue is the ordering of the soul. Many moderns, such as the Aristotelian scholar Martha Nussbaum, think that virtues are best defined as characteristics useful for achieving one's ends, whatever they may be, and that moral norms are simply good guidelines for achieving those ends. But for Aristotle and Aquinas man's natural end is happiness and virtue is the sine qua non for happiness because it is a habit that orders the soul.

It cannot be stressed too strongly that virtue has primacy over moral norms in Thomistic natural law ethics. Moral norms are grounded in an understanding of the appetites of the soul as being naturally drawn to certain objects and of the need for virtue or the control of reason over these appetites. Moral norms are simply identifications of which actions are virtuous, that is, in accord with properly ordered appetites and which actions are vicious, that is, which actions cause the appetites to be disordered. Adultery, for instance, is a violation of the virtues of justice and temperance. Thus to know what the norms are, we must know what our appetites are and what ordering of them conduces to our good. And let me pause to say that I am using the word "know" here in a very loose sense; true opinion is generally every bit as good as knowledge when one is speaking of moral behavior. The knowledge of the ethical person and the ethicist need not be the same and such a distinction is often overlooked.

Another reason that we must keep close in view that virtue ethics and natural law ethics are the same for Aquinas is that many people are more receptive to talk of virtue (a remarkable development of the last decade) than to talk of natural law. We might find it a better starting point for engaging the conversation.

Let me close by noting another source of support for natural law. Many studies both in psychology and sociology, not to mention the record of history and the stories in literature, provide substantial support for the claims of natural law. The Rockford Institute in Rockford, Illinois, is a fantastic source for such studies. Studies show that those with friends and family, those with a strong sense of right and wrong, those who remain chaste before marriage and faithful within marriage, those who practice religion, and so on, are quite measurably happier in general than those who are friendless and without family, those who have no sense of right and wrong, those who are promiscuous and divorced, and those who are without belief in God. Indeed, recent books by Lionel Tiger and Francis Fukuyama argue that contraception has been devastating to human relationships. Those with the proper anthropology hardly need such studies since simple common sense easily reveals the same, but, as we all know, simple common sense is in short supply these days and that fact goes a long way toward explaining why natural law is so out of favor.

2

THOMISTIC NATURAL LAW AND ARISTOTELIAN PHILOSOPHY

Ralph McInerny

Prologue

I shall approach my subject in an Aristotelian fashion, a fashion familiar to students of St. Thomas. First, I will make some general remarks about the attitude of Thomists to Aristotle. Second, I will indicate how misgivings about Aristotle affected thoughts on moral doctrine. Finally, I will arrive at the specific issue of Aristotle and Thomistic natural law.

Dante, at the end of *La Vita Nuovo,* tells us that in order to write of Beatrice as no woman has ever been written of before, he would first devote himself to serious study of philosophy and theology. This seems reasonable enough to us, perhaps, though not every swooning poet has followed such sane advice. Dante is said to have studied both with Franciscans and Dominicans in Florence. Among the Dominicans were two who had studied with Thomas Aquinas in Paris. Given Dante's knowledge of disputes between Thomas and Bonaventure and Siger of Brabant—the three are brought together in the Circle of the Sun in the *Paradiso*—this seems true. But another sign that Dante was influenced by Thomas Aquinas is his description of Aristotle as the master of those who know.[1] Cardinal New-

---

1. Dante, *Inferno* 4.131.

man echoed this centuries later when he said that Aristotle has expressed what we know long before we were born.[2]

Like his contemporaries, Thomas referred to Aristotle as *the* Philosopher. Whether he read any Aristotle at Montecassino, he did so at Naples and, after he joined the Dominicans, he had the inestimable privilege of studying with Albert the Great in Cologne. Albert wrote an enormous paraphrase of the Aristotleian corpus and Thomas edited Albert's commentary on the *Nicomachean Ethics*. Aristotle is present from the very beginning in Thomas's writings; moreover, he devoted five of the last six years of his life to commenting on the writings of Aristotle—twelve commentaries in all, some unfinished. These were prompted by the Averroist controversy and seek to display what in fact Aristotle taught, but Thomas brought to them a lifetime's reflection on the *corpus Aristotelicum*. Furthermore, they were written at a time when Thomas was engaged in enormous magisterial and writing projects. What is to be made of this constant, pervasive presence of Aristotle in the writings of Thomas?

Among philologists there is something called *quellenforschung*, according to which every remark in a text under study must be shown to have been borrowed from some earlier text. If an author remarks that the sun is warm and water wet, the scholarly task becomes one of discovering the previous author or authors from whom he stole such arcane lore. Nietzsche, having played this game himself, has the best credentials to lampoon *quellenforschungen*.

Now there is an opposite attitude that I would call *quellenvergessenheit* if it did not sound Heideggerian. In fact, I will call it that anyway. The central effort of the proponents of *quellenvergessenheit* is to show that nothing in the text or author being studied was ever thought of, or said, or written before. This might even better be called *quellenzuruckweisen*, the rejection of all antecedents.

Perhaps neither of these extremes is found in its pure form among students of Thomas, but both have been at least approximated.

---

2. John Henry Newman, *Idea of a University*, Discourse 5.5.

Aristotelico-Thomistic Philosophy

Among the first generation of modern Thomists—counting from the appearance of *Aeterni patris* in 1879—the philosophy of Thomas Aquinas often received a hyphenated label, meant to show his affinity with and reliance upon the Philosopher in matters philosophical. Given the philosophical origin of the cultural malaise that Leo XIII hoped a resurgence of Christian philosophy would counter, it was the realism of Aristotle that was attractive to those confronted with Cartesianism broadly construed.

We find the opposite tendency in Etienne Gilson who, during the discussion of Christian philosophy at the meeting of French Thomists at Juvisy in 1932, opposed Mandonnet, the great Dominican Thomist and medievalist. In his Aberdeen Gifford lectures, *The Spirit of Medieval Philosophy*, Gilson had made an eloquent historical argument for the influence of Christianity on philosophy. Mandonnet's position was more or less this: philosophy is one thing, theology another. While all theologians may be taken to be Christians, some philosophers are and some are not. Therefore, that a philosopher is Christian is *per accidens* and formally irrelevant to philosophical inquiry. Perhaps Jacques Maritain and Josef Pieper have given the most persuasive accounts of what Christian philosophy is. The influence of the faith on philosophizing is a fact not only of history but of personal history. But how then to keep the distinction between philosophy and theology clear? The difficulty involved in this can still be seen in *Fides et ratio*'s discussion of Christian philosophy.

I mention these things because they seem to be disposing causes of Gilson's anti-Aristotelianism. He ended by saying, "There is no greater obstacle to the spread of the thought of St. Thomas, even in the Dominican Order, than Aristotle, and Cajetan who is his prophet."[3] This came late, but one can see it building over the years. Gilson's interpretation of *esse* in Tho-

---

3. In "Cajetan et l'existence," *Tijdschrift voor Philosophie* 15 (1953): 284, Gilson had written: "... le principal obstacle à la diffusion du thomisme de saint Thomas, même à l'interior de l'Ordre Dominicain, fut l'influence d'Aristote." That same year, in a letter to Jacques Maritain, he is more forceful still: "Une chose du moins est claire dans mon esprit: le pire ennemi de saint Thomas, même dans l'Ordre Dominicain, a été Aristote, dont Cajetan est le prophete" (6 April 1953). See *Etienne Gilson-Jacques Maritain: Correspondence 1923–1971*, ed. Géry Prouvost (Paris:Vrin, 1991), 188.

mas entailed that no one prior to Thomas had grasped existence or understood the *clef de voûte* of Thomas's thought. This is not only to get rid of sources, it is to get rid of companions. With special reference to my topic, Gilson's stance comes down to this:

> *Esse* is at the heart of Thomas's thought.
> Aristotle overlooked *esse*, identifying it with essence.
> Accordingly, Aristotle's philosophy is totally different from Thomas's.

In order to show that the metaphysics of Aristotle is fundamentally different from that of Thomas Aquinas, one would have to make use of the considerations according to which sciences differ. Thomas has supplied us with all the necessary criteria. Above all, one would have to show that the subject of metaphysics for Aristotle differs from what it was for Thomas Aquinas. In a closely related matter, Thomas showed how the theology of the philosophers, the culmination of metaphysics and indeed of philosophy, differed from the theology based on revealed truths. But no similar effort was made in the case of metaphysics, so it could scarcely have been successful. Standing athwart such efforts is the undeniable fact that Thomas himself appears to be blithely unaware of any radical difference between himself and Aristotle in metaphysics. It certainly does not show up in his commentary on the *Metaphysics,* nor anywhere else. The claim thus seems to make the claimant more Thomistic than Thomas and requires an almost Straussian hermeneutic.

The Realm of Moral Philosophy

Thomists who dissociated themselves from the effort to drive a wedge between Aristotle and Thomas in speculative philosophy thought otherwise when it came to moral philosophy.

If the end is the starting point of moral argument, setting off the quest for ways of achieving it, and if man's ultimate end has been revealed to be something far beyond the dreams of the philosophers—a union with God in which we will see even as we are seen—it seems pretty clear that believers will not get much help from nonbelievers in this area, or if they do, it will be marginal and supplementary rather than substantial.

Maritain, who was unpersuaded by Gilson's position that the Christian philosophy of St. Thomas is to be found only in his theological works, and indeed that the order of philosophical discussion is identical with the order of the *Summa theologiae,* came to think that things were different in theoretical and practical reasoning. The human mind is capable of arriving at knowledge of God, that he exists and has certain attributes. There is no need for this speculative effort to be governed by or subordinated to the faith in order to succeed. But the practical order presents a different problem, and here Maritain developed a theory of "Moral Philosophy Adequately Considered" according to which moral philosophy can only be practical if it guides us to what is our ultimate end.[4] But our ultimate end is now known to be supernatural. Therefore, moral philosophy must be subalternated to moral theology in order to be truly practical. Maritain insisted that this did not destroy moral philosophy as philosophy, turning it into theology.[5] But clearly Aristotle does not look to be an adequate guide in the moral order.

Natural and Supernatural

It can be seen that the relationship between the natural and the supernatural is at the heart of such discussions. In their correspondence, Gilson and Henri de Lubac reveal themselves to be of one mind on de Lubac's conception of the supernatural.[6] (The Jesuit had come under a cloud for his views on the supernatural and is often thought to have been in the target area of *Humani generis* in 1950.) The affinity between Gilson and de Lubac is grounded in their antipathy to Cajetan. In 1948, Gilson wrote an article, "Cajetan et l'existence,"[7] in which he argued that the great commentator had missed the boat so far as the key to Thomas's thought was concerned. As it happened, de Lubac had presented a Cajetan for whom the natural order was a self-contained and self-sufficient realm to which the

---

4. See Jacques Maritain, *An Essay on Christian Philosophy* (New York: Philosophical Library, 1955), 38–42. See also the discussion of moral philosophy in Jacques Maritain, *Science and Wisdom* (New York: Charles Scribner's Sons, 1940).

5. I discussed this matter in my McGivney Lectures in 1990. See Ralph McInerny, *The Question of Christian Ethics* (Washington, D.C.: The Catholic University of America Press, 1993).

6. Etienne Gilson, *Letters of Etienne Gilson to Henri de Lubac,* annotated by Henri de Lubac, trans. Mary Emily Hamilton (San Francisco: Ignatius Press, 1988).

7. See note 3 above.

supernatural advened as something miraculous.[8] Man is said to have a natural desire for his true end, the supernatural end. How can we desire naturally that which is beyond our nature? The answer is that we have an obediential potency—a capacity that can only be actuated by a supernatural agent, God. De Lubac's charge against Cajetan turns on what I myself believe to be a serious misreading of Cajetan on obediential potency—there seems to be not a dime's worth of difference between Cajetan and the de Lubac of the second work on the supernatural.[9] But Gilson and de Lubac never saw this and accused Cajetan of holding a view that *Fides et ratio* calls separatist.

In terms of my topic, the question becomes this. If the good and *telos* of anything is read from its nature, does man have an end that is proportionate to his nature? If he does, what is the relation between that end—call it his natural end—and the supernatural end he has been revealed to have? Has the former been abrogated by the latter? Is talk of a natural end based on the presumption that man is in a state of pure nature, that is, based on a false assumption?[10]

Aristotle and Aquinas

The initial task of the *Nicomachean Ethics* is to clarify man's ultimate end. That there is such an ultimate end of all we do is taken to be self-evident. I say this because the only defense Aristotle gives of the claim that there is an overriding end or good aimed at by whatever we do is to show that its denial leads to absurdity and incoherence. But this kind of argument is the only appropriate kind of argument that can be used to defend self-evident principles.

In any case, Aristotle's account of man's overriding good or ultimate end goes like this. When we want to know whether a thing is good, we first ask

---

8. Henri de Lubac, *Augustinianism and Modern Theology*, trans. Lancelot Sheppard (New York: Herder & Herder, 1969).

9. Cf. Florent Gaboriau, *Thomas d'Aquin en dialogue* (Paris: FAC, 1993), chap. 4, "La puissance obedientielle: Un cauchemar?" (37–74). Gaboriau has treated the same controversy in *Thomas d'Aquin, penseur dan l'Eglise* (Paris: FAC, 1992) and *Entrer en théologie avec Saint Thomas d'Aquin* (Paris: FAC, 1993).

10. See the magisterial work of Denis J. M. Bradley, *Aquinas on the Twofold Human Good* (Washington, D.C.: The Catholic University of America Press, 1997). See also Steven A. Long, "Man's Natural End," *The Thomist* 64 (April 2000): 211–37.

what it is. In the case of the human agent, we ask what his proper or defining work is, and this gives us both the location and the source of criteria for determining whether or not the agent is good of his kind. The *ergon,* or defining work, enables us to say whether an artifact, a natural organ, or a human agent is good. A good eye is one that enables us to see well. A good Swiss Army knife is one that is good for cutting up the Swiss Army, and just about anything else. A good cook is one who cooks well, and so forth. Something that performs its defining function well is good.

Such reflections led Aristotle to ask whether man as such had an *ergon,* or function. If he did, we would be able to answer the question about the human good straightforwardly: a good man is one who performs well the peculiarly human function. But there is in fact such a function: it is rational activity. The perfection or virtue of rational activity is thus that which makes a good man good. This analysis is one of the great moments in the history of moral philosophy and, if we had time, we might pause and savor it. Observe a minute's silence, so to say. But we must press on. Elation soon gives way to the realization that "rational activity" is a polyvalent, or equivocal, or, as Thomas would say, analogous phrase. It gathers together in an orderly way instances of rational activity that are not univocally so-called.

Rational activity might be the activity of reason itself. But the activity of reasoning itself is of two kinds: theoretical and practical. There is also activity that is rational because it is governed by reason: in this way our emotions can come to be directed to our overall good by reason.

If the perfection of an *ergon* is its virtue, and if the human work, rational activity, has many senses, there will be a plurality of virtues following on those various senses of rational activity. This sets the agenda for the *Ethics,* which goes on to discuss first moral virtues, then intellectual virtues, and finally the supreme intellectual virtue, contemplation.

Thomas Aquinas was obviously impressed by what Aristotle had done. This is clear both from his commentary on the *Ethics* and his constant references to Aristotle in the opening five questions of the *prima secundae* of the *Summa theologiae.* This may seem surprising.

In clarifying what is meant by the human good, man's ultimate end, Aristotle was speaking of the comprehensive good of the human agent. But if it is comprehensive, it leaves nothing out. And if it leaves nothing out, there is no room for talk of a good outside it. Successful talk of the human good seems to entail that when it is had it leaves nothing to be desired. Recall the notes or properties of the ultimate end that Aristotle lists—among them its sufficiency.

That would seem to entail this. The comprehensive good articulated by Aristotle is in conflict with the comprehensive good presented by Christianity. Christ is the way, the truth, and the life. He is the one thing needful. It seems, then, that we are confronted here with two rival accounts of a good sufficient for man. But they cannot both be sufficient and ultimate. The believer knows that the end to which he is called is alone sufficient to assuage the longing of the human heart. Aristotle apparently thought otherwise.

Let me make the difficulty sharper. Among the notes of the ultimate end is that it is the sufficient good of man. If Aristotle put forward an account of the sufficient good of man, on the one hand, and Thomas Aquinas, guided by his Christian faith, judged Aristotle's account to be insufficient and that another, a different, account must be given of man's ultimate end, on the other hand, then the two men are at odds. If Aristotle is right, Thomas is wrong. If Thomas is right, Aristotle is wrong. From this it should follow that Thomas, in speaking of the ultimate end of the human person, would ignore what Aristotle said. But this he does not do. Has his grasp of logic loosened? Does he think it possible to hold simultaneously contradictory claims? But to call Aristotle's account sufficient is in contradiction to the claim that it is insufficient.

It is apparent difficulties of this sort that caused Thomas to look more carefully at the text of Aristotle. From the vantage point of moral theology, he asks whether Aristotle did indeed hold that he had given an account of the ultimate end that is sufficient. If he did think so, his view is in conflict with Thomas's. But Thomas finds a passage that makes it clear Aristotle did not think his account of the ultimate end was sufficient.

When Aristotle gives what might be called a formal account of the ultimate end and its properties, there still lies ahead of him the need to show in what that formal account is realized. Our question thus becomes: Did Aristotle think that human beings could achieve a life which saved completely and perfectly what is meant by the ultimate end? Thomas refers us to Book 1, chapter 10 of the *Nicomachean Ethics* (1101a14–20):

Why then should we not say that he is happy who is active in accordance with complete virtue and is sufficiently equipped with external goods, not for some chance period but throughout a complete life? Or must we add "and who is destined to live thus and die as befits his life"? Certainly the future is obscure to us, while happiness, we claim, is an end and something in every way final. If so, we shall call happy those among living men in whom these conditions are, and are to be, fulfilled—but happy *men*.[11]

Thomas takes this to be Aristotle's admission that the ideal of happiness can only be imperfectly realized by us men in this life. And this opens the way for him to subsume what Aristotle had to say of the good life into a richer vision of the ultimate good that overcomes the vagaries and vicissitudes and contingencies of this life.[12] Hence Thomas's frequent use of the distinction between *beatitudo imperfecta,* the happiness attainable in this life, and *beatitudo perfecta,* that which is promised us hereafter. It will not surprise you, therefore, that Aristotle is cited sixty-three times in the five questions Thomas devotes to the ultimate end.

It is because nature has not been destroyed by the supernatural that it continues to be possible to inquire about man's good, man being what he is. That the good he can achieve falls short of a full realization of the ultimate end taken formally does not prevent this.

Aristotle and Natural Law

Someone has said that life is a book in which we set out to write one story and end by writing another. You will wonder if something similar has not happened to me in writing this article. My theme is Thomistic natural law and Aristotelian philosophy. But I seem to have been talking of other matters—but not wholly unrelated matters certainly. General reflections on what have been taken to be the relation between Thomas and Aristotle led us to moral doctrine and that of course led on to discussion of the ultimate

---

11. Aristotle, *Nicomachean Ethics,* trans. W. D. Ross, in *The Basic Works of Aristotle* (New York: Random House, 1941).

12. Cf. *ST* I-II, q. 3, a. 2 ad 4. You will wonder if Thomas makes this point in commenting on the text in question. Indeed he does. "But because these things seem not to measure up in all respects to the conditions required for happiness above, he adds that those we call happy are men, subject to change in this life, who cannot attain perfect beatitude. Since a natural desire is not in vain, we can correctly judge that perfect beatitude is reserved for man after this life." See *Commentary on Aristotle's Nicomachean Ethics,* trans. C. I. Litzinger (South Bend, Ind.: Dumb Ox Books, 1993), I, lectio 16, n. 202.

end. All along, comparisons have been made between Thomas and Aristotle. But what has been undeniably missing is any allusion to natural law.

Of course natural law cannot be discussed without presupposing what was said earlier about the ultimate end. The precepts of natural law have to do precisely with the end. In its proper sense, a precept is a command to do that which will lead to the end, or a command not to do that which is destructive of the end. There have been those who wish to see an opposition between the way in which the moral part of the *Summa theologiae* begins and the later treatment of law.[13] The conception of virtue emerges quite naturally from the discussion of the ultimate end, as we have recalled earlier. The emphasis should be on prudence and the moral virtues it guides, we are told, and not on law and the application of precepts.[14]

To make short shrift of this difficulty, I offer you the following text:

The good in general is that to which will naturally tends, in the way every power tends to its object, not only the ultimate end itself which relates to things desired in the way that the first principles of demonstration relate to intelligible things, but generally whatever befits the one willing given his nature. It is not the case that in willing we will only what pertains to the power of will: we also will what pertains to each of the powers and to the whole man. Thus a man naturally wills not only the object of will but also what befits the other powers, such as knowledge of truth, which pertains to intellect, and to exist and live and other such things, which pertain to natural well being, all of which are included within the object of will as particular goods.[15]

---

13. Those who see affinities between Thomas and "virtue ethics" sometimes take prudence to be a rival of natural law. Cf. Anthony Lisska, *Aquinas's Theory of Natural Law* (Oxford, U.K.: Clarendon Press, 1996), for a good discussion of this.

14. A similar claim arose with respect to the *Nicomachean Ethics*. The end/means analysis of human decision was opposed to the account of moral decision in books 6 and 7, and the introduction of the practical syllogism. Syllogism! Some scholars who would have delighted Nietzsche argued that the order of the books was wrong, and that Aristotle wrote the later books earlier and the earlier books later, so that the end/means analysis could be seen as an advance upon and rejection of the principle/application model of the practical syllogism. Of course, this is a false opposition.

15. "Hoc autem est bonum in communi, in quod voluntas naturaliter tendit, sicut etiam quaelibet potentia in suum obiectum: et etiam ipse finis ultimus, qui hoc modo se habet in appetibilibus, sicut prima principia demonstrationum in intelligibilibus: et universaliter omnia illa quae conveniunt volenti secundum suam naturam. Non enim per voluntatem appetimus

This text is an adumbration of the discussion in q. 94, a. 2, of course, and makes clear how ill-advised is any attempt to drive a wedge between the ultimate end and natural law precepts.

Aristotle is cited forty-four times in the thirty-seven articles that make up qq. 90–97, but nowhere is his influence more obvious than in the description of natural law as providing the starting points of practical reasoning which function in a way analogous to the starting points of reasoning generally.[16] This is the basis for holding that all acting persons grasp these constitutive guidelines for good and fulfilling action. So natural, so etched in the heart are they, that the principles of natural law can never be wholly eradicated. This does not of course mean that everyone naturally knows the accounts or definitions of natural law that Thomas offers—the peculiarly human participation in eternal law; the first indemonstrable principles of practical reasoning—but we can count on anyone's being able to discern the difference between good and evil, both in general and in less general instantiations of them.

Knowing them does not entail abiding by them, of course, and bad upbringing or bad action can so obscure the mind that what is evil is taken to be good. Thomas gives an example which is peculiarly, *ut ita dicam,* applicable to our time, unnatural vices.[17]

The analogy between the speculative and the practical on the matter of starting points indicates that the precepts of natural law are the last fallback

---

solum ea quae pertinent ad potentiam voluntatis; sed etiam ea quae pertinent ad singulas potentias, et ad totum hominem. Unde naturaliter homo vult non solum obiectum voluntatis, sed etiam alia quae conveniunt aliis potentiis, ut cognitionem veri, quae convenit intellectui; et esse et vivere et alia huiusmodi, quae respiciunt consistentiam naturalem: quae omnia comprehenduntur sub obiecto voluntatis, sicut quaedam particularia bona" (*ST* I-II, q. 10, a. 1).

16. *ST* I-II, q. 91, a. 3; q. 94, aa. 2, 4.

17. In discussing whether the law of nature could ever be erased from the human heart (*ST* I-II, q. 94, a. 6), Thomas distinguishes the most common principles known to all from secondary more proper precepts that are *quasi conclusiones propinquae* of the most common. The first cannot be *erased taken as such, universally,* "but it can be in the particular thing to be done, insofar as reason is prevented form applying the common principle to the particular things to be done because of concupiscience or some other passion, as was said above. With respect to the other, secondary principles, natural law can be erased from the hearts of men, either because of bad persuasion, in the way in which errors occur in speculative matters with respect to necessary conclusions, or because of depraved customs and corrupt habits, as with those who do not think theft or even sins against nature to be sin, as the Apostle says in Romans."

position in moral argument. However at odds we may be in the moral middle distance, it is possible to find something on which disputants agree. Attempts to deny the self-evident involve incoherence and no one can be coherently incoherent. Adjudicating differences in the theoretical order, difficult as it often is, is considerably easier than it is in the practical order, because of the role appetite plays in the latter. True statements about the good are not the same thing as seeking and desiring the good—we relate to the good not only or chiefly *ut verum*, but also *ut bonum*, that is, as desirable. Still, no one can fail to want the good. A remark of Chesterton's has always seemed to me to capture the comprehensive nature of the good in Aristotle and Thomas: the young man knocking on the brothel door, Chesterton remarked, is looking for God. We can desire as good that which is actually in conflict with our motive in desiring it. Whatever is sought is sought *sub ratione boni*, but not everything which is taken to be the carrier of that *ratio* actually is.

Conclusion

My aim is not to pursue each of the matters mentioned but to suggest that their cumulative effect is to show the way in which Aristotle forms the fundamental structure of Thomas's moral thinking. A sign of this is the sheer number of times he is invoked in the course of discussing the ultimate end and natural law. (Of course I do not mean to confine his influence to these two matters.) The greatest obstacle to seeing Aristotle as an obstacle to Thomism is Thomas himself. Thomas saw Aristotle as an authority and ally. His thought would be unintelligible apart from Aristotle. Only when the role Aristotle plays in Thomas's thought is fully appreciated can we fully appreciate the extensions Thomas gives to that thought. It has been said—by Pico della Mirandola—that without Thomas, Aristotle would be mute.[18] It is also true that without Aristotle Thomas would not have found his distinctive voice.

The deeper significance of this is explored in *Fides et ratio*. Faith is not derived from reason, but reason is an indispensable presupposition of it. What the human mind can grasp by its own power continues to play the

---

18. *Sine thoma Aristoteles mutus esset* is attributed to Pico by Paul Oskar Kristeller in his *Le thomisme et la pensée italienne de renaissance* (Montreal:Vrin, 1967).

role of *praeparatio evangelica* and *praeambula fidei*. It is precisely this indispensability—grace builds on nature and does not destroy it—that has led to the paradoxical situation we see today. In our time, it is the pope who has become not merely the chief defender of the faith, but the chief defender of reason as well. The relationship of Thomas to Aristotle may be seen as a particular instance of the way the believer must engage in philosophy if he is to engage in theology.

I will end with some remarks as to why Aristotle was so attractive philosophically to Thomas that are suggested by the analogy drawn between first principles of reasoning generally and the first principles of practical reasoning in the text that has received so much deserved attention. I want to stress what would seem to be one of the principal motives behind Leo XIII's pointing to Thomas, a motive that is even clearer in *Fides et ratio*.

Descartes presided over the cultural developments that caused Leo XIII to look around him with such dismay, a dismay that is deepened in the case of John Paul II. An insufficiently stressed implication of Cartesian doubt is that it assumes that the mass of mankind cannot be said to know anything. If every candidate for true knowledge requires that it be passed through the acid bath of doubt, only those who apply this method and come up with successful survivors of the process can be said to know in any serious sense of the term. Now, this is bad news for my grandmother and the billions like her who never studied philosophy, let alone engaged in methodic doubt. With Descartes, philosophy took a fateful elitist turn. Other turns, each one more elitist than the last, have since been taken, until now we have arrived at pragmatic skepticism in theoretical thought and what Alasdair MacIntyre has called "universal emotivism" in moral matters.[19]

In *Fides et ratio*, n. 4, John Paul II speaks of what he calls "Implicit Philosophy," the truths anyone can be expected to know. His reason for enumerating these truths is that he sees them as the means of overcoming the scandal of philosophy, the dozens of radically different philosophical systems competing for our allegiance. Anyone will detect the Thomistic echoes in the list of tenets of Implicit Philosophy. The pope's procedure makes clear why he too points us to Thomas and why Thomism is not just another system. We are not being urged to be Thomists as opposed to

---

19. Alisdair MacIntyre, *After Virtue*, 2d ed. (South Bend, Ind.: University of Notre Dame Press, 1984), 21.

Hegelians or phenomenologists or whatever. We are being urged to do philosophy well.

The great presupposition of doing philosophy well is that one begin well. The beginnings of philosophy are not acquired in Philosophy 101. They are had before one begins the study of philosophy. The principles or starting points of philosophy are the truths that any human person can be expected already to know. Philosophy moves off from them, not to replace or abandon them, but to develop their implications. Any philosophical position that is at variance with these starting points has gone off the rails.

Here we see the most profound and important impact of Aristotle on Thomas in the matter of natural law. In the practical order, the first question is what can we expect everyone already to know with respect to what we ought to do and what we ought to avoid. Natural law consists of the first indisputable principles of practical reasoning. The claim that everyone knows the principles of natural law is not of course the claim that everyone, even my grandmother, knows these definitions. The natural law, as St. Paul remarks, is inscribed in our hearts.[20] But knowing natural law does not entail knowing St. Paul. The universality of the first principles of practical reasoning is manifest in the ordinary remarks and disputes that human beings engage in with respect to good and evil. When our mothers asked us how we would like it if someone did that to us, they were invoking a principle Thomas associated with natural law. Its invocation by our maternal parent brings home to us that we ourselves would not like to be hit on the head with a baseball bat. We realize that not harming others is a bedrock assumption of being a human being. I think we should pay more attention to such homely moral disputes in speaking of natural law. They prepare us for the homely handling of sophisticated errors.

When we are told that we are free to do whatever we wish so long as we respect the freedom of others, we will recognize that this is an arbitrary restriction, if I am really as free as all get out. When Justice Kennedy in the "mystery clause" tells us that everyone has the right to define life as he likes, indeed the very universe,[21] we will recognize a statement which, if it is true, is false. Perhaps our problem is not the phrase "natural law," or its

---

20. Rom 2:15.

21. "At the heart of liberty is the right to define one's own concept of existence, of the universe, and of the mystery of human life" *(Planned Parenthood of SE Pennsylvania v. Casey)*.

fortunes among scholars. Attending to what is actually operative in moral discourse by ordinary people will show the presence of what is called natural law. This is only what we would expect. If natural law theory is correct it is so not because we can persuade people to adopt a theory; rather, the theory is correct because of what people already hold.

These are simple considerations. But simplicity is what our topic calls for. However odd our discussions might sound when overheard by the janitor, he knows what we are talking about, though not perhaps our way of talking about it. Kierkegaard once asked why else do we need theologians if not to make simple things difficult. This is irony of course. But why else do we have philosophers except to show that their difficult discussions are finally parasitic on what everyone already knows, both the wise and the simple?

PART II

NATURAL LAW IN A THEOLOGICAL CONTEXT

3

MAIMONIDES AND AQUINAS ON NATURAL LAW

David Novak

Natural Law and Divine Law

It is indisputable that Moses Maimonides was an important influence on the thought of Thomas Aquinas. Whether agreeing with him or disagreeing with him, Aquinas always refers to Maimonides with the same respect he pays his Christian theological sources and his Greek and Arabic philosophical sources. A number of insightful modern studies have been written that show the depth of that influence and how deeper and more comprehensive understandings of Aquinas's thought must take it into account.[1] Furthermore, Maimonides seems to be the only Jewish thinker Aquinas took seriously, perhaps because he was the only Jewish thinker he had ever read at all.

Most studies of the influence of Maimonides on Aquinas concentrate on

---

1. See, e.g., Isaac Franck, "Maimonides and Aquinas on Man's Knowledge of God: A Twentieth-Century Perspective," *Review of Metaphysics* 38 (1985): 591–615; and Idit Dobbs-Weinstein, *Maimonides and St. Thomas on the Limits of Reason* (Albany: State University of New York Press, 1995). All of the articles collected in *Studies in Maimonides and St. Thomas Aquinas,* ed. J. I. Dienstag (New York: KTAV, 1975), deal with metaphysical similarities and differences.

metaphysics. There is good reason for that since Maimonides was an important link in the chain that brought the ontological theory of Aristotle to the attention and consideration of Christian thinkers in Europe. In metaphysics, Maimonides added his voice to the *falasifa* of Islamic thinkers like Ibn Sina. Following the example of his teacher Albertus Magnus, Aquinas was eager to appropriate this great metaphysical tradition into the type of Christian theology that takes philosophy seriously in its own constructive endeavors. As such, Aquinas could not very well ignore how this way of thinking was handled by Maimonides, whom he respectfully calls "Rabbi Moses" at all times.[2] Nevertheless, at the level of metaphysics, it is largely irrelevant whether Maimonides is *Rabbi* Moses or not. In these metaphysical discussions, it makes little difference whether one is a pagan like Aristotle, a Muslim like Ibn Sina, a Jew like Maimonides, or a Christian like Thomas Aquinas.[3] It is only when one gets to the more explicitly theological level, whether that theology be theoretical or practical, that these religious distinctions make a real difference.

Without in any way belittling the metaphysical influence, one could well argue that the influence of Maimonides on Aquinas was far more extensive in the area of practical reason, which covers the joint area of ethics and politics. This is the area where Aquinas works as a Christian moral theologian. Aquinas engages in two types of practical reason, and indeed contemporary Thomists dispute which is the more important in his moral theology. In the opening questions discussed in the first part of the second section *(prima secundae)* of the *Summa theologiae,* Aquinas engages in what we would call "virtue-based ethics" today.[4] But more of the questions dis-

---

2. In the earliest monograph on Aquinas by a Jewish scholar, *Das Verhältnis des Thomas von Aquino zum Judenthum und zur jüdischen Litteratur* (Gottingen: Vandenhock und Ruprecht's Verlag, 1891), Jakob Guttmann noted at the outset (p. 3) how respectful Aquinas was of Maimonides *(ein ehrenvolles Zeugnis).* For Aquinas's views on Jews and Judaism in general, see J. Hood, *Aquinas and the Jews* (Philadelphia: University of Pennsylvania Press, 1995).

3. Thus the great historian of ancient and medieval philosophy, Harry A. Wolfson, wrote: "The same Greek terminology lay behind the Arabic, Hebrew, and Latin terminology. . . . The three philosophic literatures were in fact one philosophy expressed in different languages, translatable almost literally into one another" (see *Spinoza* [Cambridge, Mass.: Harvard University Press, 1934], 10). For a study that insightfully demonstrates this point in the area of God-talk, see David B. Burrell, *Knowing the Unknowable God* (South Bend, Ind.: University of Notre Dame Press, 1986), esp. 1–18.

4. See, e.g., Daniel Westberg, *Right Practical Reason* (Oxford, U.K.: Clarendon Press, 1994).

cussed in this section of the *Summa* (beginning with question 90) concern what we would call "law-based ethics" today.[5] Even though Aquinas himself did not call this part of the *prima secundae* a "Treatise on Law" as it is frequently called today, one can see why his treatment of questions of law *(de Legibus)* could be seen as a self-contained work by itself. So we need to see how Aquinas structures this part of the *Summa* in order to appreciate the significant role Maimonides plays in it.

Aquinas divides law into six main categories: (1) eternal law, which is the norm whereby God governs the universe, most of which is unknowable by finite human minds; (2) natural law, which is that aspect of the eternal law that is knowable by finite human minds and applicable to human life, what my teacher Professor Germain Grisez calls "an intellect size bite of reality"[6]; (3) human law, which is how human minds apply the general principles of natural law in particular historical situations; (4) divine law, which is that aspect of the eternal law that is made known to human minds by God though historical revelation; (5) the Old Law, which is that aspect of divine law made known by God through pre-Christian revelation to the Jewish people; and (6) the New Law, which is that aspect of divine law made known by Christ to the Church.

What is most interesting, even surprising, about this arrangement is that Aquinas devotes more time to the discussion of the Old Law than he does to any of the other categories of law. And it is in these questions where we find Maimonides appearing quite regularly. That is not surprising inasmuch as this is Aquinas's most concentrated and extensive treatment of Judaism, and virtually everything he knew abut Judaism came from Scripture and the interpretations of Maimonides.[7] (How fortunate for himself and for posterity that Aquinas's engagement with Judaism was located in his engagement with the thinker whom no subsequent Jewish thinker can ever really leave behind when thinking about Judaism.) Here one sees how carefully Aquinas read Maimonides's main work in philosophical theology,

---

5. See, e.g., Russell Hittinger, "Natural Law and Catholic Moral Theology," in *A Preserving Grace: Protestants, Catholics, and Natural Law,* ed. Michael Cromartie (Grand Rapids, Mich.: Eerdmans, 1997), 1–30 .

6. Germain Grisez, "The First Principle of Practical Reason: A Commentary on the *Summa Theologiae,* 1–2, Question 94, Article 2," *Natural Law Forum* 10 (1965): 174.

7. See Guttmann, *Das Verhältnis des Thomas von Aquino zum Judenthum und zur judischen Litteratur,* 13–15.

the *Guide of the Perplexed*. In his discussion of the Old Law, Aquinas draws much from the third section of that work, which deals with what rabbinic tradition called "the reasons of the Torah" *(taʿamei torah)* and what Maimonides and the medievals called "the reasons of the commandments" *(taʿamei ha-mitsvot)*.[8] Yet I can't help thinking how much more Aquinas would have gotten from Maimonides's Jewish jurisprudence if he also had access to Maimonides's encyclopaedic codification of all of Jewish law, the *Mishneh Torah*. In the *Guide* Maimonides called this work "our great composition" *(taʿalifana al-khabir)*.[9] Aquinas could have well called it *Corpus Juris Judaeorum*, perhaps even *Summa Theologiae Judaicae*, had he been able to read it and not just hear about it.

At this point I would like to consider why Aquinas engaged in this lengthy and detailed treatment of Judaism in his own great composition, which too many forget is a summa of *theology*, not of philosophy, and where philosophy is the servant of theology *(ancilla theologiae)*, not its mistress. This consideration begins with the question: Why is Aquinas qua *Christian theologian* interested in natural law? Moreover, what is the connection between natural law and the Old Law? This is important inasmuch as it is in Aquinas's discussion of the Old Law that Maimonides plays his most extensive role in Aquinas's thought.

We need to ask these questions because a theologian's interest in natural law is not the same as that of a philosopher. For a philosopher, whom Maimonides and Aquinas would see as a human thinker to whom revelation is unavailable (or ontologically irrelevant as it was for Spinoza), the prime example being Aristotle and the Aristotelians, the interest in natural law (better "natural right" as *orthos logos* or *recta ratio*) stems from the attempt to know what remains permanent and universal in human nature as opposed to what is ephemeral and parochial in human history.[10] To discover natural law is to discover what is divine within the universe, especially as it pertains to the human condition. It is the very apex of worldly human knowledge. But for a theologian, divine law is more than natural law. As such, it is not discoverable naturally, that is, by universally accessible human reason. Di-

---

8. See *Babylonian Talmud* (hereafter "B."): Sanhedrin 21a–b; Maimonides, *The Book of the Commandments*, Introduction, root no. 5, and *Guide of the Perplexed* (hereafter "*Guide*"), 3.26.

9. *Guide*, 1.36. Arabic text: *Dalalat al-ha'irin*, ed. S. Munk (Jerusalem: n.p., 1931), 56.

10. See Leo Strauss, *Natural Right and History* (Chicago: University of Chicago Press, 1953), 81–119.

vine law is directly revealed by God in history to an elect community. It is not a dispensable element *within* the human story; instead, it is the preview of the eschatological consummation of history itself. That is why divine law is supernatural, but not irrational.[11] For a philosopher, conversely, natural law is either identical with divine law (as it is for Plato), or divine law is inferior to natural law (as it is for Kant).[12] For a theologian, natural law is at best an indispensable element within a larger divine story, what some modern theologians have called *Heilsgeschichte*.[13]

In Aquinas's thought, grace brings nature to its true perfection.[14] As such, natural law must somehow or other be seen as being contained within the divine law itself. Somewhat similarly, Maimonides had earlier said that "the [divine] Law, although it is not natural, enters into what is natural."[15] Natural law, then, can be seen as the precondition for divine grace, the greatest manifestation of which heretofore is the revelation of divine law. The humanly knowable world into which revelation can possibly enter must be a world in which natural law is discernable and respected.

I would now like to show how the constitution of this relation between divine law and natural law is generally similar in Aquinas and in Maimonides because each theologian had to deal with the question of the natural preconditions for revelation. Nevertheless, there are specific differences between them and these specific differences are important for contemporary theologians, both Jewish and Christian, to consider when rethinking natural law today.

For a variety of reasons, the more theological comparison of the views of Maimonides and Aquinas is of greater contemporary import than the

---

11. See John Courtney Murray, S.J., *We Hold These Truths: Catholic Reflections on the American Proposition* (New York: Sheed & Ward, 1960), 298.

12. See Plato, *Laws* 631B–D. Cf. Kant, *Religion within the Limits of Reason Alone*, trans. T. H. Greene and H. H. Hudson (New York: Harper & Brothers, 1960), 169–71. It is questionable, though, whether Aristotle affirmed what we call "natural law," viz., universally valid and cognizable moral norms. Note his hesitation in *Nicomachean Ethics* 1134b25–34.

13. For a study that puts Aquinas's natural law theory in the context of his biblical exegesis, hence in the context of his understanding of *Heilsgeschichte*, see Eugene F. Rogers Jr., *Thomas Aquinas and Karl Barth* (South Bend, Ind.: University of Notre Dame Press, 1995), 46–70.

14. See *ST* II-I, q. 99, a. 2.

15. *Guide*, 2.40, trans. Shlomo Pines (Chicago: University of Chicago Press, 1963), 382. For a fuller discussion of Maimonides's view of nature, see D. Novak, *The Image of the Non-Jew in Judaism* (New York and Toronto: Edwin Mellen Press, 1983), 290–94.

comparison of their more philosophical views. One of these reasons might be that one can still engage in theology, especially moral theology, similar to the way Maimonides and Aquinas engaged in it, whereas it might well be fantastic to attempt to engage in the type of Aristotelian metaphysics that occupied both of them. In moral theology it could be said we are still dealing with the same objects they both dealt with. In metaphysics, however, such objective continuity is rather implausible. In what might be termed their respective "meta-ethics," the ethics is still the same. But in their respective "meta-physics," the physics is radically different. That is a great problem for those philosophers today who think they can return to a comprehensively Aristotelian position.[16]

First, let us look at how Maimonides constitutes the relation of natural law and divine law. Next, let us look at how Aquinas constitutes that relation. Finally, let us attempt to evaluate the specific differences between their respective approaches to what might be seen as the connection of nature and grace.

Maimonides's Main Statement of Natural Law

The statements on law in the *Guide of the Perplexed,* with which Aquinas was familiar, are built upon his statements on law in his great legal compendium, the *Mishneh Torah.* (This assertion is controversial inasmuch as the late Professor Leo Strauss and his disciples see a difference in kind between the Maimonides of the *Mishneh Torah* and the Maimonides of the *Guide.* I follow those scholars who see much more unity in Maimonides's theology, the differences between the two main works being much more differences of degree.[17]) Even though Aquinas was not familiar with the earlier and larger work, it is important for us to look at it for Maimonides's most explicit statement concerning natural law. (This assertion is also controversial inasmuch as the late Professor Marvin Fox, among others, argued that the general difference between Maimonides and Aquinas is that Aquinas has a natural law doctrine whereas Maimonides denies natural law alto-

---

16. See D. Novak, *Covenantal Rights* (Princeton, N.J.: Princeton University Press, 2000), 21–23.

17. See David Hartman, *Maimonides: Torah and Philosophic Quest* (Philadelphia: Jewish Publication Society of America, 1976), 22–26. Cf. Leo Strauss, *Persecution and the Art of Writing* (Chicago and London: University of Chicago Press, 1988), 38–94.

gether.[18]) One cannot fully appreciate Maimonides's treatment of natural law in the context of the "reasons of the commandments" in the *Guide* without seeing its precedent in *Mishneh Torah*.

Even though Maimonides does not use the term "natural law," it is clear he means something quite similar when he refers to some norms as being required "because of the inclination of reason" *(mipnei hekhre ha-daʿat)*.[19] This term could be literally translated into Aquinas's Latin as *inclinatio rationalis*, which for humans is the prime *inclinatio naturalis*.[20] This term is employed within a larger discussion of possible Jewish governance of gentiles in chapter 8 of "the Laws of Kingship" of *Mishneh Torah*. What are the types of this possible governance?

The most obvious form of Jewish governance of gentiles is when gentiles convert to Judaism. This type of governance is the most complete, so complete in fact that the gentiles cease to be gentiles at all and are totally absorbed into the Jewish people. It is the equivalent in Roman law of someone of non-Roman birth becoming adopted by the people of Rome that he could now say with them "I am a Roman citizen" *(civus Romanus sum)*. Maimonides mentions this option (which may not be forced upon gentiles against their will), but that is not his main concern here, which is with the gentile "other."[21] The forms of Jewish governance of the gentile "other" with which Maimonides is concerned here are threefold.

First, according to the Talmud, any gentile living under Jewish rule is required to accept upon himself (or herself) seven norms that are seen as binding on all humankind. They are called "the seven commandments of the children of Noah" *(sheva mitsvot bnei Noah)*.[22] The core of these commandments are three general prohibitions: the prohibition of idolatry, the prohibition of killing innocent human life, and the prohibition of sex outside a permanent heterosexual union.[23] Acceptance of these basic prohibi-

---

18. See Marvin Fox, *Interpreting Maimonides* (Chicago: University of Chicago Press, 1990), 124–51.

19. *Mishneh Torah* (hereafter "MT"): Kings 8.11. (The entire *Mishneh Torah* is available in English translation in the Yale Judaica series [New Haven, Conn.: Yale University Press].)

20. See *ST* II-I, q. 91, a. 2. Quotations taken from *Summa theologiae,* trans. Thomas Gilby et al. (Cambridge, U.K.: Blackfriars, 1964–1974).

21. MT: Kings, 8.10.

22. *Tosefta:* Avodah Zarah 8.4; B. Sanhedrin 56a–b.

23. B. Sanhedrin 57a. See 74a where these same three commandments are designated those a Jew is to die for as a martyr rather than transgress.

tions is required for any gentile to become a resident alien *(ger toshav)* in a Jewish polity.[24] Since these requisite norms are administered by Jewish authorities, and since these norms seem to be universally justifiable by reason, several scholars have compared this type of Jewish rule over gentiles domiciled in their midst to the Roman political institution of *ius gentium*.[25] This was the form of law used by Roman officials to govern non-Roman peoples who had long lived under Roman rule. (In later Roman law it designated law seen as internationally prevalent, that is, by *consensus gentium*.) *Ius gentium* was more general and less specific than Roman law for Roman citizens *(ius civile)*.

Second, Maimonides speaks of gentiles who accept the Noahide laws, not because of Jewish rule but because of acceptance of what Judaism regards as rationally binding on all humans. These are persons who practice these basic laws because of "the inclination of reason."[26] Here we have a distinction between general moral obligation and specific Jewish political obligation. Those who follow reason need not live under a Jewish regime at all, and Jewish tradition recognizes their moral status as law-abiding persons nonetheless. Thus valid morality does not need Jewish enforcement or supervision. Such persons Maimonides calls "their [i.e., the gentiles'] sages."[27] Undoubtedly, this category of persons includes both those who can arrive at moral truth through their own reasoning and those who follow the teachings of their own sages as participants in a venerable moral tradition. Some scholars have seen this type of rule to be akin to the Roman notion of *ius naturale*, which is the law that is prior to the founding of any human polity.[28]

Finally, there is a third category, one that is quite problematic, being the subject of great debate among students of Maimonides for centuries. Here is what Maimonides says:

---

24. B. Avodah Zarah 64b.

25. See Novak, *The Image of the Non-Jew in Judaism*, 11–14.

26. For the rabbinic sources of this concept, see *Tosefta:* Hullin 8.1; *Palestinian Talmud:* Sanhedrin 1.1/8b; also see M. Guttmann, "Maimonide sur l'universalité de la morale religieuse," *Revue d'etudes juives* 99 (1935): 41.

27. MT: Kings, 8.11.

28. See D. Novak, *Natural Law in Judaism* (Cambridge, U.K.: Cambridge University Press, 1998), 122–42.

Whoever accepts the seven commandments and is obligated [*nizhar*] to perform them, this person is one of the pious of the nations of the world [*me-hasidei ummot ha'olam*] and has a portion in the world-to-come. But this person is one who accepts them because [*mipnei*] God has commanded them in the Torah. And He [God] has let us know through [*ve-hodi'enu al yedei*] Moses our Master that the Noahides had been commanded concerning them in the past [*me-qodem*].[29]

Many scholars have interpreted this statement of Maimonides, especially, as the clearest indication that he is opposed to the idea of natural law. They have read it to mean that only those who accept Mosaic revelation and what it requires of gentiles can be said to be law-abiding gentiles.[30] Furthermore, they accept the reading of the printed texts of *Mishneh Torah*, which have Maimonides saying that those who only accept the Noahide laws because of rational inclination are "neither pious nor wise" *(ve-lo me-hakhmeihem)*. Spinoza made much of this text, using it to show that there is no universal ethic in Judaism, indeed, that such an ethic could not be constituted even by one so committed to the reconciliation of Scripture and reason as was Maimonides.[31]

In this view, the only law-abiding gentiles, for Maimonides, are those who are willing to live according to that department of Jewish law designated for them. That would include any gentiles actually living under Jewish political rule, or any gentiles willing to accept the moral authority of Jewish teaching from books. This latter type of law-abiding gentile might also include Christians, who see the general moral teachings of the Old Testament to still be authoritative even after the coming of Christ and the New Covenant.[32] And, by a somewhat more inclusive reading, it might even include Muslims, whose basic morality seems to be close enough to that of Judaism, and who also revere Moses as a genuine prophet.[33] Never-

---

29. MT: Kings, 8.11.

30. See Fox, *Interpreting Maimonides*, 130–39.

31. Spinoza, *Tractatus Theologico-Politicus*, chap. 5, trans. S. Shirley (Leiden: E. J. Brill, 1991), 122–23.

32. See D. Novak, *Maimonides on Judaism and Other Religions* (Cincinnati: Hebrew Union College Press, 1997), 4–10; also see D. Novak, *Jewish-Christian Dialogue* (New York: Oxford University Press, 1989), 57–72.

33. See D. Novak, "The Treatment of Muslims and Islam in the Legal Writings of Maimonides," *Studies in Islamic and Jewish Traditions*, ed. W. M. Brinner and S. D. Ricks (Chico, Calif.: Scholars Press, 1986), 233–50.

theless, it would not include those whose morality stems from their own rational discovery of natural law. A more careful reading of this text, however, plus a look at the overall *Tendenz* of Maimonides's understanding of practical reason, give a different impression altogether.

First and most important, Maimonides says that some of the laws of the Torah are rationally evident (what Aquinas would call *ratio quoad nos*), and that the seven basic Noahide laws fall into this category.[34] Second, the best manuscripts, unlike the printed texts, do not have Maimonides's saying that those who keep the Noahide laws are not even wise. Instead, they have Maimonides saying that those who keep these laws because of rational inclination may not be pious "but they are wise" *(ela me-hakhmeihem)* nonetheless.[35] This makes much more sense in the context of this whole chapter in the *Mishneh Torah* about gentile obligations. The lowest level of gentile is one who accepts what Judaism regards as universally mandated because that is the way for him or her to gain a permanent and protected status in a Jewish polity. This makes one eligible to become a resident alien *(ger toshav)*. The next highest level is one who accepts what Judaism regards as universally mandated because that is what he or she reasons is right. This makes one a wise Noahide. The highest level is the one who accepts what Judaism regards as universally mandated because he or she believes this is a divine law. This makes one pious. Only this last person is worthy of the world-to-come along with all Jews who accept (or, minimally, do not deny) the Mosaic Torah to be divine law. But, it is important to keep in mind, this pious gentile does not have to convert to Judaism in order to attain the world-to-come.

After this analysis of the text, it would seem that Maimonides does affirm natural law and that the natural law is known by practical wisdom. The only difference between one who keeps natural law and one who keeps divine law is that the keeper of natural law only has a respected status in this world, but the keeper of divine law also has a respected status in the world-to-come.

It would seem that the difference between the two is that the keeper of divine law must accept it via Mosaic revelation, whereas the keeper of nat-

---

34. See *ST* I, q. 2, a. 1.

35. See I. Twersky, *The Code of Maimonides* (New Haven, Conn.: Yale University Press, 1980), 455, n. 239.

ural law need only keep it via rationally perceived human nature. However, even this distinction may not be what Maimonides means.

A careful reading of the text shows that Maimonides is not saying that the pious gentiles are pious *because* they accept Mosaic revelation. He only says Mosaic revelation "informs us"—the Jews—*that* the universal moral laws have already been accepted as divine law by humankind in the past. In other words, the *Torah* they discover need not be the specifically Mosaic Torah. As such, the Mosaic Torah given to the Jews confirms what the gentiles have or could have been doing since time immemorial *(me-qodem)*. It is not that the Noahides need to learn their basic morality *from* Jewish revelation; Jewish revelation need not be prescriptive for them. Instead, Jewish revelation is simply descriptive of what has been prescribed for the gentiles elsewhere. And, if they accept divine law from this other source, then they are worthy of joining normative Israel in the world-to-come. But what is this other source? Haven't we already eliminated both reason and Mosaic revelation? Must it be some other revelation like that of Christianity or Islam, or is there another alternative?

The only key we get from this text in our quest to answer the above questions is that Maimonides says that the Jews know about Noahide/human normativeness from what God revealed to us through Moses. But where is this to be found in Mosaic revelation? The few biblical verses brought up by the talmudic rabbis when explicating these commandments are only allusive rather than being strictly prescriptive.[36] That is undoubtedly why Maimonides does not cite them. So what Maimonides means here by Mosaic revelation is the Oral Tradition, which for him is the long history of Jewish teachers reasoning about what the meaning and application of the Torah is to be.[37] That reasoning sometimes even includes speculation as to what the universal preconditions for the acceptance of the specific Mosaic Torah must be. This discursive tradition is initiated by Moses, and it is carried on by all who participate in it and contribute to it. They are functioning as Moses did, and with Mosaic warrant.[38]

I do not think it is implausible to infer from his words about Mosaic revelation that Maimonides might mean that Jews learn of what the

---

36. See B. Sanhedrin 56b–57a.
37. See Novak, *Natural Law in Judaism*, 95–99.
38. MT: Rebels, chap. 1.

Noahides have been commanded by reasoning about what are the basic requirements of a decent life for any human being. Those are the things which, according to the Talmud, "had they not been written, they would have to have been written [*hayu le-kotvan*]."³⁹ Indeed, according to rabbinic tradition, the Jews themselves were Noahides before their status was elevated when they accepted the Written Torah (i.e., the fundament of Scripture) at Mount Sinai.⁴⁰ In other words, Jews learn about the obligations of Noahides/humans the same way all humans are to learn of their moral obligations, that is, by reasoning about what the fulfillment of human nature essentially requires. This is taken to be divine law when one reasons that this must be what God intended for humans to do by creating them. But, if that is so, why does Maimonides dismiss rational inclination as a sufficient way to learn how to attain the world-to-come?

The answer to this last last question cannot be inferred from the texts we have been examining so carefully. For this answer we must turn to the *Guide*, the Maimonidean work Aquinas knew quite well, and where Maimonides himself is much more explicit philosophically. What we see from the *Guide* is that there are two distinct types of human reason, and their respective use determines what kind of law we get.

Accordingly, if you find a law the whole end of which . . . [is] directed toward the ordering of the city . . . you must know that that Law is a nomos. . . . If, on the other hand, you find a Law all of whose ordinances are due to attention being paid . . . to the body and also to the soundness of belief . . . with regard to God . . . and

---

39. B. Yoma 67b. In his response to this paper, Prof. Martin D. Yaffe points out that Maimonides cites this very talmudic text to argue against the "dialectical theologians" (*mutalkallimun*) who speak of "rational commandments" (*mitsvot sikhliyot*). Based on this text (*Commentary on the Mishnah*: Avot, Introduction [*Eight Chapters*], chap. 6), Prof. Yaffe concludes, "[t]his passage alone evidently decides the question of whether Maimonides has a natural law teaching. By his own lights, at least, he does not" (Yaffe, p. 71). However, considering the earlier distinction between rational commandments and revealed commandments (*mitvot shimiʿyot*) could Maimonides, who continually emphasizes the reasons of the commandments, not affirm rational commandments? So it seems that it is better to interpret Maimonides's criticism of the distinction of the earlier theologians as being that they limit the category "rational" to only some of the commandments. However, a more sufficient metaphysical foundation would have enabled them to affirm, as does Maimonides himself, that all the commandments are rational, albeit some having reasons more evident than others. See Novak, *The Image of the Non-Jew in Judaism*, 285–87.

40. B. Nedarim 31a.

that desires to make men wise . . . you must know that this guidance comes from Him, may he be exalted, and that this Law is divine [al-shariyah al-alahiyah].[41]

What we see from this is that ordinary human reason, which is directed to purely political matters, might satisfy the immediate practical demands of rational inclination, but it does not lead rational inclination to its true object. That true object of the intellect is apprehending that what is good for human life is the result of the divine governance of the whole universe. I think Maimonides would have agreed with Bernard Lonergan when he said, "One can go beyond common sense and present science, to grasp the dynamic structure of our rational knowing and doing, and then formulate a metaphysics and an ethics."[42] For Maimonides, that metaphysics and that ethics are "natural," understanding the *nature* that makes them *natural* to be cosmic and not just the general structure required by earthly politics. For him, the world-to-come is not a future historical event; instead, it is the eternal realm of God which those of highest rational ability can apprehend even while they are living in the physical world.

Some scholars have seen this higher type of reason to be a more Platonic than Aristotelian correlation of practical and theoretical reason.[43] The Judeo-Christian-Islamic idea that nature is the lawful creation of the divine creator/lawgiver gives a new and more satisfying grounding to the process whereby ethics presupposes metaphysics and metaphysics entails ethics.[44] This is a far cry from the type of practical reasoning that is satisfied with what appears to be politically useful. It is also a far cry from the type of theoretical reason that sees the universe as a place indifferent to what human do or do not do. And, even though these truths are available to human reason, since they are not evident to most human minds, Jewish and Christian and Islamic revelations (the only historically recorded revelations of the one creator God) make them dogmatically, even if not demonstrably, available for large communities of humans.[45]

---

41. *Guide,* 2.40, 383–84 = Arabic, p. 271.

42. Bernard Lonergan, *Insight* (New York: Harper & Row, 1978), 635.

43. See Shlomo Pines's introduction to *Guide,* lxxxviii. Cf. Aristotle, *Nicomachean Ethics* 1177a25–30; Thomas Aquinas, *Commentary on Aristotle's Nicomachean Ethics,* 10, lect. 2087–97, trans. C. I. Litzinger (South Bend, Ind.: Dumb Ox Books, 1993), 624–26.

44. See Novak, *Natural Law in Judaism,* 113–21.

45. See Menachem Kellner, *Dogma in Medieval Jewish Thought* (Oxford, U.K.: Oxford University Press, 1986), 10–49.

Finally, as a Jewish theologian, Maimonides believes that Judaism presents the divine law in the best possible way, that it is the best coordination of theoretical and practical wisdom available in the world. It is rationally knowable, even if not immediately evident (what Aquinas would call *ratio per se*).[46] However, as his most astute commentator noted, when Maimonides indicated that the attainment of the world-to-come does not require conversion to Judaism (although apostasy from Judaism could forfeit it), he was accepting one rabbinic view over its opposite.[47] The opposite view is a Jewish version of *extra ecclesiam nulla salus,* namely, only Jews can attain the life of the world-to-come.[48] Maimonides clearly denies that.

At most, Judaism's superiority to the other monotheistic religions and to the philosophical coordination of ethics and metaphysics is one of degree rather than one of kind. Prophetic revelation is a propensity of human nature, and only philosophers can become prophets, even though there is no natural necessity that they actually do become prophets.[49] Prophecy is not confined to Israel (as Maimonides's predecessor, Judah Halevi, had argued), but Moses is unique among all the prophets and will never be surpassed.[50] The recognition of natural law, especially as it operates in human nature, is the beginning of a process that could possibly end in prophetic revelation, which grants us vision of the larger created nature of which human nature is a part. But to see natural law apart from its metaphysical ground is to make human reason rather than divine wisdom the measure of all things. That is why Maimonides is reticent to treat natural law apart from the full Law itself. To concentrate on what is only immediately evident could easily lead to the erroneous conclusion that what we call natural law at the political level is not only necessary but sufficient for the fulfillment of human nature. Natural law can be abstracted from the full Law itself, but it cannot be constituted in any adequate way independent of it. As Maimonides notes with good Aristotelian reasoning, the natural/Noahide law is "completed [*ve-nishlamah*] by the Torah of Moses."[51]

---

46. *ST* I, q. 2, a. 1.
47. Joseph Karo, *Kesef Mishneh* on MT: Kings, 8.11.
48. See *Tosefta:* Sanhedrin 13.2 and B. Sanhedrin 105a re Ps. 9:18.
49. See Novak, *Jewish-Christian Dialogue,* 129–38.
50. MT: Foundations of the Torah, 7.1–6; *Guide,* 2.36, 39. Cf. Halevi, *Kuzari,* 1.95, trans. H. Hirschfeld (New York: Pardes, 1946), 31.
51. MT: Kings, 9.1.

Aquinas on the Old Law

Although Aquinas was unaware of Maimonides's constitution of Noahide law as natural law (since Maimonides does not discuss Noahide law in the *Guide*), one could make the following analogy: Maimonides's view of the relation of Noahide law to Mosaic law is logically quite similar to Aquinas's view of the relation of the Old Law to the New Law. That general similarity is best seen in the fact that like Maimonides, Aquinas regards the relation of the earlier law to the later law to be one of potency and act. That is, the Old Law functions as potential for its full actualization in the New Law. Both of them learned much from Aristotle in their respective teleologies.

As a Christian theologian, Aquinas had to deal with a problem that has troubled Christians ever since the time when Christianity separated itself from Judaism. One might see this problem as how does a Christian steer clear of the Scylla of Marcionism and the Charybdis of Judaization. Because Christianity's claims are primarily based on the revelation of the Old Testament (the "Jewish" Scriptures), to advocate the total supersession of Judaism, as did Marcion and his followers (in all ages), is to destroy the very basis of Christianity. That basis is the claim that Jesus of Nazareth is the promised Messiah of Israel, and that God became incarnate in the body of this Torah-observant Jew.[52] (That is why the core of the Jewish-Christian debate is located in the rival claims made by Jews and Christians about the meaning of the Hebrew Bible as the prime criterion of truth: *torat emet*.) Something significantly Jewish must remain within Christianity and its teaching. On the other hand, if Christianity is not selective in its incorporation of Judaism, then how can it be regarded as anything more than an heretical Jewish sect (since the vast majority of Jews have refused to accept Christian claims upon them)? So, where does a Christian theologian draw this crucial line?

In Aquinas's view, Judaism's continued validity for Christians lies in its superior constitution of natural law. Natural law is what humans discover in their "natural inclination to know the truth about God and to live in society; and in this respect, whatever pertains to this inclination belongs to natural law."[53] Aquinas says that "the Old Law was in accordance with reason,"

---

52. Mt 5:17.   53. *ST* II-I, q. 94, a. 3.

and that "the Old Law was good, but imperfect."[54] The imperfection of the Old Law is not seen, however, until the revelation of the New Law in the same way, let us say, the immaturity of an acorn is not seen until it grows into a mature oak tree. In other words, the imperfection of the old is only seen retrospectively after the appearance of the new. Taken in and of itself, the Old Law intends "a sensible and earthly good, and to this man was directly ordained."[55] In fact, Aquinas is so serious about the earthly sufficiency of the Old Law that he argues that "the Old Law is said to be forever [*esse in aeternum*] unqualifiedly and absolutely as regards its moral precepts."[56] Moreover, "it is clear that the Old Law provided sufficiently concerning the mutual relations of one man with another."[57] Indeed, it is only because there are "things in which human reason may happen to be impeded" that natural law had to be given the stamp of divine (i.e., revealed) law in ancient Israel.[58]

Aquinas insists that natural law is "fully contained" not only in the New Law, but even in the Old Law.[59] Indeed, it might even be more evident in the Old Law than it is in the New Law inasmuch as Aquinas goes so far as to suggest that "the form of government established by the divine law" (i.e., the divine law as the Old Law) was the best example in human history of a mixed political constitution, combining what is best in monarchy, aristocracy, and democracy.[60] That is highly significant inasmuch as it could

54. *ST* II-I, q. 98, a. 1.
55. *ST* II-I, q. 91, a. 5.
56. *ST* II-I, q. 103, a. 3 ad 1. See *ST* II-I, q. 100, a. 1.
57. *ST* II-I, q. 105, a. 2. See *ST* II-I, q. 91, a. 5.
58. *ST* II-I, q. 99, a. 2 ad 2. In his response to this paper, Prof. John Goyette rightly points out that Aquinas saw the need for natural law to be part of the revealed Old Law (citing *ST* I, q. 95, a. 1) "because of original sin . . . man does not possess the knowledge he needs to fulfill the natural law and it was necessary, therefore, for God to give the Old law to the Jews so that nature might be restored" (Goyette, p. 77). But for Maimonides, conversely, it would seem that if there is any "original sin," it is the falling away of Adam (and his descendants) from the *vita contemplativa* and being solely concerned with the bodily goods that are the subject of the *vita activa* (see *Guide*, 1.2). Hence, there is a natural cure for this human predicament. Nevertheless, for a rabbinic view of original sin and the need for grace/revelation to cure humans of its consequences, see B. Yevamot 103a–b regarding Gn 31:24.
59. *ST* II-I, q. 94, a. 4 ad 1. Cf. John Calvin, *Institutes of the Christian Religion*, 2.7.10 and 4.20.16.
60. *ST* II-I, q. 105, a. 1.

be argued that the New Testament itself has no distinct political teaching. Jesus proclaims to Pontius Pilate, the representative of Roman imperial authority, "my kingdom is not of this world."[61] Before that he differentiated between the this-worldly realm of Caesar and the other-worldly realm of God.[62] Both Peter and Paul advocate obedience to temporal authority as long as one is still living in this world.[63] At most, beginning with Augustine, especially, one can see Christian political theory as functioning as a negative limit on the authority of the state whenever it tends to regard itself as divine.[64] That is why Aquinas seems to suggest that it is a good thing for an earthly sovereign to attempt to positively model his realm on biblical ideas of polity and its structures, as long as he does not present this political program as a literal reinstitution of the Old Law per se.[65]

Aquinas's selectivity of the Old Law is seen in the way he divides its precepts into three categories: moral, ceremonial, and judicial. Only the moral precepts, which turn out to be those contained in the Decalogue, are seen as the perpetual precepts of natural law, which have in no way been superceded by the precepts of the New Law. The ceremonial precepts and the judicial precepts, conversely, have been superceded by the New Law, but they have been superceded by it in quite different ways.

The ceremonial precepts of the Old Law have been superceded by the sacraments ordained by the New Law, which is the New Testament as interpreted by the magisterium of the Church.[66] In the past these ceremonial precepts functioned as the way Israel legitimately worshiped God, that is, until the coming of Christ. As such, their meaning today is that of a memory of God's faithfulness to Israel by seeing how God enabled Israel to worship Him in great detail. And, even more importantly, they are to be seen as a foreshadow of the complete worship of God brought about by Christ's institution of the sacraments. In this view, their meaning is symbolic, in contrast to the sacraments whose meaning, for Christians, is literal, even if mysterious by the standards of this world.[67] However, since they have been practically superceded *in toto* by the sacraments, Aquinas insists that it would be spiritual regression to observe them after the coming of

---

61. Jn 18:36.
62. Mt 22:21 and parallels.
63. Rom 13:1–7; 1 Pt 2:13–17.
64. See Augustine, *De Civitate Dei* 19, c. 17.
65. *ST* II-I, q. 104, a. 3. See *ST* II-I, q. 98, a. 5.
66. *ST* II-I, q. 104, a. 3.
67. *ST* II-I, q. 104, a. 4.

Christ in the way they were (properly) observed before the coming of Christ. In fact, "it would be a mortal sin now to observe those ceremonies which the fathers of old fulfilled with devotion and fidelity," and thus they are "not only dead, but deadly [*mortifera*] to those who observe them after the coming of Christ."[68] Here Aquinas's intention seems to be directed against those Christians who think they can practice Judaism and Christianity in tandem. (It is hard to ascertain, however, what he thinks of the legitimacy of Jews continuing to practice these commandments.)

The judicial precepts, though, have not been superceded as much as they have been relativized. That is, their connection to the everlasting moral precepts can be seen as their having been historically relative means to absolute ends. Their function must be seen as what some Aristotelians have called "instrumental ends."[69] Regarding the Old Law, Aquinas speaks of the judicial precepts as "the determination of those things . . . according to the different states of mankind."[70] By *determinatio*, he means something similar to what Kant meant by "schematization," namely, "the *application* of a category to appearances."[71] These judicial applications are much closer to the perpetual precepts of natural law that govern interhuman relationships than the ceremonial precepts are to the perpetual precepts of natural law that govern the divine-human relationship. One needs to see this view of the historical function of the judicial precepts and their closer connection to the moral precepts as originating in Aquinas's natural law theory per se.

In writing about the precepts of natural law, which are known in themselves *(per se nota)*, Aquinas does not want to claim that these precepts are sufficient to govern any real human society in history.[72] They require precise application to the moral/political situation at hand. Thus he writes that

---

68. *ST* II-I, q. 104, a. 3.

69. See Aristotle, *Nicomachean Ethics* 1094a1–5. There Aristotle distinguishes between ends where the activity *per se* is the end *per se* and ends where the activity is a means to something separate from it. Clearly the former are superior to the latter; in fact, if all ends were instrumental, we would be left with the absurdity of an infinite regress (see *Metaphysics* 994b10–15). For further clarification, see Aquinas, *Commentary on Aristotle's Nicomachean Ethics*, 1, lect. 12–14, pp. 4–5.

70. *ST* II-I, q. 104, a. 3 ad 1.

71. Immanuel Kant, *Critique of Pure Reason* B177, trans. N. Kemp Smith (New York: Macmillan, 1929), 180.

72. *ST* II-I, q. 100, a. 4.

"those things which are derived from the law of nature [*lege naturae*] by way of particular determination belong to the civil law, according as each state decides on what is best for itself [*aliquid sibi accomode*]."[73] Here I think we need to make a clear distinction between the specificity of laws and the particularity of cases. For Aquinas, it seems, civil law is derived from natural law in the institution of specific laws in a specific society. They are designed to function as means to the general ends of justice. Civil law is then applied to particular cases within that specific society.

The choice between good and evil is occasionally so stark that one's moral decision can be made on the basis of the primary precepts of natural law. But in most cases these primary precepts need to be mediated by the specifics of the civil law. And the civil law is the human law that is necessary for the proper administration, legislation, and adjudication of justice. Whereas "the natural law contains universal precepts which are everlasting [*quae semper manent*], human law contains certain particular precepts, according to various circumstances [*secundum diversos casus qui emergent*]."[74] As such, the determinations of the natural law are formulated in a historically contingent way by human authorities. And "these determinations which are made by human law are said to be, not of natural, but of positive law [*de iuro positivo*]."[75]

Nevertheless, positive law is not confined to human law. There is also a divinely ordained positive law *(ius divinum positivum)*.[76] Picking up on his statement about human law just quoted above, Aquinas says "so the determinations of the precepts of natural law effected by the divine law are distinct from the moral precepts which belong to natural law."[77] Therefore, there is some divine law that is perpetual because it is identical with either natural law or the supernatural reality of Christian revelation (the difference being between earthly and heavenly ends), while there is some divine law that is brought by prophets for a limited period of time.[78] This aspect of divine positive law, in the form of the judicial precepts, may even have great analogical (as distinct from symbolic) meaning as long as it is justified by

---

73. *ST* II-I, q. 95, a. 4.
74. *ST* II-I, q. 97, a. 1 ad 1. See *ST* II-I, q. 96, a. 2; q. 98, a. 2 ad 1.
75. *ST* II-I, q. 99, a. 3 ad 2. See *ST* II-I, q. 108, a. 2 ad 4.
76. *ST* II-I, q. 104, a. 1.
77. *ST* II-I, q. 99, a. 3 ad 2.
78. *ST* II-I, q. 102, a. 2.

natural law rather than by pre-Christian revelation. After Christ, for Aquinas, only one revelation qua revelation is immediately normative.[79] That revelation, together with the precepts of natural law, is now totally sufficient to attain both earthly and heavenly ends.

The Differences between Maimonides and Aquinas

The main point in common between Maimonides and Aquinas is their admission, mutatis mutandis, that the divine law contains the natural law. Both Maimonides and Aquinas had to battle against the fideists in their respective communities, those who seemed to think that ascribing reason to God's law limits the infinity of God's power and will.[80] And both Maimonides and Aquinas have been suspected by subsequent fideists in their respective traditions as being too philosophical to be trusted by the faithful.[81] This commonality of both their friends and their enemies should not be underestimated. Any retrieval of natural law by either Jews or Christians has a lot to learn from Maimonides and Aquinas and the roles they played in history, both in their own times and in later times. Nevertheless, their differences must be appreciated in order for Jews and Christians to be able to have a greater diversity of teachers about natural law. What are these differences?

The first difference is not only theological, it is religious. As a posttalmudic Jew, Maimonides could not very well accept a new law to supercede the Torah of Moses (and the whole Jewish tradition built upon it). The law of God, centered in the Torah of Moses, is permanent and perfect, from its most general precepts to its particular minutiae.[82] Rejecting one earlier rabbinic view that those aspects of the Torah which Aquinas (and others) called "ceremonies" will be abrogated when the Messiah comes, Maimonides stressed that God will never change any aspect of His law.[83] (And, moreover, he denied that Jesus of Nazareth was the Messiah.[84]) In fact, the

---

79. *ST* II-I, q. 103, a. 3 ad 4; q. 103, a. 4; q. 107, a. 2 ad 1.

80. See *Guide,* 3.31.

81. See J. Sarachek, *The Conflict over the Rationalism of Maimonides* (New York: Hermon Press, 1970).

82. See Maimonides, *Commentary on the Mishnah:* Sanhedrin, chap. 10: Foundations, no. 8.

83. MT: Kings, chap. 11 (uncensored ed.), ed. Y. Rabinowitz (Jerusalem: Mosad ha-Rav Kook, 1962), 416.

84. Ibid.

role of the Messiah is not to abrogate the law, but rather to provide the political realm in which the law can and will be fully observed in every detail. For him, then, there is no normative difference between the moral precepts and either the ceremonial precepts or the judicial precepts. There is no divine positive law in the sense of positive law being law that admits of abrogation or repeal. It is only that the present political circumstances of the Jews do not enable them to observe some aspects of the Law like the Temple rituals, for example. However, the reign of the Messiah will once again enable the Jews to observe all the precepts of the Law, which themselves have never lost their perpetual normative force.[85]

The positive law of revelation, as distinct from the natural law in revelation, mostly pertains to certain details of the law, especially in its ritual aspects, which cannot be rationally inferred from the overall ends of the law.[86] As for their nonrational (although never irrational) character, Maimonides and Aquinas would be in agreement. Their difference here would be whether this nonrationality makes them temporary (which would be Aquinas's view) or not (which would be Maimonides's view).

Positive law in any temporally limited sense is only human. For Jews, it is the law made by the rabbis functioning as the legislators of and for all Israel.[87] (And it is clear from the history of Jewish law, this rabbinic authority had to be responsive to popular needs in the formulation of the law and to popular opinion in the persuasion of the community to accept the law.[88]) Furthermore, these human-made laws admit of repeal if and when it is decided subsequently that they no longer serve the end for which they were originally formulated.[89] (After the demise of the Sanhedrin as the central legislative-judicial body of the Jewish people, repeal de jure became impossible. However, repeal de facto took the form of more conservative judicial review and reinterpretation of the old laws.) For Maimonides, the only thing roughly comparable to Aquinas's notion of divine positive law would be the ad hoc commandments found in Scripture that are addressed to particular prophets for their particular times.[90] Jewish tradition does not consider them to be among the six hundred and thirteen permanent commandments of the Written (Mosaic) Torah. But one would have to see these

---

85. MT: Kings, 12.1.
87. See MT: Rebels, chaps. 1–2.
89. See *Mishnah:* Eduyot 1.5.
86. *Guide,* 3.26.
88. See B. Avodah Zarah 36a–b.
90. See Maimonides, *Book of the Commandments:* Introduction, root no. 3.

commandments as being particular applications of more general principles rather than being specifications of them in the form of common laws. Sometimes they are even particular dispensations from Torah laws, which are requited for very limited situations, what the rabbis called "decrees of the hour" *(hora'at sha'ah)*.[91]

The second difference between Maimonides and Aquinas is theological, and it is one where Maimonides not only differs from Aquinas, but where he also differs from some other important Jewish theologians. Unlike Aquinas, it seems that Maimonides would make no real distinction between natural law and supernatural law. Such a distinction, as we have seen in Aquinas, is teleological. For Maimonides, natural law leads to natural ends attainable either physically or spiritually. The life of the world-to-come is attainable by ordinary acts of body and soul that are performed in this world. Indeed, it seems that Maimonides saw the world-to-come as the highest aspect of nature, being what is everlasting and beatific.[92] In principle, all the laws of the Torah have universalizable reasons that can be rationally intended here and now. All of them are thus natural law in principle. But in this type of rationalism, Maimonides was very much opposed by the kabbalistic theologians. For a few of them, such as Maimonides's most systematic theological critic, Nahmanides (d. 1270), while some of the commandments pertaining to interhuman relationships do have mundane reasons, almost all of the commandments pertaining to the divine-human relationship have supernatural reasons.[93] That is, their effects must be considered the work of grace, not of nature. From this perspective, Maimonides elided the difference between theology and philosophy.

For many of the kabbalists, however, the difference with Maimionides is even greater. All of the commandments are the work of grace, not of nature. In fact, in what could be termed their acosmic theology, there is no nature at all; everything real is a direct participation in the life of God. All of reality is panentheistic.[94] Everything is very much what Aquinas would call a sacrament.[95] And even those kabbalistic theologians, like Nahmanides,

---

91. See B. Yoma 69b; also, B. Sanhedrin 46a.

92. See MT: Repentance, chap. 8.

93. See D. Novak, *The Theology of Nahmanides Systematically Presented* (Atlanta, Ga.: Scholars Press, 1992), 107–113. See *ST* II-I, q. 91, a. 4; q. 100, a. 5.

94. See Novak, *The Image of the Non-Jew in Judaism,* 265–68.

95. See *ST* III, q. 62, a. 1. See *ST* III, q. 62, a. 4.

who did recognize the limited reality of nature, are highly critical of what they see as Maimonides's pannaturalism/panrationalism. In Nahmanides's case, that allowed him to affirm natural law, but it was a much more minimal natural law than that affirmed by Maimonides (and, for that matter, even by Aquinas). Finally, even those Jewish theologians who would not see the commandments as sacraments in the kabbalistic sense (which also tends to ascribe theurgic powers to them) would ascribe to them a far greater historical particularity than would Maimonides. And since that historical particularity intends a salvific consummation of all human history, it does not share the pitfalls of modern historicism and the relativism it so obviously presupposes. In this view, *Heilsgeschichte* fulfills nature; it does not destroy it or deny it. But Maimonides refuses to assign any supernatural significance to history, even to sacred history.[96]

The Contemporary Retrieval of Natural Law

Natural law theory lies at the border of philosophy and theology. Without theology, it tends to become the type of rationalism that overlooks the fundamental religious thrust of human nature, that humans are essentially and uniquely God-seeking creatures. Without philosophy, natural law theory tends to become a mere apologetics for specifically religious doctrine, namely, rationalization rather than reason in its teleological quest.[97] By concentrating our look at the natural law theories of Maimonides and Aquinas in their understanding of the normative significance of the Hebrew Bible, Jews and Christians have the most to learn from both of them. After all, the most basic claims of Maimonides's Judaism and Aquinas's Christianity come from the common and rival interpretations of that book. Since that book teaches us about the creation of the world and especially the creation of the human person as having one nature and one destiny, natural law theory by Jews and Christians must ultimately find its theological justification there or nowhere at all. Who understood that better than Moses Maimonides and Thomas Aquinas?

---

96. See D. Novak, "Does Maimonides Have a Philosophy of History?," in *Studies in Jewish Philosophy*, ed. N. M. Samuelson (Lanham, Md.: University Press of America, 1987), 397–420.

97. See Novak, *Natural Law in Judaism*, 174–78.

❋ RESPONSE ❋

NATURAL LAW IN MAIMONIDES?

Martin D. Yaffe

To begin with, I must express my admiration for the serious efforts of David Novak in raising the question of the kinship between Thomas Aquinas and Maimonides in matters concerning our common well-being as law-abiding citizens nowadays. I have in mind that our Founding Fathers appealed to the "Laws of Nature and of Nature's God" and to the "Protection of Divine Providence" in establishing a government of laws dedicated to the proposition that all human beings are "created equal and ... endowed by their Creator with certain unalienable Rights," and also bequeathed a constitution designed, among other things, to "secure the Blessings of Liberty."[1] Can there be any doubt, then, that in laying the foundations for our laws, they counted as well on the ongoing flourishing of the way of life taught by the Bible, in spite or perhaps because of the multiplicity of sectarian paths leading to and from the Bible?[2] Given the comparable stature of Aquinas and Maimonides as authoritative teachers in their respective religions, and given that Aquinas looks to "Rabbi Moses" in turn for understanding the pre-Christian roots of *sacra doctrina,* it follows that we do well to consider Aquinas's proximity to Maimonides with respect to Aquinas's teaching of natural law in particular. If, unlike Novak, I have lingering doubts over whether we can attribute a teaching of natural law, strictly speaking, to Maimonides, it is not because I doubt that Maimonides, like Aquinas, sees a need to appeal to nature and nature's God in order to clarify our understanding and practice of law-abidingness. It is be-

---

1. I have followed the punctuation of these phrases from the Declaration of Independence and the Constitution of the United States as found in George Anastaplo, *The Constitution of 1787: A Commentary* (Baltimore: Johns Hopkins University Press, 1997), 239, 243, 266.
2. Consider *The Federalist,* No. 51.

cause I have difficulties fitting a teaching of natural law as we find it in Aquinas to the details of Maimonides's *Guide of the Perplexed* and related writings.

My difficulties arise at several points during Novak's argument. Let me outline the difficulties as they occur by respectfully imitating, to the extent of my modest powers, the literary practice of Aquinas in his *Summa theologiae* and elsewhere, and articulating those difficulties in the form of a disputed question. Or rather, given my inability to adduce convincing arguments for the other side of the question, let me simply list a series of objections to Novak's own position, and invite anyone who wishes to defend that position further to supply an appropriate *sed contra, respondeo dicendum,* and point by point answers to my objections, wherever possible.

So: It seems that there is no natural law teaching in Maimonides.

In the first place, Novak argues that "[t]o discover natural law is to discover what is divine within the universe, especially as it pertains to the human condition" (Novak, p. 46); and he goes on to suggest that the notion of the divine law as inclusive of the natural law affords us adequate entry into Maimonides's theological teaching, as it may be said to afford us adequate entry into Aquinas's theological teaching. My difficulty here has to do with the fact that Maimonides nowhere uses the term "natural law." So my objection amounts to asking in turn: If we are to construe Maimonides as speaking about natural law, why doesn't it *look* as if he is speaking about natural law? Shouldn't we be guided by what Maimonides appears to be saying, before going on to ascribe to him what he is *not* exactly saying? Let me subdivide this objection into three points.

First, Novak says that the theological view that the natural law is part of the divine law is preferable to the strictly philosophical view that the divine law is either the same as the natural law or inferior to the natural law. The second of these three views he ascribes to Plato and Aristotle, the third to Kant (Novak, p. 47f.). Leaving aside the Kantian view as anachronistic for present purposes, it appears that Maimonides's own view is much closer to that of Plato and Aristotle, who likewise do not seem to take their bearings by the notion of a natural law.[3] For Maimonides, as for Plato and Aristotle, law is, first and foremost, a political phenomenon. Maimonides understands "divine law" in contradistinction to *nomos* (he uses the Greek term), the

---

3. Cf. Plato, *Gorgias* 483e, *Timaeus* 83e; Aristotle, *Rhetoric* 1373b4–18, *De Caelo* 268a10–15.

law or set of laws governing a political community. *Nomoi,* according to the Maimonidean passage Novak quotes in part, are

> . . . directed exclusively toward the ordering of the city and of its circumstances and the abolition in it of injustice and oppression; and if in that Law attention is not at all directed toward speculative matters, no heed is given to the perfecting of the rational faculty, and no regard is accorded to opinions being correct or faulty—the whole purpose of that Law being, on the contrary, the arrangement, in whatever way this may be brought about, of the circumstances of people in their relations with one another and provision for their obtaining . . . a certain something deemed to be happiness—you must know that that Law is a nomos. . . .[4]

A "divine law," on the other hand, is "a Law all of whose ordinances are due to attention being paid, as was stated before, to the soundness of the circumstances pertaining to the body *and also* to the soundness of belief—a Law that takes pains to inculcate correct opinions with regard to God . . . and with regard to the angels, and that desires to make man wise, to give him understanding, and to awaken his attention, so that he should know the whole of that which exists in its true form."[5] For Maimonides, a "divine law" is a divinely enhanced *nomos,* a set of political laws specifically differentiated from other law codes since it is revealed by God and dedicated to wisdom and understanding about all things, including divine as well as human things.

Second, we should hardly expect to find in Plato and Aristotle the view that God reveals natural laws, since this view is, as Novak says, of theological rather than strictly philosophical provenance. But that Maimonides resembles Plato and Aristotle rather than Aquinas here is evident from Maimonides's discerning the proper standards for political laws by looking, as we have just seen, to "the soundness of the circumstances pertaining to the body," that is, to the natural needs of the human body, including its interdependence with other bodies in political life. Unlike Aquinas, Maimonides does not derive the need for political life from the human rational capacity apart from the body—that is, from what Aquinas calls "the inclination to the good according to the nature of reason, which is proper to him."[6] Mai-

---

4. Moses Maimonides, *Guide of the Perplexed* II.40 (trans. Shlomo Pines [Chicago: University of Chicago Press, 1963], 383f.).

5. *Guide of the Perplexed* II.40 (Pines 384, emphasis added); cf. III.27–28 (Pines 510–14).

6. *ST* I-II, q. 94, a. 2. (all translations of Aquinas are my own, M.Y.).

monides takes his bearings by "nature" without the benefit, such as it may be, of an appeal to laws that originate independently of the circumstances of political life, although or because those laws are in tandem with a divine revelation that originates independently of the circumstances of political life.[7]

Third, in following Plato and Aristotle rather than the tradition of natural law, Maimonides is also far from identifying divine law with natural law, if only because Plato and Aristotle do not do so either. Aristotle, for example, defines "nature" *(phusis)* as the governing principle or cause inherent in things that move or change of their own accord; in this way, he distinguishes nature from "art" *(techne),* which concerns the principles governing the changes imposed on things by human artisans.[8] Aristotle seems to have in mind Homer's *Odyssey,* where that term makes its first appearance: when the god Hermes digs up the moly plant on Circe's island and shows Odysseus its "nature," he shows what links the blackness of its root with the whiteness of its flower; *phusis,* in other words, is the cause of the togetherness of black and white, root and flower in the growth *(phuein)* of the plant—a cause independent of the arbitrary will of humans and (Homeric) gods alike.[9] Aristotle preserves Homer's understanding when he distinguishes between natural things (e.g., plants, animals, stars), which move or change on their own, and God or pure intelligence *(nous),* which is altogether exempt from change.[10] There is, in all this, no "law" *(nomos)* common to God and nature according to Aristotle, except perhaps in the myths introduced, as he says, "for the persuasion of the many and for use in the *nomoi* and in matters of [political] convenience."[11] Be that as it may,

---

7. Cf. Raymond L. Weiss, *Maimonides' Ethics: The Encounter of Philosophic and Religious Morality* (Chicago: University of Chicago Press, 1991), 178–85.

8. Aristotle, *Physics* 192b21–23. Cf. Martin D. Yaffe, "Myth and 'Science' in Aristotle's Theology," *Man and World* 12 (1979): 70–88.

9. Homer, *Odyssey* 10.303. Cf. Seth Benardete, *The Bow and the Lyre: A Platonic Reading of the Odyssey* (Lanham, Md.: Rowman & Littlefield, 1997), 86f.

10. Aristotle, *Metaphysics* 1069a30–1069b2, 1071b3–1076a4, esp. 1074b15ff.

11. *Metaphysics* 1074b3–5. For the difference between "natural law" as understood by Aquinas and the law "according to nature" as understood by Aristotle at *Rhetoric* 1373b7, see Harry V. Jaffa, *Thomism and Aristotelianism: A Study of the Commentary by Thomas Aquinas on the Nicomachean Ethics* (Chicago: University of Chicago Press, 1952), 168–69; Leo Strauss, "On Natural Law," in *Studies in Platonic Political Philosophy* (Chicago: University of Chicago Press,

Maimonides finds a remarkable similarity between Aristotle's rationally demonstrable, nonbodily God and the God of the Hebrew Bible; the biblical God, he adds, differs only in having created the world ex nihilo, though much else follows from this difference as well. Although Maimonides does not find creation ex nihilo to be rationally demonstrable, he does not find it unreasonable either;[12] even so, he does not think that it entails a God who is bound by natural (or what he calls, as we shall see, "rational") laws.

My second major objection can now be stated briefly. Novak says in passing that "it might well be fantastic to attempt to engage in the type of Aristotelian metaphysics that occupied both [Maimonides and Aquinas]" (Novak, p. 48). But if the points that I have just raised are to be addressed properly, it seems that, somewhere down the line, we shall need to look once again at Aristotle in toto. The "comprehensively Aristotelian position" to which Novak alludes (ibid.) may turn out to be more viable than is often said by those who no longer take him seriously. In particular, Aristotle may prove helpful for our coming to grips with such pressing issues as concern for the natural bonds supporting marriage and the family, the violation of natural right in human slavery, and current attempts to extend the conquest of nature into the terra incognita of human cloning.[13] As Novak himself says in a different context, "to see natural law apart from its metaphysical ground is to make human reason rather than divine wisdom the measure of all things" (Novak, p. 56).

My third and final objection concerns the question Novak raises about whether Aquinas's understanding of Maimonides, and so of Judaism, would have been improved by acquaintance with Maimonides's strictly legal writings. My difficulty here is threefold.

First, as to whether Maimonides's strictly legal writings support Novak's claim that there is a natural law teaching in Maimonides as there is in Aqui-

---

1983), 139–40; and Larry Arnhart, *Aristotle on Political Reasoning: A Commentary on the "Rhetoric"* (DeKalb: Northern Illinois University Press, 1981), 103–5.

12. See *Guide of the Perplexed*, II.13–24.

13. On the first two issues, see esp. Larry Arnhart, *Darwinian Natural Right: The Biological Ethics of Human Nature* (Albany: State University of New York Press, 1998), 89–210, with 238–48; on the last issue, see esp. Leon R. Kass and James Q. Wilson, *The Ethics of Human Cloning* (Washington, D.C.: AEI Press, 1998), and Kass, *Toward a More Natural Science: Biology and Human Affairs* (New York: Free Press, 1985), 275.

nas, the same talmudic dictum Professor Novak cites ("had they not been written, they would have to have been written";[14] p. 54) is cited as well by Maimonides in one of his legal writings, his *Commentary on the Mishnah,* though to exactly the opposite effect. Maimonides cites it in the course of rethinking the views of Aristotle and others concerning whether virtue is superior to continence or vice versa, that is, whether it is better to restrain an immoral desire (continence) or not to have it in the first place (virtue). Maimonides's understanding of the talmudic dictum, it seems, contradicts Novak's. Here are Maimonides's words: "For the bad things to which the philosophers referred when they said that someone who does not desire them is more virtuous than someone who does desire them and restrains himself—these are the things generally accepted [*sic*] by all the people as bad, such as murder, theft, robbery, fraud, harming an innocent man, repaying a benefactor with evil, degrading parents, and things like these. They are the laws about which the *sages,* peace be upon them, said: *If they were not written down, they would deserve to be written down.* Some of our modern wise men who suffer from the sickness of the dialectical theologians [*mutakallimun*] call them rational laws."[15] Maimonides cites the foregoing talmudic dictum in support of the view, which he amplifies in the *Guide,*[16] that the basis for calling those bad things bad is that they are generally accepted as being bad, rather than that they are bad because they contravene any "rational" (or natural) laws.[17] This passage alone evidently decides the question of whether Maimonides has a natural law teaching. By his own lights, at least, he does not.

Second, I wonder whether Aquinas's view of the relation between the

---

14. Babylonian Talmud, *Yoma* 67b.

15. Maimonides, *Introduction to Pirqei Avot,* chap. 6, in *Ethical Writings of Maimonides,* ed. Raymond L. Weiss, with Charles Butterworth (New York: Dover, 1975), 79f.

16. See esp. *Guide of the Perplexed,* I.2 (on Adam), and III.22–23 (on Job).

17. Contrast Aquinas, *ST* I-II, q. 94, a. 3 ad 2: ". . . the nature of a human being can be said to be either that which is proper to a human being—and according to this, all sins insofar as they are contrary to reason are also contrary to nature . . .—or that which is common to a human being and the other animals—and according to this, some specific sins are said to be contrary to nature, as homosexuality [*concubitus masculorum*], which is specifically said to be a vice contrary to nature, is contrary to heterosexuality [*commixtionem maris et feminae*], which is natural to all animals." I am indebted to Dr. Joshua Parens of the University of Dallas for alerting me to this and other passages under discussion here.

Old and the New Laws, and so between Judaism and Christianity, is adequately described as being tantamount to that between "potency and act" (Novak, pp. 57ff.). Aquinas himself, in the very first question of the *Summa,* starts with the distinction between the literal meaning of Scripture, which spells out the Old Law, and the figurative meanings, which point to the New Law; at the same time, he insists on the integrity of the literal meaning as the one originally intended by the author of Scripture, namely God.[18] Later on, when practical questions come up in the *Summa* concerning the treatment of the Jews, Aquinas bends over backward—if I may speak metaphorically—to avoid giving Christians any excuse for forcing Jews to convert or otherwise harrassing them.[19] Evidently the Old Law, whatever its strictly theological shortcomings, is not just the material for the New. Given Aquinas's focus in the Treatise on Law on the distinction between exterior and interior law,[20] the "Jewish" layer of the *Summa*—if that is the right term—seems meant to be approached via philosophical wonderment about the scope and limits of law as such, a wonderment Aquinas shares with, say, Plato and Aristotle and, of course, Maimonides.[21]

Finally, as for whether Maimonides's strictly legal writings stand more in continuity than in discontinuity with the *Guide of the Perplexed,* it seems that Maimonides himself calls attention to their discontinuity. He calls the former "the legalistic study of the Law," while he says that the *Guide* in contrast is about the meaning of biblical terms and parables, that is, about the infralegal and supralegal complement to the legalistic study of the law.[22] The *Guide,* as opposed to Maimonides's strictly legal writings, is about the

18. *ST* I, q. 1, a. 10; also see *ST* I-II, q. 107, a. 3. For a defense of Aquinas's exegetical practice in expounding the Book of Job in particular, see Martin D. Yaffe, "Interpretive Essay," in Thomas Aquinas, *The Literal Exposition on Job: A Scriptural Commentary Concerning Providence,* trans. A. Damico (Atlanta, Ga.: Scholars Press, 1989), 1–65.

19. E.g., *ST* II-II, q. 10, aa. 8, 11; III, q. 47, a. 5; see *De regimine Judaeoru* ("On the Governance of the Jews"; in Thomas Aquinas, *Selected Political Writings,* ed. A. P. D'Entrèves [New York: Macmillan, 1959]). See also Martin D. Yaffe, review of *Aquinas and the Jews* by John Hood (Philadelphia: University of Pennsylvania Press, 1995), *Association for Jewish Studies Review* 22 (1997): 122–25.

20. *ST* I-II, q. 98, a. 1; q. 99, a. 3; q. 100, a. 2.

21. Consider *Guide of the Perplexed,* III.34, with I.34.

22. *Guide of the Perplexed,* I Introduction (trans. Pines 5f.).

foundations of law. The relation between Maimonides's strictly legal writings and the *Guide* is something like the relation between the Declaration of Independence and the Constitution of the United States and related writings, on the one hand, and, say, Locke's *Two Treatises of Government* or, for that matter, Aquinas's treatment of law in the *Summa theologiae,* on the other.

✣ RESPONSE ✣

NATURAL LAW AND THE METAPHYSICS OF CREATION

John Goyette

I would like to offer three relatively brief comments on David Novak's stimulating comparison of Maimonides and Aquinas: First, I want to raise a question about his assertion that Maimonides has a natural law doctrine. Second, I have a question about his suggestion that one can defend natural law without engaging in metaphysics. And third, I want to highlight the importance of his claim that "Judaism's continued validity for Christians lies in its superior constitution of natural law" (Novak, p. 57).

Can one find a natural law teaching in Maimonides? Martin Yaffe has raised some questions about finding a natural law teaching in Maimonides by examining certain texts in Maimonides. I would like to raise a question from the perspective of Aquinas. In *Summa theologiae* II-I, q. 91 Aquinas defines natural law as the rational creature's participation in the eternal law, the law by means of which God governs "all actions and movements of the whole of nature" (*ST* II-I, q. 93, a. 5). The upshot of this definition is that natural law, for Aquinas, presupposes that the world is governed by divine providence and that this providence extends to particular events (note: Aquinas's treatment of natural law in the *Summa contra gentiles* is found within his treatment of divine providence). To put it quite simply, natural law presupposes a divine lawgiver. Without it we are left with nothing more than natural right. The prohibition against murder, for example, may be contrary to reason, and therefore contrary to human nature, but it can only be understood as a violation of natural law if the natural order is established by a divine lawgiver. Since, however, divine providence can only extend to particular events if the world is created by God, for St. Thomas natural law presupposes that God is a creator. But, and this is the crucial point, since natural law pertains to what is knowable apart from divine revelation, it presupposes that we can know by unaided human reason that the world is created by God. Thomistic natural law, then, presupposes what we might call a metaphysics of creation, that is, a philosophic demonstration of creation ex nihilo, a demonstration Aquinas claims to supply earlier in the *Summa theologiae* (*ST* I, q. 44, oo. 1, 2). But this raises the following question in regards to a putative natural law doctrine in Maimonides: How can Maimonides hold a natural law doctrine if he explicitly denies, as he does in the *Guide of the Perplexed,* that we can know by unaided human reason that the world is created by God?

One might reply to this question by pointing out that for Aquinas the natural law, or at the least the first principles of the natural law, are known to all men but that according to Aquinas most men do not possess a philosophic demonstration of the existence of God. Indeed, Aquinas follows Maimonides in claiming that one of the reasons that divine revelation is necessary is that demonstrative knowledge of the existence and nature of God is possessed by only a few, and that such knowledge is attained by them only after a lifetime of study and with the admixture of many errors (*ST* I, q. 1, a. 1; See *Guide* 1.33). Aquinas seems to acknowledge, then, that the natural law can be known apart from a demonstration of the existence of a creator God. Nonetheless, Aquinas would insist that the existence of a creator God can be known, at least in principle, apart from divine revelation and that this knowledge is ultimately necessary to defend the distinction between natural law and divine law. If the creation of the world can only be known by means of divine revelation, it becomes difficult to assert that what unaided human reason judges to be necessary for human happiness has the binding character of law.

This brings me to the second point I wish to address, Professor Novak's suggestion that we can defend natural law without engaging in metaphysics. In his paper he compares the views of Maimonides and Aquinas as moral theologians partly because he believes that the metaphysical speculations of both Maimonides and Aquinas are based upon Aristotelian natural science which, he suggests, can no longer be defended in light of the apparent success of modern science. I should make clear that Novak does not deny that natural law presupposes a metaphysical ground. Later in his paper he acknowledges that "ethics presupposes metaphysics" and that "to see natural law apart from its metaphysical ground is to make human reason rather than divine wisdom the measure of all things" (Novak, p. 56). What he seems to question is whether we can or should attempt to supply the metaphysical ground by means of unaided human reason.

I wonder about this. Even if we suppose, for the sake of argument, that it is not essential to be able to positively demonstrate creation ex nihilo since one can know the truth about God by means of faith, I wonder whether one can dispense altogether with metaphysics. However true it may be that the practical knowledge of the natural law that most men possess can be had independent of a metaphysics of creation, this practical knowledge will always be endangered by false accounts of the whole. The moral life of the many will always be endangered by those who deny that God is provident over human affairs or who deny God altogether by asserting, for example, that the ordered whole is the product of blind chance. The practical knowledge of the natural law is always in need of defense against such opinions and this defense must be made by means of metaphysics. Thus, while Maimonides does not claim to be able to prove creation ex nihilo, as does Aquinas, he considers it essential to the defense of the law that one be able to refute, by means of philosophy, any argument that claims to show the *impossibility* of creation (*Guide* 2.15). In our own time, the apparent victory of modern science over Aristotelian natural science should not lead the defenders of natural law to abandon traditional metaphysics; rather, the challenge posed by modern science renders metaphysics all the more necessary today. To abandon the metaphysical speculation that might supply the theoretical ground for a natural law teaching seems, to me at least, to promote the view that natural law theory is "mere apologetics for specifically religious doctrine," a view that Professor Novak explicitly seeks to avoid (Novak, p. 65). While I agree with Novak's suggestion that Aquinas's natural law doctrine is often taken as something that can simply be abstracted from its theological context, I do not think we should lose sight of the fact that theology's handmaiden is indispensable.

By insisting upon the importance of metaphysics, I do not mean to take issue with Novak's basic thesis that natural law is most fruitfully viewed in the context of divine revelation, or sacred theology. This brings me to the third point I would like to address, Novak's assertion that "Judaism's continued validity for Christians lies in its superior constitution of natural law" (Novak, p. 57). As he points out, the longest treatment of law in the *Summa theologiae* is the treatment of the Old Law. Indeed, I would argue that the most important question dealing with the natural law in the *Summa thelogiae* is not q. 94, which is explicitly devoted to the question of natural law per se, but q. 100, which is devoted to the moral precepts of the Old Law. It is in q. 100 that we learn not only that the moral precepts of the Old Law are part of the natural law, but we also get a detailed discussion of the relation between the various kinds and gradations of the natural law as well as the order among the various precepts of the natural law. Why is this? Why does Aquinas choose to treat the details of the natural law in his treatment of the Old Law? I believe that the answer to this question is closely connected to a point I made earlier, that is, that most men in their natural condition do not possess the knowledge necessary to know the natural law. This is most obvious in the case of those precepts that pertain to divine worship, for example, the prohibition of idolatry. Since most men do not naturally possess knowledge of the existence of God or of the fact that he is a creator and providential governor of the cosmos, they are incapable of worshipping him as is required by the natural law. But how can this be? How can we speak of the precepts pertaining to divine worship as part of the natural law if they are unknowable in man's natural condition? The answer to this question lies in the fact that for Aquinas there is no pure state of nature although he expressly considered such a state possible (*ST* I, q. 95, a. 1). For Aquinas the "natural" in natural law refers to nature in the existing order of providence, that is, nature having been created in the state of grace, weakened by original sin and repaired by means of grace and divine revelation. As Aquinas makes clear in his treatment of the Old Law, it is because of original sin that man does not possess the knowledge he needs to fulfill the natural law, and so it was necessary for God to give the Old Law to the Jews so that nature might be restored. Thus, knowledge of the natural law is made available to man, after original sin, by means of the Old Law. Thus, the moral precepts of the Old Law, which for Aquinas are reducible to the ten precepts of the Decalogue, are part of the natural law even though some of these precepts—for example, the prohibition of idolatry—are necessarily known to most men by means of divine revelation. Thus, I think Aquinas would concur with Professor Novak's assertion that "[n]atural law theory lies at the border of philosophy and theology" (Novak, p. 65) Still, Aquinas differs from Maimonides to the extent that he defends the possibility of knowing, in principle, the content of the precepts of the natural law by means of unaided human reason. For Aquinas natural law can be known de jure in abstraction from the Old Law even though natural law is known de facto by means of God's revelation to the Jews.

4

WHY AQUINAS LOCATES NATURAL LAW WITHIN THE *SACRA DOCTRINA*

Romanus Cessario, O.P.

The purpose of this paper is to show that the theologian can speak with competence about the natural law.† This proposal may seem like an odd exercise until it is recalled that in the recent literature constructive attention to natural law derives mainly from Christian philosophers and professors of jurisprudence. Yves Simon, Ralph McInerny, Russell Hittinger, John Finnis, and Robert P. George are some names that come immediately to mind. It is of course possible to cite a theologian or biblical scholar who has turned his or her attention to the topic of natural law, for example, in the context of commenting on the opening chapters of the Letter to the Romans, but their number is not large. What is more important, the purpose of these theological interventions may be described for the most part as revisionist. As the professors who so kindly responded to my paper will point out, what follows may be described as a presentation of natural law according to its classical formulation, drawn principally from the thought of St Thomas Aquinas.

† A version of this paper forms part of chap. 2 of Romanus Cessario, *Introduction to Moral Theology* (Washington, D.C.: The Catholic University of America Press, 2001).

Christ and Divine Wisdom

For the purposes of moral theology, we can distinguish a twofold objective in divine wisdom. First, wisdom denotes an image or exemplar, namely, the ruling notion that governs the activity of created things. It is in this sense that the Scriptures refer explicitly to the preexistent Christ, the divine Word, as the true pattern by which "all things in heaven and on earth were created, things visible and invisible" (Col 1:16). Second, wisdom denotes a teleological principle, namely, one that moves every being toward its proper end or goal through the sovereign attractiveness of the end. In this meaning, Christ, "in whom are hidden all the treasures of wisdom and knowledge" (Col 2:3), accomplishes par excellence not only the task of efficiently guiding human activity to its completion, but also of attracting and summoning this activity to himself as its sovereign and consummate end. To associate divine wisdom personally with the incarnate Son introduces another distinction about God's wise government of the world. Though the theologian may suitably appropriate "the power of God and the wisdom of God" (1 Cor 1:24) to the eternal Son by reason of his origin and relation within the intra-Trinitarian life of God, it belongs to the divine nature itself to govern the universe and to ordain whatever is necessary for the well-being of humankind.[1] In other words, "the Father, the Son, and the Holy Spirit are not three principles of creation but one principle."[2]

When Aquinas discusses the eternal law in the *Summa theologiae,* he draws attention to a very important distinction for understanding Christ's relationship to the created moral order. It is simply in an appropriated sense, that is, by way of an illustrative theological convention, that we identify only the second divine Person of the Trinity with the eternal law. Why? Aquinas argues for this appropriation on the basis of the affinity between the personal name for the second Person in God—namely, Word or *Ver-*

---

1. This doctrine is substantially represented in the encyclical letter *Veritatis splendor,* no. 43, which quotes the Second Vatican Council's Declaration on Religious Freedom, *Dignitatis humanae,* no. 3: "the supreme rule of life is the divine law itself, the eternal, objective and universal law by which God out of his wisdom and love arranges, directs and governs the whole world and the paths of the human community."

2. *Catechism of the Catholic Church,* no. 258, quoting the fifteenth-century Council of Florence (*DS* 1331) and referring back to the sixth-century Second Council of Constantinople (*DS* 421).

bum—and the notion of an exemplar or image.³ The appropriation of essential divine attributes, such as wisdom, to one of the Persons of the blessed Trinity serves only to bring out a particular aspect of the faith.⁴ Forasmuch as the eternal law represents the exemplar of God's wisdom and power actually directing and moving all that exists toward perfection, it fulfills the conditions required for formal exemplar causality. So because of his divine status as the Logos-Son, Christ, "the image of the invisible God, the first born of all creation" (Col 1:15), embodies and displays the definitive shape or form that the order of human existence should take in the world. The Second Vatican Council's "Pastoral Constitution on the Church in the Modern World" puts it this way: "Only in the mystery of the incarnate Word does the mystery of man take on light."⁵

From the start of theological deliberation on the incarnation of the eternal Logos, Christian apologists and theologians have sought to further the quest for the ultimate *logos* or intelligibility that undergirds and directs the created order. It is axiomatic for Christian moral theology that the regulative pattern for all right human conduct ultimately lies within the blessed Trinity. As a principle of divine life for human beings, our Trinitarian origins also display an order toward a final goal, that "most high calling" that is bestowed graciously on the human race.⁶ Since this pattern especially sug-

---

3. See *ST* I-II, q. 93, a. 1 ad 2: "Whatsoever the word you can consider first, the word itself, and secondly, what it expresses. A spoken word is something uttered by the mouth of man, and expresses what it is meant to signify. The same applies to man's mental word, which is nothing other than a concept of mind expressing what he is thinking about. So it is in the life of God; the Word itself, conceived by the Father's mind, is a personal term. As appears from Augustine (*De Trinitate* XV, 14) whatsoever is in the Father's knowledge, whether it refers to the divine nature or to the divine Persons or to the works of God, is expressed by this Word. Included in what is there expressed is the Eternal Law. All the same it does not follow that the Eternal Law is used as a personal term in our vocabulary about divine things, though in fact it is specially attributed to the Son on account of the close agreement exemplar has with word."

4. *ST* I, q. 39, a. 7 ad 2: "In truth the Son's name is 'wisdom of the Father,' because he is wisdom from the Father as wisdom, for each one is wisdom in himself and both together are the one wisdom."

5. *Gaudium et spes*, no. 22, as quoted in *Fides et ratio*, no. 60, where Pope John Paul II also acknowledged that this conciliar doctrine has served since his first encyclical "as one of the constant reference points" of his papal teaching.

6. *Fides et ratio*, no. 13, quoting *Gaudium et spes*, no. 22, makes the point explicitly: "Christ,

gests the second divine Person, who perfectly images the Father, there is something appropriate about referring to it as a Logos pattern. It belongs especially to Christian moral theology to discern and explicate this Logos pattern as it shapes the action of free creatures and guides human conduct.

Confusion about the manner in which the eternal Word provides the pattern for right moral conduct leads some theologians to speak about the incarnate Christ as if he were involved in the created moral order even prior to the free and gracious divine self-donation that occurs in the Incarnation. This sort of mythological Christocentrism distracts, however, from the full transcendence of the divine wisdom. The New Testament asks, "Where is the one who is wise? Where is the scribe? Where is the debater of this age? Has not God made foolish the wisdom of the world?" (1 Cor 1:20). To affirm the transcendence of the eternal law is not to depreciate the central and indispensable importance of the incarnate Word for the Church. For the ultimate regulation of the moral order finds its preeminent expression in the freedom that Jesus Christ, the incarnate Son, communicates to those believers who remain personally united with him. In an effort to concretize this union, some theologians speak about the *sequela Christi,* or the following of Christ. But the appropriation of eternal law to the Word of God, the eternal Son of the Father, implies much more for the Church than that the incarnate Son offers an example of good behavior for his followers to imitate.

The Swiss theologian Hans Urs von Balthasar referred to Christ as the "concrete norm" of the moral life.[7] By this he meant that the *exitus-reditus,* which marks out the human person's itinerary toward God, actually

---

the Lord 'in revealing the mystery of the Father and his love, fully reveals man to himself and makes clear his supreme calling,' which is to share in the divine mystery of the life of the Trinity." The relationship of Christ both to creation and to the eternal law that directs it depends on a common notion of manifestation or image. We find this notion verified both in Christ's personal Trinitarian name, the Word of God—a manifestation of a concept—and the eternal law's definition as a plan or *ratio*—the manifestation of God's wisdom. For a good analysis of how St. Thomas understands the doctrine of *circulatio,* e.g., *Scriptum super libros Sententiarum Petri Lombardiensis* I, d. 14, q. 2, a. 3, see Jan Aertsen, *Nature and Creature: Thomas Aquinas's Way of Thought,* trans. H. D. Morton (Leiden: E. J. Brill, 1988).

7. See Hans Urs von Balthasar, "Nine Theses in Christian Ethics," in *International Theological Commission: Texts and Documents 1969–1985,* ed. Michael Sharkey (San Francisco: Ignatius Press, 1989), 105–28, esp. Thesis One: "Christ as the Concrete Norm."

centers on the person of Jesus Christ. In making this assertion, moreover, von Balthasar echoed teachings of the Second Vatican Council that we have already cited:

> It is Christ, the last Adam, who fully discloses humankind to itself and unfolds its noble calling by revealing the mystery of the Father and the Father's love. . . . He who is "the image of the invisible God" (Col 1:15), is the perfect human being who has restored to the offspring of Adam the divine likeness which had been deformed since the first sin. Since the human nature which was assumed in him was not thereby destroyed, it was by that fact raised to a surpassing dignity in us also. For by his incarnation the Son of God united himself in some sense with every human being.[8]

This conciliar text not only alludes to the concrete and historical realization in Christ of the eternal law, but what is more important, it also exhibits the organic link in the common nature assumed that exists between the incarnate Son and the moral life.

St. Augustine accustomed the Western theological tradition to identify eternal law as a permanent expression of God's wisdom when he wrote that "that law which is named the supreme reason cannot be otherwise understood than as unchangeable and eternal."[9] And Aquinas amplified this notion when he squarely affirmed that that which establishes the origin of all that derives from the eternal law lies within God himself. In the *Summa theologiae,* Aquinas further argues that the eternal law, which he sometimes calls the *lex divina,* or divine law, embodies the "ruling idea, the *ratio,* of all things which exist in God as the effective sovereign of them all."[10] In the

---

8. *Gaudium et spes,* no. 22: "Christus, novissimus Adam, in ipsa revelatione mysterii Patris eiusque amoris, hominem ipsi homini plene manifestat eique altissimam eius vocationem patefacit. . . . Qui est 'imago Dei invisibilis' (Col 1:15), Ipse est homo perfectus, qui Adae filiis similitudinem divinam, inde a primo peccato deformatam, restituit. Cum in eo natura humana assumpta, non perempta sit, eo ipso etiam in nobis ad sublimem dignitatem evecta est. Ipse enim, Filius Dei, incarnatione sua cum omni homine quodammodo se univit."

9. See *ST* I-II, q. 91, a. 1, *sed contra:* "'Lex quae summa ratio nominatur, non potest cuipiam intelligenti non incommutabilis aeternaque videri.'" For the citation from St. Augustine, see his *De libero arbitrio* I.6 (*PL* 32:1229).

10. *ST* I-II, q. 91, a. 1: "Dicendum quod . . . nihil est aliud lex quam dictamen practicae rationis in principe qui gubernat aliquam communitatem perfectam. Manifestum est autem, supposito quod mundus divina providentia regatur . . . quod tota communitas universi gubernatur ratione divina. Et ideo ipsa ratio gubernationis rerum in Deo sicut in principe

sense both of exemplar and of guiding principle, we can speak about divine or eternal law as an analogical expression of the divine wisdom. Because Aquinas associates this doctrine with God's providence for the world, the order of divine government directly relates to the notion of the eternal law. This divine *ordo rerum,* or order of things, undergirds the whole of the created moral order. The proposal is a large one, and cannot be compressed easily to fit the contours of a narrow-minded moralism. Eternal law represents how God knows the world to be, how he effectively conceives the ordering of everything that exists within creation.[11]

How God Knows the World to Be

Because the eternal law principally reflects the divine intelligence, it stands in relationship to divine providence as a theory of practice stands in relationship to a conclusion for practical action.[12] Consider this example. For a general to master the elements of military science, that is, to learn a theory of practice, does not therefore imply that the same general will win a specific military campaign, that is, that he will successfully execute a practical action. The contingencies involved in human knowing and acting disallow positing such a necessary connection between human theory and practice. On the other hand, because God abides in utter simplicity, so that there is no real distinction between what he knows and what he does, his practical theory about things remains one with their practical realization.[13]

As much as all human language falls dramatically short of representing divine truth, theology is limited in the use that it can make of univocal

---

universitatis existens legis habet rationem. Et quia divina ratio nihil concipit ex tempore, sed habet aeternum conceptum . . . inde est quod huiusmodi legem opportet dicere aeternam." Because of the central importance of this and the preceding text, the Latin is given.

11. In a very good study of the foundations and implications of a natural law order, Oscar J. Brown, *Natural Rectitude and Divine Law in Aquinas* (Toronto: Pontifical Institute of Medieval Studies, 1981), 1–12, makes this point with reference to eternal law.

12. When Aquinas describes the nature of prudence, he takes pains to assert that the reason prudence shapes practical reason is because its *imperium* ("actus eius praecipere") moves into the order of practical reasoning, to do something. See *ST* II-II, q. 47, a. 8, "Utrum praecipere sit principalis actus prudentiae."

13. For comment, see John Finnis, *Natural Law and Natural Rights* (New York: Oxford University Press, 1980), 391, n. 35.

terms. For example, the theological deployment of the term "nature" retains a variety of analogical meanings that include the life of the blessed Trinity, the physical cosmos, and the sphere of human activity. The notion of law pertains to our human experience, and in particular to the field of jurisprudence.[14] When theologians employ the term "law," its analogical capabilities include a wide range of meanings, as one author puts it, "from the pure and eternal exemplar in the mind of God to the unsteady beat of lust in human nature."[15] In each analogical application of the term, the common note that allows for the broad deployment of the term "law" centers on the notion of regulation. Thus, as objective beatitude, God remains the end point that regulates all moral activity, and as the intelligent origin of all that exists, God serves as the beginning of every action which, when freely ruled by grace, leads to the beatific fellowship of heaven.

There are historical reasons that persuade the moral realist to describe eternal law as how God knows the world to be. For example, a realist theologian wants to avoid interpreting eternal law by appeal to the distinction between divine "absolute" and "ordained" powers that late fourteenth-century nominalists such as Gabriel Biel introduced into Western theology. Biel defines the *potentia absoluta Dei,* the divine absolute power, as God's power to do whatever does not imply a contradiction, without regard to whether God has in fact committed himself to this activity—that is, without regard to *de potentia ordinata,* to the ordained power. In contrast to the infinite range of possibilities that the *potentia absoluta* foresees, the "ordained power" signifies that course of action to which God has in fact freely committed himself.[16] While voluntarism represents a basically Christian phenomenon, born of meditation upon a God who acts freely and a Christ who announces the will of the same God, its unlimited volitional emphasis does not suggest an appropriate context for understanding eternal law as an expression of the divine creative wisdom.

Since the voluntarist position seeks to ensure that God does not become subject to created morality, voluntarist theologians affirm that God does

---

14. For a further discussion, see Edward Damich, "The Essence of Law According to Thomas Aquinas," *American Journal of Jurisprudence* 30 (1985): 79–96.

15. See Thomas Gilby, "Appendix 2: The Theological Classification of Law," in St. Thomas Aquinas, *Summa theologiae* (Cambridge, U.K.: Blackfriars, 1966), 28:162.

16. For further details, see Heiko Oberman, *The Harvest of Medieval Theology: Gabriel Biel and Late Medieval Nominalism* (Cambridge, Mass.: Harvard University Press, 1963), 37 and n. 25.

not will something because it is essentially good and right, but rather the converse. That is, in voluntarist accounts the divine willing itself determines the objects of the divine will with respect to their being good and right. Thus for such a theory it is not the divine knowledge—how God knows the world to be-that establishes the intrinsic goodness of the created moral order. But by interpreting divine wisdom as a contingent reality within God himself, voluntarist theologians must face the embarrassment that the "lawlessness" of God causes for those who argue that "the Creator of the universe and Ruler of the world can do whatever he wants to without injustice to his creatures."[17]

Because practitioners of moral realism understand that God is the fullness of wisdom, they outrightly reject the voluntarist construal of how God establishes a moral order in the world. On the other hand, for realist theology to possess confidence in the Logos pattern of the created order, in which every person can uncover an exemplar for leading a happy and fulfilled life, does not mean that Christian theology espouses a form of determinism. To put it differently, to affirm the givenness of the eternal law does not gainsay the reality of human freedom. The eternal law instead rather opens up the mystery of human participation in God's providence through the free disposition of our human wills "according to the purpose of him who accomplishes all things according to his counsel and will, so that we, who were the first to set our hope on Christ, might live for the praise of his glory" (Eph 1:11–12).

In every good action that merits eternal life, God and the human person fully exercise distinct but related causalities. The pattern whereby human activity and divine grace cooperate reflects a providential design for our salvation. "With all wisdom and insight he has made known to us the mystery of his will, according to his good pleasure that he set forth in Christ, as a plan for the fullness of time, to gather up all things in him, things in heaven and things on earth" (Eph 1:8–10). Although some writers esteem that the Thomist notion of predestination depreciates the place of human autonomy in the appropriation of merit, Aquinas himself warrants no such undifferentiated judgment when he analyzes the diverse exercises of human and divine freedom.[18] Rather, he advances the view that human freedom

---

17. Oberman, *The Harvest of Medieval Theology*, 97, n. 26.
18. E.g., see *ST* I, q. 15, a. 3; I-II, q. 91, a. 1, q. 93, a. 1. There are obvious affinities here to

itself remains instrumentally related to the exercise of the divine omnipotence. In this construal of grace and freedom, the Thomist tradition respects the full integrity of both divine causality and human autonomy, and at the same time avoids reducing their interaction to a mutual complementarity within the same category of being, as if God does his part and we do ours.

God's wise providence active in the world covers every circumstance of human life. The eternal law applies to a world of free, and therefore defective, fallible human beings. In the ministry of Jesus Christ, God's wisdom provides even for those moments when the human person makes a bad choice. The Gospel of John records Jesus' encounter with a Samaritan woman, who, we are told, was not living according to the determinations of the eternal law. But we also learn that the "drink" that Christ requests of the Samaritan woman becomes in the believer a "spring of water gushing up to eternal life" (Jn 4:14). The catechetical purpose of the passage is clear: no personal history or present condition excludes a person from living according to God's truth. Christ himself announces this consoling message: "Let anyone who is thirsty come to me, and let the one who believes in me drink. As the scripture has it, 'Out of the believer's heart shall flow rivers of living water'" (Jn 7:38). For the one who believes in Christ, conformity to God's truth causes human freedom without constraining it. Conformity with Christ purifies the soul.

Eternal Law and Salvation

While it is true that Christ alone manifests the full revelation of the Father's plan for our salvation, theologians err when they imply that knowledge of the eternal law belongs only to those who are the beneficiaries of this divine revelation. Rather, the recognition of a ruling idea, or *ratio,* operative in nature derives from the notice taken of its effects in the world. "For what can be known about God is plain to [men], because God has shown it to them. Ever since the creation of the world his invisible power and deity, has been clearly perceived in the things that have been made" (Rom 1:19–20).

Aquinas clearly demonstrates his sympathy for the Pauline instruction

---

what *Veritatis splendor* calls "theonomy." For further discussion, see chap. 5 of my *Introduction to Moral Theology* (Washington, D.C.: The Catholic University of America Press, 2001).

about what can be known apart from God's revelation to Israel and in Christ. In fact, in the text of the *Summa theologiae* we can observe a special Latin term that Aquinas uses to distinguish the way that the eternal law becomes known to us from the way intelligent creatures grasp other kinds of truths. Our knowledge of the eternal law does not emulate the ordinary mode of gaining knowledge, which the Latin verb *scire* and its cognates designate. Rather, such knowledge develops in a way similar to the way the mind grasps the first principles of speculative reasoning. In Aquinas's Latin, the eternal law is said to be "*nota*," from the Latin stem, *notare*, which approximates the English verb "to perceive."[19] It is interesting to remark that Descartes also speaks about the *imago Dei* "as the *nota* of the artificer which is impressed on his work," but Aquinas's usage does not approximate a Cartesian doctrine of innate ideas.[20]

The eternal law manifests itself with greater clarity in certain creatures than in others. Participation in the eternal law, however, is not restricted to the world of nature, for, to the extent that artificial things reflect human intelligence, they also manifest divine wisdom. Because they cannot choose to place themselves outside of the order of divine providence, infrarational creatures are also bound up with eternal law. However, when some material defect impairs their participation in the divine plan the result causes less harm than when a free creature mars the divine order by willful sin. On this account, the saint better reflects the plan of divine wisdom by living a good life than the sinner does by following bad paths.[21]

Since its purpose is to direct human conduct toward the good, all human positive laws should be measured against divine truth. There exists a real sense in which bad civil legislation of any kind amounts to a violent disruption of God's providence. In modern Western legal cultures, natural law is typically invoked as a principle of autonomy that subordinates the authority of positive laws.[22] Open and sincere proponents of natural law

---

19. According to *The New Shorter Oxford English Dictionary* (1993), one definition of the English verb *note* is "perceive."

20. Descartes, *Meditations,* III (ed., Adam-Tannery, VII, 51): "tamquam *nota* artificis operi suo impressa."

21. See Aquinas's discussion as to "whether all human affairs are subject to the Eternal Law" in *ST* I-II, q. 93, a. 6.

22. For a development of this consideration, see Russell Hittinger, "Theology and Natural Law Theory," *Communio* 17 (1990): 402–8.

are unlikely to receive key positions in liberal governments. Rather than discerning natural law as participating in eternal law, and as embracing the common good of society together with the hierarchy of ends that define this good, Western legal cultures instead are prone to invoke natural justice as vindicating the autonomous expression of disordered individual appetites that are contrary to the common good of civil society. Of course, Aquinas did not encounter this antinomian usage of "natural justice" and "natural right."[23] His influence on contemporary legal theory accounts in some measure for the fact that naturalist legal philosophy today challenges certain "autonomist" assumptions of liberal jurisprudence. To the extent that these assumptions have led to outright frustrations of God's plan for the world, for example, in countenancing the heinous crime of abortion, the task of renewal is urgent.[24] The Roman pontiff has even spoken about constructing "civil salvation."

Those who consider both law and morality as properly subject to the directive function of the eternal law are to be distinguished from those who endorse the principal tenets of secular humanism and ethical idealism. First, secular humanism affirms the self-sufficiency of human resources with respect to directing the course of human development and, second, ethical idealism maintains that rational categories of understanding are sufficient for founding moral precepts. Authentic Christian moral theology, on the other hand, first recognizes the profound relationship between nature and law as part of the divine plan for drawing men to beatific union, and second, acknowledges that the intrinsic basis for morality reposes in the

---

23. For further discussion, see Ernest Fortin, "On the Presumed Medieval Origin of Individual Rights," in Fortin, *Collected Essays*, Vol. 2, *Classical Christianity and the Political Order: Reflections on the Theologico-Political Problem,* ed. J. Brian Benestad (Lanham, Md.: Rowman & Littlefield, 1996), 243–64.

24. The Church has encouraged this reform at various moments, for example, in the Sacred Congregation for the Doctrine of the Faith, "Declaration on Abortion" (18 November 1974): "It is at all times the task of the State to preserve each person's rights and to protect the weakest. In order to do so the State will have to right many wrongs. The law is not obliged to sanction everything, but it cannot act contrary to a law which is deeper and more majestic than any human law: the natural law engraved in men's hearts by the Creator as a norm which reason clarifies and strives to formulate properly. . . ." (no. 21). The appeal takes on stronger tones in the 1995 encyclical *Evangelium vitae*, where Pope John Paul II argues this point (see no. 90) and further stresses the urgency of promoting a just society (no. 20).

whole person, precisely in its imaging of the blessed Trinity. On this point Aquinas speaks explicitly when he affirms that in a primary way, "the order of nature does not mean the ordering of nature itself, but the existence of order in the divine Persons according to natural origin."[25] He leaves no room for rationalist reductions about nature.

As a theological concept, the eternal law undergirds the economy of Christian salvation that is accomplished definitively by the promulgation of the new law of grace. Aquinas is equally explicit on this point when he compares St. Augustine's teaching on the eternal law with St. Paul's remark, "But if you are led by the Spirit, you are not subject to the law" (Gal 5:18). These words of the Apostle, Aquinas says, can be understood in two senses:

> One, that being under the law means that, while an individual is unwilling to meet its obligations, he is yet subject to its burden. So . . . one is under the law who refrains from evil deeds through fear of the punishment threatened, not from love of righteousness. In this sense spiritual persons are not subject to the law for, through charity shed in their hearts by the Holy Spirit, they fulfil the law of their own will. Second, the words can be taken to mean this, that what one does by the Holy Spirit are the deeds of the Spirit rather than of the individual human being. Since the Spirit is not under the law, as neither is the Son . . . it follows that such deeds, in so far as they spring from the Spirit, are not under the law.[26]

The point of view represented in this text assumes a particular conception of the Old Law in salvation history, and the correlative thesis that Christ's Passion fulfills the Old Law.[27]

It is important to avoid a theological anachronism; Aquinas remains entirely innocent of the controversies concerning the alleged antinomy of law and freedom that arose several centuries after his death. The theological issue of justification as developed by sixteenth-century reformers put this antimony in a strong and public light. Though its antecedents can be discovered in the work of late medieval theologians, as the refutatory work of the fif-

---

25. *ST* I, q. 42, a. 3. For further information on the ontological foundations of the *imago Dei*, see D. Juvenal Merriell, *To the Image of the Trinity: A Study in the Development of Aquinas's Teaching* (Toronto: Pontifical Institute of Medieval Studies, 1990), 170–90.

26. *ST* I-II, q. 93, a. 6 ad 1.

27. For more on this topic and its contemporary significance, see Matthew Levering, "Israel and the Shape of Thomas Aquinas's Soteriology," *The Thomist* 63 (1999): 65–82, as well as the author's more developed presentation in his forthcoming book.

teenth-century French Thomist Jean Capreolus demonstrates, these controversies come to occupy the center of theological debate during and after the sixteenth century.[28] In the period of baroque scholasticism, Thomists defended Aquinas's views against the interpretations of Luis de Molina, which repristinated certain of the reformers' themes about freedom and law. But for Aquinas, and for the medieval theologians in general, the question arose in a different light. They held that the disclosure of the eternal law and its design for human happiness opens up a way that allows divine love freely to take root in the world. Their vision was symphonic. And while in the actual order of salvation, this divine love derives preeminently from the Person of Jesus Christ, Aquinas, as we have seen, considers the Trinitarian dimensions of the eternal law to establish the grounds for this harmony or, in the case of unrepentant sinners, the conspicuous lack of this harmony.[29]

Catholic doctrine illuminated by the work of Aquinas accepts as axiomatic the harmonious workings of law and grace in the Christian life. The New Testament does not place actions that proceed from theological charity "under the law." The Gospel rather announces a reign of liberty: "Now the Lord is the Spirit, and where the Spirit of the Lord is, there is freedom" (2 Cor 3:17). Caritative actions do, however, conform to the designs of the eternal law insofar as through them Christian believers freely accomplish the work of the Holy Spirit in the world. "For the whole law is summed up in a single commandment, 'You shall love your neighbor as yourself'" (Gal 5:14). However, attempts to fulfill this commandment without due respect to the givens of the eternal law fail precisely to the extent that they disregard the order of generation in the Trinity. The Person of Love, the Holy Spirit, cannot proceed from an action that does not conform to the perfect image of the Father's goodness. We can thank St. Augustine for reminding us of the importance of the Trinitarian dimension of

---

28. For further information, see the relevant essays in *Jean Capreolus en son temps (1380–1444), Mémoire Dominicaine,* numéro spécial, 1, ed. Guy Bedouelle, Romanus Cessario, and Kevin White (Paris: Les Éditions du Cerf, 1997).

29. "And this also is a natural thing, that the mind can use its reason to understand God, according to which we have said that the image of God always remains in the mind; 'whether this image of God is so overthrown,' as if overshadowed, 'that it is almost annihilated,' as in those who do not have the use of reason, 'or it is darkened and deformed,' as in sinners, 'or it is shining and beautiful' as in the just, as Augustine says in *De Trinitate,* Book 14" (*ST* I, q. 93, a. 8 ad 3).

the moral life: "In the Trinity there is the Holy Spirit, the suavity of the begetter and the begotten, who showers us with an unmeasurable generosity and richness."[30]

In imitation of Christ who accomplished the work that the Father gave him to do (see Jn 17:4), Christian life unfolds within a pattern of obedience to the will of the Father. In his commentary on this Gospel, Aquinas even speaks about Christ as the "doctrine of the Father."[31] This means that Christ himself supplies to each of his members the concrete measure or starting point for a moral life lived under the inspiration of the Holy Spirit. The Trinitarian rhythms of the moral life reveal that the final end of human perfection coincides with the first movement of our freedom. The Book of Wisdom anticipates this slant on human destiny. We are in the hand of God, we and our words. It is he who has granted me to know both the beginning and the middle of events, the sequence of the solstices, and the succession of the seasons, the passing of the year and the place of the zodiac (see Wis 7:16–19). This movement from and toward the divine goodness arises from the depths of one's being—*interior intimo meo*. "For you did not receive a spirit of slavery to fall back into fear, but you have received a spirit of adoption. When we cry, 'Abba! Father!' it is that very Spirit bearing witness with our spirit that we are children of God, and if children, then heirs, heirs of God and joint heirs with Christ—if, in fact, we suffer with him so that we may also be glorified with him" (Rom 8:15–17). It is possible to elaborate a properly theological appreciation of natural law only within the context of the Trinitarian ordering of human existence in conformity with the rhythms established within the eternal law.

Since as Son of the Father, Jesus Christ fulfilled the complete will of the Father, that is, everything that must be done, he remains the concrete measure or starting point of moral life lived under the inspiration of the Holy Spirit.[32] Thus, in God's eternal plan, the last end coincides with the first movement of our freedom, a movement that arises from the depths of one's being; and so the tradition places the movement toward God at the heart of the human person—*interior intimo meo*. What else explains St. Paul's admonition? "For you did not receive a spirit of slavery to fall back into fear, but

---

30. *De Trinitate*, Bk. 6, chap. 10 (*PL* 42, col. 931).

31. See his *Commentary on the Gospel of St. John (Lectura super Ioannem)*, 7.1.3.

32. See William J. Hill, *The Triune God* (Washington, D.C.: The Catholic University of America Press, 1982).

you have received a spirit of adoption. When we cry, 'Abba! Father!' it is that very Spirit bearing witness with our spirit that we are children of God, and if children, then heirs, heirs of God and joint heirs with Christ—if, in fact, we suffer with him so that we may also be glorified with him" (Rom 8:15–17). A properly theological appreciation of natural law arises only within the context of the Trinitarian ordering of human existence that flows from what the tradition has identified as the eternal law. It was Aquinas's recognition of this truth that led him to place natural law within the framework of the *sacra doctrina,* the articulation of which we have inherited as the *Summa theologiae.*

What the Church teaches about the human good is not the equivalent of promoting a sectarian enterprise. If there is conflict, it is over how a community dwells under the eternal law, not about the merits of the moral values espoused by a particular religious tradition. This explains why Pope John Paul II has affirmed that *Evangelium vitae* must guide the construction of "civil salvation."[33] He knows that the truths of divine and Catholic faith are meant for everyone. Revelation makes us privileged participants in the *sacra doctrina,* which may be described as everything that God knows about himself and communicates to those blessed ones who already enjoy the vision of God.

This revelation safeguarded in the Catholic Church has already changed the way that persons in the world think about God. In other words, Christ has already changed the way that people think about God. In the 1970s, the late French Dominican A.-J. Festugière observed on this novelty that Christian revelation has introduced: "Even though one may be as unhappy as before, and though there may have been as many crimes and sufferings in the year 1972 as in the time of Tiberius or Nero, an extraordinary phenomenon took place during the first century of our era: man came to believe that God loved him."[34] Only the theologian can announce this truth. And it expresses the most important truth that God knows about himself.

33. The Holy Father addressed a group assembled in Rome to commemorate the fifth anniversary of his encyclical letter *Evangelium vitae.* In this discourse ("Let us offer the world new signs of hope," *L'Osservatore Romano* N. 8 [23 February 2000]: 4) he asserted that the message of *Evangelium vitae* provides not only true and authentic guidelines for moral rebirth, but also a "reference point for civil salvation."

34. André-Jean Festugière, "Appendice," *Mémorial André-Jean Festugière. Antiquité païenne et chrétienne,* Vingt-cinq études publiées et réunies par E. Lucchesi et H.-D. Saffrey, *Cahiers d'orientalisme* X (Geneva: Editions P. Cramer, 1984), 275.

RESPONSE

NATURAL REASON IN THE SERVICE OF FAITH

Robert Fastiggi

Father Cessario's paper is rooted not only in Scripture and the writings of Aquinas, but he makes a constant effort to situate his reflections within the central mysteries of the Christian faith: the Trinity and the Incarnation. It is this recognition of the Christological and Trinitarian "ordering of human existence" that leads Cessario to his central thesis. Aquinas places natural law within the framework of the *sacra doctrina* because the natural law flows out of the eternal law that is the wisdom of the Triune God revealed in Christ who is the exemplar of all creation and the teleological principle guiding all beings toward their proper ends.

As a general thesis, I think that Cessario has presented a compelling argument woven within the fabric of Scripture, Vatican II's *Gaudium et spes,* and the insights of Pope John Paul II, especially those of *Veritatis splendor* and *Fides et ratio.* There are numerous points that are provocative and stimulating and which, in another context, could be treated with more attention and development. Let me explore five of these: (1) the meaning of *sacra doctrina;* (2) the preeminence of Christ; (3) the question of voluntarism; (4) grace and free will; and (5) the uniqueness of the Christian revelation.

The Meaning of *Sacra Doctrina*

It would be helpful if Father Cessario could be more specific about what he (or Aquinas) means by *sacra doctrina.* I say this because the very phrase "sacred doctrine" could suggest to many that order of knowledge distinct from natural reason. This, of course, would be the order of knowledge identified by Vatican I as that of divine faith in which "there are proposed for our belief mysteries that are hidden in God, which cannot be known unless they are divinely revealed" *(nisi revelata divinitus).*¹ If this is what is meant by *sacra doctrina,* then the placement of natural law within its compass would be problematic since it would seem to undercut the usual understanding of natural law as the law of "right reason" that is "written and engraved in the soul of each and every man"² (apart from or prior to divine revelation in its proper sense).

There are, however, good reasons why natural law can be placed under *sacra doctrina* when we understand that for Aquinas *sacra doctrina* is a broader term than the order of divine faith as set forth by Vatican I. As Father Thomas Gilby observes, *sacra doctrina,* for Aquinas, is not a rigid term, but rather one with a certain "plastic" quality to it.³ This is why "St. Thomas chose *sacra doctrina* instead of *theologia* for his opening title in the *Summa*" because "the highest part of metaphysics is also called theology."⁴ For the Angelic Doctor grace and reason work together. As he writes: "Since grace does not take away nature but perfects it, it is thus fitting that natural reason should serve faith and the inclination of the natural will submit to charity" *(Cum igitur gratia non tollat naturam sed perficiat, oportet quod naturalis ratio subserviat fidei sicut et naturalis inclinatio voluntatis ratio obsequitur charitati).*⁵

For Aquinas, *sacra doctrina* is the "highest wisdom above all other human wisdoms" *(doctrina maxime sapientia est inter omnes sapientias humanas).*⁶ But this "highest wisdom" embraces both natural reason and divine faith. Thus, in a recent article in *The Thomist,* Lawrence J. Donohoo observes that *sacra doctrina* employs "both its revelation-dependent and reason-punctuated modes, in order to investigate in turn natural and supernatural knowledge."⁷ Apparently, it was only in later Thomists such as John of St. Thomas (1589–1644) that a sharper distinction between *sacra doctrina* in the general sense and *sacra doctrina* in the more specific sense of theological teaching on

---

1. Denzinger-Hünermann, *Enchiridion Symbolorum* (37th ed.) [henceforth DH], 3015 (unless otherwise indicated, all translations from Latin or French are my own).

2. See *Catechism of the Catholic Church,* nos. 1956 and 1954.

3. Thomas Gilby, "Appendix 5: Sacra Doctrina," in St. Thomas Aquinas, *Summa theologiae* (Cambridge, U.K.: Blackfriars, 1964), 1:63.

4. Ibid.   5. *ST* I, q. 1, a. 8 ad 2.

6. *ST* I, q. 1, a. 6.

7. Lawrence J. Donohoo, "The Nature and Grace of *Sacra Doctrina* in St. Thomas's *Super Boetium de Trinitate,*" *The Thomist* 63 (July 1999): 398.

revealed truths began to emerge.[8] However, even when the order of reason and the order of revelation are distinguished, the natural law is still a matter of theological concern. As Father John J. Reed writes:

> From the fact, therefore, that the natural law is said to be the object of the order of reason, it does not follow that it is not the object of revelation. The mode of cognition is a question of methodology; the constitutive element of natural law is the divine reason and will. Obviously, therefore, natural law is not only an object of philosophy; it is also an object of theological inquiry.[9]

All this helps to explain why Aquinas can place the natural law within *sacra doctrina*.

The Preeminence of Christ

Father Cessario is supremely Christocentric, and he begins his paper with a Scripture-based meditation on how and why divine wisdom refers to Christ as both eternal Word and the incarnate Son. However, he also notes how confusion about the relation of the eternal Word to the moral order results in "mythological Christocentrism" which "speak[s] about the incarnate Christ as if he were involved in the created moral order even prior to the free and gracious divine self-donation that occurs in the Incarnation" (Cessario, p. 82). But who does Cessario have in mind when he mentions this "mythological Christocentrism?" One possibility might be the Jesuit Pierre Teilhard de Chardin (1881–1955). In his book *Synthèse dogmatique* the Dominican theologian Jean-Hervé Nicolas writes:

> According to the conception of Teilhard, this primacy of Christ, in order to be realized, must consist in an organic union of Christ with the world. Blondel reproached Teilhard for this insistence on speaking about a physical union. In truth, this "organicism" is not an intelligible theory (this physical penetration of Christ, in his physical reality, at the heart of things, is not thinkable) but a myth. It is a projection, in a purely imaginative scheme, of a certain truth: the ordination of all things to Christ.[10]

As Father Cessario makes clear, the centrality of Christ to the moral order need not result in this "mythological Christocentrism." However, the

---

8. Gilby, "Appendix 5: Sacra Doctrina," 64.
9. John J. Reed, "Natural Law, Theology and the Church," *Theological Studies* 26 (1965): 44.
10. Jean-Hervé Nicolas, *Synthèse dogmatique* (Fribourg: Editions Universitaires, 1986), 460.

belief in the preeminence of Christ in the created moral order even prior to the Incarnation is not something alien to the Catholic tradition. Usually, it is expressed in the Scotist belief in the predestination of the Incarnation prior to the Fall. While this is a view identified with the Franciscan rather than the Dominican-Thomist tradition, there is one passage in Aquinas, namely, *ST* II-II, q. 2, a. 7, that seems to suggest a type of predestination of the Incarnation:

> Before the state of sin man had explicit faith in the Incarnation of Christ insofar as it was ordered towards the consummation of glory but not as it was ordered towards the liberation from sin through the Passion and Resurrection: for man did not have foreknowledge of future sins. However, it seems as if he did have foreknowledge of the Incarnation of Christ when, in Genesis, it is said: "For this reason a man shall leave his father and mother and cling to his wife" and the Apostle says in Ephesians: "A great mystery is in this: Christ and the Church."[11]

While this particular passage of Aquinas does not seem to be in complete harmony with what he says in *ST* III, q. 1, a. 3, it should be noted that even there he does not limit the purpose of the Incarnation only to the redemption of sin. It would seem that the significance of Christ for the created moral order—even prior to the Incarnation—was not something foreign to the mind of Aquinas.

The Question of Voluntarism

Father Cessario rightfully contrasts the voluntarist position of late medieval nominalism with that of Aquinas who perceives an intrinsic rationality in the created moral order. In its most extreme form, nominalism maintains that God does not will something because it is good, but that it is good because God wills it. As Luther puts it, "What God wills is not right because He ought to or was bound to so will. On the contrary, what takes

---

11. "Nam ante statum peccati homo habuit explicitam fidem de Christi Incarnatione secundum quod ordinabatur ad consummationem gloriae, non autem secundum quod ordinabatur ad liberationem a peccato per Passionem et Resurrectionem, quia homo non fuit praescius peccati futuri. Videtur autem Incarnationis Christi praescius fuisse quod dixit, 'Propter hoc reliquet homo patrem et matrem et adhaerit uxori suae,' ut habetur Gen. II:24, et hoc Apostolus ad Ephes., dicit, 'sacramentum magnum esse in Christo et Ecclesia' . . ." (*ST* II-II, q. 2, a. 7).

place must be right because He so wills it."[12] Thus the "creator of the universe can do whatever he wants to without injustice to his creatures."[13] Luther, therefore, could assert: "If it should please you that God rewards the undeserving, it should not displease you that he damns the innocent" *(Si placet tibi Deus indignos coronans, non debet discplicere immeritos damans).*[14] This position, of course, is in marked contrast to the "confidence in the Logos pattern of the created order" (Cessario, p. 86) that Cessario finds in the realist theology of Aquinas.

While the extreme forms of voluntarism have obvious dangers, I think it is necessary to note the importance of God's will in the establishment of the moral law within the created order. In discussions of natural law, fears of voluntarism have, at times, led Thomists to criticize the natural law theory of the Jesuit Francisco Suarez (1548–1617) as placing too much emphasis on law as an expression of the *imperium* (authority or sovereignty) of the divine will.[15] This alleged voluntarism of Suarez is contrasted with the view of Aquinas that "law is an ordination of reason to the common good" *(Lex est ordinatio rationis ad bonum commune).*[16]

A careful reading of Suarez's *De Legibus,* however, shows that God's will acts in harmony with his intellect and there should be no fear of an arbitrary or irrational exercise of his legislative *imperium.* The first point to consider is that in any rational mind (including God's), there must be both intellect and will. As Suarez writes:

> We must first assume that law is that which pertains to an intellectual nature, insofar as it is, and therefore, to its mind: for under mind are comprehended intellect and will (for this is how I now speak). This, in itself, is sufficiently noted, since law indicates a moral order towards something to be performed: but no nature except the intellectual is capable of this ordering.[17]

---

12. Luther, *De servo arbitrio,* 709, in *Erasmus-Luther: Discourse on Free Will,* trans. Ernst Winter (New York: Frederick Ungar, 1961), 130.

13. This is from Heiko Oberman's *The Harvest of Medieval Theology: Gregory Biel and Late Medieval Nominalism* (Cambridge, Mass.: Harvard University Press, 1963), 97, n. 26 (cited by Cessario).

14. Luther, *De servo arbitrio,* 174 (a text not included in Winter's abridged edition).

15. See William E. May, "The Natural Law Doctrine of Suarez," *New Scholasticism* 58 (Autumn 1984): 409–23.

16. *ST* I-II, q. 90, a. 4.

17. "Primum ergo supponimus legem esse aliquid pertinens ad naturam intellectualem,

For Suarez, therefore, it is proper to speak of the natural law as an *ordo rationis*. However, law not only requires an intellectual judgment but also a command of the will. As he observes: "The natural law not only points to good and evil but also contains its own prohibition of evil and command of the good" *(Lex naturalis non tantum est indicativa mali et boni, sed etiam continet propriam prohibitionem mali, et praeceptionem boni)*.[18]

Suarez, though, should not be understood as if the reason for goodness or evil of certain acts rests totally in God's commanding will. In his own words:

The prohibition or command of God's will is not the whole reason of the goodness and evil of that which relates to the observing or the transgressing of the natural law, but it presupposes in the acts themselves the necessary righteousness or deformity and to these it adds the obligation of particular divine laws.[19]

I bring forward the case of Suarez only to emphasize that in the natural law, as with any expression of divine law, there is a complementarity between God's intellect and his will. This is seen most clearly in the divine positive laws of the Decalogue. God does not merely point to the rational moral order and observe: "It is wrong to steal." Rather, he commands: "Thou shall not steal."

Grace and Free Will

Father Cessario is correct, I believe, to note that in Aquinas there is no conflict between the natural law and the new law of grace. Likewise, I think he is correct to understand Aquinas as maintaining the harmony between grace and human freedom. However, I was somewhat surprised by his description of the controversy between the Dominican Thomists and the Jesuit Molinists as a revival of "the reformers' themes about freedom

---

quatenus talis est, atque adeo ad mentem ejus: sub mente intellectum et volunatem comprehendo (ut enim nunc loquor). Hoc per se satis notum est, quia lex dicit moralem ordinem ad aliquid agendum: nulla autem natura est capax hujus ordinationis nisi intellectualis" (Suarez, *De Legibus ad de Deo Legislator*, I, 4.2).

18. Ibid., II, 6.5.

19. "Haec Dei voluntas, prohibitio, aut praeceptio non est tota ratio bonitatis et malitiae, quae est observatione vel transgressione legis naturalis, sed supponit in ipsis actibus necessariam quandam honestatem vel turpitudinem, et allis adiungit specialis legis divnniae obligationem" (ibid., II, 6.11).

and law" (Cessario, p. 91). This controversy, which resulted in the papal commission *De Auxiliis* (1598–1607), is not usually understood as a conflict over freedom and the law but rather as a conflict over how best to harmonize the truths of divine foreknowledge, human free will, and the necessity of grace. The controversy likewise involved a discussion of how sufficient grace is made efficacious. The Dominican Domingo Bañez (1528–1604) maintained that sufficient grace is made efficacious by the intrinsic power of the grace itself *(ab intrinseco)*, while the Jesuit Luis de Molina (1535–1600) believed that sufficient grace is made efficacious by the free consent of the will. The Dominicans accused the Jesuits of being semi-Pelagians and the Jesuits accused the Dominicans of being Calvinists. In 1607 and 1611, Pope Paul V closed the debate by allowing the freedom of either side to teach its respective position.[20]

The Uniqueness of the Christian Revelation

Father Cessario ends his paper with a quote from the late Dominican scholar A. J. Festugière: "An extraordinary phenomenon took place during the first century of our era: man came to believe that God loved him." He then comments: "Only the theologian can announce this truth. And it expresses the most important truth that God knows about himself" (Cessario, p. 93).

I certainly would agree that the Christian revelation is a revelation of God's love for us. Indeed, God's very nature is love (cf. 1 Jn 4:16, "God is love"). However, this insight into the loving nature of God does not seem to have occurred only in the first century of our era. One need only turn to the great affirmation of God's *hesed* (loving kindness) found in Psalm 103. But even outside of the biblical revelation, witness to God's love for human beings is not absent. In the *Bhagavad Gita* (c. 400–200 B.C.) Krishna tells his devotee Arjuna:

---

20. DH, 1997–1997a; see also W. J. Hill, "Bañez and Bañezianism," in *The New Catholic Encyclopedia* (Washington, D.C.: The Catholic University of America Press, 1967); 2:48–50, F. L. Sheerin, "Molinism," in *The New Catholic Encyclopedia* (Washington, D.C.: The Catholic University of America Press, 1967), 9:1011–13; and Raoul de Scorraile, *François Suarez de La Compagnie de Jesus* (Paris: Lethielleux, 1912), 2:402–67.

I have revealed to you a knowledge more mysterious than any secret. Reflect on it fully, and then do as you wish.... Listen again to my final word, the most secret of all. I love you deeply and so I will tell you your good. (*Gita* 18:63–64)

Be intent on me, love me, sacrifice to me, worship me. You will come to me, I promise you truly, for you are dear to me. (*Gita* 18:65)[21]

The witness of other religions to the great mystery of God's love, I think, provides support for Father Cessario's central thesis: that the natural law should be placed under *sacra doctrina*. For Aquinas, I believe, would not hesitate to support the affirmation of Vatican II that the many diverse religions "often reflect the ray of that Truth which enlightens all men" *(haud raro referunt tamen radium illius Veritatis, quae illuminat omnes homines)*.[22] As a Christian, I embrace the Christological and Trinitarian "ordering of existence" witnessed to by Father Cessario. However, I maintain that the gift of reason, which enables us to know the natural law apart from divine revelation proper, is our link with all men of goodwill. And what a gift it is!

From a Christian perspective, to be sure, "only in the mystery of the Incarnate Word does the mystery of man take on light."[23] But the light of that Word has been shining since the dawn of creation, and as Father Cessario puts it: "[T]he quest for the ultimate *logos* or intelligibility ... undergirds and directs the created order" (Cessario, p. 81). It is within God's *logos*—which is also God's *Sophia*—that the natural law is established. As Aquinas writes, "The natural law is nothing other than the light of understanding placed in us by God" and "God has given this light or law at creation."[24] But the light of reason is also the law of love. The Almighty Creator has given us this marvelous gift of the natural law for one reason and one reason only: he loves us.

---

21. The translations are those of Prof. José Pereira of Fordham University. In the book *Salt of the Earth* (San Francisco: Ignatius Press, 1997), Cardinal Joseph Ratzinger states that the Hindu deity Krisha comes closest to Jesus and the Christian belief in the Incarnation. However, the Cardinal notes that the Hindu belief in the descent of God in Krisha "is conceived in a completely different way from the Christian belief in the definitive union of the one God with a definitive historical man, through whom he draws the whole of humanity to himself" (258).

22. *Nostra aetate*, no. 2.

23. *Gaudium et spes*, no. 22.

24. Aquinas, *De praesc.* I (cited in *The Catechism of the Catholic Church*, no. 1955).

❈ RESPONSE ❈

THE CHRISTOLOGICAL FOUNDATION OF NATURAL LAW

Earl Muller, S.J.

Father Romanus Cessario has situated Thomas's discussion of the natural law squarely within the Thomistic understanding of *sacra doctrina*. This location, as Cessario rightly observes, necessitates the correlate location of "the regulative pattern for all right human conduct ultimately . . . within the blessed Trinity" (Cessario, p. 81). I concur whole-heartedly with these two points and propose to pursue this issue in the comments that follow. I must necessarily return to the topic of a previous paper, the anthropological foundations of the natural law. The reason is clear: those anthropological foundations themselves are placed by Thomas within the context of *sacra doctrina*. This, I will argue, necessitates understanding natural law within a fundamentally ecclesial context, which is to say, within a fundamentally Christological context. Thomas himself provides the linkage between *sacra doctrina* and Christ when he tells us that Christ is the "doctrine of the Father."[1] Jesus Christ is *sacra doctrina*. Locating natural law within the context of *sacra doctrina* simultaneously locates it within a Christological, and ultimately an ecclesialogical, context. Given his comment about mythological Christocentricism, Father Cessario, I suspect, would be reluctant to go this far.

One cannot understand the place of the Angelic Doctor's anthropology within the *Summa theologiae* without also considering the place of the *tertia pars* and thus of the overall structure of Thomas's masterwork. The modern discussion of this was initiated by Marie-Dominique Chenu's article, "Le

---

1. *Commentary on the Gospel of St. John* 7.2.4 (1037). I am grateful to Richard Nicholas for bringing this text to my attention in his 2002 Marquette University dissertation.

plan de la Somme théologique de saint Thomas," which came out in 1939.² Chenu's own suggestion that the first two parts of the *Summa* are patterned on a Neoplatonic *exitus-reditus* pattern has remained influential down to the present day.

Etienne Gilson, in his review of Chenu's *Introduction à l'étude de Saint Thomas d'Aquin*,³ was enthusiastic in his assessment of Chenu's discussion of the plan of the *Summa*.⁴ He singled out particularly, and this defines one pole of the subsequent debate, Chenu's comments on the attempt by some commentators to effect a Bonaventurian or Scotist *Summa* "after the form and the plan of" Thomas's.⁵ Of particular importance in this is the contrast that is drawn between Thomas's theology and the Christocentric theology of Duns Scotus which resists being treated as a science. There is, according to Chenu and Gilson, no such Christological metaphysics possible. Grace, for instance, treated without explicit reference to the Incarnation by Thomas, "has its own nature, its own structure, its own laws, beyond the temporal conditions of its realization."⁶ This is, to their minds, a necessitarian structure to which the concrete manifestations of the economy of salvation conform. "Here as elsewhere," Gilson wrote, "history presupposes nature, from which it is not deduced, but to which it conforms."⁷ Grace follows on and conforms to nature. Their contention is that the Incarnation in its gratuitous historicity is not minimized by being "inserted" into such an ontology of grace.⁸ "Humanity," Chenu likewise wrote, "is encountered in the

2. Marie-Dominique Chenu, "Le plan de la Somme théologique de Saint Thomas," *Revue thomiste* 47 (1939): 93–107.

3. Marie-Dominique Chenu, *Introduction à l'étude de Saint Thomas d'Aquin* (1950; reprint, Paris: Vrin, 1954); English translation by A. M. Landry and D. Hughes, *Toward Understanding Saint Thomas Aquinas* (Chicago: Henry Regnery, 1964).

4. Etienne Gilson, *Bulletin thomiste* 8 (1951): 7: "pages littéralement sans prix dans leur simplicité."

5. Chenu, "Le plan," 106–7; Chenu, *Introduction*, 272; Chenu, *Understanding*, 317. Gilson, of course, was pleased at Chenu's refusal to amalgamate different theological systems, something Gilson had been insisting on for years.

6. Chenu, "Le plan," 104–5; Chenu, *Introduction*, 270; Chenu, *Understanding*, 314–15. Cf. Gilson, *Bulletin thomiste*, 9.

7. "Ici comme ailleurs, l'histoire présuppose des natures, dont elle ne se déduit pas, mais conformément auxquelles elle arrive" (Gilson, *Bulletin thomiste*, 9).

8. Chenu, "Le plan," 105; Chenu, *Introduction*, 270; Chenu, *Understanding*, 314–15. Cf. Gilson, *Bulletin thomiste*, 9.

Summa, not primarily as the mystical body of Christ, but as part of a cosmology."[9] (I will sharply contest this idea in what follows.) He summed up what is at issue when he affirmed that "the transition from the *Secunda* to the *Tertia Pars* is a passage from the order of the necessary to the order of the historical, from an account of structures to the actual story of God's gifts." Theology "as a science" is thus understood to be concerned primarily with these necessary structures and only secondarily with the concrete events of salvation. It follows that the natural law will be similarly understood. Human nature is understood to participate, not in the God-man Jesus Christ, but in the eternal Word considered apart from the Incarnation.

André Hayen developed the first extensive response to Chenu's position in his little work entitled *Saint Thomas d'Aquin et la vie de l'Église*.[10] Hayen's main point was that the *Summa theologiae* is Christologically structured. Divinity, humanity, and their union all pertain to Christ. The place of Christ in the thought of Thomas "is total," he wrote, "[m]ore total than Father Chenu would wish . . . more total also than for Father Rondet."[11] Hayen reiterated this Christological focus in a subsequent article, "La structure de la Somme théologique et Jésus," where he affirmed that "Jesus Christ is not only the central point of the *Summa theologiae*. He is the substance itself of it."[12]

Rondet, for his part was also critical of Chenu's vision of the plan of the *Summa* and particularly of the characterization of the Incarnation as merely the concrete historical manifestation of an ontological structure otherwise independent of it. "Christ is the way [Chenu's view]," he wrote, "but

---

9. Chenu, "Le plan," 104; Chenu, *Introduction,* p. 269; Chenu, *Understanding,* 314.

10. André Hayen, *Saint Thomas d'Aquin et la vie de l'Eglise* (Louvain and Paris: Publications universitaires, 1952), 75; cf. also p. 88. He is referring to Etienne Gilson, "Maimonide et la philosophie de l'Exode," *Medieval Studies* 8 (1951): 223–25. Cf. "la vie," 80–81, for the former point; he cites *ST* II-II, q. 27, a. 4 ad 2, and *De Potentia* q. 9, a. 9, for examples of changed meanings. Cf. also note 13 above.

11. "La vie," 95: "Ce qu'on vient de dire permet de préciser avec exactitude la place du Christ dans la pensée de saint Thomas. Cette place est totale. Plus totale que ne le veut le P. Chenu . . . Plus totale aussi que pour le P. Rondet." Cf. Chenu's response in his review of this work in *Bulletin thomiste* 8 (1947–1953): 771–72, no. 1346.

12. "La structure de la Somme théologique et Jésus," *Sciences ecclésiastiques* 12 (1960): 61: "*Jésus-Christ n'est pas seulement le point central de la Somme théologique. Il en est la substance même.*" Cf. also p. 68.

he is also the term; one is not able, without discussion, to oppose the mystery of Christ to the mystery of God [or as he notes later, biblical theology to speculative theology, history to science]; it is in Christ that God reveals Himself to man, everything, in fact, has been created for Christ."[13]

He also accused Chenu of missing the point on the subalternation of the sciences. All sciences are not oriented only to the general. "The whole edifice of knowledge," he wrote, "if it is coherent with itself, if each particular science does not usurp the place of the superior science, this whole edifice will culminate in the affirmation of one fact: the primacy of Christ in whom, by the divine will, all things find their consistancy."[14] (He was citing Colossians.) To the response that theology is first and foremost about God as he is in himself and not human history, Rondet rejoined that God is only revealed to us in salvation history.[15]

Two other works are worth briefly mentioning. The first is Ghislain Lafont's *Structures et méthode dans la Somme théologique de Saint Thomas d'Aquin*, originally published in 1961, which has been fairly influential in the subsequent discussion.[16] Lafont accepted the critique of Chenu's Neoplatonic motif and shifted the consideration to more Aristotelian causes. In the end his scheme is not all that different from Chenu's—instead of a Neoplatonic *exitus* that governs the first part of the *Summa* Lafont saw efficient causality; instead of the Neoplatonic *reditus*, there was final causality. However, he undermined his rather lengthy study from the very first. He began with a consideration of question 2 of the *Summa*, the proofs for the existence of God, and completely ignores the first question in which Thomas himself

---

13. Henri Rondet, "Bulletin de théologie historique: Etudes médiévales," *Recherches de science religieuse* 38 (1951): 154: "Le Christ est la voie, mais il est aussi le terme; on ne peut, sans explications, opposer le mystère du Christ au mystère de Dieu; c'est dans le Christ que Dieu se révèle à l'homme, pour le Christ que, de fait, tout a été créé."

14. Ibid., 155: "Si bien que, finalement, tout l'édifice du savoir, s'il est cohérent avec lui-même, si chaque science particulière n'usurpe pas la place des sciences supérieures, tout cet édifice culminera dans l'affirmation d'un fait: la primauté du Christ en qui, de par la volonté divine, toutes choses trouvent leur consistance: *Christus, in quo omnia constant* (Col 1:17). Entrer dans ces perspectives ne sera nullement renoncer à la théologie comme science, ce sera seulement reconnaître que la fonction théologique a de multiples aspects."

15. Ibid., 156.

16. Ghislain Lafont, O.S.B., *Structures et méthode dans la Somme théologique de Saint Thomas d'Aquin*, reprint with new preface (Paris: Les Éditions du Cerf, 1996).

sets out what he is doing. This is a rather stunning methodological mistake even if it has been very influential.

Michel Corbin in his *Le chemin de la théologie chez Thomas d'Aquin*, a work far less known than Lafont's, did not make this mistake.[17] He examined the first question in detail and showed how it is worked out throughout the *Summa theologiae*. He concluded that the three parts are strictly parallel—God and his works, man and his works, Christ and his works. Christ, the God-man, is composed. His divinity actualizes this composite; divinity is considered in the first part of the *prima pars*. His humanity stands in potency to the actualizing divinity; this humanity is considered in the latter part of the *prima* and in the *secunda*. The complete substance is the Christ himself and this is treated in the *tertia pars*. The unity of the whole enterprise, then, resides in Christ, the God-man. The *tertia* is not an appendix, as in Chenu; it is in considerable measure the point of the *Summa theologiae*. The subject of *sacra doctrina* is God, not as the philosopher considers him, that is, as being qua being, but in his concreteness. God is concretely the Trinity; God is concretely Jesus Christ. It is this twin affirmation that is necessary for salvation and Thomas demands that even those who preceed Christ must believe explicitly in the Incarnation if they were to be saved.

Let us examine these claims. First, is there additional evidence in the *Summa* to support the claim that act/potency/union-of-act-and-potency structures the work in its entirety? There is. In the treatises on creation the order of emanation is not a Neoplatonic order. Thomas consistently follows an Aristotelian order, treating first the general and then the specific: creation as it proceeds from God and then created things in themselves. There is no orderly progression from highest level to lowest level as one might expect in a Neoplatonic chain of being. The first specific reality created are the angels—pure spirits, pure forms (qq. 50–64). Then, after general questions regarding corporeal bodies and their derivation from God (q. 65), the first thing treated is formless matter (q. 66). There follows the seven days of creation in which all other things, all corporeal except for light, are created (qq. 67–74). Finally, Thomas discusses the creation of man who is the union of spirit and body.

The Aristotelian character of this structure is clear as well as Thomas's

---

17. Michel Corbin, *Le chemin de la théologie chez Thomas d'Aquin*, Bibliothèque des Archives de Philosophie, n.s., vol. 16 (Paris: Beauchesne, 1974).

concern to treat things in the order suggested by the discipline. Man is a composed creature. The composite is considered only after the constituent elements of that composition are considered: first that which actualizes the composition, which is to say, spiritual reality; then that which stands in potency, which is to say, corporeal reality. If Thomas follows the same procedure in the whole of the *Summa theologiae* as he does in the tractates on creation, then one can only conclude that Thomas's primary interest in discussing humanity in the *Summa* is in setting out that which is in potency in Christ. Humanity is not treated as some pure nature in isolation from Christ. The humanity of the *Summa* is humanity that has fallen and been assumed and redeemed by Christ. It is humanity as it actually exists; it is "in Christ."

There is a second indication that Thomas understands the humanity in the *secunda* in terms of Christ. In question 8 of the *tertia pars* Thomas considers the grace of Christ as the Head of the Church. In the third article he asks whether Christ is the Head of all men, noting the objection that unbaptized individuals are in no way members of the Church. His response is that everyone, apart from the damned in hell, is, in point of fact, in the Church, at least potentially. The damned have irrevocably severed themselves from Christ but even here the fundamental reference point is Christ. Humanity in its entirety, concretely understood, is or was potentially part of the Body of Christ. The natural law, inherent to humanity, is the law inherent in the Body of Christ. This law, as Cessario points out, is the human participation in divine Wisdom; it is rooted in the Trinitarian reality of God; it is also rooted in Wisdom incarnate.

There is a third indication that Thomas understands the humanity of the *secunda* in terms of the Body of Christ and this is the choice of topics to cover that Thomas makes. There has always been an awkwardness felt in the treatment of grace in the *secunda* without any explicit mention of Christ. This certainly led Chenu, but also many others, astray. Thomas, on the other hand, is explicit on the point. Christ is the Head of the Church, of all of humanity, in order, perfection, and power because "His grace is the highest and first, though not in time, since all have received grace on account of His grace. . . . He has the power of bestowing grace on all the members of the Church." Thomas explicitly extends this to all of humanity as noted above.

Thomas distinguishes five kinds of law in q. 91 of the *prima secundae*:

eternal law which is God's governance of creation, natural law which is human participation in the eternal law proportionate to the capacity of human nature, human laws, and two types of scripturally revealed divine law found respectively in the Old and the New Testaments to aid men in the attainment of their supernatural end. They are all relevant to the same humanity, and the inclusion of the New Law makes it clear that Thomas has the humanity of which Christ is the Head in view.

Finally, the inclusion of discussions, at the end of the *secunda secundae,* of prophecy, tongues, the episcopal state, and religious life make it clear that it is humanity understood as, in principle, which is to say in potency, the Church. This, among other things, grounds the capacity of the Church to speak authoritatively about natural law since she is fundamentally talking about herself, not indeed of her supernatural destiny, but of her concrete existence in this life in ways other than supernatural—the property rights of her members, the corporeal propogation of her members, the civil governance of her members either actual or potential.

The ecclesial context for Thomas's natural law theory suggests that problems will be encountered when one tries to leave that ecclesial context. This may have something to do with the disarray among proponents of natural law and the difficulty of convincing those who are either outside that context altogether or who have taken on postures of dissent from within. The further that one departs from a full acceptance of Jesus Christ, who is Wisdom itself, and the Church who testifies to him, the further one concretely departs from the sort of rationality—fallen but healed by the grace of Christ—in which natural law theory works. A similar situation exists with regard to natural theology. As Thomas notes, "the fool says in his heart there is no God." If one choses to abandon that rationality that is specifically human, as is done, for instance, by those who would reduce human reality to nothing other than the material or who would so insist on autonomy to the detriment of the communitarian character of human rationality, if one thus chooses to abandon this rationality then no argument in the world will be effective.

Is, then, the development of natural law theory primarily a theological rather than a philosophical task in which there is reliance on Scripture and the Tradition of the Church as well as on the canons of reason? In principle the answer is no. Natural law is the participation in the eternal law that is proportionate to the human mind. In practice, however, the answer is yes because the human mind that is presupposed is one that has been redeemed by Christ. Natural law theory can only be successfully pursued by someone who has been converted to Christ, by someone who is part of the ecclesial context that is the primary referent of Thomas's understanding of natural law.

Still, Thomas is also aware of the strategy of apologetics. If the *Summa theologiae* is structured for the needs of believing students, the *Summa contra gentiles* is structured for use with those who are not believers. The further one's audience is located away from the ecclesial context, the more one will need to work with restricted principles and presuppositions as one tries to find common ground with them. With other Christians one can still use the Scriptures and parts of the Tradition as well as reason for moral discussions. But the further one moves from this center the more will recourse to the canons of reason be necessary and yet the more will the nature of human rationality be contested. Natural law pursued in this extraecclesial context will end by being more art than science, more persuasion about fundamental principles than scientific exposition. And, of course, with fools nothing will be of avail.

Are the canons of reason sufficient for the task? In the hands of a believer, yes, but it must be recognized that philosophical systems devised outside the Christian context will almost invariably require transformation in order to be somewhat adequate to the truth. An untransformed system will at best be an approximation to the truth—at best because even within the Church theological understandings of revealed truth are only approximations. Outside the ecclesial context natural law theory will have to take on a pluriform character to match the plurality of regnant philosophical systems. There will have to be, not simply Thomistic versions of natural law, but Kantian versions, pragmatic versions, phenomenological versions, and so on. Within the explicitly ecclesial context natural law theory may still have a pluriform character but it would also share in the unity of the faith.

There are many other things that could be said on this topic but I have no time in which to say them. Let this much suffice for now.

PART III

THE NEW NATURAL LAW THEORY

5

CONTEMPORARY PERSPECTIVES ON THOMISTIC NATURAL LAW

William E. May

Many significant studies offering new perspectives on Thomistic natural law cry for attention. I believe that an in-depth study and comparison of a few of the more important such studies will give us a far better grasp of what natural law, and in particular natural law in the Thomistic tradition, is all about and why it is of central importance to our lives as moral beings than would a survey of a host of different viewpoints. I have therefore decided to center attention on the work of Pamela Hall, Benedict Ashley, Ralph McInerny, and Germain Grisez and his school of thought.

Hall and McInerny explicitly intend their studies to be, at least in part, authentic interpretations of St. Thomas's teaching on natural law, and Ashley regards his own view as fully compatible with that of St. Thomas. Grisez and his collaborators, among whom the most important are John Finnis, Joseph Boyle, Robert George, and Patrick Lee, do not present their natural law theory primarily as an interpretation of St. Thomas. Nonetheless, on key aspects of their natural law theory where others, including Hall, McInerny, and Ashley, claim that their thought is incompatible with that of St. Thomas, Grisez et al. are adamant in affirming that on these issues *they*, and not their adversaries, are being faithful to the Common Doctor.

After reviewing and briefly commenting on the positions of these authors I will focus attention on significant areas of disagreement, in particular, areas where Hall, Ashley, and McInerny agree among themselves but differ from Grisez et al. In addressing these areas of disagreement there are two separate issues to consider. The first is the fidelity of the authors to the thought of St. Thomas; the second is the truth of the positions set forth. Another matter of considerable importance to consider, which I will address is this: If there is a natural law whose normative truths are in principle accessible to human reason, how can we account for the fact that reasonable persons, presumably intelligent and morally earnest, so vehemently disagree on so many issues of critical importance to human civilization: abortion, euthanasia and assisted suicide, sex outside of marriage, and so on?

Pamela M. Hall's Interpretation of Thomistic Natural Law

Hall offers her interpretation of Thomistic natural law in her book *Narrative and the Natural Law: An Interpretation of Thomistic Ethics*.[1] Hall maintains that St. Thomas's teaching on natural law cannot be understood properly unless it is set into the context of its relationship to God's providence over the universe, the eternal law, to the virtues both acquired or natural and infused or supernatural, and to the human and divinely revealed law, both the Old and the New. She believes that we can come to understand how natural law is promulgated or made known only by providing an account of natural law that does "full justice" to its historical development, which presupposes the activity of prudence "operating on both the individual and political levels."[2]

What the Natural Law Is

Toward the close of chapter 2 Hall writes as follows:

Thomas calls natural law the rational creature's way of participating in eternal law. This partaking occurs in human beings' directedness to specific goods by their nature. But men and women also partake in the eternal law by their knowledge and

---

1. Pamela M. Hall, *Narrative and the Natural Law: An Interpretation of Thomistic Ethics* (South Bend, Ind.: University of Notre Dame Press, 1994).
2. Ibid., 1–2.

choice: (1) they must recognize certain *inclinationes* as normative, as ordering them toward specific goods; and (2) they must discover and choose the means by which they can achieve the goods to which they are so directed.[3]

a. Natural law as a set of natural inclinations. Hall believes that "it is clear from how Thomas speaks of natural law that it comprises principally forms of directedness towards our proper ends or goods."[4] Indeed, "Thomas's own emphasis on the natural law is first in terms of *inclinationes,* ways of being directed to our end."[5] Hall maintains that our natural "*inclinationes* are the *primary* constituents of the natural law."[6] Natural law is, as it were, *in* us, at least in substantial part, as innate, naturally given tendencies or inclinations or drives toward our ends or the goods that contribute to our fullness of being. Indeed, Hall says that this is "our possession of the natural law (in terms of our being directed to our proper end)."[7] Our possession of natural law through our natural *inclinationes* is, Hall insists, as we shall see more clearly below, the *primary meaning* of natural law in St. Thomas.

b. Natural law as known. For rational creatures such as men natural law has a rational character consisting in "our knowledge of that directedness [provided by the natural *inclinationes*]."[8] If we take seriously the rational character of natural law, we will realize that "natural law also affords us understanding of the goods to which we are so [i.e., naturally] directed. We must see and assent to pursue in specific ways the goods to which we are inclined by our natures.... rational creatures recognize their *inclinationes* for what they are, as law."[9] Our rational apprehension of the precepts that are to guide us in realizing the goods to which we are naturally inclined is, Hall maintains and as we shall see more clearly below, the *secondary meaning* of natural law for Aquinas.

Precepts and "Rules" of the Natural Law and Our Knowledge of Them

a. First principles or precepts of natural law. The fundamental principles (precepts) of natural law are known to us through *synderesis,* a natural *habitus* whose basic principles or precepts "form the core knowledge of natural law

---

3. Ibid., 37.
4. Ibid., 29.
5. Ibid., 28.
6. Ibid., 31. Here I have added emphasis to the word "primary."
7. Ibid., 28.
8. Ibid.
9. Ibid., 29.

within us, and these principles . . . are 'indelible,' persisting even in the most vicious."[10] The very first of these principles, the precept that "good is to be done and pursued and evil is to be avoided," renders human actions intelligible and purposeful. Hall, noting how this first practical principle is analogous to the first principle of theoretical reasoning (the principle of non-contradiction), emphasizes that "[j]ust as one cannot think intelligibly without upholding the truth that something cannot be and not be at the same time and in the same way, so one cannot act intelligibly, i.e., deliberately and rationally, without acting purposively, for the sake of some end understood as good."[11]

b. Primary precepts and a hierarchy of human inclinations and goods. The other primary precepts of natural law, rooted in this fundamental principle, relate us to the goods to which we are oriented by our natural *inclinationes*. In interpreting the key text of *Summa theologiae,* I-II, q. 94, a. 2, concerning the primary precepts of natural law, Hall holds that for St. Thomas the goods toward which we are naturally inclined are hierarchically ordered. There are "three sets of precepts," corresponding to

> the hierarchy of the *inclinationes* themselves. The first set . . . guides the preservation of human life, a good which we share with all living things. The second set pertains to the begetting and rearing of offspring, goods which we share with other animals. Third are precepts that govern the goods to which humans incline as specifically rational beings. . . . In so sketching the goods to which we are ordered naturally, Thomas presents us with a natural human end which is "inclusive." . . . But this inclusive natural end is also hierarchical in the structure of its constituent goods. . . . Those goods to which we are inclined as rational creatures have greatest value. Among these, knowledge about God, even within the limited reach of natural contemplation, is the highest and best good.[12]

Hall, moreover, holds that the "lesser goods," those we share with other living things and with animals are "constituents of the human end" only if they are "enjoyed in a specifically rational way."[13]

The crucial point here, in Hall's view of Thomistic natural law, is that men first participate in the eternal law as intelligent and willing beings (what I termed earlier our *formal* participation through natural law in the eternal law) by "recogniz[ing] certain *inclinationes* as normative, as ordering

10. Ibid., 29.
11. Ibid., 30.
12. Ibid., 32.
13. Ibid.

them toward specific goods."[14] In addition, Hall maintains that our rational grasp of "natural law's primary precepts, which pertain to the goods to which our inclinations direct us by nature," which, she says "is the *primary sense* of *natural law* for Aquinas," constitutes "the *secondary* sense of natural law, the sense of its *rules*."[15]

c. "Secondary" natural law precepts or rules and the role of prudence. Hall notes that in his core treatment of the natural law in I-II, q. 94, Aquinas does not "spell out the actual rules of the natural law" but is rather occupied with showing the fundamental bond between any natural law precept and the goods to which the precepts are ordered.[16] How do we come to know such actual precepts or rules?

Hall gives her answer to this partly in chapter 2, where she comments on natural law as law and on the articles in q. 94 of the *prima secundae* devoted to human knowledge of natural law, and again in chapter 3, where she relates Thomas's understanding of natural law to the precepts of the Old Law.

In chapter 2 she says that such "actual" precepts entail "an articulation of which actions are conducive toward, or destructive of, those goods to which the *inclinationes* direct us." But—and here we come to a key theme in Hall's interpretation—in articulating such actions and rules based on them, *the exercise, both individual and political, of the virtue of prudence is essential*. We come to understand, "through individual and social reflection . . . what actions promote attainment of our good and what actions damage or destroy attainment. We may then express this understanding and render it practically efficacious, through the formulation of rules prescribing or proscribing certain actions."[17] The discovery of these rules, Hall says, "takes place . . . within the narrative context of experiences that engage a person's intellect and will in the making of concrete choices. . . . This process of inquiry is . . . one of practical reasoning . . . which must be carried on individually and communally. And in so mentioning practical reasoning, the operation of some measure of prudential deliberation is implied."[18]

Hall then says that in order for one to grasp the truth of a "particular rule" such as "Never murder," the virtue of prudence is necessary. This, at

14. Ibid., 37.
15. Ibid., 32.
16. Ibid., 33.
17. Ibid.
18. Ibid., 37.

any rate, seems to me to be the proper way to understand the following passage:

> An understanding of particular rules of the natural law, e.g., "Never murder," is inseparable from an understanding of the rule's point and purpose, on Aquinas's view. One cannot reason down to specific cases without some apprehension of the goal of a precept. To attempt to do so would be to separate the rules from their real function: to help secure the goods of human life. . . . *And only prudence can give such an understanding of the end or purpose of law.* . . . Thus to divorce natural law from the virtues is to misunderstand how both the law and the virtues alike conduce human beings to their proper goods. *It would also be to misunderstand how one arrives at the specific rules of the natural law in the first place. Given that only prudence can yield a realization of the ends we pursue as genuine goods, it seems it must operate in the discovery of the natural law.*[19]

Here Hall seems to say that, on St. Thomas's understanding of natural law, one needs the virtue of prudence in order to grasp the truth of such particular "rules" as "Never murder." Yet in the following chapter, where she considers how St. Thomas relates the natural law to the Old Law, and in particular to the *moral* precepts of the Old Law as found in the Decalogue (see in particular I-II, q. 100, a. 3), she notes that for St. Thomas more particular moral precepts (rules) proceed from the primary precepts of natural law in two different ways: first, those moral precepts known immediately and with a modicum of consideration—and Aquinas includes all the precepts of the Decalogue here, including the Fifth Commandment, "Thou shalt not kill"—and, second, those moral precepts known only by the "wise" and after much consideration of diverse circumstances.[20] From this text it seems that one does *not* need the virtue of prudence in order to understand the truth of the precept that we are not to murder. Hall, in my opinion, is somewhat inconsistent on this matter. It surely is true, however, as she insists, that for St. Thomas the virtues, and in particular the virtue of prudence, are necessary for grasping the truth of many moral precepts.

---

19. Ibid., 38; emphasis added.
20. Ibid., 56.

Some Critical Observations

Although other aspects of Hall's account of Thomistic natural law could fruitfully be taken up—for instance, the relevance of the ceremonial and the juridical, as well as the moral, precepts of the Old Law—the basic elements of her interpretation of Thomistic natural law have now been identified. I now want to focus attention on some key theses Hall maintains and comment on them.

First of all, Hall is incorrect, I believe, in claiming that for Aquinas natural law is understood primarily in terms of our natural *inclinationes*. St. Thomas *never* says this. To the contrary, he emphasizes that for rational creatures participation in the eternal law is *properly* called *law* because law is something pertaining to reason. More specifically, law pertains to reason precisely as a *universal proposition of practical reason as ordered to action*.[21] And it is precisely in this sense that the natural law is called *law*. This matter is put beyond doubt by the discussion in I-II, q. 93, a. 6, where Thomas sharply distinguishes between participation in eternal law by way of "a natural inclination to that which is conformable to eternal law" and "the natural knowledge itself of the good." What differentiates natural law from natural inclination and makes it law in the proper sense is the fact that it is the work of practical reason, expression, not impression.[22] As present in our natural *inclinationes*, natural law allows us to participate *passively* in God's eternal law, as being ruled and measured by it, in the same way that nonrational creatures participate in the eternal law. But precisely as *rational beings,* human persons *actively* participate in God's eternal law, ruling and measuring their own actions by the normative truths or precepts of natural law. Aquinas is very clear about this.[23]

---

21. See *ST* I-II, q. 90, a. 1, and, in particular, the response to the second objection.

22. On this topic, see D. O'Donoghue, "The Thomist Concept of the Natural Law," *Irish Theological Quarterly* 22 (1955): 93–94.

23. See, for instance, *ST* I-II, q. 91, a. 2: "lex, cum sit regula et mensura, dupliciter potest esse in aliquo ... uno modo, sicut in regulato et mensurato, quia inquantum participat aliquid in regula vel mensura, sic regulatur et mensuratur. Unde cum omnia quae divinae providentiae subduntur [and this "omnia" includes human beings] a lege aeterna regulentur et mensurentur. ... Inter cetera autem rationalis creatura excellentiori quodammodo divinae providentiae subiacet, inquantum et ipsa fit providentiae particeps, sibi ipsi et aliis providens." Previously, in q. 91, a. 1 ad 3, Thomas had said: "etiam animalia irrationalia pariticipant

Hall's error here is closely linked with her interpretation of the very first article in the *prima secundae* devoted to natural law itself and the *habitus* of *synderesis*. One reading Hall's account legitimately concludes that for St. Thomas natural law, understood as precepts about what is to be done, is best regarded as the *habitus* of *synderesis*. *But Thomas's teaching in this article is precisely the opposite.* He argues that "properly and essentially, natural law is *not* a habit." His point is that natural law, formally and properly understood, is something that practical reason brings into being, namely, a set of universal propositions of the practical reason ordered to action. But a habit is not such a set. He grants that natural law can be called the *habitus* of *synderesis* in an accommodated, secondary sense, as our habitual knowledge of such propositions.[24]

Another problem with Hall's interpretation is her claim that we come to know the goods to which we are directed by our natural inclinations by "reflecting on our natures" and on the "*inclinationes*." I do not believe that any texts of Aquinas support this reading. It is not necessary for us first to know our inclinations and then, reflecting on them, to come to know the goods to which we are ordered. According to St. Thomas, our practical reason "naturally apprehends as good and therefore to be pursued in action, all those things toward which we are naturally inclined."[25] Thus it seems that the natural inclinations themselves may be unknown to the person, but they dynamically orient the person toward the goods perfective of him and his practical reason naturally, that is, without engaging in a reasoning process or a process of *inferring* some conclusions from antecedently known truths. Hence, the person spontaneously recognizes these goods as the goods to be pursued through his deliberate actions and their contraries as realities to be avoided.

---

rationem aeternam uno modo, sicut et rationalis creatura. Sed *quia rationalis creatura participat eam intellectualiter et rationaliter, ideo participatio legis aeternae in creatura rationali proprie lex vocatur. . . .*"

24. Ibid., I-II, q. 94, a. 1: "Aliquid potest dici esse habitus dupliciter. Uno modo, proprie et essentialiter, *et sic lex naturalis non est habitus*. . . . Alio modo potest dici habitus id quod habitu tenetur . . . et secundum hunc modum potest dici quod lex naturalis sit habitus." On this matter, see William E. May, *An Introduction to Moral Theology*, rev. ed. (Huntington, Ind.: Our Sunday Visitor, 1994), 45–47.

25. "omnia illa ad quae homo habet naturalem inclinationem ratio naturaliter apprehendit ut bona et per consequens ut opere prosequenda et contraria eorum ut mala et vitanda" (*ST* I-II, q. 94, a. 2).

The issue seems to be this: Do we first have to know our natures and our natural inclinations and then, by reflecting on our natures and our inclinations, come to know the precepts or "rules" of natural law? Hall seems to say yes. But does St. Thomas?

A third problem with Hall's interpretation is her contention—at least if I have read her correctly—that in order to grasp the truth of "secondary" precepts of natural law, of "rules" such as "Never murder," one needs the virtue of prudence. I grant that for St. Thomas prudence *is* required if one is to grasp the truth of "more remote" conclusions from the first or common precepts of natural law, but, as noted before, he clearly holds that everyone (whether good or bad) is able to grasp the truth of the "proximate" or "immediate" conclusions from those principles.

Benedict Ashley on Thomistic Natural Law

Benedict Ashley, a learned and erudite man, student of St. Thomas, and teacher, has written voluminously on theological and philosophical issues. In many of his books and articles he has taken up in depth the meaning of the natural law, and he regards St. Thomas, to whom he seeks to be faithful, as a fundamental source. Recently Mark S. Latkovic completed a doctoral study of Ashley's fundamental moral theology and even more recently contributed an exceptionally helpful overview of Ashley's thought on the natural law. My presentation is heavily indebted to Latkovic's careful study.[26]

---

26. Mark S. Latkovic, *The Fundamental Moral Theology of Benedict Ashley, O.P.: A Critical Study. Toward a Response to the Second Vatican Council's Call for Renewal in Moral Theology* (Ann Arbor, Mich.: University Microfilms, 1998). This doctoral study was completed at the John Paul II Institute for Studies on Marriage and Family, Washington, D.C. See also Latkovic, "Natural Law in the Moral Thought of Benedict Ashley, O.P.," *Fellowship of Catholic Scholars Quarterly* 22 (Fall 1999): 2–5.

In his *Fellowship* article Latkovic lists the following works as those containing Ashley's most extensive discussions of natural law: Benedict Ashley, *Theologies of the Body: Humanist and Christian*, 2d ed. (St. Louis: Pope John Center, 1995), 360–72, 386–482; Ashley, *Living the Truth in Love: A Biblical Introduction to Moral Theology* (Staten Island, N.Y.: Alba House, 1996), esp. Part 1; Ashley (coauthored with Kevin O'Rourke), *Health Care Ethics: A Theological Analysis*, 4th ed. (Washington, D.C.: Georgetown University Press, 1997), chaps. 1 and 7; Ashley, *Justice in the Church: Gender and Participation* (Washington, D.C.: The Catholic University of America Press, 1996), 7–9, 35–43; Ashley, "What Is the Natural Law?," *Ethics and Medics* 12, no. 6 (June 1987): 1–2; Ashley, "Scriptural Grounds for Concrete Moral Norms," *The Thomist* 52 (1988):

In common with all commentators on Aquinas, Ashley affirms that the highest law is God's eternal (divine) law, his wise and loving plan directing us to our happiness and that the natural law is our intelligent participation in God's law, our "human sharing in God's own wisdom about what kind of living will best fulfill the nature which the Creator has given us by creating us as bodily beings who also in our spiritual intelligence and free will image God (Gen 1:27)."[27]

I will consider the following aspects of Ashley's thought on natural law: (1) its basic content; (2) how we come to know this content; (3) the hierarchical ordering of basic human needs and goods and of the basic precepts of natural law; (4) its fundamental moral principle; and (5) prudence and the movement from the first principles of natural law to specific norms, of which some are absolute.

The Basic Content of the Natural Law

God's eternal law, in which we intelligently participate by means of the natural law, orders us to our proper end, happiness. Thus ethics, for Ashley, is fundamentally teleological. Because it is so, in his consideration of natural law Ashley seeks to discover what fulfills us as human persons. Unlike Aquinas, Ashley does not ordinarily speak of basic human "goods," but rather speaks of "needs." Latkovic suggests that in using this term Ashley has been influenced by his mentors at the University of Chicago, Yves Simon and Mortimer Adler.[28]

Frequently, as Latkovic observes, Ashley is content to identify basic human needs with the four basic human goods identified by St. Thomas as life, mating and the procreation and education of children, living in society with others, and coming to know the truth, particularly the truth about

---

1–22, esp. 13–22; Ashley, "Dominion or Stewardship?: Theological Reflections," in *Birth, Suffering, and Death: Catholic Perspectives at the Edges of Life,* eds. Kevin M. Wildes, S.J., et al. (Boston: Kluwer Academic Publishers, 1992), 85–106, esp. 90–92; and Ashley, "What Is the End of the Human Person?: The Vision of God and Integral Human Fulfillment," in *Moral Truth and Moral Tradition: Essays in Honor of Peter Geach and Elizabeth Anscombe,* ed. Luke Gormally (Dublin: Four Courts Press, 1994), 68–96.

27. Ashley (and O'Rourke), *Health Care Ethics,* 156–57; also see Ashley, "What Is the Natural Law?," 2; and Ashley, *Living the Truth in Love,* 28.

28. Latkovic, *The Fundamental Moral Theology of Benedict Ashley,* 266–71.

God (cf. *ST* I-II, q. 94, a. 2). When he does so, Ashley refers to them as "life, reproduction, truth, and society." At other times he expands on this list by dividing the good of life into the need for "food" and "security" and by adding the need for "creativity," thus arriving, as Latkovic points out, at *six basic needs:* "*food* (appropriate nourishment, water, and air), *security* (i.e., protection against injury by natural forces, animals, and other humans; it includes the need for physical freedom), *sex* (i.e., our need to reproduce and to bond with a member of the opposite sex in marriage), *information* (including sense and intellectual knowledge and our need to communicate it), *society* (i.e., the need for community to meet our needs and to share goods in friendship), and *creativity* (i.e., our need to be creative in the arts and sciences in order to advance culture; it includes our need to seek the 'Ultimate Totality')."[29] Ashley notes that the basic human needs, whatever their precise number, are satisfied by human goods or values.[30] Indeed, "the satisfaction in an integral manner of these basic needs," Ashley writes, is "the primary condition of a good human life and indeed of a Christian life."[31]

Our Knowledge of This Content

Ashley maintains that ethical knowledge (knowledge of the natural law and its requirements), although formally distinct from philosophical anthropology, is nonetheless materially dependent upon it. Ethics rests on some understanding of what it is to be human, and if we are to be morally good persons our actions must conform to human nature.[32] Ashley holds that "we can *derive* a natural law morality in the strict sense of the term" from our knowledge of human nature.[33] Ashley recognizes that the inner

---

29. Latkovic, "Natural Law in the Moral Thought of Benedict Ashley, O.P.," 2; see also Latkovic, *The Fundamental Moral Theology of Benedict Ashley*, 262–88. Latkovic, in his *Fellowship* essay, refers to the following sources in Ashley for a listing of these "needs"/"goods": *Theologies of the Body*, 396, and *Health Care Ethics*, 18, where Ashley (and O'Rourke) relate basic human needs to the four dimensions of the human person as biological, psychological, social, and spiritual.

30. Ashley, *Health Care Ethics*, 17.

31. Ashley, *Theologies of the Body*, 396.

32. See Ashley, "What Is the End of the Human Person?," 74; Ashley, *Living the Truth in Love*, 5, n. 11.

33. See Ashley (and O'Rourke), *Health Care Ethics*, 141.

nature of an entity is never known exhaustively and is always open to further research,[34] and that because of human sinfulness "in some times and cultures the knowledge of natural law is very rudimentary or distorted."[35] In addition, human persons always exist "as members of a particular community with its particular culture, in a given place, at a given time in history," with the result that "what it means to be human is variously manifested and can be either developed and enriched or distorted and trivialized by culture."[36] What this means, as Latkovic notes, is that our nature is historical and that our knowledge of natural law is accordingly subject to historicity, which simply means that at any given time period "for any group of people their moral understanding will be profoundly conditioned by their history."[37]

But this in no way means that we cannot come to know an objective and universal natural law based on our human nature. Indeed, there would be no human history "unless the human race shared a common nature that was at least relatively stable for vast periods of time; there would be no human history . . . [unless] human persons all have some basic common needs that characterize them as human and make possible cooperation as a human family."[38] Indeed, Ashley declares, moral norms "imply some concept of our *common human nature*, its *innate needs* and the *values* by which these needs are satisfied."[39]

Our knowledge of human nature, to which our actions are to conform if they are to be morally good, and of basic human needs and the goods that satisfy them, is basically a matter of philosophical anthropology and natural philosophy and science. Latkovic points out that for Ashley the following three conclusions of natural philosophy/natural science are necessary as a foundation for ethics: "(1) Humans are animals, living, sentient, having biological drives to eat, rest, defend themselves, mate, and reproduce; (2) Species-specific humans are intelligent, free, and social in a way that requires language and the invention of culture and technology; (3) Hu-

---

34. Ashley, *Theologies of the Body*, 266–88.
35. Ibid., 366.
36. Ashley (and O'Rourke), *Health Care Ethics*, 142.
37. Ibid. See Latkovic, "Natural Law in the Moral Thought of Benedict Ashley, O.P.," 3; and Latkovic, *The Fundamental Moral Theology of Benedict Ashley*, 240ff.
38. Ashley (and O'Rourke), *Health Care Ethics*, 142.
39. Ashley, *Theologies of the Body*, 372.

man intelligence is dependent on the body to supply the instruments by which it is able to learn about the environment and the human person itself, but is not identical with the activity of the body or any bodily organ, not even the brain, nor is it subject to the mortality of the body."[40]

Ethics thus presupposes and is dependent on natural philosophy or philosophical anthropology which, "beginning with the generic study of human beings as natural objects, and then as animals, proceeds to show that animals of this sort are intelligent, free persons who understand their own activities both theoretically and practically. The human nature (natural moral law) to which we must conform to be morally good persons is a nature that requires us to make decisions about the unconditionally is-to-be [i.e., the purpose or end of a human act]."[41] Knowledge of natural law, to put it another way, is derived from knowledge of human nature.

All human persons, of whatever period of history or of whatever culture, "have some basic common needs that characterize them as human and make possible cooperation as a human family."[42] Knowledge of these needs and the goods that satisfy them gives us our basic understanding of what it means to be human, and this basic understanding can be subsequently developed and enriched by further discoveries in the natural sciences, the philosophy of nature, and philosophical anthropology. Divine revelation, for instance, as found in the Genesis story of Adam and Eve, likewise provides us with "a profound anthropology which is consistent both with what we now know to have been the evolutionary history of our species, and with the ethical doctrine of a universal moral law rooted in human nature as that of a bodily being capable of spiritual acts of intelligence and free decision."[43]

The Hierarchical Ordering of Basic Needs and Goods

Ashley claims that basic human needs/goods are hierarchically ordered, and he insists that this is the teaching of St. Thomas. Thus he writes: "Aquinas, rightly we believe, though he holds that each of his four basic goods

---

40. Ashley, "What Is the End of the Human Person?," 73. See Latkovic, "Natural Law in the Moral Thought of Benedict Ashley, O.P.," 2–3.
41. Ibid., 76.
42. Ashley (and O'Rourke), *Health Care Ethics*, 142.
43. Ashley, *Theologies of the Body*, 416.

[life, reproduction, truth, and society] is a good in itself and not a mere means, also believes that they are mutually ordered in the way indicated, so that the first three are subordinated to the last, supreme good. Thus the ultimate goal of human life to which all other goods are ordered is friendship with God in his kingdom, which includes all other persons who are God's friends."[44] The needs/goods are hierarchically structured insofar as "we need life to be able to strive for other goals. We need propagation of the race because without it we cannot preserve the human community. We need community because without it we cannot achieve the other goals nor share our achievements with others. We need truth, because it is necessary to guide our lives and to give them their ultimate meaning in the knowledge and love of God, ourselves, and other persons in the Kingdom of God."[45]

The basic needs/goods, hierarchically ordered, are unified by the ultimate good, identified in the text just cited as "knowledge and love of God, ourselves, and other persons in the Kingdom of God," and at times designated simply as "contemplation."[46]

Corresponding to the hierarchy of basic needs/goods is a hierarchy of basic natural law precepts or principles. According to Ashley, the basic principles of natural law direct us to "seek bodily health, the preservation of the human species, the common good of society, and truth as the highest element of the common good, *in ascending order of importance,* and avoid whatever is contrary to these goods."[47]

The Fundamental Moral Principle of Natural Law

We have just seen how Ashley thinks the primary precepts of the natural law are internally ordered in a hierarchy. Given this understanding of these precepts, his way of formulating the first principle of morality follows. Ashley believes that this principle can be expressed, particularly in a Christian context, as "Seek the true goal of life in all your actions,"[48] or "Do those acts, and only those acts, which are appropriate means to the supreme good of true knowledge and love of God, oneself, and the human community in

---

44. Ashley (and O'Rourke), *Health Care Ethics,* 168.
45. Ibid. See Ashley, *Living the Truth in Love,* 93.
46. Ashley, "What Is the End of the Human Person?," 86–88.
47. Ashley, *Living the Truth in Love,* 108; emphasis added.
48. Ibid.

time and eternity."⁴⁹ These would seem to be Ashley's ways of expressing in philosophical and theological language the basic normative principle familiar to Jews and Christians as the twofold commandment to love God above all things and one's neighbor as oneself.

If I am properly interpreting Ashley here, he is claiming that the first principle of practical reasoning, "good is to be done and pursued and its opposite is to be avoided," if taken together with the basic principles ordering us to the goods that satisfy our basic needs, is to be regarded as the *first moral principle,* articulated as indicated in the previous paragraph.

Prudence and the Derivation of Specific Moral Norms

Like Hall, Ashley, who with O'Rourke terms his moral methodology "prudential personalism,"⁵⁰ maintains that we come to know specific moral norms, such as that adultery is always wrong and that we ought never intentionally kill innocent human persons, through the virtue of prudence. It is also through prudence that we apply these more specific norms to concrete situations. He says that "the basic needs and values which satisfy them . . . constitute the *first principles* of moral reasoning, i.e., of natural law. . . ." But "their application to the particular problems of life which constitute the *means* to this goal [i.e., knowledge and love of God, oneself, and the human community in time and eternity] are [sic] the work of practical wisdom or prudence."⁵¹

An interesting illustration of how "prudential personalism" functions to show how one comes to know the truth of a specific moral norm is provided by Ashley and O'Rourke in their discussion of the immorality of abortion, where they contrast their methodology with "rule centered" or "deontological" forms of ethical reasoning and with utilitarianism/consequentialism/proportionalism.⁵² In light of the virtue of prudence, they de-

---

49. Ashley (and O'Rourke), *Health Care Ethics,* 171.

50. The method of "prudential personalism" is developed at length by Ashley (and O'Rourke) in *Health Care Ethics,* esp. on 137–90.

51. Ashley, *Living the Truth in Love,* 93. See also 107–10, on how moral wisdom (prudence) builds on the first principles or goals of human life and "applies them to form the judgment of conscience . . . to particular decisions that must be made." On 112–15, Ashley describes the "eight steps of moral prudence."

52. Ashley (and O'Rourke), *Health Care Ethics,* 173–76.

velop five key principles relevant to bioethical issues.[53] What is most important to note, however, is that for Ashley the virtue of prudence is the indispensable means for both grasping the truth of specific moral norms and applying them to specific situations of life.

Some Critical Observations

a. The hierarchical ordering of human goods. Like Hall, Ashley insists that for St. Thomas the goods of human persons are *hierarchically* ordered. Thus the good of human life is, for instance, a lower good or a less valuable good than fellowship in human society or knowledge of the truth. Nonetheless, Ashley holds that *all* of the basic goods of human persons are *inviolable,* and he thus holds that "acts which directly contradict these goods are intrinsically evil and cannot serve as means to the ultimate end, although they are not equal but form a hierarchy."[54] But he also holds that lesser goods can be *sacrificed* for the sake of a higher good under two conditions. The good of bodily life, he holds, is "the least in the hierarchy of basic goods and can be sacrificed to the higher goods, but only on the condition that the sacrificial act (1) does not involve an injustice; (2) is not intrinsically evil."[55]

I will return later to this question of a hierarchy of basic goods, but here I want to point out the danger of regarding the so-called lesser goods of human persons, in particular, the good of human life, as *instrumental* to higher goods and therefore no longer worthy of protection if the so-called higher goods are no longer capable of being instantiated or realized. Ashley himself does not make human bodily life merely instrumental, but that this danger is present in his thought is illustrated, I believe, by the *reasoning* he uses to conclude that we are obligated to preserve bodily life "only when it gives the person opportunity to strive to achieve the spiritual purpose of life [our ultimate end, the highest of the hierarchically ordered goods]. In order to strive for the spiritual purpose of life, one needs some degree of cognitive-affective function." Thus "mere physical survival" offers no "possibility of spiritual advance" if it is no longer possible for one to perform "acts of faith, of love, and of hope," since "consciousness and freedom have

---

53. Ibid., 181–200.
54. Ashley, "What Is the End of the Human Person?," 92.
55. Ibid.

been irrevocably lost."[56] Ashley applies this rationale to justify his conclusion that it is not morally necessary to provide food and water artificially to persons in the so-called persistent vegetative state because doing so does not enable them to pursue the spiritual goal of life. This reasoning would also justify the decision not to stop arterial bleeding in an infant suffering from trisomy 13, who has no cognitive abilities. But this is surely wrong.

b. Prudence and knowledge of the truth of specific moral norms. I think that Ashley, like Hall, is mistaken in claiming that only the virtue of prudence shows the truth of specific moral norms. First of all, prudent persons can themselves disagree over ethical issues, and their disagreements can be contradictory, with one, say, claiming that the GIFT procedure "assists" the marital act and does not substitute for it and is therefore morally permitted, and with another holding that GIFT clearly substitutes for the marital act and is therefore not morally permissible. Both parties cannot be correct: one must be right and the other wrong. There are no objective reasons for holding one person more prudent (virtuous) than the other. Thus the virtue of prudence will not settle the dispute; rather, appeal to relevant moral principles and to the *arguments* and evidence marshaled by the virtuous persons can alone show who is correct.

Ralph McInerny and Thomistic Natural Law

Ralph McInerny is widely recognized as an outstanding Thomistic scholar.[57] He has articulated his understanding of Thomistic natural law in several key essays.[58] I will here attempt to provide a synthesis of his thought

---

56. Ashley (and O'Rourke), *Health Care Ethics,* 426.

57. Recently a festschrift in his honor, focusing on his endeavors to make the thought of St. Thomas relevant to contemporary philosophical issues, has been published: *Recovering Nature: Essays in Natural Philosophy, Ethics, and Metaphysics in Honor of Ralph McInerny,* ed. John O'Callaghan and Thomas J. Hibbs (South Bend, Ind.: University of Notre Dame Press, 1999). None of the essays included, however, seeks to recapitulate his thought on natural law.

58. The writings of Ralph McInerny on which I will draw are the following: (1) "The Principles of Natural Law," *American Journal of Jurisprudence* 25 (1980): 1–15, reprinted in *Natural Law,* ed. John Finnis (New York: New York University Press, 1991), 1:325–39; (2) chap. 3, "Ultimate End and Moral Principles," in his *Ethica Thomistica: The Moral Philosophy of Thomas Aquinas* (Washington, D.C.: The Catholic University of America Press, 1982), 35–62 (this chapter basically reproduces [1] with some modifications); (3) chap. 5, "Natural Law," in

by examining the following aspects of it: (1) practical reason and the is/ought question; (2) the essential meaning of natural law; (3) the meaning of the first principle (precept) of natural law and its articulation in primary precepts "telling us how to act"; (4) the hierarchy of human goods; and (5) the movement from first principles (precepts) of natural law to "quasi conclusions" and to "conclusions" of the natural law.

Practical Reason and the Is/Ought Question

McInerny insists that it is possible to understand what Thomas has to say about law in *Summa theologiae* I-II, qq. 90ff., only within the context provided by what preceded in *ST* I-II, especially in qq. 1–5, on human happiness. There Aquinas had stressed that the aspect under which something is thought when it is deemed good is goodness, the *ratio boni,* the ultimate end, happiness. Of necessity all men desire their ultimate end, understood as happiness, and of necessity also we desire not only the ultimate end but also whatever is necessary for it, for instance, life itself, existence, and so on. Aquinas's discussion of our ultimate end and happiness puts emphasis on the will, since the will's object is the good. But the good must first be grasped as a truth, *ut verum,* before it can be desired as a good, *ut bonum,* for knowledge guides the will. It is in this context that we must consider Aquinas's teaching on natural law.[59]

If we do so, we will realize that the first principles of natural law (to be examined below), although *indemonstrable* and therefore *not deduced* from speculative or theoretical truths or from our knowledge of human nature, are nonetheless dependent upon speculative truths, implied in them, and in this sense derived from them: it is not, in other words, fallacious to derive an "ought" from an "is." This can be seen by thinking about what we mean when, with Aquinas, we affirm that whatever we do we do for some purpose or end. The aim of action is the good, and the principle or starting-point in thinking about human action is the *good,* the formality under

---

Aquinas on Human Action: A Theory of Practice (Washington, D.C.: The Catholic University of America Press, 1992), 103–32; (4) chap. 6, "Carrying On," in *Aquinas on Human Action,* 133–60; and (5) "Portia's Lament: Reflections on Practical Reason," in *Natural Law and Moral Inquiry: Ethics, Metaphysics, and Politics in the Work of Germain Grisez,* ed. Robert P. George (Washington, D.C.: Georgetown University Press, 1998), 82–103.

59. McInerny, *Aquinas on Human Action,* 103–6.

which we desire whatever we actually desire. The good, in other words, is the desirable. But the "desirable," even if this is taken to refer to what we *in fact* desire (desirable$_1$), involves the judgment that what is desired perfects the one who desires it, that is, that the desirable is what *ought* to be desired (desirable$_2$), and desirable$_2$ preserves the formality of the meaning of the good or the *ratio boni*.

Commenting on this, McInerny has this to say: "Any account [of human action] assumes that desirable$_1$ is desirable$_2$. If we learn that desirable$_1$ is not desirable$_2$ we already have a motive for desiring what truly is desirable$_2$. . . . What [this means] is that merely factual desire does not exist. The supposedly troublesome transition from Is to Ought suggests that the formality of goodness, that which is perfective and fulfilling, is not already present in any desire."[60]

McInerny brings all this to our attention because it is relevant to the transition that St. Thomas makes in I-II, q. 94, a. 2, from "the good is that which all men seek" to "the good is to be done and pursued and evil avoided." "This," McInerny says, "is exactly the move we have been discussing with regard to the desirable and is no more mysterious. The link with previous discussions of ultimate end is clear."[61]

McInerny further emphasizes that the practical and the speculative intellects are *not* different powers but *one* power of the human person, accidentally differentiated by being ordered to action and not being so ordered, and in fact St. Thomas held that the speculative intellect becomes practical by extension. The very first principle of speculative thinking, the principle of contradiction, is the first principle of thinking as such and reigns over the practical as well as the speculative order. Because of this the principles of the practical order, although nondemonstrable, are dependent for their intelligibility on speculative truths, in the way that "good is to be done and pursued and its opposite is to be avoided" is dependent for its intelligibility on "the good is that which all men seek."[62]

---

60. McInerny, *Ethica Thomistica*, 37–38.

61. Ibid., 38.

62. Here I have sought to illustrate McInerny's point by showing how the practical truth, "good is to be done and pursued and its opposite avoided," is dependent on the theoretical truth, "the good is that which all men seek." On this issue, see McInerny, *Aquinas on Human Action,* 117–18. There McInerny writes: "It is sometimes said that if there are self-evident principles of the practical order they must stand on their own without any relation or

McInerny also calls attention to *Summa theologiae* I, q. 14, a. 16, where St. Thomas speaks of the degrees of practical thinking. These degrees depend on three criteria: (1) the nature of the objects known (theoretical or practical); (2) the way they are known (an operable or practical considered either theoretically or practically); and (3) the intent, aim, or purpose of the knower (to make or do something [practical] or simply to know about it [theoretical]). After emphasizing that for St. Thomas *practical truth* or the truth of the *practical intellect* requires conformity of the intellectual judgment with right appetite, that is, appetite rectified by virtue,[63] he then concludes: "It is only practical knowledge in the full sense, completely practical knowledge, that is true with practical truth. *The other modes of practical knowledge, if true, will be true with speculative truth—that is, insofar as their judgments are in conformity with the way things are.*"[64] Thus, the *truth of the principles of the natural law, the principles of practical reasoning,* is *not*, on this view, *practical*. It is rather *speculative* or *theoretical* in character, true because in conformity with the way things are. The "ought" of these practical principles thus follows from or is derived from the "is" of theoretical judgments about the way things are. This, it seems to me, is McInerny's principal claim here.

The Essential Meaning of Natural Law

Natural law, our intelligent participation in God's eternal law, essentially consists in the *first principles (precepts) of practical reason*. These principles express nondemonstrable truths (but, as we have seen, truths whose truth is theoretical, not practical). McInerny emphasizes that

by natural law Thomas means the principles in practical reason that function in a way analogous to principles in speculative reason. . . . Natural law is reason's natural grasp of certain common principles which should direct our acts. Just as speculative intellect moves from common and certain truths toward ever more particular truths

---

dependence on theoretical truths. . . . This seems a view quite alien to that of Thomas. . . ." Then, after citing the text (*ST* I, q. 79, a. 11) where Thomas had said that practical and speculative intellects are one power, he then criticizes those who, in light of Kantian-inspired notions of the autonomy of practical reason, come to conclude that Thomas must be interpreted to say that the truths of practical intellect are utterly independent of the way the world is. This is not Aquinas's view.

63. McInerny, "Portia's Lament," with reference to *ST* I-II, q. 57, a. 5 ad 3.
64. Ibid., 97; emphasis added.

about things that are, so practical reason moves off from basic, common, and certain directives toward ever more particular guides for choice and action. The starting points of speculative reason are indemonstrable, so are those of practical reason.[65]

Natural law, or our intelligent participation in God's eternal law, essentially consists in or is made up of universal propositions of practical reason ordered to action,[66] and "Aquinas takes natural law to refer to the first principles of practical reason, *not* to practical reason's grasp of those principles."[67] McInerny notes that the term used to designate practical reason's grasp of those principles is *synderesis*[68] but natural law in its primary and proper sense for Thomas is *not synderesis* nor does it consist in our natural inclinations, but is rather a set of universal propositions of practical reason ordered to action. We see here how McInerny differs from Hall.

The Meaning of the First Principle (Precept) of Natural Law and Its Articulation in Primary Precepts "Telling Us What to Do"

The first principle or precept of natural law is that "good is to be done and pursued and its opposite is to be avoided." This first precept, McInerny affirms,

"expresses with sweeping generality the end of human acts. In acting, we must seek and do the good and avoid its opposite.... We must, in acting, seek that which is truly fulfilling and perfective of us, our good, and avoid what thwarts or stunts the flourishing of our nature."[69]

This first precept of natural law is the basic moral norm: it "is formed by human reason and it is meant to be directive of human action. The addressee is the human agent, and the first directive is: The perfection, the completion, the good *in the sense of the ultimate end,* is to be pursued and whatever is incompatible with that end is to be avoided."[70] This ultimate end is the good proper and exclusive to human beings, that is, contemplation of the truth about God.

---

65. McInerny, *Aquinas on Human Action,* 110–11, with reference to *ST* I-II, q. 91, aa. 2 and 3.
66. Ibid., 108–9, with reference to *ST* I-II, q. 90, a. 1 ad 2.
67. Ibid, 113, with reference to *ST* I-II, q. 94, a. 1.
68. Ibid.   69. Ibid., 136.
70. McInerny, "The Principles of Natural Law," 4 (in Finnis, *Natural Law,* 328).

The very first precept of natural law, then, directs us to our ultimate end. McInerny raises the question, "What is the field over which further precepts will range?" He next cites I-II, q. 94, a. 2 ad 2, where Aquinas instructs us that "all the inclinations of whatever part of human nature, for example, the concupiscible and irascible, pertain to natural law insofar as they are regulated by reason, and they are reduced to one first precept," and continues by affirming that "precepts telling us how to act will bear on the ends of these inclinations. Obviously, since the inclinations are natural . . . it is not our choice whether to have them or for them to have the objects they do. What does fall to us is to regulate the pursuit of these goods, and the precepts [i.e., primary precepts of natural law] do this by ordering these goods to the good of the whole man, to the common good."[71]

The several precepts of natural law are "directives aiming at constituents of the human good or ultimate end." The very first precept directs us toward our ultimate end, while its specifications direct us to "constituents of the end."[72] These "constituents" are the ends or goods of our natural inclinations, which are all components of the final or ultimate end. "There are," McInerny notes, "three levels of inclination—those we share with everything, those we share with other animals, and those peculiar to us as men—and there are also levels of precepts among and within these three orders. The first and most common in the three orders would be, respectively, that our pursuit of food and drink should be regulated by reason, that our sexual lives should come under the governance of reason, and that we should not harm our fellows or wallow in ignorance."[73] In other words, "We should preserve life in a way appropriate to a rational agent. We should engage in sexual activity in a way appropriate to a rational agent. We should rationally pursue the good of reason itself and particularly truth about the most important things."[74] To put the matter another way, "Precepts of natural law are rational directives aiming at the good for man. The human good, man's ultimate end, is complex, but the unifying thread is the distinctive mark of the human, i.e., reason."[75]

---

71. McInerny, *Aquinas on Human Action*, 136.
72. McInerny, *Ethica Thomistica*, 47; McInerny, "The Principles of Natural Law," 5.
73. McInerny, *Aquinas on Human Action*, 136–37.
74. McInerny, *Ethica Thomistica*, 47; McInerny, "The Principles of Natural Law," 5.
75. McInerny, "The Principles of Natural Law," 5.

The Hierarchy of Human Goods

With Hall and Ashley, McInerny holds that for St. Thomas the goods perfective of human persons are hierarchically ordered. Thus he says that "man is a complex whole comprising a number of inclinations, each of which will have an appropriate good or end. If we enumerate these inclinations and *notice their hierarchy,* we will be able to glimpse the natural law precepts which take them into account."[76] The good or perfection of reason, a good peculiar and specific to man, is man's end. But if this is so, then "why does Thomas mention the inclination to self-preservation, common to all creatures and thus to man, and the inclination to reproduce and have offspring, common to all animals and thus to man?" McInerny answers this query by saying: "The goods aimed at by these inclinations are part of the human good, *but only insofar as they are humanized, that is, insofar as they are pursued . . . as the aim or goal of conscious action. . . .* by coming under the guidance of reason."[77] In short, goods such as human life itself, the union of male and female, and the having and rearing of children are human *goods* only insofar as they come under the rule of reason, that is, insofar as they are willed in accordance with reason.[78]

---

76. Ibid., 4, emphasis added; see McInerny, *Ethica Thomistica,* 44.

77. McInerny, *Ethica Thomistica,* 45–46.

78. An illuminating text summarizing McInerny's thought here is found in McInerny, *Aquinas on Human Action,* 119–20. There he writes: "Practical reason is concerned with perfecting activities other than its own reasoning, and the theater of its directing and guiding activity contains the other inclinations which enter into the human makeup, some of them unlike reason in that we share them with other beings. The most widely shared inclinations are the most basic, the most natural. The natural drive to preserve itself in being is taken by Thomas to be true of anything. As present in us, it comes down chiefly to pursuing food and drink and avoiding harm. These are not inclinations we choose to have. The human task is to guide such inclinations so that they achieve their end or good in a way compatible with and even enhancing the good of the whole man. . . . In much the same way, like other animals we do not decide to be attracted to the opposite sex or feel an impulse to mate; nor is continuing concern for offspring simply the result of a decision. If the first inclination is ordered to the preservation of the individual, this second level of inclination is ordered to the preservation of the species. Sexual activity and the raising of children must be rationally guided in such a way that they achieve their natural ends and contribute to the good of the agent as a whole. The ends of these inclinations, like the ends of the first, are particular goods, which must find their setting within the comprehensive good stated in the most basic precept of all."

The Move from Primary Natural Law Precepts to "Quasi-Conclusions" and "Conclusions"

We have already seen that on McInerny's interpretation, St. Thomas teaches that the first "precepts" of natural law, which are rooted in the fundamental principle that good is to be done and pursued and its opposite avoided, direct us to pursue in a human way the goods to which we are naturally inclined. He observes that Aquinas himself does not provide us in I-II, q. 94, a. 2 with any list of first principles of natural law. "Indeed," he notes, "the only things that look like precepts are found at the end and might be formulated: One ought to avoid ignorance; one ought not cause harm to his fellows." These precepts bear on the goods to which we are directed by the inclination specific to us as human beings. McInerny thinks that we can "discern the shape of the [primary] precepts that would be formulated with regard to the first and second levels of inclination," and he then offers the following formulas: "The pleasures of food and drink should contribute to the good of man as a whole." "Sexual congress should further the good of procreation in a way contributing to the whole good of man."[79] But how do we go from precepts such as these to more specific moral norms, norms such as those prohibiting the killing of the innocent, adultery, and so on?

In *Summa theologiae* I-II, q. 100, a. 1 and a. 3, cited by McInerny, St. Thomas made it clear that one can readily appeal to the "first and common principles" of natural law, and with minimum consideration immediately recognize the truth of some specific norms, those found for instance in the second tablet of the Decalogue, whereas to show the truth of other specific moral norms a more diligent inquiry is necessary, one that only the "wise" are capable of carrying out. Thomas calls the first and common principles of natural law, among them the Golden Rule and such principles as that we ought not do evil to anyone, *per se notae* truths of natural law, and he calls the precepts of the Decalogue, known readily by appeal to these first and common principles their proximate conclusions.[80]

In I-II, q. 94, a. 6, a text which McInerny does not cite, Thomas had used the expression *quasi conclusiones* in referring to these "secondary precepts"

---

79. McInerny, *Aquinas on Human Action*, 121.
80. See *Aquinas on Human Action*, 128–30.

closest to the "primary precepts." McInerny then asks about the status of such specific precepts as "Do not lie" and "Do not murder" (which relate, respectively, to the Eighth and Fifth Commandments of the Decalogue): "Is it the case that they are not *per se nota* precepts? Or is the phrase '*quasi conclusiones*' [used in q. 94, a. 6, but *not*, it should be noted, in q. 100, a. 1 and a. 3] meant to suggest a discursive derivation less than argument and demonstration?"[81] McInerny believes that certain prohibited forms of conduct can be shown to be as incoherent as behavior at odds with the *per se notae* precepts of natural law. He thinks that reducing certain specific precepts, the "*quasi conclusiones*" from the first principles, to those principles is possible "in the case of suicide ... of drunkenness, of wholesale slaughter, and the like. If this is true, then the *quasi conclusiones* are themselves *per se notae*."[82]

McInerny, if I have properly understood him, thus holds that the specific moral norms found in the Decalogue, known immediately and with a minimum of consideration, are not, properly speaking, truths *demonstrated* by appeal to first principles of natural law but are rather so closely related to those first principles that they can be reduced to them and regarded as *per se notae* precepts. *Further moral precepts*, such as those requiring us to return items we have borrowed, and—I would assume—the norm requiring that new life be given only through the conjugal act—are truths demonstrated by appeal to the first principles and to their proximate conclusions and are known only through the diligent inquiry of the "wise."

McInerny believes that in his discussion of marriage St. Thomas shows clearly that the goods to which we are naturally inclined are hierarchically ordered and that precepts directive of them reflect this. He then considers at some length St. Thomas's thought on polygamy, as found in his early *Commentary on the Sentences of Peter Lombard*, where St. Thomas argued that polyandry, having many husbands, is ruled out by a primary precept of natural law insofar as having a plurality of husbands totally thwarts attainment of the primary end of marriage, the having and raising of children, whereas polygyny, having more than one wife, does not, although it does impede attainment of marriage's secondary end, the mutual help spouses give one another in domestic affairs, and where St. Thomas also gave his reasons for

---

81. Ibid., 130.
82. Ibid., 131.

thinking that the Golden Rule, a primary precept of natural law, does not rule out polygyny.[83] McInerny's point is that for St. Thomas natural law is not a set of intuitions, but rather the rational direction of human actions, the formulation of precepts, some common and universal, others in the form of *quasi conclusiones* from such common and universal precepts having the same universality, and still others valid only for the most part. Moreover, the various levels of natural inclinations and natural law precepts are hierarchically ordered.[84]

Some Critical Questions

In the concluding section of this paper, after examining the thought of Grisez and his school, I will return to the Is/Ought question. Here I wish to comment briefly on the following: (a) McInerny's understanding of the first principle of practical reason; (b) his claim that the goods to which we are naturally inclined are hierarchically ordered and that they must be brought under reason's rule to become truly components of the human good; (c) the derivation of specific norms from the primary precepts of natural law; and (d) St. Thomas on marriage and polygamy.

a. McInerny's understanding of the first principle of practical reason. According to McInerny, the first principle of practical reason, good is to be done and pursued and its opposite is to be avoided, must be understood as directing us to the good *in the sense of the ultimate end.* This principle, he says, means that "in acting, we must seek that which is truly fulfilling and perfective of us, our good, and avoid what thwarts or stunts the flourishing of our nature." He maintains that this principle directs us to *morally good* action.

Yet St. Thomas himself insists, in I-II, q. 100, a. 1, that "*every* judgment of practical reason proceeds from some principles that are naturally [i.e., nondiscursively and nondemonstrably] known" *(omne iudicium rationis practicae procedit ex quibusdam principiis naturaliter cognotis).* In other words, even morally bad judgments of practical reason proceed in some way from the first principle of practical reasoning. Immoral action is not *irrational* action; it is rational behavior, and wrongdoers frequently rationalize their immoral

---

83. The text of this article in St. Thomas's *Scriptum super libros Sententiarum Petri Lombardiensis* IV is reprinted in *ST* Suppl., q. 65, a. 1.

84. McInerny, *Aquinas on Human Action,* 149–50.

behavior by appealing to real goods as the motives behind their choices. In other texts St. Thomas noted that sinful operations of practical reason are attributed, as are its virtuous operations, to one's grasp (but misuse) of the first principles of practical reason.[85] St. Thomas, as McInerny himself recognizes, drew an analogy between the first principle of practical reasoning and the principle of noncontradiction in the speculative order. If this analogy is valid, then the first principle of practical reasoning governs the practical reasoning of people who do evil as well as the practical reasoning of those who do good. Thus, for Aquinas, the first principles of practical reason (including the very first and primary one) govern the actions of the bad as well as the good. Hence this principle directs us to do and pursue the good in general, not what is morally good.

b. McInerny on the hierarchy of basic goods and claim that the goods toward which we are naturally inclined must be brought under reason's sway if they are to be truly good. We have seen these claims. St. Thomas surely recognized an order of natural inclinations and of goods toward which those inclinations direct us. But McInerny assumes and in no way proves that this order establishes a hierarchy. The principle of order that Aquinas identifies is simply "what man has in common with all substances," "what he has in common with animals," and "what he has specifically to himself." In saying this Thomas is not saying what McInerny says when he affirms that "if we enumerate [man's] inclinations and notice their hierarchy we will be able to glimpse the natural law precepts that take them into account." What Thomas does say is that "all those things to which man has a natural inclination, reason naturally grasps as goods and, in consequence, as things-to-be-pursued by action and their opposites as evils and things-to-be-avoided,"[86] and this seems quite different from what McInerny says.

Although Thomas, in connection with the goods proper to us and human beings, does articulate as primary precepts "ignorance is to be avoided" and "one ought not offend those with whom one lives," he nowhere

---

85. *Quaestiones disputatae de veritate*, q. 16, a. 2 ad 6: "sicut in speculativis ratio falsa, quamvis originem sumat a principiis, non tamen a principiis primis falsitatem habet sed ex malo usu principiorum, sicut in operativis accidit."

86. *ST* I-II, q. 94, a. 2: "omnia illa ad quae homo habet naturalem inclinationem ratio naturaliter apprehendit ut bona, et per consequens ut opere prosequenda, et contraria eorum ut mala et vitanda."

gives the kind of precepts McInerny proposes with respect to the goods of the other inclinations, namely, that "we should preserve life in a way appropriate to a rational agent. We should engage in sexual activity in a way appropriate to a rational agent. We should rationally pursue the good of reason itself and particularly truth about the most important things." Rather it seems that the primary precepts bearing on these goods should be formulated as: life is a good to be pursued and protected and its opposite an evil to be avoided; the procreation and education of children is a good to be pursued and done; knowledge is a good to be pursued. Practical reason naturally, that is, nondiscursively, apprehends these as *goods* to be pursued and done. They are intrinsically good, not instrumentally so.

McInerny, however, claims that the "goods aimed at by these inclinations are part of the human good . . . *only insofar as they are humanized, that is, insofar as they are pursued . . . as the aim or goal of conscious action.*" This claim seems to be far from Thomistic. On this view, one dangerously near to a dualism that views human sexual capacity as a subpersonal or subhuman good, a good *for* the person and not *of* the person, goods such as human life itself, bodily health, and the procreation and education of children are not, as Thomas held, *intrinsically good* but only instrumentally so.[87]

c. The derivation of specific moral norms from the primary precepts. McInerny distinguishes too sharply, it seems to me, between precepts that are *quasi conclusiones* and precepts termed simply *conclusiones* from the primary precepts of natural law and holds that the precepts of the Decalogue, which St. Thomas does call "proximate conclusions" from the primary precepts are in fact reducible to the primary precepts and are thus *per se notae* truths. This seems to me to be mistaken. Although in one text (I-II, q. 94, a. 6) he does call the "more proper secondary precepts" "*quasi* conclusions close to the principles," in the principal text where he is explicity concerned with the way the precepts of the Decalogue are related to the primary precepts of natural law (I-II, q. 100, a. 3), he refers to these precepts simply as "proximate conclusions" from such primary precepts as "man ought do evil to no one." Moreover, it is not irrational, and therefore directly contrary to the principle that good is to be done and pursued and its opposite avoided or

---

87. See, e.g., *Scriptum super libros Sententiarum Petri Lombardiensis* I, d. 48, q. 1, a. 4, where knowledge, health, and virtue are listed as goods intrinsic to the human person; and *ST* I-II, q. 2, a. 4, on bodily life as intrinsically good. See also *ST* I-II, q. 73, a. 3.

to the specifications of this principle, to ask why it is *always wrong* to kill an innocent person or to lie. It is, of course, wrong to do so, but the truth of these specific moral norms needs to be demonstrated by showing how these kinds of human actions entail violation of better known truths (e.g., primary precepts of the natural law). The question is, which principles best serve as *premises* in light of which the truths of the Decalogue's precepts can be shown.

McInerny, moreover, does not consider the significance of two important Thomistic texts relative to the derivation of specific moral norms from *primary* precepts. The first is I-II, q. 100, a. 3 ad. 1, where Thomas says that the commands that we are to love God above all things and our neighbor as ourselves are "the first and common precepts of natural law," and that therefore "*all* the precepts of the Decalogue are related to these two as conclusions are related to their common principles." The second text is in *Summa contra gentiles,* 3, ch. 122, where St. Thomas, in speaking of simple fornication (an act proscribed by the Sixth Commandment), says that we offend God only by acting contrary to our own good *(non enim Deus a nobis offenditur nisi ex hoc quod contra nostrum bonum agimus)*. This indicates that, for St. Thomas, to show the truth of specific norms such as those found in the Decalogue, one should show what good of human persons is being intentionally violated.

d. Aquinas on marriage and polygamy. To support his claim that goods are hierarchically ordered McInerny appeals to St. Thomas's justification of polygamy as opposed to polyandry and the different "ends" or "goods" at stake. Here the comparison was between the good of procreating and educating children—one of the basic goods to which we are naturally inclined—and the mutual help spouses give to one another in domestic life, clearly a more instrumental good. But Thomas's teaching in his commentary on the *Sentences* was by no means his last discussion of marriage. He returned to marriage in *Summa contra gentiles,* 3, in particular in chapters 123 and 124. In chapter 124, where he is explicitly speaking of the need for marriage to be between *one* man and *one* woman, he speaks about the special *friendship* (a basic good to which we are naturally inclined) that should exist between husband and wife, and clearly contends that if a woman cannot have more than one husband because this is contrary to the good of the child's parenthood, neither ought a husband to have more than one wife because this is incompatible with the equal and freely given friendship meant to exist between husband and wife. Here the comparison is between two different basic goods, one to which we are directed by the inclination with other animals (the good of procreation), the other a good to which we are inclined by our specific nature, the good of marital friendship. Each is intrinsically good, nor does one take precedence over the other, as one would if there were an objective hierarchy between them.

The "New" Natural Law Theory of Germain Grisez, John Finnis, Joseph Boyle and Their School

Beginning with his book *Contraception and the Natural Law*, published in 1964, Germain Grisez[88] has developed a theory of natural law widely referred to today as the "new natural law theory." In a succession of publications from that time to the present, Grisez and his associates, preeminent among them John Finnis and Joseph Boyle, have deepened and clarified this theory of natural law.[89]

Since I regard myself as a member of this school and since I have elsewhere[90] set forth in detail its understanding of natural law, my presentation here will be concise. In my earlier treatment of this theory I concluded by offering a synoptic view of it.[91] I will present this synopsis, here expanded slightly and clarified, comment on certain of its features, and end by looking at some of the major criticisms made of it by Pamela Hall, Ralph McInerny, and Benedict Ashley. Although others have criticized this theory, among them Russell Hittinger and Jean Porter, these other criticisms will not be considered here; other writers have adequately responded to them.[92]

---

88. On Grisez, see *Natural Law and Moral Inquiry: Ethics, Metaphysics, and Politics in the Work of Germain Grisez*, ed. Robert P. George (Washington, D.C.: Georgetown University Press, 1998).

89. For a list of the principal sources of the new natural law theory, see Appendix.

90. See, e.g., William E. May, *An Introduction to Moral Theology*, rev. ed. (Huntington, Ind.: Our Sunday Visitor, 1994), 68–89. The Second Edition of this book, published in 2003, considers recent developments in Grisez's thought, particularly the developments of his position elaborated in his *American Journal of Jurisprudence* 46 (2002); see Appendix under I. Works by Grisez Alone.

91. May, *An Introduction to Moral Theology*, 86–87.

92. Russell Hittinger's critique is set forth at length in his book *A Critique of the New Natural Law Theory* (South Bend, Ind.: University of Notre Dame Press, 1987), and more briefly

A Synthetic Overview of the New Natural Law Theory

The natural law, as law, consists of ordered sets of true propositions of practical reason. The first set (1) includes the first principle of practical reasoning, *good is to be done and pursued and its opposite, evil, is to be avoided,* and the specific determinations of this first principle identifying the basic human goods, to which we are naturally inclined, that are the goods to be pursued and done. There are eight such goods, five reflexive or existential insofar as choice enters into their very definition and thus lie within our power and which perfect us as agents through deliberation and choice, and three substantive insofar as they do *not* require choice for their existence and perfect us as organic substances, as rational, and as simultaneously rational and animal. The five existential or reflexive goods, which have harmony as a common theme, are (i) marriage; (ii) harmony between and among individuals and groups of persons—living at peace, friendship, justice; (iii) harmony among one's feelings, judgments, and choices, or inner peace; (iv) harmony among one's judgments, choices, and actions, or peace of conscience; and (v) harmony with God or the more-than-human source of meaning and value or religion. The three substantive goods are (vi) life itself, including health, bodily integrity and the transmission of human life; (vii) knowledge of the truth and appreciation of beauty; and (viii) excellence in work and play. These principles of practical reason are used in some way or another by everyone who considers what to do, however unsound his conclusions. These principles, therefore, govern the practical

---

in his essay "The Recovery of Natural Law and the Common Morality," *This World* 18 (Summer 1987): 62–74. Hittinger's critique, which in many ways seriously misrepresents the thought of Grisez, has been devastated, in my opinion, by Robert George, "Recent Criticism of Natural Law Theory," *University of Chicago Law Review* 55 (1988): 1371–429; and by William Marshner, "A Tale of Two Beatitudes," *Faith and Reason* 16, no. 2 (1990): 177–99. In addition, Grisez himself gave an extended critique of Hittinger's critique, detailing instances where Hittinger had misstated his views; see Grisez, "A Critique of Russell Hittinger's Book, *A Critique of the New Natural Law Theory*," *New Scholasticism* 62 (1988): 62–74.

Jean Porter presents her critique in "Basic Goods and the Human Good in Recent Catholic Moral Theology," *The Thomist* 47 (1993): 27–41. Gerard V. Bradley and Robert George have shown how inadequate and misleading Porter's presentation of the theory is and how off-the-mark her criticisms are in "The New Natural Law Theory: A Reply to Jean Porter," *American Journal of Jurisprudence* 38 (1994): 303–15.

reasoning of the morally upright and the not morally upright; they are not, as such, *moral* principles because they do not enable us to determine, prior to choice, which alternatives are morally good and which are morally bad.

The second set (2) consists of (i) the first principle of morality or basic moral principle and (ii) its specifications or modes of responsibility. The first principle of morality, formulated in religious language as the twofold commandment to love God above all things and one's neighbor as oneself, is more adequately expressed for ethical purposes as follows: *in voluntarily acting for human goods and avoiding what is opposed to them, one ought to choose and otherwise will those and only those possibilities whose willing is compatible with a will toward integral human fulfillment.* The specifications of this first moral principle, called "modes of responsibility," identify specific ways of choosing *not* compatible with a will toward integral human fulfillment. There are eight such "modes of responsibility," and they exclude ways of choosing and acting that ignore, slight, neglect, arbitrarily limit, or damage, destroy, or impede a basic human good, excluding as well emotional and nonrationally grounded choices and actions.

The third set (3) consists of specific moral norms, whose truth can be shown in light of the first principle of morality and its modes of responsibility. These norms identify kinds of human acts, specified by their object of moral choice, that are reasonable all-things-considered (and not merely relative to a particular purpose) and acts that are unreasonable all-things-considered, that is, between specific alternatives of choice that are morally good and morally bad. Of the specific moral norms included in this set some are absolute and admit of no exceptions, whereas many are not and admit of exceptions in the light of the moral principles (set 2) that gave rise to them to begin with.

In addition, the integral directiveness of the first principles of practical reasoning, expressed in the first principle of morality that directs us toward the ideal of integral human fulfillment, provides us with a criterion for establishing moral priorities among our interests in the basic goods of human existence. When these goods are considered from the perspective of this integral directiveness, the directiveness of unfettered practical reason, the good of religion, or of harmony between human persons and God or the more-than-human source of meaning and value is seen to have a priority insofar as commitment to this good offers to human persons an overarching purpose in terms of which they can order their lives as a whole. Thus a commitment to religious truth emerges as the commitment that can integrate the whole of human life when this is conceived in the light of the demands of moral truth.

Comment

a. Grisez and his school seek to follow St. Thomas in identifying the basic goods of human persons to which they are naturally inclined. Aquinas himself had not sought to provide an exhaustive list in I-II, q. 94, a. 2, as shown by the fact that he used the expression *et similia* (and others of like kind) after providing his identification of the goods on the three levels of human existence. Moreover, in I-II, q. 94, a. 3, he included as another good to which we are naturally inclined to act in accordance with reason, a good that can be called "practical reasonableness *(bonum secundum rationem esse).*"[93] Grisez et al. deem it important to identify *all* the basic human goods, all the goods to which we are naturally inclined and which practical reason naturally, that is, nondiscursively, grasps as the goods to be pursued and done, because a morally upright person is one who is open to *all* human goods.

b. The basic goods of human persons are *not* hierarchically ordered. *Each* is a good *of* the person, not merely a good *for* the person, and each fulfills a distinct aspect or level of a person's being. This means that there is no rational way of comparing goods of different categories or of comparing individual instantiations or realizations of goods in the same category.

c. They emphasize that in I-II, q. 100, a. 3, Aquinas *explicitly* identified the twofold command to love as *the first and common principle* on which the truth of the precepts of the Decalogue depend. They accept this as a sound way of expressing the first *moral* principle in religious language, but maintain that for philosophical ethics it can be more adequately formulated as noted above. They do so because this way of formulating the first moral principle refers to the many basic human goods that generate the need for choice and moral judgment. This first principle is more clearly and fully expressed by being more closely related to the first principles of practical reasoning (the first set of natural law principles), that is, the integral direc-

---

93. On this issue, see John Finnis, *Aquinas: Moral, Political, and Legal Theory* (New York: Oxford University Press, 1998), 83–84.

tiveness of the first principles of practical reasoning working together harmoniously in full concert.

d. The "integral human fulfillment" to which we are directed by the first moral principle is *not* itself a basic human good alongside of or in addition to the basic goods identified in the first set of principles. Unlike basic goods it is not a *reason* for acting, but rather an ideal whose attractiveness depends on *all* the goods that can appeal to persons and serve as reasons for acting. It is the "object" of "unfettered human reason," that is, right reason, and as such rectifies the will. The will of a person committed to choosing and acting in accord with the requirements of integral human fulfillment is the will of a person inwardly disposed to choosing well, to choose in accord with right reason.

e. They believe that St. Thomas's account of the movement from the first and common moral principles of natural law to specific moral norms, such as those found in the Decalogue, needs to be clarified. They note that he identified principles less general than the love commandments but more particular than specific moral precepts, principles such as the Golden Rule. Seeking to develop and clarify his thought on the movement from the first principle of morality to specific moral norms, they identify ways of choosing that are *not* compatible with integral human fulfillment, the "modes of responsibility" noted above. These modes, along with the first principle of morality, furnish us with the premises needed to show the truth of specific moral norms and to show why some specific moral norms are absolute whereas others admit of exceptions.

Critiques of the New Natural Law Theory by Hall, McInerny, and Ashley

The Critique of Pamela Hall

Hall characterizes the new natural law theory as "natural law without nature."[94] She says moreover that Grisez and Finnis have renounced teleology and that "since without teleology the natural law would be without foundation . . . [they] have certainly given up any claim that their natural law is Aquinas's."[95]

---

94. Hall, *Narrative and Natural Law*, 16.
95. Ibid., 18.

In my opinion Hall's critique is based on a misrepresentation of the thought of Grisez et al. Take her claim that because they reject teleology they cannot be faithful to Aquinas. To support this claim she cites a passage from p. 101 of the essay jointly authored by Grisez, Finnis, and Boyle, "Practical Principles, Moral Truth, and Ultimate Ends" in which they reject teleological ethical theories. But the theories they reject are teleological in the sense of *consequentialist/proportionalist* theories which deny that any actions are intrinsically immoral and not in accord with universally binding principles of natural law. Since this meaning of teleological theory is widely used today, and since it is crystal clear that this is what they reject and *not* a teleology recognizing that human persons act for basic goods understood as *ends* of human action, Hall's charge here in my view is grossly inaccurate; she could not have been unaware that the teleology they reject is simply utterly other than the teleology she claims they reject. Thus I find this "critique" totally misses the mark and misrepresents the thought of Grisez et al.

Hall's claim that Grisez et al. propose a natural law without nature is in some ways similar to a criticism made by others, including McInerny, and was addressed to some extent in my critique of McInerny. But here I wish simply to cite a not-untypical passage from Grisez that clearly shows that he has a deep understanding of human nature, a profound grasp of philosophical anthropology, and affirms and does not deny that morality is *grounded in human nature*. In it he says:

> [M]oral thought must remain grounded in a sound anthropology which maintains the bodiliness of the person. Such moral thought sees personal biological, not merely generically biological, meaning and value in human sexuality. The bodies which become one flesh in sexual intercourse are persons; their unity in a certain sense forms a single person, the potential procreator from whom the personal, bodily reality of a new human individual flows in material, bodily, personal continuity.[96]

It is surely not accurate to claim that the author of this passage has a natural law without nature, as Hall does. Her critique on this matter is again based on a grotesque misunderstanding and/or misrepresentation of the view she criticizes.

---

96. Germain Grisez, "Dualism and the New Morality," in *L'agire morale,* Vol. 5, *Atti del Congresso sul Settimo Centenario di Santo Tomasso d'Aquino* (Naples: Edizioni Domenicane, 1975), 325.

Ralph McInerny's Critique

McInerny faults Grisez et al. as being non-Thomistic on three major issues: (1) the dichotomy between facts and values (the Is/Ought question); (2) their claim that the basic goods and first principles of practical reasoning are "premoral," not moral; and (3) their denial of an objective hierarchy among the goods.[97]

a. Excessive dichotomy between facts and values. According to McInerny, Grisez, Finnis and their associates think that knowledge of the world as it is is irrelevant to practical reason,[98] and that they consider the proposition "knowledge is a good for man" as a metaphysical truth having nothing to do with practical judgments. He claims that Grisez "says that in theoretical thinking the world calls the turn, [whereas] in practical thinking the mind calls the turn. Often he [Grisez] suggests that practical reason turns upon a malleable world which it can remake pretty much at will."[99]

In their response to this criticism[100] Finnis and Grisez insist first of all that they have constantly affirmed that the "basic forms of good are opportunities of *being:* the more fully a man participates in them, the more he is what he can be. And for this state of being fully what one can be, Aristotle appropriated the word *physis,* which was translated into Latin as *natura.* . . . So Aquinas will say that these requirements [are] requirements not only of reason, and of goodness, but also (by entailment) of (human nature)." Nor do they claim, as McInerny had charged, that knowledge of the world is irrelevant to practical reason. They say that "in the *practical* principle that knowledge is a good to be pursued, 'good' is understood practically in the light of the first *practical* principle, Good is to be done and pursued. If 'Knowledge is a good for man' were understood theoretically, simply as a truth of metaphysical anthropology, then it would have no more normative implication than 'Knowledge is a good for angels' has practical implication for us." They never claim that it is not possible to pass from metaphysical

---

97. This critique is given in McInerny's essay, "The Principles of Natural Law." See note 58 above for bibliographical details.

98. Ibid., 11.

99. Ibid., 9.

100. John Finnis and Germain Grisez, "The Basic Principles of Natural Law: A Reply to Ralph McInerny," *American Journal of Jurisprudence* 26 (1981): 21–31, reprinted in *Natural Law,* 1:341–52.

and/or factual truths together with principles of practical reasoning to normative conclusions. Their point "was that there can be no valid deduction of a normative conclusion without a normative principle, and thus that *first* practical principles cannot be derived from metaphysical speculations."

Finnis and Grisez hold that epistemologically or gnoseologically, first practical principles and normative propositions are *not dependent* on better known theoretical or factual truths. But they vigorously affirm that there is an *ontological* or *anthropological* dependence of practical truths on human nature. The goods perfective of us and which, when grasped nondiscursively by practical reason, serve as *first principles* of practical reasoning would be other than they are if our nature were other than it is. In other words, their natural law is not without nature. It totally depends on nature ontologically and anthropologically, but there is an epistemological nondependence of practical principles on theoretical truths, and here Finnis and Grisez claim that they, and not McInerny, are faithful to Aquinas.

b. The "premoral" nature of the basic goods. McInerny, as we have seen, claims that the first principle of practical reason as formulated by Aquinas—good is to be done and pursued—is a moral norm directing us to our ultimate end and that the various goods of the person noted in I-II, q. 94, a. 2 are "components of the ultimate end"; he likewise claims that a proper understanding of Aquinas requires us to recognize that goods such as bodily life itself, the procreation of children, and so on are goods *of* the person *only when brought under the rule of reason*. He faults Grisez and Finnis for not regarding the first principle of practical reason as a moral principle and for not recognizing the *moral* value of the basic goods. He claims that they "want principles that ... must split the difference between moral and immoral."[101]

In reply Finnis and Grisez say that McInerny, in claiming that the *bonum* in the first principle of practical reasoning refers to our *ultimate* end, drops the "to be done" *(faciendum)* in the way this principle is formulated, and that "this suppression of *faciendum* certainly facilitates the interpretation of *bonum* as *ultimus finis*," but it is not faithful to the text of St. Thomas. Nor is it clear, as McInerny claims, that for Thomas all the goods to which man is naturally inclined are components of the "ultimate end." Most importantly, however, if the analogy Aquinas draws between the first principle of practi-

---

101. McInerny, "The Principles of the Natural Law," 10.

cal reasoning and the first principle of theoretical reasoning is true, then the first principle of practical reasoning governs the practical reasoning of people who do evil. McInerny's charge that they want principles that "split the difference between the moral and the immoral" is simply false. Insisting that here they are following Aquinas (and they refer to I-II, q. 94, a. 2 ad 2; q. 100, a. 5 ad 1), they stress that "the basic principles of practical reasoning do underlie and make possible the reasoning of good people and bad people alike. The price for denying this is to say that the immoral are sheerly irrational, and thus free of moral responsibility." Moreover, they never held that the immoral person responds to all the principles of practical reasoning and pursues goods consistently with all of them. "The difference between moral good and evil arises just at this point. Practical principles do not 'split the difference between the moral and the immoral'; rather, the less than upright conscience shapes action by some practical principles while ignoring others which are also relevant."[102]

c. The hierarchy of basic goods. This issue has been handled sufficiently above, in my critique of McInerny.

Benedict Ashley's Critique

Ashley calls the understanding of natural law developed by Grisez, Finnis, Boyle, and their collaborators a "polyteleologism" and identifies three "theses" it affirms that in his judgment are erroneous.[103] The three "theses" are the following: "(1) Ethics is independent of a philosophical anthropology; (2) the human person, even if as Christians believe it now has a supernatural ultimate end, still also has a natural end; (3) the ultimate end of the human person is not a single good, but integral human fulfillment jointly constituted by several incommensurable basic goods."[104]

It is, first of all, not accurate to call the new natural law theory "polyteleologism" or "plural-goals-ism." It is not accurate and actually misrepresents the position. Grisez et al. do say that the diverse human goods are *ends* in the sense that people recognize that they are worth pursuing *for their own sake*. But they avoid calling these ends "goals" precisely because "goal" sug-

---

102. Finnis and Grisez, "The Basic Principles of Natural Law," 26–27.
103. Ashley develops his critique in his essay, "What Is the End of the Human Person?," 68–96.
104. Ibid., 70.

gests a sought-after state of affairs that can be attained once and for all, at which point one's desire is satisfied. But the basic goods of human persons are not ends in this sense. They are *not* concrete states of affairs one seeks to bring about as a result of one actions. A sign of this is that one *never* reaches a point of having "enough" knowledge, friendship, health, and so on.

In "Practical Principles, Moral Truth, and Ultimate Ends," Grisez, Finnis, and Boyle explain that emotional motives accompany rational motives. The former are tied not to the *intelligible good* that reason seeks, that is, the good perfective of the person and rationally sought, but to the concrete aspect of the purpose or to something psychologically associated with that purpose that one can imagine. Thus a purpose has two aspects: emotional, the purpose desired as a concrete and imaginable goal, a state of affairs; and rational, the purpose desired as an *intelligible good* or *end*. But it is precisely because the basic goods are *ends,* that is, *intelligible* goods that they serve as motives for purposeful human choices and actions.[105] Thus in my opinion Ashley's basic way of characterizing the view of Grisez et al. is highly inaccurate and conveys a misunderstanding of it to people not familiar with it.

With regard to the three "theses," Ashley says he finds in the new natural law theory, I maintain that its authors hold *none* of the theses he attributes to them.

(re Thesis 1). As we have seen already, Grisez and his associates hold, *with St. Thomas,* that the *first principles of practical reason* are *underived,* gnoseologically or epistemologically independent of prior known truths of the speculative intellect or of prior knowledge of human nature, from which their truth could be derived. However, as we have already seen, they never deny but rather vigorously affirm that there is an *ontological* and *anthropological* foundation of ethics or natural law inasmuch as the *goods* perfective of human persons and which, when grasped by practical reason, function as starting points or principles for thinking about what-is-to-be done would be other than they are were human *nature* other than it is.

(re Thesis 2). Grisez et al. make it clear that they do *not* think that man has a natural end in any strong sense of that term, that is, some definite good that of itself fully perfects man. The "integral human fulfillment" to which the first moral principle directs one is *not* a supergood, *not* the ulti-

---

105. Grisez, Finnis, and Boyle, "Practical Principles, Moral Truth, and Ultimate Ends," 104f.

mate reason why one chooses or should choose all one chooses; it is, rather, an ultimate end in the sense that it is the object of a rectified will, the object of "unfettered practical reason."[106]

(re. Thesis 3). Grisez, Finnis, and Boyle explicitly teach that a good life is a complex not of incommensurable goods connected together but rather is a complex of *morally good actions* in and through which human persons give themselves their identity as moral persons, in and through which they give themselves their moral *character*. Such a life is unified by the commitment one makes to seek the truth about God or the more-than-human source of meaning and value and to shape one's entire life in accord with that truth.[107]

More can and should be said in reply to Ashley's critique, but the points already noted suffice to indicate why his analysis is off the mark.

My Own Concerns

For years I have been associated with the Grisez school of thought on natural law and I am in basic agreement with it. But there are two issues that puzzle and trouble me. The first has to do with the *moral good* of the person; the second, with their account of the virtues.

The Question of the "Moral Good"

Is not there in man, the human person, a natural inclination to the *moral good, or the good of virtue?* Is not this a perfection of the human person, and does not the moral good function as a *basic reason* for acting? As John Finnis has noted, in I-II, q. 94, a. 3, St. Thomas himself had identified a natural inclination not noted in q. 94, a. 2, namely, the inclination to act according to reason. And the corresponding good, which Aquinas speaks of often and centrally, is the "good of [practical] reasonableness [*bonum rationis; bonum secundum rationem esse*], the good of ordering one's emotions, choices, and actions by intelligence and reason. The *bonum rationis* is both an intelligible good *and* the good of that person's being interested in it and sufficiently well integrated [mind integrated with will and each with subrational desires and powers] to choose it and put it into practice. Another name for it,

---

106. Ibid., 131–32.
107. Ibid., 135–36, 145–46.

then, is virtue."[108] The principle directing us to this good seems to me to function in the natural law thought of St. Thomas in the way that the ideal of integral human fulfillment functions in the later work of Grisez et al., for it is the good of "unfettered practical reason," the hallmark of the person committed to choosing with a will toward *all the goods of human existence*, with a will toward integral human fulfillment.

Moreover, in his *Natural Law and Natural Rights* Finnis himself had identified this as a basic good of human persons, speaking of its "requirements," which, in that work, performed the functions of what later were called by Grisez, Finnis, Boyle, and others the "modes of responsibility."[109]

In fact, in "Practical Principles, Moral Truth, and Ultimate Ends," Grisez, Finnis, and Boyle note that in some of their previous writings moral value had been imported into the good Finnis described as "practical reasonableness," a good which in their later work they identify as harmony among one's judgments, choices, and performances, and which they call the good of "peace of conscience." But in this later work they emphasize that this is not to be regarded as a *moral good* and that it is a mistake to import moral value into it insofar as one can participate in this good *immorally* by bringing one's judgments into harmony with one's immoral choices and performances and not by bringing one's choices and performances into harmony with one's judgments.[110]

Nonetheless, it seems to me that the good Aquinas identified as the good according to reason, the good of virtue, is indeed a basic good of human persons and one to which they are naturally inclined. Grisez considers this objection in his 2001 essay "Natural Law, God, Religion, and Human Fulfillment." He denies that the good of virtue is a basic good of human persons and that there is a natural inclination to the good of virtue. He argues that, if there were such a natural inclination, people would be virtuous by nature. However, they are not, and consequently there is no such natural inclination nor is the good of virtue a basic good of human persons.[111]

I disagree with Grisez here. We have a natural inclination to seek knowl-

---

108. Finnis, *Aquinas*, 83–84. Finnis, in a lengthy note, r, on 98–99, refers to numerous texts in St. Thomas on this good (e.g., I-II, q. 30, a. 1; q. 55, a. 4; q. 59, a. 4; q. 80, a. 1).

109. See Finnis, *Natural Law and Natural Rights*, chap. 3.

110. Grisez, Finnis, and Boyle, "Practical Principles, Moral Truth, and Ultimate Ends," 139–40.

111. Grisez, "Natural Law, God, Religion, and Human Fulfillment," 8, note 9.

edge of the truth, but not everyone is learned by nature. It seems strange to me that the moral good, the good that makes a person unqualifiedly good, is not a basic good and that it perfects persons as intelligent, choosing subjects. It also seems to me that John Finnis has returned to the view he held when he published *Natural Law and Natural Rights* in 1980, namely, that the good of practical reasonableness or virtue is a basic good of human persons insofar as he develops Aquinas's teaching on this issue to some length in his 1998 volume *Aquinas: Moral, Political, and Legal Theory*.[112]

Virtues in the New Natural Law Theory

Grisez et al., despite what some of their critics maintain, affirm the need of virtues for the moral life and provide a rich treatment of the virtues.[113] Still they do not continue the Thomistic tradition regarding the cardinal virtues of prudence, justice, fortitude, and temperance and the way in which Aquinas related these virtues to specific powers of the human person, "seating" the virtues in those powers, the powers, namely, of intellect (prudence), will (justice), the concupiscible appetite (temperance), and the irascible appetite (fortitude), and the way in which they name and consider virtues seems to be extraordinary flexible and ad hoc. But it seems to me that Aquinas was on to something of great importance in "seating" specific virtues in specific powers of the human person. Thus the chaste person "feels" differently about sexual matters than does the unchaste person. Grisez et al. would agree with this, but their account of it is not as clear, in my opinion, as Aquinas's. I believe that the Thomistic schema *can*, however, be integrated into their thought. But this is the subject of another paper.

Final note: In this paper, originally written in the spring of 2000, I did not consider the understanding of Thomistic natural law developed by Martin Rhonheimer in his work *Natural Law and Practical Reason: A Thomist View of Moral Autonomy*, trans. Gerald Malsbary (New York: Fordham University Press, 2000), a translation from the German text *Natur als Grundlage der Moral: Eine Auseinandersetzung mit autonomer und teleologisher Ethik*, pub-

---

112. On this matter, see the second edition of my *An Introduction to Moral Theology*, chap. 3 (see note 90 above).

113. See, e.g., Grisez, Finnis, and Boyle, "Practical Principles, Moral Truth, and Ultimate Ends," 129–33.

lished in 1987. Rhonheimer's understanding of natural law is very faithful to St. Thomas and his own views are much more in agreement with the Grisez school of thought than with the other authors considered here. Rhonheimer, however, places central importance on the basic good of virtue to which we are naturally inclined, as Thomas himself taught in I-II, q. 94, a. 3, and differs greatly from Grisez. I consider Rhonheimer's position at length in the second edition of my *An Introduction to Moral Theology*.

Appendix: Principal Sources for the New Natural Law Theory

(Listed by author and authors and chronologically)

I. Works by Germain Grisez Alone

1. "The First Principle of Practical Reason: A Commentary on the *Summa Theologia*, 1–2, Question 94, Article 2," *Natural Law Forum* 10 (1965): 168–201 (the abridged version of this essay, printed in *Modern Studies in Philosophy: Aquinas: A Collection of Critical Essays*, ed. Anthony Kenny [Garden City, N.Y.: Doubleday, 1969], 340–82, includes significant and unauthorized editing by Kenny and hence should not be used by critics).
2. *Contraception and the Natural Law* (Milwaukee: Bruce, 1964), 46–106.
3. *Abortion: The Myths, the Realities, and the Arguments* (New York: Corpus Books, 1970), chapter 6.
4. *The Way of the Lord Jesus*, Vol. 1, *Christian Moral Principles* (Chicago: Franciscan Herald Press, 1983); chapters 2 through 12 offer the most mature statement of the theory as a whole.
5. "Natural Law and Natural Inclinations," *New Scholasticism* 61 (1987): 307–20.
6. *The Way of the Lord Jesus*, Vol. 2, *Living a Christian Life* (Quincy, Ill.: Franciscan Press, 1993). In this volume, devoted to the common responsibilities of all Christians whether lay or clergy or religious, substantive chapters apply the principles set forth in *Christian Moral Principles* to such issues as the search for moral truth; the requirements of justice, love, and mercy; bioethical or life issues; marriage and sexual morality.
7. "Natural Law, God, Religion, and Human Fulfillment," *American Journal of Jurisprudence* 46 (2002): 3–35.

II. Works by Grisez with Other Authors

1. With Joseph Boyle, *Life and Death with Liberty and Justice: A Contribution to the Euthanasia Debate* (South Bend, Ind.: University of Notre Dame Press, 1979).
2. With John Finnis, "The Basic Principles of Natural Law: A Reply to Ralph McInerny," *American Journal of Jurisprudence* 26 (1981) 21–31; reprinted in *Natural Law*, ed. John Finnis (New York: New York University Press, 1991), 1:341–52.

3. With John Finnis and Joseph Boyle, "Practical Principles, Moral Truth, and Ultimate Ends," *American Journal of Jurisprudence* 32 (1987) 99–151; reprinted with table of contents in *Natural Law*, 1:236–89.

III. Works by John Finnis Alone

1. *Natural Law and Natural Rights* (New York: Oxford University Press, 1980).
2. "Natural Law and the 'Is'-'Ought' Question: An Invitation to Professor Veatch," *Catholic Lawyer* 26 (1981): 266–77; reprinted in *Natural Law*, ed. John Finnis, 1:313–24.
3. *Fundamentals of Ethics* (Washington, D.C.: Georgetown University Press, 1983).
4. "Natural Inclinations and Natural Rights: Deriving 'Ought' from 'Is'" According to Aquinas," in *Lex et Libertas: Freedom and Law According to St. Thomas Aquinas*, Studi Tomistici, Vol. 30, eds. L. J. Elders and K. Hedwig (Vatican City: Libreria Editrice Vaticana, 1987), 43–55.
5. *Moral Absolutes: Tradition, Revision, and Truth* (Washington, D.C.: The Catholic University of America Press, 1991).

IV. Works by Finnis with Others:

1. With Joseph Boyle and Germain Grisez, *Nuclear Deterrence, Morality, and Realism* (New York: Oxford University Press, 1987). Chapter 10 in Part 4 offers a fresh, philosophical presentation of the theory.

In addition to these works, in which the basic theory is set forth, developed, clarified, and defended in the light of criticism, the following work of Finnis is very relevant to the theory and understanding of Aquinas's thought: *Aquinas: Moral, Political, and Legal Theory* (New York: Oxford University Press, 1998).

❊ RESPONSE ❊

NATURAL LAW AND SPECIFIC MORAL NORMS

Mark S. Latkovic

Introduction

William E. May's paper shows us that the Thomistic natural law tradition is very much alive and well. Over the last twenty years or so, especially with the publication of John Finnis's *Natural Law and Natural Rights*,[1] but also due to the writings of May himself and the authors that he treats in his paper, and others left untreated such as Jacques Maritain and Yves Simon, as well as many of the other authors in this volume, natural law thinking has experienced a well-deserved revival.

How does one respond to a paper with which one is in fundamental agreement? I thought it might be helpful to first briefly summarize May's overview of the positions of Pamela Hall, Benedict Ashley, Ralph McInerny, and Germain Grisez, John Finnis, and Joseph Boyle by grouping their respective positions together under the main topics, common to all of them, that May treats: What is the natural law? How do we know the first principles of the natural law? What is the nature of the first principle of practical reasoning: moral or nonmoral? Are the goods/needs of the natural law hierarchically ordered? How does one derive specific moral norms from the first principles of the natural law? I will not, however, take up May's discussion of the various criticisms (including some of his own) of the Grisez school and his responses to them at the end of his paper.

Second, I will focus in depth on the last mentioned of these topics: the derivation of specific moral norms from the first principles of the natural law. I will accomplish this aim by comparing the view of St. Thomas Aqui-

---

1. John Finnis, *Natural Law and Natural Rights* (New York: Oxford University Press, 1980).

nas with both Martin Rhonheimer in *Natural Law and Practical Reason: A Thomist View of Moral Autonomy*[2] and with the views of Hall, Ashley, and McInerny that May has summarized. I will also compare the views of these authors with the position of the Grisez school.

May on the Thought of Hall, Ashley, McInerny, and Grisez et al.

What is the natural law? May notes that for all of these authors, with the exception of Hall, the natural law is primarily a work of reason, that is, it is a rational guide for human action. Thus, they would all agree that natural law in its proper sense is a set of universal propositions of practical reason ordered to action, and not our natural inclinations, as it is for Hall.

How do we know the precepts of the natural law? On this topic, May observes that all of the authors he considered, except for Grisez et al., think that our knowledge of the first principles of the natural law is dependent on natural philosophy or philosophical anthropology. May sums up this view as follows: one first needs to know human nature and its natural inclinations and then, by reflecting on them, come to know the precepts of the natural law, that is, the first principles of the natural law, which include the goods which our inclinations direct us to. Although McInerny's position is somewhat more nuanced, it is still quite different, if I understand him correctly, from the position of Grisez et al., who hold that while the goods of the natural law are surely *ontologically* or *anthropologically* grounded in human nature, they are not *epistemologically* or *gnoseologically* dependent on prior knowledge of human nature. In the end, however, as May shows, McInerny's view is the following: "The 'ought' of [natural law's] practical principles . . . follows from or is derived from the 'is' of theoretical judgments about the way things are" (May, p. 132).

What is the nature of the first principle of practical reasoning: moral or nonmoral? On this issue, we find Hall taking a position that is very close to that of Grisez et al.: the first principle of the natural law ("good is to be done and pursued and its opposite, evil, avoided") is a *practical* norm rather than a *moral* norm. On this contested point of Thomistic exegesis, May argues that Grisez's view, in fact, is closest to that of St. Thomas himself: "the first prin-

---

2. Martin Rhonheimer, *Natural Law and Practical Reason: A Thomist View of Practical Reason*, trans. Gerald Malsbary (New York: Fordham University Press, 1999).

ciples of practical reason (including the very first and primary one) govern the actions of the bad as well as the good. Hence this principle directs us to do and pursue the good in general, not what is morally good" (May, p. 139). This is why, for Grisez et al., one is in need of a *first principle of morality* that will enable one to distinguish alternatives of choice that are morally good from those choices that are morally bad. However, as May notes, both Ashley and McInerny hold that the first principle of the natural law requires us to do *moral* good, with McInerny adding the notion that we are to pursue *in a human way,* that is, according to reason, the goods to which we are naturally inclined.

Are the goods/needs of the natural law hierarchically ordered? For all of the authors that May examines, apart from Grisez et al., the goods/needs of the natural law are arranged in a hierarchy. Moreover, for Hall, Ashley, and McInerny, the hierarchy of the goods corresponds to a hierarchy of general natural law principles. But this position does not have such firm support in the texts of St. Thomas, as has been assumed by these authors, as May is at pains to argue. Additionally, May thinks, the hierarchy-of-goods position can easily slide into a form of dualism that disparages the bodily goods of the person, inclining persons to more readily perform actions such as direct sterilization, which harm a basic good like human sexual capacity.

From the First Principles of the Natural Law to Specific Moral Norms

The issue of how one proceeds from the first or general principles of the natural law down to specific moral norms, that is, what Thomas calls the "proximate conclusions" or "secondary precepts" of the natural law such as the Ten Commandments, does not often receive the attention it merits. However, each of the authors May analyzes does indeed consider the problem.

Contrary to Hall, as May points out, St. Thomas does not say that one needs the virtue of prudence to understand the truth of such "secondary precepts," as she calls them. That is, for St. Thomas, the specific moral norms found in the Ten Commandments, are truths grasped, as he says, "immediately, with little consideration."[3] Prudence *is* necessary, however, to grasp

---

3. *ST* I-II, q. 100, a. 3. English translation from the *Summa theologiae* is by the Fathers of the English Dominican Province (New York: Benziger, 1948).

the truth of "more remote" conclusions from the first principles of the natural law, for example, principles such as the Golden Rule.[4]

For McInerny, at least in May's interpretation, the specific moral norms of the Decalogue are not truths that we *demonstrate* "by appeal to first principles of natural law but are rather so closely related to those first principles that they can be reduced to them and regarded as *per se notae*" (May, p. 137). Prudence it would seem, in this view, has the role here of discerning the truth of *further moral precepts* such as the norm requiring borrowers to return items to their owners.

May, however, believes that the virtue of prudence, although absolutely essential to a good moral life, is inadequate to show the truth of specific moral norms. As he states in his critique of Ashley's (and Kevin O'Rourke's) "prudential personalism," "prudent persons can themselves disagree over ethical issues, and their disagreements can be contradictory . . ." (May, p. 129). Moreover, I would add, even a Jack Kevorkian can think, oddly enough, that he is "loving" his neighbor by *killing* his neighbor in physician-assisted suicide. Thus, there is a great need, especially today in our "culture of death," to show the underlying truth of the specific moral norms found in the Decalogue, that is, of showing why we do not, for example, love our neighbor—and indeed cannot do so—by killing our neighbor.

Though the moral norms of the Decalogue might appear to be self-evident truths to good Christians and Jews, it is obvious that for many of our contemporaries this cannot be assumed. As May expresses it, the question then is this, "which principles best serve as *premises* in light of which the truths of the Decalogue's precepts can be shown" (May, p. 141).

For St. Thomas, as we have seen, one is able to derive specific moral norms without going through a detailed process of moral reasoning, for he maintained that the precepts of the Decalogue follow as immediate and proximate conclusions from the first moral principle to love God and neighbor. Grisez et al., however, think that St. Thomas moved too quickly from natural law's first principles down to specific moral norms. Thus, as Finnis says, St. Thomas thinks that the way from the highest moral principle(s) to specific moral norms "is short, but however short it needs more than one premise, and the needed premises he does not systematically display."[5]

---

4. See *ST* I-II, q. 100, aa. 3 and 11.

5. John Finnis, *Aquinas: Moral, Political, and Legal Theory* (New York: Oxford University Press, 1998), 138.

Now, before going on to discuss the views of Rhonheimer and Grisez et al., let me first ask about the role that prudence will play in all of this for St. Thomas's moral theory. As John Finnis admits in *Aquinas: Moral, Political, and Legal Theory*, according to St. Thomas, "the way down from first and most general principles to specific moral norms is a way which will not be clear to those in whom a habit of vice has supplanted *prudentia*." Indeed, as Finnis continues, prudence "is nothing other than the disposition to guide one's choices and actions by practical reasonableness. So it is informed and directed at every stage by every relevant practical principle and true moral norm." And, as Finnis observes, "in the first instance *prudentia* will be guided by the [specific] norms which identify and exclude wrongful killing, adultery, false witness, and other offences against justice."[6]

Hence, as I hope this discussion has made clear, prudence, although absolutely essential for choosing well, is not sufficient to generate specific moral norms that can direct one's free choices in a morally upright way. Rather, one must appeal to relevant moral principles. Indeed, it is by first choosing consistently in accord with true moral principles that one develops the virtue of prudence (or any other virtue for that matter).

The view of the Swiss priest and philosopher Martin Rhonheimer is, unfortunately, probably less well known to English-speaking audiences. But with the translation of his book *Natur als Grundlage der Moral*[7] into English, more will have access to his valuable understanding of St. Thomas—an understanding sympathetic to the Grisez school, but one that departs from it on a number of key points, as Rhonheimer himself notes.

According to Rhonheimer, Thomas sums up his teaching about the explication of the natural law through the *ratio naturalis* in *ST* I-II, q. 100, a. 11. Here the moral commandments of the Old Covenant are, as Rhonheimer puts it, natural law in a "threefold gradation." In fact, Rhonheimer finds a threefold gradation of natural law precepts in St. Thomas very similar, I believe, to that laid out in the work of William E. May.[8] For Thomas, then, there are "(1) first principles ('to love God and neighbor'); and then

---

6. Ibid., 168.

7. Martin Rhonheimer, *Natur als Grundlage der Moral: Eine Auseinandersetzung mit autonomer und teleologisher Ethik* (Tyrolia: Verlag, 1987). See note 2 above for the English translation.

8. See William E. May, *An Introduction to Moral Theology*, second edition (Huntington, Ind.: Our Sunday Visitor, 2003), 76–80.

(2) precepts (the commandments of the Decalogue) that are proximate and 'more determined' *(magis determinata),* but understandable to all, as conclusions drawn from the very first principles; and (3) the 'more remote' and more difficult precepts, recognizable only by the wise."[9] Rhonheimer too, however, insists that it is the task of prudence and "the moral virtues always attached to prudence—to judge concrete situations rightly for their objective meaning, which is to order human actions to their goal—to the good—according to the order of reason." The act of prudence, he insists, "is nevertheless fundamental and not originally regulated by 'norms.'"[10] While here I am unable to go into the arguments Rhonheimer gives for his position, we can see that it is one very similar to that of Hall and Ashley, already criticized by May.

The view that has the most merit on this question, in my judgment, is that of the Grisez school. For these authors, it is necessary to articulate so-called intermediate principles—what they call "modes of responsibility"—which enable us to show the truth of more specific moral norms, such as those requiring us not to kill the innocent, not to lie, not to steal.[11] That is, these principles, among them the principle of fairness or the Golden Rule and the principle that we are not to repay evil with evil (both of which Thomas clearly articulated) enable us to show why specific moral norms indeed follow as conclusions from the first moral principle or norm. This first principle of morality is formulated by Grisez et al. as follows: "In voluntarily acting for human goods and avoiding what is opposed to them, one ought to choose and otherwise will those and only those possibilities whose willing is compatible with a will toward integral human fulfillment."[12] That is, morality's first principle directs us to choose in such a way that we respect every human good, in every human person.

9. Rhonheimer, *Natural Law and Practical Reason,* 238, note omitted.

10. Ibid., 526.

11. For a listing of the modes of responsibility, see, e.g., Germain Grisez, *The Way of the Lord Jesus,* Vol. 1, *Christian Moral Principles* (Chicago: Franciscan Herald Press, 1983), 225–26.

12. Ibid., 184; John Finnis, Joseph Boyle, Germain Grisez, *Nuclear Deterrence, Morality, and Realism* (New York: Oxford University Press, 1987), 283. This way of formulating the first moral principle is a more technical way of expressing in philosophical language the first moral principle as found in Aquinas ("to love God and neighbor"). This principle, along with the modes of responsibility (i.e., the kinds of principles that comprise the natural law), will be transformed by Christian faith and charity into specifically Christian moral principles and norms. On this matter, see Grisez, *The Way of the Lord Jesus,* 1:599–659.

The modes of responsibility, as described by May in *An Introduction to Moral Theology*, "are normative principles more specific than the first principle of morality, but they are more general than specific moral norms identifying kinds of human choices as morally good or morally bad." Such specific norms, he continues, "are discovered by considering the ways a proposed course of human action relates a person's will to basic human goods and by considering such a proposed human action in light of the first principle of morality and its specifications."[13]

In my view, then, and in agreement with May, the approach of the Grisez school on this question is sounder than those approaches that primarily rely on prudence to show the truth of specific moral norms.

13. May, *An Introduction to Moral Theology*, 79.

6

NATURAL LAW OR AUTONOMOUS PRACTICAL REASON

Problems for the New Natural Law Theory

Steven A. Long

The authors of the "new natural law theory"[1] famously distance natural law—as something putatively merely practical—from speculative knowledge, metaphysics, and theology. While moral truth is ontologically rooted in nature, they argue, it is epistemically independent of any natural truth.

It has been the gravamen of many arguments against their doctrine that this separation has no parallel in the classical account of natural law to be found in the writings of St. Thomas Aquinas. Practical reason derives its principles from the unfolding teleological inclinations of nature. However, these inclinations themselves presuppose *knowledge of their ends,* a knowledge that is speculatively adequated as the basis for practical agency.

Further, the doctrine of natural law is not merely a function of practical

---

1. The chief progenitors of this school of thought are of course Germain Grisez and John Finnis, although several other authors of note endorse aspects of their analyses. Because I am most familiar with the formulations of Finnis, I here emphasize his treatment of these matters, which, however, I do not understand to be significantly opposed to the teaching of Grisez.

reason. Whereas the new natural law theorists clearly think of the natural law as a purely practical affair generating answers to ethical problems, for St. Thomas the natural law is *nothing other* than the creature's rational participation of the governing wisdom of God.[2] Natural law is not merely the *product* of practical reason but the *precondition* for its right exercise—it is the normative theological and metaphysical order that undergirds, makes possible, and flows into our moral logic. Through our practical moral reason we do actively participate in the divine government of our own actions. This ordering is of enormous practical import because acts that are not directed to the due end are not good acts, and to know what the due end is is prior to desire for that end—the very desire to which all right action must be conformed. The directive character of moral precepts regarding the good does indeed presuppose prior knowledge of the good.

While these points are without doubt correct—Thomas *defines* the natural law as *nothing other than a rational participation of the eternal law*, leaving one to meditate that the *definition of a thing* is hardly *accidental thereto*—the intellectual necessity for this position is something that contemporary philosophers need to retrieve. The reason, of course, is that the very reality of the eternal law is (as a philosophic matter) a function of speculative metaphysics, whereas for most contemporary philosophers such a science is unknown territory.

In a previous paper,[3] I addressed the new natural law theory in an effort to show how its characteristic propositions lead to further and further remotion from the teaching of Aquinas. In that work, I pointed out certain teachings of the new natural law theory whose provenance seems largely analytic: in particular, doctrines such as the incommensurability of basic goods, and the nominalist and instrumentalist reduction of the common good. In this paper I want to highlight another tendency of the new natural law theory. This tendency is that which finds expression in Kant's argument for an ethic founded on purely practical reason, in which the law is conceived not as a subjection to divine government, but as promulgated solely by the rational agent itself. Of course, the new natural law theorists are philosophic theists. Yet they argue that God is not only not first in our

2. *ST* I, q. 91, a. 2 ad 1.
3. Steven A. Long, "St. Thomas Aquinas through the Analytic Looking-Glass," *The Thomist* 65 (April 2001): 259–300.

knowledge of the natural law—which any Thomist would affirm—but that God is not essential to natural law as such (a proposition hard to square with the text of St. Thomas, and which I will argue below is speculatively insufficient).[4]

Hence, in this paper, I will attempt two things that not only address the new natural law theory, but which obliquely address the more general re-motion of thinkers from Thomas's method in the context of the modern and postmodern predilection toward ethical *autonomy* in the rationalist sense of the term. The *first* is to highlight the essential importance St. Thomas accords—both formally and materially—to the priority of the speculative to the practical in moral philosophy (the formal element being the necessity for speculative knowledge antecedent to right appetite, and the material element being the essential hierarchy of ends as defined in relation to God). The second point is that a strongly theonomic doctrine of natural law—such as that of St. Thomas Aquinas—requires and implies that the liberty of the rational moral agent is subject to divine causality and therefore to divine providence.[5]

Point A: The Priority of the Speculative

In many respects the priority of speculative knowledge is the most slippery and difficult of all the issues broached by the new natural law theo-

4. Hence John Finnis writes, in his work *Natural Law and Natural Rights* (New York: Oxford University Press, 1980), 49, referring to what he calls "the fact that natural law can be understood, assented to, applied, and reflectively analyzed without adverting to the question of the existence of God. . . ." But, on the contrary, while the natural law may be partially understood with respect to some of its material content, apart from adverting to God, this is not true of all the material content of the natural law; and, as regards the form of the natural law, this cannot be understood without adverting to God since the *form* of the law is, as St. Thomas insists, nothing other than the rational participation of the eternal law. Hence, natural law cannot accurately be formally defined without reference to God.

5. This addresses a historically and doctrinally critical point that I am persuaded is an intra-Catholic root of the turn toward pure practical reason, and that also is related to the antinomianism about the higher law corrected by *Veritatis splendor*. Those interested in seeing this proposition explicated more fully from St. Thomas's texts, defended against the innovations of J. Maritain regarding God and the permission of evil, and thence applied with respect to the theonomic character of St. Thomas's doctrine of natural law, should see Steven A. Long, "Providence, liberté et loi naturelle," *Revue thomiste* 102 (December 2002): 355–406.

rists. Surely, they point out, the datum that there are *per se nota* truths of practical reason suffices to indicate that practical knowledge is not epistemically *derived* from speculative knowledge? The difficulty here reaches the definitional level, since one must understand what it is that makes *an act of reason* to be either speculative or practical. Notice here that we are identifying the speculative or practical with respect to the use of reason itself, rather than speaking of practical or speculative *objects*. For an object is practical when it essentially concerns doing or making, but such an object may be *considered* either practically (for the very *purpose* of doing or making) or *speculatively* (for the purpose simply of understanding the structure of this essentially practical activity). So when is an act of reason speculative, and when is it practical?

Regarding the first practical principles, Finnis writes:

> Nor, of course, can the genuine first practical principles be "speculative" ("theoretical," i.e. non-practical) propositions about what is the case, e.g. about human nature. Some commentators on Aquinas have imagined that they are such propositions, on which a "practical," i.e. directive, character is conferred by the intervention of some act of will. Such a view not only contradicts Aquinas' conception of the first practical principles as "founded on" an absolutely first practical principle whose form—the form which makes every practical principle and proposition *practical*—is neither indicative nor imperative, but gerundive and directive. It also hopelessly contradicts his basic and pervasive understanding of will—that it is response to reasons. Practical intelligence is not slave to the will any more than it is the slave of the passions. . . . In short, the "ought" of first practical principles is not deducible from "is," whether from "is willed by God" or from "has been prescribed by me myself."[6]

In his earlier work too Finnis held that propositions about the "primary goods" are not derived "from any . . . propositions of speculative reason."[7] This is not, however, what St. Thomas has to say about the matter. He does not equate the speculative exclusively with the "theoretical," nor identify some class of propositions in which the primacy of speculative adequation of mind to being is not presupposed in knowledge of the good. He teaches consistently that there are *not* two intellectual powers—one speculative, one

---

6. John Finnis, *Aquinas, Moral, Political, and Legal Theory* (Oxford, U.K.: Oxford University Press, 1998), 89–90.

7. Finnis, *Natural Law and Natural Rights*, 46.

practical—and that the difference between the speculative and practical intellect is accidental and hence does not alter the adequation to reality that attends knowledge as such. Thus St. Thomas in the following two quotations from the same article of the *Summa theologiae* articulates, with precision, both the nature of, and the distinction between, the speculative and the practical:

> Now, to a thing apprehended by the intellect, it is accidental whether it be directed to operation or not, and according to this the speculative and practical intellects differ. For it is the speculative intellect which directs what it apprehends, not to operation, but solely to the consideration of truth; while the practical intellect is that which directs what it apprehends to operation.[8]

> The object of the practical intellect is good directed to operation, and under the aspect of truth. For the practical intellect knows truth, just as the speculative, but it directs the known truth to operation.[9]

While the speculative intellect is ordered simply to the consideration of truth, *practical* knowledge adds a *further ordination toward operation*. Inasmuch as the practical intellect knows truth "just as the speculative" but is distinct from the speculative only in "directing the known truth to operation," it would appear that the notion of a truth with no speculative content whatsoever is alien to the thought of Aquinas: a contradiction in terms.[10] More-

---

8. *ST* I, q. 79, a. 11: "Accidit autem alicui apprehenso per intellectum, quod ordinetur ad opus, vel non ordinetur. Secundum hoc autem differunt intellectus speculativus et practicus. Nam intellectus speculativus est, qui quod apprehendit, non ordinat ad opus, sed ad solam veritatis considerationem: practicus vero intellectus dicitur, qui hoc quod apprehendit, ordinat ad opus." I have taken the English predominately from the translation of the *Summa theologiae* by the Fathers of the English Dominican Province (New York: Benziger, 1948).

9. *ST* I, q. 79, a. 11 ad 2: "ita obiectum intellectus practici est bonum ordinabile ad opus, sub ratione veri. Intellectus enim practicus veritatem cognoscit sicut speculativus; sed veritatem cognitam ordinat ad opus."

10. One notes on this score—ensconced in a treatment of art—Thomas's cognate observation in *De veritate* q. 2, a. 8: "Sed sciendum, quod artifex de operabili habet duplicem cognitionem: scilicet speculativam et practicam. Speculativam quidem, sive theoricam cognitionem habet, cum rationes operis cognoscit sine hoc quod ad operandum per intentionem applicet; sed tunc proprie habet practicam cognitionem quando extendit per intentionem rationes operis ad operationis finem; et secundum hoc medicina dividitur in theoricam et practicam, ut Avicenna dicit. Ex quo patet quod cognitio artificis practica sequitur cognitionem eius speculativam, cum practica efficiatur per extensionem speculativae ad opus. Remoto autem

over, it is exclusively the rational intent to direct the known truth to operation that causes the accident (vis-à-vis *truth* as such) of some knowledge being practical.

The new natural law theorists confuse the truth that certain propositions by their nature bear essentially upon action—and hence are practical—with the distinct character of the knowing that is *presupposed by* such propositions *in order that they may be able to bear upon action*.[11] That a certain proposition refers essentially to operation simply concerns the content of the proposition: but that it be able to refer essentially to operation depends on prior *adequatio* regarding the nature of the end.

The speculative considered precisively and formally is simply the knowing of an object apart from any accident of desire it may spark. The known object may accidentally (from the vantage of speculation) spark desire, and in doing so cause a new and rationally distinct practical engagement with the object. In this practical engagement the object is sought no longer simply for the sake of knowing it but as the terminus of desire and operation. Nonetheless at root this practical knowing is speculatively adequated.

The precisive sense of the speculative is most formal because a thing is not properly defined by accidental relations, and it is an accident vis-à-vis

---

posteriori remanet prius." "But the knowledge that an artist has about something that can be made is of two kinds: speculative and practical. He has speculative or theoretical knowledge when he knows the intimate nature of a work but does not have the intention of applying the principles to the production of the work. His knowledge is practical, properly speaking, when by his intention he ordains the principles of the work to operation as an end. In this way, as Avicenna says, medicine is divided into theoretical and practical. *It is clear that the practical knowledge of an artist follows his speculative knowledge, since it is made practical by applying the speculative to a work. But when the practical is absent, the speculative remains*" (emphasis added). These remarks once more indicate that for St. Thomas Aquinas practical knowledge always presupposes this underlying speculative element: precisely the point at issue in the discussions with the theorists of the new natural law theory.

11. Lawrence Dewan, "St. Thomas, Our Natural Lights, and the Moral Order," *Angelicum* 67 (1990): 283–307. As he puts it: "Can there be any doubt that for St. Thomas the knowledge of the one ('the good') derives from the knowledge of the other ('a being')? St. Thomas teaches, in *ST* 1–2.9.1, that the practical intellect has its priority with respect to the will, as mover of the will, precisely inasmuch as its (the intellect's) vision of 'the good' flows from its vision of 'a being' and 'the true'. The practical intellect views goodness under the aspect of being and truth, sees *what* goodness *is*. If goodness were not being viewed under the aspect of being, it would not be being 'understood' at all."

any speculative object that it should spark desire. But this is only accidental vis-à-vis the speculative object as such, and not vis-à-vis human nature. It is not an accident that the subject is appetitive, nor that its inclinations are hierarchically ordered. And hence, rectitude with respect to the means must conform to right appetite of the end, and this right appetite of the end *presupposes prior knowledge of the end.* And so Thomas writes, in q. 19 of the *prima secundae* of the *Summa theologiae,* that:

> Now in regard to the means, the rectitude of the reason depends on its conformity with the desire of a due end: nevertheless the very desire of the due end presupposes on the part of reason a right apprehension of the end.[12]

And, as St. Thomas also writes:

> Now the first formal principle is universal "being" and "truth," which is the object of the intellect. And therefore by this kind of motion the intellect moves the will, as presenting its object to it.[13]

In other words, rationally to desire a good is already to have been speculatively adequated to its truth.

Thus the practical employment of the intelligence requires a prior speculative apprehension of the object. *This priority of speculative adequatio governs intellectual knowledge as such: speculative adequation is not something that can be temporarily left behind, only to be reconnected to later.*[14] Moral good is a species

---

12. *ST* I-II, q. 19, a. 3 ad 2. Leonine *ST*: "In his autem quae sunt ad finem, rectitudo rationis consistit in conformitate ad appetitum finis debiti. Sed tamen et ipse appetitus finis debiti praesupponit rectam apprehensionem de fine, quae est per rationem."

13. *ST* I-II, q. 9, a. 1: "Primum autem principium formale est ens et verum universale, quod est obiectum intellectus. Et ideo isto modo motionis intellectus movet voluntatem, sicut praesentans ei obiectum suum."

14. This is how the arguments adduced by Robert P. George in his essay "Natural Law and Human Nature," in *Natural Law Theory: Contemporary Essays,* ed. Robert George (Oxford, U.K.: Clarendon Press, 1992), 31–41, strike the Thomistic ear. He argues strenuously that one may epistemically prescind from what is nonetheless the given ontological ordering of nature. Of course, such abstraction is possible, but there is no particular reason to view the result of such abstraction as yielding "the natural" in any definitive sense—i.e., the sense required if one is to invoke the naturalistic fallacy against adversion to the teleological structure of the good. One cannot derive in the conclusion what is not in the premises, but abstracting from what is proper to the natural and then arguing that the abstracted residue should be treated as the normative sense of "nature" is a *petitio principii.* Nor—to refer to the issue under discussion in the text above—is there any reason to suppose that *per se nota*

of transcendental good, and transcendental good is merely being as appetible. *One cannot know it as appetible without knowing it.* This is a foundational element of St. Thomas's teaching. The basic goods schema of the new natural law theory in effect promulgates a category of truth with no speculative content, while at least for St. Thomas Aquinas the apprehension of speculative content—even by the practical intellect—is required by the very nature of knowledge itself. As Thomas argues in the *Summa contra gentiles,* the first active principle in moral actions is the thing apprehended, followed by the apprehensive power, the will, and the motive force carrying out the command of reason.[15] Further, command, or *imperium,* is chiefly an act of the intellect, not of the will.[16]

Suppose that one's knowledge bears upon doing or making, that is, suppose that it bears upon an *object* essentially practical. Even in this case, the *act of reason by which* one regards this practical object *may do so in one of two ways:* (1) it may order this knowledge of a practical object *to action,* in which case not only the object of the knowledge *but the act of knowledge itself* will be practical; or (2) it may merely seek to know the nature of this practical object for its own sake, in which case while the object is practical the ordering of the knowledge thereof is speculative. Hence ethics may be studied—as a practical object—both with a view to guiding particular conduct *hic et nunc,* or with a view to contemplative wisdom regarding the basic structure of the human good.

Or, consider an essentially speculative object: mathematical science. The object of mathematical science is, as such, speculative. Yet one might further order speculative mathematical knowledge to action as part of a practical engagement, for example, in order to facilitate running calculations necessary for fixing a piece of high-tech equipment on whose proper functioning lives depend. Or one might study this essentially speculative object simply for its own sake without ordering it to further doing or making. Surely mathematics is objectively a speculative discipline. But the act of reason engaging in it, while necessarily speculative, may either be further ordered to action or ordered simply to the contemplation of truth.

---

practical knowledge occurs without precisely that speculative knowledge of the end that is naturally prior to appetite.

15. *SCG* III, c.10.

16. *ST* I-II, q. 17, a. 1: "Command is an act of the reason presupposing, however, an act of the will" (Dicendum quod imperare est actus rationis, praesupposito tamen actu voluntatis).

Does the accidentality of the practical/speculative distinction render our intellect a "slave to the will"? That we can view the very same practical objects *contemplatively* is a sign *not* of slavery to the will, but of the transcendence of the intellect—and of truth. Why should desire to know the nature of the good contemplatively not signify liberty rather than "slavery"—a manifestation of the dignity of practical rationality as rooted in the order of truth, truth that may then fecundate the entire moral life?

But the matter is not at rest. For it is not only that we may know *practical* objects in a speculative manner. As I said above, *the chief point* is rather that at the font of practical knowing necessarily lies the adequation of the intellect to the real that is presupposed by truth as such and hence also by practical knowing. This is a prior speculative knowledge of the end that (owing to our appetitive and volitional natures) ignites our desire and the ensuing essentially practical deliberations. *Whereas purely speculative knowledge of practical objects is possible, practical reason is necessarily indebted to speculative reason in the adequation of mind to the good that is necessary if there is to be right appetite of the end.*

Without knowledge of the end, and indeed of the ordering of ends, practical reason cannot even "get started"—it has no "startup capital." No rational action occurs save in the light of the *finis ultimus,* and the natural ordering of sublunary ends to the *finis ultimus* is precisely what renders these to be ends—it is repugnant to nature that there be diverse final ends. As St. Thomas puts it, "It is impossible for one man's will to be directed at the same time to diverse things, as last ends."[17] The same thing that makes goods to be goods, makes them to be in an order vis-à-vis the final end.[18]

---

17. *ST* I-II, q. 1, a. 6.

18. Even from the vantage point of the hypothesis of pure nature (e.g., articulated by St. Thomas Aquinas in *Quod.* I, q. 4, a. 3), the intensive perfection of reason in the most comprehensive and profound contemplation of the order of the whole universe in relation to its transcendent principle—God—is the chief element in human felicity, together with that ethical rectitude that is nothing other than the extensive perfection of reason. Since everything has as its end in some way to be like God, there can be no question of denying that the most profound natural knowledge of God—which requires and implies the most profound and comprehensive knowledge of the universe—is naturally speaking the *finis ultimus*. Hence the *superadditum* of grace perfects the natural dynamism of man toward the end within a higher and essentially supernatural order—in a beatifically direct, rather than indirect, knowledge and love of God. But were there nothing to stand in the place of the final end naturally

Hence, the fundamental ethical question is always: what is the nature of the good? And this question is tantamount to asking: what is the natural order of ends? Growth in wisdom regarding the nature and ordering of ends is possible, and this growth in wisdom has *practical* implications (clearly one may wrongly construe power, or wealth, or sexual gratification to be the final end, whereas this is not true). Although the natural evidence at the font of wisdom is accessible to all, insight into the natural order of ends—insight *into* this font of natural evidence—is not automatic. Hence it is possible for persons even to fail to refer their acts to God, or to fail to be aware that wisdom, or fidelity in friendship, are nobler ends that surpass health or play.

The essential hierarchy of ends prior to choice—a teaching of St. Thomas[19] contrary to the teaching of the new natural law theory that basic goods are incommensurable (i.e., not normatively ordered prior to choice)—is the material element vouchsafed us through the formal priority of the speculative in moral philosophy. Thus it is wholly intelligible that having disseevered moral philosophy from the truth of the order of ends the new natural law theorists should be constrained to hypothesize that such an order must be extraneous to ethics. Yet this is not so. Although knowledge of the order of ends cannot replace the role of authentic prudence, without the order of ends serving as the principal element in our knowledge right appetite is impossible, and ethical discrimination would become merely an ad hoc weaving together of wholly incomparable elements. But if goods putatively "basic" are wholly incomparable, then why should we denominate them as *goods*? It seems that they do indeed fall under a common *ratio*,

---

speaking, then there would be either an infinite regress of ends, or—which comes to the same thing in terms of action—no end at all. For an infinite regress of ends never attains a final end, and so offers no sufficient reason for action; and no end at all provides the same scenario. One respect in which sympathy is owed the new natural law theorists is in their suspicion of *la nouvelle theologie* and its denial of the hypothesis of pure nature. But that the felicity proportionate to pure nature is less determinate than the supernatural *finis ultimus* does not mean that—had man been created in a state of pure nature—there would have been no final end. For man is ordered to God as a final end either naturally (as transcendent principle of the whole universe contemplated through and in relation to the universe) or supernaturally (intellectually beheld in direct beatific vision).

19. One notes that in *ST* I-II, q. 94, a. 2 Thomas speaks of the *order* of ends, and not of a mere "list," and that this order ascends from what man shares with all being, to what man shares with all animals, to the properly rational goods such as knowing the truth about God. This is, indeed, a normative hierarchy.

and that they do not share equally in this *ratio,* that is, they are not all equally distant from the final end, but some are closer and others more remote. For example, life is not *merely instrumental,* we desire it in itself; but we do not desire it only for itself, but precisely as further ordered to essentially higher ends such as friendship and wisdom.

In any case, the *per se nota* truths of practical reason *presuppose* precisely this prior speculative knowledge, a knowledge that—given our appetitive nature—brings forth *inclinatio*. The right ordering of inclinations follows the ordering of ends. *Inclinatio* cannot be incited in a vacuum—it is not objectless—nor is the *end* that incites rational desire initially known simply through our desire, for this desire cannot exist without prior inciting knowledge. This prior knowledge is of its nature speculative—it is accidental *to such knowledge* that we be or act as appetitive agents, although it is not accidental to us that we are such appetitive agents, and so *inclinatio* is sparked.

Articulating a central theme of the new natural law theory, Finnis argues:

> So the epistemic source of the first practical principles is not human nature or a prior, theoretical understanding of human nature (though a theoretical knowledge of the efficacy, as means, of certain choosable conduct is relevant to our knowledge of the first practical principles). Rather, the epistemic relationship is the reverse: any deep understanding of human nature, i.e. of the capacities which will be fulfilled by action which participates in and realizes those goods, those *perfections,* is an understanding which has amongst its sources our primary, undemonstrated but genuine practical knowledge of those goods and purposes.[20]

But, on the contrary, the epistemic source of the first practical principles will be the actual ordering of human nature as known by the intellect, a knowledge that is speculatively adequated as a root condition for its practical reference. As to whether the speculative or the practical is prior, consider what St. Thomas has to say about the true (which is, *simpliciter,* the formal object of knowledge) and the good (which is that which one seeks through directing knowledge to operation) in the following two passages:

> I answer that, although the good and the true are convertible with being, as to suppositum, yet they differ logically. And in this manner the true, speaking ab-

---

20. Finnis, *Aquinas,* 91.

solutely, is prior to good, as appears from two reasons. First, because the true is more closely related to being than is good. For the true regards being itself simply and immediately; while the nature of good follows being in so far as being is in some way perfect; for thus it is desirable. Secondly, it is evident from the fact that knowledge naturally precedes appetite. Hence, since the true regards knowledge, but the good regards the appetite, the true must be prior in idea to the good.[21]

A thing is prior logically in so far as it is prior to the intellect. Now the intellect apprehends primarily being itself; secondly, it apprehends that it understands being; and thirdly, it apprehends that it desires being. Hence the idea of being is first, that of truth second, and the idea of good third, though good is in things.[22]

In short, being and truth are prior to good, and the practical operation of the intellect presupposes and builds upon the speculative. Practical intellect apprehends the true of the good, ordered to operation, and adds to that speculative adequation of mind to object that defines knowledge as such this accidental ordering to operation and concern for the operable for the sake of operation.

The speculative horizon of all ethical choice together with the order of ends implicit in any and every ethical decision provides the fragrance of genuine grandeur in moral philosophy, enabling it to rise to the contemplation of the nature of the good life. It is precisely this genuinely philosophic character that is lost to moral thought by its absorption in a *praxis* separated from truth. But contemplating the true of the good is not servile, and authentic freedom does not reside in liberty from the need to conform one's mind to the order of being. This brings us to the verge of another—and arguably crucial—failure not alone of contemporary moral theory, but within the historic unfolding of Catholic understanding with respect to the nature and limits of moral agency.

This is the error of supposing that moral responsibility requires a liberty of indifference with respect to divine causality. And lest it be supposed that, as a merely speculative issue, this question is devoid of practical implications, to the contrary, it is the source of that antinomian disposition with

---

21. *ST* I, q. 16, a. 4.

22. ST I, q. 16, a. 4 ad 2: "Dicendum quod secundum hoc est aliquid prius ratione, quod prius cadit in intellectu. Intellectus autem per prius apprehendit ipsum ens; et secundario apprehendit se intelligere ens; et tertio apprehendit se appetere ens. Unde primo est ratio entis, secundo ratio veri, tertio ratio boni, licet bonum sit in rebus."

respect to the normativity of the natural law that constitutes the chief and outstanding characteristic of moral reflection in the twentieth and early twenty-first centuries. Indeed, it is a remote reflection of this error that lies at the base of the new natural law theorists's reluctance to speak of the natural law[23]: for the natural law implies that the human agent is naturally subject to the author and promulgator of the law. But if our freedom is indeed absolute with respect to divine causality as such, then in what sense can the rational creature be *naturally subject* to divine governance?[24] It is to this question and its moral implications that I now turn, aware that in doing so the limits of the new natural law theory are surpassed in the direction of showing the essentially speculative character of the doctrine of the natural law.[25]

---

23. See, e.g., Finnis who, writes that "'[n]atural law' . . . is only analogically law in relation to my present focal use of the term: that is why the term has been avoided in this chapter on Law" (*Natural Law and Natural Rights*, 280). When it comes to the *type* of the analogy involved, note also his seeming approbation of the thesis of Mortimer Adler that natural law is law only by an extrinsic analogy of attribution, because, in other words, it contributes moral elements and reference to the processes and substance of positive law (*Natural Law and Natural Rights*, 294), although he also states that this account is "not in every respect beyond cavil." Still, since in analogy of extrinsic attribution only one of the beings compared intrinsically possesses the perfection analogically shared, it follows from the Adlerian reading that in the strict sense there is no natural law. This is not only "not in every respect beyond cavil," but it is inconsistent with any genuine doctrine of natural law—for the eternal law whose rational participation is the natural law is more truly law than is any ordinance of mere positive law.

24. This is truly an intra-Catholic source for philosophic conclusions bearing an amazing symmetry with the moral conclusions drawn by Kant, for whom the prime *autonomy* of the moral agent is an absolute prerequisite of moral worthiness.

25. Of course, the argument is not that to be moral requires one consciously to advert to the truth that natural law is nothing but a rational participation in the eternal law, but rather (1) that the normativity of the natural law resides in the eternal law, and (2) that any adequate understanding of the moral life requires reference to God both materially (there are natural duties to God, such as the duty to worship God simply as a matter of justice) and formally (natural law is nothing other than a rational participation of the eternal law; and, indeed, the passive participation of the eternal law manifests the primacy of God in the promulgation of the natural law). Natural law as law, if "law" is not to be a metaphor, requires a promulgator. Indeed, properly speaking law is the express articulation of one mind directed to another mind for the sake of its government—which clearly requires that an authentically natural law reflect and participate the mind of the Author of creation. On these points, see Russell Hittinger's excellent work *The First Grace: Rediscovering the Natural Law in a Post-Christian World*

Point B: Our Passive Participation in the Natural Law as the Necessary Condition of Our Preceptive Participation

Speculative and practical considerations nowhere more powerfully converge than in the teaching of St. Thomas that acts of rational will are both free and caused by God. Thomas's account is bound to be misunderstood as long as one treats God simply as a terrestrial cause. Hence there is no *tertium quid* which of its own created nature has the power to determine the human will, but only the transcendent principal causality of God.

The importance of this teaching that human freedom is subject to divine causality is decisive. Only this proposition places the human will natu-

---

(Wilmington, Del.: ISI Books, 2003). This collection of essays provides exemplary analysis and instruction. See especially the first two essays of Section 1, "Natural Law and Catholic Moral Theology," and the essay "Natural Law as 'Law'" which is even more formally to our point here. Of course, I do not suppose that the full case for the theistic character of the doctrine of natural law is contained in the present essay—for this case seems to presuppose the proofs for the existence of God and (arguably) the metaphysics undergirding these. Rather, here I presuppose the proofs and the doctrine of the eternal law that follows—both of which I believe are eminently defensible—and focus chiefly upon what is arguably the neuralgic point at the heart of resistance to theistic natural law theory both within and without the Catholic tradition. I also wish to note here—an exiguous recognition for so protean and insightful a philosopher—that this approach does not deny the efficacy of natural law accounts such as those offered by Henry Veatch (e.g., Henry Veatch, *For an Ontology of Morals: A Critique of Contemporary Ethical Theory* [Evanston, Ill.: Northwestern University Press, 1971]). Aquinas himself makes an argument for the reality of God *predicated on the natural teleological order*, the famed fifth way of the *Summa theologiae*. While I consider the teleological, natural kind reasoning exemplified by the work of Veatch to be excellent and necessary for a full account of natural law, finally I believe that both the normativity and the being of natural law require adversion to eternal law. But arguing this through sufficiently is the task for another, and different, essay. The present essay is focused upon that crucial point that moves and has moved many minds to the rejection of natural law—rejection even of natural law construed on a footing that is not expressly theistic. For the adverse critics see ahead, and know that unified teleology cannot help but imply God as First Efficient and Final Cause, as well as an order that must encompass human freedom. Hence the modern and postmodern drive to construe human freedom as a liberty of indifference to divine causality comes to distort the doctrine of natural law, cutting it adrift from the eternal law and Providence, and transforming liberty into a naturally autonomous jurisdiction immune from Higher Law. And, at least implicitly, this is a worm turning well inside even many materially Catholic reflections on this subject. Arguably the primordial fear of compromising a chimerical autonomy stands at the root of the modern and postmodern revolt against the very idea of natural law.

rally within the divine causality and government, such that the human creature rationally participates, and is naturally subject to, the eternal law. And it is this participation that defines the natural law: it is not an accident, nor a mere speculative supervention upon something that is, after all, an affair originally and naturally devoid of reference to God and eternal law.

The point must be narrowed and sharpened: one grants that natural law is, as it were, chiefly a cognitive affair in the sense that the precepts of the natural law are directive of the intelligence and only so reach the will. Yet, for the natural law to direct the human creature, this creature must be subject to direction. But if the will of the creature is such as to move itself from potency to act, then it is independent in being, and not subject to direction from without—just as God, who is independent in being, is not subject to direction from without. Or, to put the matter differently: according to St. Thomas Aquinas, the volition of the end is not among the things of which man is master. Why? Because the end is *natural*. If the end is not naturally willed but rather *chosen*, then *in terms of what could it be chosen?* The end would become wholly arbitrary and hence every act would be as choiceworthy as every other.

Hence, clearly the will is moved to its end *naturally*. But it might be thought that outside of this natural motion of the will to its end—which clearly it receives from God—the human will moves itself to act, applying this natural motion by itself in any particular choice, and so moving from potency to act wholly on its own. It was, after all, the famous formulation of Molina in the *Concordia* that the will is free only when, all requirements being retained, the will could indeed act otherwise.[26] But this proposition of Molina's—which is true of all terrestrial causes—is impossible with respect to the hypothetical but immutable divine willing of created effects. For what changes with this hypothetical but immutable divine willing—owing to the divine simplicity—*is not God,* but rather *only the creature itself.* The creature is really related to, and dependent upon, God, but not vice versa. Hence the only difference between God efficaciously willing a created effect, and God *not* efficaciously willing some created effect, is that the efficaciously willed effect actually *is*. Thus one cannot retain the requirement that God cause the creature freely to act while the creature is not caused freely to act, *because this is a contradiction in terms.*

Molina's formulation presuppposes that because the will is not causally

---

26. Cf. Molina's *Concordia,* q. 14, a. 13, disp. II.

determined by terrestrial causes—with respect to which it is objectively free—that therefore it is not causally determined in its free act by God. This error traces to an erroneous definition of "freedom" itself. For no created being, howsoever noble, can move itself from potency to act.[27] Every creature is such that it depends upon God in order to act. And, if this dependence does not obtain, then quite literally there is a creature whose *being* and whose *action* lie outside the scope of the eternal law. A thing can only *act* as it *is*: *operatio sequitur esse, agere sequitur esse,* the maxims converge on the same point. The actuality of the creature is limited by potency. Were the creature absolutely self-activating it would be a being *a se*, not a creature.

The consideration above leads to a further point, namely, that God's providence extends only so far as God's power (a power that, flowing from the infinitude of *ipsum esse subsistens per se*, extends to all that may be willed without self-contradiction). Remove the application of the creature's volitional act from the divine power, and one forthwith removes the application of the creature's volitional act from the divine providential governance. Of course, this *application* is not only a matter of the will's *rational specification* but of its *exercise*. If the creature's application of the natural motion of the will to act *is ineluctably rationally specified,* but this application of the natural motion is not *in its exercise* subject to divine causality, then the action of the creature lies outside the providential governance, and so lies outside the scope of the eternal law. But, to the contrary, no creature can apply itself to act without first having been moved by God. If this were possible, the inference would be that God is not the first cause of every being and good and truth, but rather only one "precondition." Whereas, to the contrary,

---

27. One recollects *ST* I-II, q. 109, a. 1: "Manifestum est autem quod sicut motus omnes corporales reducuntur in motum caelestis corporis sicut in primum movens corporale; ita omnes motus tam corporales quam spirituales reducuntur in primum movens simpliciter, quod est Deus. Et ideo quantumcumque natura aliqua corporalis vel spiritualis ponatur perfecta, non potest in suum actum procedere nisi moveatur a Deo. Quae quidem motio est secundum suae providentiae rationem; non secundum necessitatem naturae, sicut motio corporis caelestis. Non solum autem a Deo est omnis motio sicut a primo movente, sed etiam ab ipso est omnis formalis perfectio sicut a primo actu. Sic igitur actio intellectus et cuiuscumque entis creati dependet a Deo inquantum ad duo: uno modo, inquantum ab ipso habet perfectionem sine formam per quam agit; alio modo, inquantum ab ipso movetur ad agendum." Of course, one must be clear that Molina did not intend to deny that freedom is subject to divine providence, howsoever necessarily this implication flows from his account. But this is, indeed, the effect of denying that the positive perfection of our acts of free choice are caused by God.

God actually brings it about that this act performed by me is performed by me, by moving me from potency to act with respect to the very act of my own free self-determination.

Hence if the rational will is held to enjoy a liberty of indifference with respect to the divine causality, it is implicitly construed as a being *a se,* and so will naturally appropriates the sublunary world of natural ethics to itself as though it were its own kingdom. It is difficult to understand how even revelation could make a difference to this implication: why should a being *a se* either stand in need of—or be subject to a desire for—divine revelation, when it itself is putatively absolutely independent? But, if the manifest facts of the human condition conflict too much with the project of treating the finite rational creature as a god, then deflecting these perceptions to revealed religion and putatively keeping moral philosophy free of them is a strategy well known to history: rationalist philosophy compounded with fideist error.

Thus it is not alone the natural desire of the end that is within the divine governance, but the whole motion of the human creature toward its end. And this motion includes our free self-determination with respect to particular actions. Why should we call an act of choice subject to divine causality "free"? We call it free because the formal object of the rational will is the universal good, good in general. But no finite good is such as to constitute in its own right the subsistent universal good. Every finite good is known, precisely as being finite or limited, as being in some respect *not good*. Even when something constitutes our authentic good here and now, it is a limited good and therefore may be conceived as in that respect *not good*. My obligation to attend Mass is clearly on some Sunday my authentic good, but this does not prevent me from judging that I am too tired, or the homily too vexing, or other goods more attractive, even though in fact these judgments if acted upon will prove harmful to me. Hence the will enjoys a sovereign liberty of indifference with regard to such goods. Even at the moment of choosing to act for the sake of such a good, the rational agent is free and retains sovereign indifference with respect to it. Not even God can make the finite good as such to be in itself compelling, for the intellect presents this good to the will as finite and so as in some way potentially not-good. Thus no finite good can compel the will: with respect to the contingent objects of the human will, the will is objectively free.[28]

28. Cf. *ST* I, q. 82, a. 2 ad 2; or *Quaestiones Quodlibetales,* Quodlibet 6, q. 2, a. 2.

Yet, since the will must be activated in order to choose any good, and since it cannot activate itself absolutely speaking, it must receive its activation from God. In this it is no different than any other creature: for as Thomas makes very clear, no creature, howsoever noble, can even so much as proceed to its act unless it first be moved by God.[29] This *motio* from God is not merely the natural motion of the will, for the natural motion of the will must be applied for any particular willing to occur—the human will is not always and everywhere in act. That is to say, at times we potentially will something, and then consequently we actually come to will it. And it is this transition from potency to act that no creature can achieve apart from prior divine motion.

The motion imparted by God to the rational creature is the very motion whereby the creature freely determines itself. *Hence the creature is not free with respect to this motion, because this motion constitutes and defines the actual exercise of freedom.* I cannot at one and the same time be moved freely to act and not be moved freely to act. It is impossible insofar as I am doing X that simultaneously I am not doing X, howsoever much it is true that there is nothing about X as such that compels my will. This is of course the foundation for the famous distinction introduced by St. Thomas Aquinas between the divided and the composite senses of freedom. Just as Socrates cannot in the *composite sense* sit and stand simultaneously, so that in this sense we deny that Socrates has the power to stand whilst he sits, so the free rational agent cannot simultaneously and in the same respect *be* moved freely to act and *not be* moved freely to act: so that in this composite sense we deny that the agent has the power to act differently. Yet, we do say that Socrates whilst sitting has the *power* to stand *in the divided sense,* that is, in *the sense* of meaning that for him to sit here and now does not keep him from having a *power* susceptible of diverse actuation whereby he may stand *later*. And so likewise we say that the free rational agent is by nature not compelled by any finite good, so that this agent has the *objective power to do otherwise* than God is moving it to do now—that is, nothing about its present object is such as to necessitate the will, and the will can indeed at another time choose differently than it is now choosing.

But, someone might argue, *to the contrary,* that even an animal can act dif-

---

29. Again, see *ST* I-II, q. 109, a. 1. For St. Thomas, "Quod movetur ab alio movetur" is an evident principle.

ferently than it is now doing, and this does not make the animal to be free. So, even less can this be a satisfactory account of human freedom. I respond that the animal can indeed act differently, but not in the *pertinent respect*. For the respect in which the rational creature is free lies in its rational liberty of indifference to any finite good whatsoever. Hence, that it be willing one finite good here and now does not alter the fact that nothing about the good so willed constrains the rational agent to will it, and that the rational agent may will otherwise at another time. By contrast, the mere animal has operative powers prefixed to a narrow range of objects to which it instinctually moves, and it cannot do other than be moved within this range of objects.[30] And although this instinctual movement may be such that it comprises a degree of spontaneity, the mere animal is indeed constrained by its instinctual ordination in a fashion that the rational agent is not.

Whereas no finite good may constrain or compel the rational will, the animal is ordered instinctually and cannot abstract from this ordering to act contrary to it, as is clear in many distinct ways. For the rational agent, on the contrary, the respect in which it may act otherwise is simple and absolute, not limited and instinctually conditioned: the rational will is not compelled by any finite good, each of which is presented to the will by the intellect as limited and hence in some respect not-good. Physiological harm may impede the use of reason, because reason extrinsically depends upon an object abstracted from the senses, and without adequate sensory contact such abstraction becomes impossible. Emotional and physical dependencies may likewise impede or distort an adequate rational deliberation. But insofar as rational deliberation occurs, no finite good may of its own nature compel the rational will.

Hence, objectively speaking, the rational will is not determined or compelled by finite goods. But this does not mean that the will can freely act and freely not act at the same time and in the same respect; nor does it

---

30. Cf. *ST* I, q. 22, a. 2 ad 4: "Dicendum quod in hoc quod dicitur Deum hominem sibi reliquisse, non excluditur homo a divina providentia; sed ostenditur quod non praefigitur ei virtus operativa determinata ad unum, sicut rebus naturalibus; quae aguntur tantum, quasi ab altero directae in finem, non autem seipsa agunt, quasi se dirigentia in finem, ut creaturae rationales per liberum arbitrium, quo consiliantur et eligunt. Unde signanter dicit: 'In manu consilii sui.' Sed quia ipse actus liberi arbitrii reducitur in Deum sicut in causam, necesse est ut ea quae ex libero arbitrio fiunt, divinae providentiae subdantur; providentia enim hominis continetur sub providentia Dei, sicut causa particularis sub causa universali."

mean that the will is a self-activating being that can move itself from potency to act altogether apart from prior divine activation. It is not a being *a se* and hence it cannot act apart from the Prime Efficient Causality of God. All creation is divinely ordered in wisdom and measure, and this includes the very positive substance of our own free volition, which like existence itself is most our own and yet is most a gift. The entire universe of causation presupposes divine activation, and this activation is not terrestrial but the precondition for each and every terrestrial causality.

Clearly, this does not deny the objective freedom of the human will. But it does deny that either the human will or any other creature can move itself from potency to act, and it does deny that the rational creature is the first cause of that surplus of perfection constituted by its own free self-determination. The very motion imparted by God is the motion whereby the will determines itself freely. That the motion of the will is contingent does not mean that the omnipotence of God does not extend to it, nor that if God wills its act that the certainty of this free act is doubtful. Denial of this proposition that the rational will must first be moved by God in order to act will leave us with a self-actualizing being who must wholly escape the divine providence. But it is not aimlessly that Thomas points out, in *ST* I-II, q. 91, a. 2, that "since all things subject to divine providence are ruled and measured by the eternal law, as was stated above; it is evident that all things partake somewhat of the eternal law, in so far as, namely, from its being imprinted on them, they derive their respective inclinations to their proper acts and ends." If the human will is not subject to divine providence, then it is not ruled and measured by the eternal law. But as St. Thomas himself notes, Providence extends so far as power[31]: the will cannot be subject to divine providence if it lies outside the divine causality. Hence, if we affirm a theonomic conception of natural law, we need also to affirm that the human will is autonomous neither in being nor in action, but is moved to its act from without, yet in such a manner that this motion is its own motion: which is to say that the very motion that is received by the will is that whereby it moves itself in free self-determination.

One may profitably consider the matter from the opposite side: if we maintain that the will possesses a liberty of indifference with respect to God, then this not only denies the divine omnipotence and treats God as a

---

31. See *ST* I, q. 22, a. 2.

merely terrestrial cause, but it renders natural law nothing other than the rules of thumb generated by a practical reason promulgating the law to itself. For on such a hypothesis the human agent does not receive *its* motion from God, and so this motion of the agent will not naturally be subject to eternal law. But the natural law is "nothing other" than a rational participation of the eternal law, which is to say, that those who do not center their account of moral law on the ordinance of God do not according to St. Thomas Aquinas so much as *possess* a doctrine of natural law. It is for this reason that in *Fides et ratio* (#83) Pope John Paul II speaks of:

> ... the need for a philosophy of genuinely metaphysical range, capable, that is, of transcending empirical data in order to attain something absolute, ultimate and foundational in its search for truth. This requirement is implicit in sapiential and analytical knowledge alike; and in particular it is a requirement for knowing the moral good, which has its ultimate foundation in the Supreme Good, God himself.

One savors the words that "a philosophy of genuinely metaphysical range" is needed and indeed is "a requirement for knowing the moral good, which has its ultimate foundation in the Supreme Good, God himself." This sapiential dimension of natural law is not an alien speculative intrusion on an exclusively practical consideration, but a defining thematic element in Thomas's account of the natural law.

Consequent on treating the rational agent as a totally self-activating source of being, good, and truth, it may come to be thought that the precepts of natural law are rules of thumb constructed by practical reason and manifesting no higher order of law or authority, a mere *index of likely uses for natural human tendencies:* the "Standard & Poor's Index of Inclinations." Such a tendency seems to be what is in play in the idea that incommensurable "basic goods" may replace the natural moral *order,* that is, the natural *order* of ends defining the order of inclinations and the order of moral precepts. The teaching that basic goods are incommensurable asserts that these goods are not objectively ordered prior to choice. Thus for example, "play" is said not to be ordered to truth or religion, but to be simply incomparable with respect to these.

Yet in the teaching of St. Thomas life is based upon truth in a way that renders truth wholly superordinate vis-à-vis play; likewise, the truth of God (*not* mere *religion,* as though merely any putative religion counted as *good* altogether apart from its *truth*) is likewise naturally superordinate. Such ordering does not suffice in the absence of prudence to vouchsafe ethical directives *hic et nunc,* but it is a necessary condition for such directives to be sound. Yet one must cede the new natural law theory this much: in distinguishing "basic" from "nonbasic" goods, it just so far honors natural teleology (*why* are the basic goods *basic?*—because of the *ordering of human nature*). Yet, unfortunately, the claim that there is no normative natural teleological order *among the basic goods* is almost as damaging as the lack of any teleological ordering whatsoever: for if only an imperious subjectivity assigns order to basic goods in choice, then it is not natural order and wisdom that are finally determinative, but private and incommensurable willing. We are vaulted to a scenario wherein—lacking any final cause for action—the whole practical realm is deprived of natural intelligible order, for the basic goods are in this case normatively further ordered to nothing whatsoever.

At the other extreme from the reduction of natural law to a mere index of natural inclinations, natural law stripped of its metaphysical and teleological foundations may become a rationalism that rigorously imposes a disembodied law whose idolatrous center is practical reason itself. Of course, this was the Kantian strategy, forced upon him by his denial of metaphysics, natural theology, and natural teleology. Since the natural order of ends was not defined in relation to any natural finality, all inclinations toward ends became for Kant merely contingent and empirical, manifesting no normative order, and embracing only that which is knowably lower than the rational agent. Whereas for Aristotle (and St. Thomas) there is not only the merely contingent object of wish, but also the normative object of wish flowing from the normative ordering of ends and inclinations, for Kant wish and appetite are ineluctably contingent and empirical and of no normative worth. For, given the absence of metaphysics and natural theology, the ends of human inclinations are things lower than the rational agent or at least no higher, and thus understood the rational agent becomes the highest knowable principle in the cosmos. Far from being moved by God to its own free act, for Kant the rational agent is both the first agent and the first promulgator of the moral law.[32]

---

32. See, e.g., Immanuel Kant, *Grounding of the Metaphysic of Morals,* trans. James W. Ellington (Indianapolis, Ind.: Hackett, 1993), 39–45, or in the Prussian Academy edition (hereafter cited as Ak), 433–41.

And so, by indirection, we find ourselves once more in the courtyard of the teaching of the new natural law theory. For according to this theory too, there is no ethically significant natural order among ends as more remote or more proximate to the final end, the *finis ultimus*. And just as Kant erected his doctrine as one of pure practical science with no entangling foundation in speculative metaphysics, the new natural law theorists claim to have discovered that this (or at least something similar to it) has all along been the understanding of natural law—as though Aquinas ever defined natural law in this modern, anthropocentric, and rationalist fashion. The lone difference appears to be that the new natural law theory does refer to basic natural goods, as opposed to the pure formalism of the categorical imperative, and so to constitute a materially richer and perhaps more flexible form of deontological moral theory. Nonetheless, this theory refuses to acknowledge the ethical normativity of the metaphysical and teleological order that defines St. Thomas's doctrine of natural law.

If this view of the new natural law theorists were simply a rejection of the view that natural desire is properly speaking for supernatural beatitude—the teaching associated with de Lubac and other proponents of what came to be called *la nouvelle theologie*—one might sympathize. But the new natural law theory denies that there exists any ethically significant order among "basic" ends prior to choice whatsoever.[33]

The profundity of St. Thomas's doctrine of natural law is only harvested

---

33. Clearly Thomas is correct that even efficient causality becomes unthinkable in the absence of final causality, for efficient causality requires that one thing be ordered to bring about another. Were there no final causality, either action would never begin—for there would be no *reason* for it—or it would never end (for as it were not ordered toward any determinate end, there would be no reason for it to terminate). Contrary to these alternatives, the universe everywhere displays action ordered toward ends, a fact about which to be dismayed only if one has mistakenly confused our capacity to abstract from this order with its putative nonexistence. This is, of course, the key to the claim that propositions of "mere fact" are devoid of "reasons for action"—namely, that this construction of what a proposition of fact is, is an erroneous construction, since it *is a fact that nature is ordered to an end that has the nature of the Good*. Of course, it is alike implicitly the answer to those continental rationalists who simply cannot fathom that the end *is* an end because it is either the self-subsisting Good—God—or because it participates and to some degree irradiates his goodness. Certain theorists such as Dietrich von Hildebrand simply never realize that the ordering to the end is the immanent seam of a transcendent Good rather than a naturalist *reductio* confining the rational creature to the cage of "nature" construed as ineluctably "lower."

when it is realized that natural law is not something different from the eternal law,[34] but a mode of the divine government through secondary causality. And this government occurs not only by way of the cognitive direction given by the law, but also by way of the divine motion whereby the creature freely determines itself to act, such that the actual exercise of the will is brought forth from the creature so as to enable the creature to incline toward, and actually to move toward, its end. When Thomas says that *all* creatures passively participate the eternal law, that includes *rational* creatures, whose *active and preceptive* participation is built upon this passive participation and presupposes it.[35] All creatures receive from God their being, their natures, their natural powers, the ordering of their powers by way of natural inclination, *the application of their powers to act,* and of course the hierarchy of ends that specifies these acts. If any part of this passive participation in the eternal law is excised, then just so far does one subtract it from the governance of the eternal law.

In fact, for several hundred years it is arguably the case that Westerners have been drawing out the consequences of the fable that, alone of all the known cosmos, the rational agent is demiurgically self-activating and in no essential dependence upon God in the use of its freedom. This "Ur-myth" of rationalism has irradiated its implications throughout the moral and social life of the West. That skepticism regarding ethical objectivity whose redress preoccupies the inheritors of the deontological tradition is chiefly generated from the same source as this myth itself—for moral skeptics frequently intuit that ethical objectivity implies some order *transcending and governing* the individual predilection. But if this transcendent normative order is not first known speculatively, it is not clear how it can define our action. The intellect is a *measured measure.* If the intellect does not first conform to the order in nature, then it cannot serve as a yardstick for human action—knowledge of the order of ends is presupposed by right practical judgment. Granted that practical rectitude about the means requires the conformity of our judgment with right appetite, right appetite requires prior knowledge of the end, and of the order of ends. This order of ends must repose from a *finis ultimus* even in the natural order, just as the order of agents in the natural order must proceed from a First Efficient Cause.[36]

34. *ST* I, q. 91, a. 2 ad 2.
35. See *ST* I-II, q. 91, a. 2, which articulates this vision with concision and profundity.
36. Granted, again, that had man been created in a state of pure nature the natural end

By comparison with the issue of the existence or nonexistence of moral objectivity, *this issue of the relation between human and divine agency is both doctrinally and historically determinative for the course of moral thought in the West.* Its import is decisive, as it directly concerns that passive participation in the eternal law that is the precondition for the active, rational, and preceptive participation that is the natural law. *The ordering of ends to the ultimate end—God*[37]*—and the ordering of acts to the ultimate end—God—is determined by the*

---

would not have been the beatific vision, it does seem that the natural end is a natural contemplative knowledge of the universe in relation to the highest possible natural knowledge of God, joined by whatever virtues befit the active life. Hence, although one may sympathize with John of St. Thomas in holding that the ultimate end for man naturally speaking is not determined concretely but only vaguely and generally, nonetheless, there is an imperfect felicity whose crown is the speculative contemplation of the ordered whole of the cosmos in relation to its transcendent cause. Thus, for example, the proper function of man of which Aristotle wrote exhibits a threefold ascending nature comprising acts of moral virtue, of prudence and *neosis*.

37. It must be kept in mind that the ultimate end of the whole universe consists in a certain *imitatio* of God, and this is true even naturally speaking and in precision from the *superadditum* of grace and the beatific call of the rational creature, whose natural end (the contemplative life fixed upon the widest and most profound knowledge of the universe in relation to the highest possible natural knowledge of God, in a life whose practical activity extensively realizes the perfection of reason) is thus in a certain respect (according to the natural mode of *imitatio*) said to be God. Hence *SSC* III, c. 17–20. To use the language of but one of the arguments: "The particular good is directed to the common good as its end: for the being of the part is on account of the whole: wherefore the good of the nation is more godlike than the good of one man. Now the supreme good, namely God, is the common good, since the good of all things depends on him: and the good whereby each thing is good, is the particular good of that thing, and of those that depend thereon. Therefore all things are directed to one good, namely God, as their end. Again. Order among ends is consequent to the order among agents: for just as the supreme agent moves all second agents, so must all the ends of second agents be directed to the end of the supreme agent: since whatever the supreme agent does, it does for its own end. Now the supreme agent is the active principle of the actions of all inferior agents, by moving all to their actions, and consequently to their ends. Hence it follows that all the ends of second agents are directed by the first agent to its proper end. Now the first agent in all things is God, as we proved in the Second Book. And His will has no other end but His own goodness, which is Himself, as we showed in the First Book. Therefore all things whether they were made by Him immediately, or by means of secondary causes, are directed to God as their end. But this applies to all things: for as we proved in the Second Book, there can be nothing that has not its being from Him. Therefore all things are directed to God as their end" (*SCG* III, c. 17). In passing one must note that the premotive character

eternal law, and wholly governed by the plan of God's providence, and by the divine decrees that execute this providential plan.

Natural law is not principally the *minima natura* of conversation with those who deny subjection to any wider normative order, nor is it the residue of natural integrity required for deontology to have human reference. One recollects, on the one hand, Kant's point that any applications of moral reason presupposing anthropology are secondary to pure practical reason,[38] and, on the other hand, the new natural law theory's doctrine of "basic" but naturally unordered goods that strikes down any claim that one putatively basic end is objectively nobler or superordinate to another. While the new natural law theory is materially more ample, neither acknowledges unified natural teleology as definitive for the moral life, nor passive participation of the eternal law as essentially definitive for the natural law.

Difficult moral questions implicate our knowledge of natural teleology, and while we all share the same natural ordering that makes the evidence accessible, wisdom with respect to this evidence is not equally distributed. Knowing the right order of ends requires us to know the relation of subordinate ends to the final end—and this knowledge is only partially and incoherently achievable apart from knowledge of the existence and providence of God.[39] Natural law without God is thus, as I have had occasion to say

---

of this passage is arresting: "the supreme agent is the active principle of the actions of all inferior agents, by moving all to their actions, and consequently to their ends." This is the ontological language that is utterly forgotten by most contemporary moral theorists, for whom the moral agent is indeed not moved but absolutely self-moving: which is impossible.

38. Kant, *Grounding for the Metaphysic of Moral*, 23, or Ak 412: "The principles should not be made to depend on the particular nature of human reason, as speculative philosophy may permit and even sometimes finds necessary; but, rather, the principles should be derived from the universal concept of a rational being in general, since moral laws should hold for every rational being as such. In this way all morals, which require anthropology in order to be applied to humans, must be entirely expounded at first independently of anthropology as pure philosophy."

39. Cf. Yves Simon, *The Tradition of Natural Law*, ed. Vukan Kuic (New York: Fordham University Press, 1992), 62. Inasmuch as natural law is not finally intelligible apart from theistic principles, its content may be accessible to all, but it can be a source of theologically neutral and minimal consensus only when it is left incoherent. In his great work *The Tradition of Natural Law* the philosopher Yves Simon perhaps put it best. Speaking of certain truths of the moral law that we discover before we naturally discover the existence of God, he states: "from this logical priority in the order of discovery it does not follow that the understanding of

elsewhere,[40] like opera without voices: that is, it is a contradiction in terms that even were it possible still could command no normative attention. It is, then, not wholly surprising to find the new natural law theorists reluctant to use the *language* of natural law, a respect in which their reserve appears wholly warranted given their general views.[41]

Natural law—which is nothing other than a rational participation in the eternal law—is the normativity of that *order* that is divinely impressed upon, defines, and permeates the rational nature. For the rational creature *passively* receives from God its being, nature, natural powers, order of powers to end, hierarchy of ends reposing from the *finis ultimus,* and even the actual application of its natural volitional power to act. Only insofar as these are passively received—including rational nature itself and the very motion whereby the rational agent freely determines itself—may reason then participate or receive this order *rationally* as providing reasons to act and not to act. If the creature is to be normatively governed toward its end, it must be subject to divine causality. Natural law moral doctrine grows in the fertile loam of causally rich metaphysics and theism. It could be no other way. Human reason does not turn the water of mere *inclinatio* into the wine of *lex,* but is subject to an order of law by the very being and order that it passively participates and which it is *ordered* to receive rationally and preceptively.

It is a contradiction in terms for an agent whose act absolutely traces no further than itself to receive its direction from another, for an agent whose act derives from no higher causal principle than itself is an agent *a se;* the act of such an agent is outside the power, and hence outside the providence, of any other cause; and it neither needs nor can receive extrinsic di-

---

natural law can be logically preserved in case of failure to recognize in God the ultimate foundation of all laws." Not only are the remoter inferences ensuing from the ordering of ends—even those inferences whose scope is universal—not necessarily drawn by all, but further, since all are not in the same prudential circumstances, the moral stance required *hic et nunc* may be significantly different (i.e., as Thomas puts it *ST* I-II, q. 94, a. 4, it may be different both with respect to rectitude, and with respect to knowledge).

40. Steven A. Long, "Reproductive Technology and the Natural Law," *National Catholic Bioethics Quarterly* 2 (Summer 2002): 221–28.

41. Of course, I refer to Finnis's reluctance to use the term, and to his generally approbatory citation of Mortimer Adler, in his earlier work *Natural Law and Natural Rights* (see note 22 above for citation).

rective principles. On such a view the finite agent is the creator ex nihilo of the perfection of its own free acts, and is naturally outside the governance of any higher principle or law. Yet whether theorists deny the intelligibility of being—like Kant himself—or affirm it, it is today common for moral theorists to insist upon the necessity of upholding the absolute autonomy of the will[42] as necessary for moral responsibility. But, to the contrary, this affirmation constitutes the implicit denial of natural law as such. The essential choice in ethics lies between participated theonomy and autonomism, the latter of which has skeptical modalities as well as ethically objectivistic ones. Put in historical terms, the genie of absolute autonomy does not escape the bottle of law primarily for the sake of morality but for the reveries of an anthropocentric *telos*. As Gilson notes in his work *The Unity of Philosophical Experience*:

> As we read the notes published in 1920 by Erich Adikes under the title of *Kant's Opus Posthumum,* we are led to suspect that, had he lived a little longer, even Kant might have finally given way to some sort of mystical urge. Having proved in his youth that we know nothing about God, old Kant was beginning to suspect that he himself might be God: "God is not a being outside me, but merely a thought in me. God is the morally practical self-legislative reason. Therefore only a God in me, about me, and over me." A God who is both in us and above us, as moral law itself, is either nothing, or the legislative power of practical reason in us. "God can be sought only in us," says Kant, and further: "There is a Being in me which, though distinct form me, stands to me in relations of causal efficacy, and which, itself free, i.e., not dependent upon the law of nature in space and time, inwardly directs me (justifies or condemns), and I, as man, am myself this Being."[43]

Conclusion

The doctrine of the natural law propounded by St. Thomas is theonomic in its very essence. It requires speculative knowledge of the order of ends—including the *finis ultimus*—and a robust metaphysics of the relation of created to divine causality. It is a doctrine according to which natural order is a finite and inadequate but real manifestation of Uncreated Wisdom,

---

42. Cf. Kant, *Grounding for the Metaphysics of Morals,* 58–59, or Ak 459–460.
43. Etienne Gilson, *The Unity of Philosophical Experience* (New York: Charles Scribner's Sons, 1965), 239.

and in which not even rational creatures are self-activating but rather dependent upon the divine largesse for each *motio* toward the Good. One can understand the difficulties that arise with respect to metaphysics. But to suppose that one can create a purely practical doctrine that will dispense with the need for speculative metaphysical premises at the font of one's moral philosophy while somehow still achieving the same conclusions stretches credulity. Kant, who thought himself to have utterly incinerated metaphysics in his *Critique of Pure Reason,* knew better: it would never be possible to develop the normative ethics of natural law doctrine in the absence of its metaphysical requisites. A purely rational ethic, divorced from prior speculative knowledge of unified natural teleology and the reality of God, would afford only the most formal, and naturally the thinnest, of rationales: a purely practical science.[44] In this respect, the contrast between the new natural law theory with its praxic, antiteleological tendency, and the classical Thomistic doctrine of natural law, is instructive. This contrast is such as to challenge us to rediscover, and reimmerse ourselves within, the tradition of reflection that—from Plato and Aristotle, through Boethius, Augustine, and Aquinas—is definitive for the tradition of Catholic theology and philosophy.

44. Kant, *Grounding of the Metaphysic of Morals,* 22, or Ak 410: ". . . there had better be adopted the plan of undertaking this investigation as a separate inquiry, i.e., as pure practical philosophy . . ."

PART IV

LAW AND POLITICS

7

THOMISTIC NATURAL LAW AND THE AMERICAN NATURAL LAW TRADITION

Christopher Wolfe

Introduction

In this paper, I would like to ask, "What is the relation between classic natural law, in the Thomistic tradition, and the American natural law tradition?"

A preliminary question that might be asked is: "Why should we care?" The reason I think we should care is that (1) Thomistic natural law provides the best rational framework for understanding political and social life. It embodies the *truth* about human beings living together in community and points out the best way to attain the common *good*. (2) We should, therefore, want to know where contemporary American political life stands vis-à-vis Thomistic natural law, both (a) because such knowledge is a good in itself, and (b) because we need that knowledge in order to be able to more effectively pursue the goal of bringing our political life into line with it.

Moreover, a better understanding of the *past* American natural law tradition, and how it relates to Thomistic natural law, is valuable for understanding how we have gotten to where we are today. Besides that knowledge being valuable in itself, it is important because understandings of our past to some extent shape our sense of what is right and possible in the present.

That is, understanding the American natural law tradition is an important element in American public philosophy.[1] For example, the commitment of the Founders, and virtually all subsequent Americans (though in different forms), to *limited government* plays a significant role in how current Americans think and talk about politics. On the other hand, the past may sometimes serve to provide us with negative models, as it did in the movement from the Gilded Age of strong property rights and limited government to the New Deal of more limited property rights and expansive government with social welfare obligations, and in the movement from slavery to segregation to the civil rights movement. Understandings of our past are constantly influencing our understandings and actions in the present.

Clear ideas about the common good and American public philosophy are especially important today, because contemporary political discussions and decisions—especially those involving so-called culture war issues—constitute an extremely important "moment" in the development of American public philosophy. How these debates are resolved will determine today's answer to the question that Aristotle posed for all polities: To what extent can a good citizen be a good person?[2]

In order to answer the question I have posed about the relation between Thomistic natural law and the American natural law tradition, I first will, briefly describe Thomistic natural law, contrasting it with a later form of thought often referred to as natural law, but more properly called natural rights theory; second, I will briefly summarize some high points in the American natural law tradition; and third, I will discuss some contemporary issues in Catholic natural law teaching, contemporary political and legal philosophy, American law, and natural law theory.

The basic answer to the question I have posed is (1) that Thomistic natural law and the American natural law tradition are fundamentally different, and yet (2) they have had enough in common to have made a significant difference in (i.e., a positive contribution to) the quality of the American polity, but (3) the overlap between them has been diminishing in modern America.

---

1. See my "Issues Facing Contemporary American Public Philosophy," in *Public Morality, Civic Virtue, and the Problem of Modern Liberalism*, ed. T. William Boxx and Gary M. Quinlivan (Grand Rapids, Mich.: Eerdmans, 2000).

2. Aristotle's *Politics*, Bk III, chap. 4. See also *The End of Democracy?*, ed. Richard John Neuhaus (Dallas, Tex.: Spence, 1997).

Thomistic Natural Law

The greatest representative of the classic natural law tradition is Thomas Aquinas, whose teaching on law is developed in the *Summa theologiae*. But Thomas was not operating in a vacuum. He was the heir to centuries of reflection on nature and morality, which came to him through various strands of thought. Indeed, it may be said that classic (Thomistic) natural law theory is part of a "family" of doctrines/concepts/ethical and political theories that share certain fundamental features. Among the most important were the natural right tradition of Plato and Aristotle,[3] the Stoic tradition (described, e.g., in certain works of Cicero),[4] Roman law, and Augustine.[5] Thomas drew on all of these sources (and others) in forming his natural law doctrine.

Aquinas on Natural Law

Thomistic natural law, paradoxically, is a teaching developed in a theological rather than a philosophical work, the *Summa theologiae*. St. Thomas's treatment of law in *ST* I-II, qq. 90–108, set in the discussion of man's moral life, is the first of two parts (together with the following section on grace) regarding "extrinsic principles" of men's action. It follows an earlier general discussion of intrinsic principles (powers of the soul, and good and bad habits—virtues and vices), and precedes a discussion of virtues in particular (the theological virtues and the cardinal virtues).

Thomas's definition of law in general is that it is "an ordinance of reason for the common good, made by him who has care of the common good, and promulgated"[6] (*ST* I-II, q. 90, a. 4). The most comprehensive law is God's eternal law; other forms of law include natural law, human law, and divine positive law (*ST* I-II, q. 91).

---

3. See, in particular, Aristotle's *Rhetoric*, Bk I, chaps. 10 and 13.

4. See esp. Cicero's *Republic* and *Laws*. The extent to which Cicero's views are accurately stated by any of the particular participants in these dialogues is a subject of scholarly debate. See Ernest Fortin, "Augustine, Aquinas, and the Problem of Natural Law," *Mediaevalia*, 4 (1978): 183–86.

5. Augustine develops his doctrine, not of natural law, but of the eternal and human laws, in *De libero arbitrio*.

6. English quotations from the *Summa theologiae* are by the Fathers of the English Dominican Province (New York: Benziger, 1948).

Thomas describes the natural law as the rational creature's "share of the Eternal Reason, whereby it has a natural inclination to its proper act and end; and this participation of the eternal law in the rational creature is called the natural law . . . the light of natural reason whereby we discern what is good and what is evil, which is the function of the natural law, is nothing else than an imprint on us of the Divine light. It is therefore evident that natural law is nothing else than the rational creature's participation of the eternal law" (*ST* I-II, q. 91, a. 2).

The precepts of the natural law are the first principles of the practical reason.

> The first principle in the practical reason is one founded on the notion of good, viz. that *good is that which all things seek after*. Hence this is the first precept of law, that *good is to be done and pursued, and evil is to be avoided*. All other precepts of the natural law are based upon this; so that whatever the practical reason naturally apprehends as man's good (or evil) belongs to the precepts of the natural law as something to be done or avoided. (*ST* I-II, q. 94, a. 2)

But since good has the nature of an end,

> all those things to which man has a natural inclination, are naturally apprehended by reason as being good, and consequently as objects of pursuit . . . Wherefore according to the order of natural inclinations, is the order of the precepts of the natural law. (*ST* I-II, q. 94, a. 2)

There are various inclinations in man. First, in accordance with the nature of all substances, we seek the preservation of our own being, according to its nature, so that "whatever is a means of preserving human life, and of warding off its obstacles, belongs to the natural law." Second, according to the nature we share with animals, things "which nature has taught to all animals, such as sexual intercourse, education of offspring and so forth" belong to the natural law. Third, according to man's own nature, man has "an inclination to the good, according to the nature of his reason," which includes a natural inclination "to know the truth about God and to live in society" (*ST* I-II, q. 94, a. 2), so that the natural law includes whatever pertains to this inclination (e.g., shunning ignorance, avoiding offending those among whom one has to live).

All virtuous acts *as such* belong to the natural law, since virtue is nothing other than acting according to reason. But specific virtuous acts may or may not be prescribed by the natural law, since nature inclines to some of them at first, while others are the result, not of immediate inclination, but of the "inquiry of reason" which shows them "to be conducive to well-living" (*ST* I-II, q. 94, a. 3).

As "regards the general principles of practical reason, truth or rectitude is the same for all, and is equally known by all." As "to the proper conclusions of the practical reason, neither is the truth or the rectitude the same for all, nor, where it is the same, is it equally known by all." So, for example, it is right for all to act according to reason, and from this principle it follows that "goods entrusted to another should be restored to their owner." But this is true only "for the majority of cases"—there may be cases where it is not true, as when someone tries to reclaim property for the purpose of engaging in treasonous acts. (And the more the application of a principle descends into matters of detail, the greater the likelihood of exceptions.)

So "the natural law, as to general principles, is the same for all, both as to rectitude and as to knowledge. But as to certain matters of detail, which are conclusions, as it were, of those general principles, it is the same for all in the majority of cases, both as to rectitude and as to knowledge, and yet in some few cases it may fail, both as to rectitude . . . and as to knowledge" (through being perverted by, for example, passion or evil habit) (*ST* I-II, q. 94, a. 4).

The first, most general, principles of the natural law are known to all and cannot be blotted out of the heart of man, though their application to a particular action may be (on account of concupiscence or some other passion). But the secondary and more detailed principles of the natural law "which are, as it were, conclusions following closely from first principles" can be blotted out of the heart, by evil persuasions or vicious customs and corrupt habits (*ST* I-II, q. 94, a. 6).[7]

Key Features of Classic Natural Law

What are the key features of classic natural law theory? Let me offer the following as some possibilities:

---

7. I confine myself mostly to the brief discussion of natural law in *ST* I-II, q. 94. It should be noted that much of what Thomas has to say about the natural law can be found in his comments on the moral precepts of the Old Law (which he treats as a statement of natural law precepts) in *ST* I-II, q. 100.

1. Natural law is an *objective* moral theory; it is discovered, not created.

2. Natural law principles are *permanent* (not simply reflections of a particular time), because they are based on a stable or permanent human nature.

3. Natural law principles are *universal* (not bound to a single culture or set of cultures), because they are based on a nature common to all human beings.

4. Natural law is founded on *epistemological realism:* that is, it is based on the mind's contact with reality, rooted in something more than the "structures of the mind itself" (vs. Kant).

5. Natural law is *reason-based,* rather than will-based.

6. Natural law is based on a notion of reason that goes *beyond instrumental rationality:* it involves the intellect's capacity to "grasp" the human good and what conduces to it; it is not about pleasure, or a utilitarian calculus thereof.

7. Natural law involves an orientation toward *happiness,* but it is also a matter of *obligation* or command (though it is not reducible simply to command).

8. Natural law theory has an essential focus on *human acts,* but it also emphasizes *habits* or *virtues.*

9. Natural law theory is intertwined with (though it is *not a deduction from*) an *anthropology* that includes (a) *an internal ordering of the human faculties:* reason-spirit-desire (in the earlier, natural right tradition), or intellect-will-passions, in the Thomistic tradition; and (b) *an integration of mind and body,* which is neither reductionist (materialist or naturalist), nor dualist.

10. Natural law is intimately connected with (though not simply derived from) *a natural theology,* which helps to justify the use of the term "law," by identifying a lawgiver.

The Natural Rights Tradition

The natural law tradition ultimately transmogrified into a new and different tradition: to the modern tradition of natural rights.[8] Thomas Hobbes was the first great exponent of the new doctrine. He argued that the most

---

8. A particularly interesting account of the change may be found in Michael Zuckert, *Natural Rights and the New Republicanism* (Princeton, N.J.: Princeton University Press, 1994).

fundamental "law of nature" was the desire for self-preservation. In the state of nature, each man had to enforce his own right to self-preservation, and the result was the war of all against all, with life being "solitary, poor, nasty, brutish, and short." Under such circumstances, men found it worthwhile to establish a social contract, by which their power to enforce their own right to self-preservation was handed over to an absolute ruler whose task was to protect everyone's rights by the fear he instilled in all subjects.[9]

John Locke, the greatest exemplar of the classic natural rights tradition, had similar starting points, beginning with a state of nature, but one that is described in somewhat less brutal terms. The first law of nature is still self-preservation, and men have the executive power to enforce this law. If this state of nature is not quite as fearsome as Hobbes's, it has considerable "inconveniences" that lead men out of it into the social contract and civil society, with government having the job of protecting life, and the allied rights of liberty and property (which are essential to self-preservation, not only vis-à-vis other men, but also vis-à-vis a somewhat ungenerous nature). "Comfortable self-preservation" is perhaps a fuller description of Locke's great *desideratum*.[10]

This natural rights tradition employed the language of "the law of nature," and Locke added to the appearance of continuity by explicit invocations of God and by his citations of the "judicious Hooker," an Anglican divine generally considered to be in the old natural law tradition.[11] But a close examination of the content of this philosophy shows a fundamental change: from the natural law's orientation toward the positive fulfillment of the capacities of human nature—toward the *summum bonum* of virtue—we have moved to an orientation toward a *summum malum,* the loss of self-preservation, with questions regarding man's ultimate fulfillment being relegated to a very private sphere.[12]

---

9. Thomas Hobbes, *Leviathan*.

10. John Locke, *The Second Treatise of Government*.

11. Thomas Hibbs, in his response to the paper on which this chapter is based, pointed out that Daniel Westberg has raised serious questions about this assumption about Hooker. See Westberg "Thomistic Law and the Moral Theory of Richard Hooker," *American Catholic Philosophical Quarterly* 68 (1994): 203–14.

12. This theme of the shift from natural right and natural law, on one hand, to natural rights, on the other, was an important theme in Leo Strauss, *Natural Right and History* (Chicago: University of Chicago Press, 1953).

(As with natural law, there is a larger family of natural rights doctrines—using the term less strictly. Hobbes and Locke are the founders, but the family includes many others, who depart from them as Locke departs from Hobbes on very important matters. They include thinkers as varied as Montesquieu, Rousseau, and Kant.)

Some (borrowing from later Rawlsian political theory) might argue that the most important difference between natural law and natural rights doctrines is that the former claims to be a comprehensive moral philosophy, while natural rights doctrine should be understood as a narrower, "political" doctrine, about the limits of government rather than the full range of moral possibilities for human beings. But it is doubtful that natural rights doctrine can be confined so easily, for several overlapping reasons. First, to the extent that certain ethical or metaphysical or religious positions impinge directly on this political doctrine, the latter trumps the former. (The salience of this point was limited at the time classical liberalism was being developed by the assumption that the ethical/metaphysical/religious views most widespread in late-seventeenth-century England would not be in conflict with Locke's political views. It was only relatively small and unpopular groups, like Catholics and certain minority sects, that would feel the brunt of the limits of liberal tolerance.) Second, the political doctrine of liberalism might be thought to require certain fundamental ethical positions. Some of the most obvious ones (at least to people like Locke himself) were the prohibitions of murder, theft, adultery, and libel (private and seditious). Third, implicit in the political doctrine of natural rights is a priority for certain goals, above all, peace and security. But whether peace and security are the highest goals (even merely politically) is not so clear. The distinction between a comprehensive moral doctrine and a merely political doctrine, then, is not so sharp as it might seem.

While natural rights theory was fundamentally different from natural law, however, it did have certain important features in common: it was (1) objective, (2) permanent, (3) universal, (4) generally understood as based on a "realist" epistemology (even if its main proponents may have had different views), and (5) also reason-based (though the content of that "reason" was truncated, relative to natural law). In these respects, despite the profound differences between natural rights theory and natural law, they have some important points in common, vis-à-vis other, modern forms of political thought (e.g., utilitarianism, pragmatism, and the array of forms of postmodernism).

The American Natural Law Tradition

There is no doubt that one strand of American political thought has been a "natural law" teaching of some form. But what is the nature and content of that natural law doctrine?

I have discussed various uses of "natural law" doctrine in American history elsewhere, describing (1) early "natural justice" judicial review, (2) the rise and decline of substantive due process and property rights, and (3) the post–New Deal "incorporation" debate between Supreme Court Justices Black and Frankfurter.[13] In what follows I would simply like to supplement that earlier treatment by adding brief discussions of natural law in three other "moments" of American history (the Founding, several late-nineteenth and early-twentieth-century Supreme Court cases on the family, and the mid-twentieth-century confrontation with totalitarianism) and to make some general observations about the use of "natural law" in America.

The Founding

The first major form of "American" political thought was that of the Puritans who established the New England colonies. Some scholars believe that Puritan thought was the primary force that shaped American political thought.[14] But by the time of the American founding, the dominant stream of political thought was based on the Enlightenment.

The central figure for the political philosophy of the Founding was John Locke. His natural rights version of natural law provided the most important element in the philosophical framework of the American Constitution. This can be seen clearly, I think, in the Declaration of Independence, especially the "self-evident truths" laid out in its first part, which is difficult to see as anything other than a substantially Lockean version of political philosophy. (Note that the *Federalist* draws on this philosophy too, in justifying the authority of the convention that produced the Constitution.

---

13. See Christopher Wolfe, "Natural Law and Judicial Review," in *Natural Law and Contemporary Public Policy,* ed. David Forte (Washington, D.C.: Georgetown University Press, 1998), 157–89.

14. On this early political thought, see Willmoore Kendall and George Carey, *Basic Symbols of the American Political Tradition* (Baton Rouge: Louisiana State University Press, 1970). As the text makes clear, I disagree with these authors' estimation of the vitality of this earlier tradition in the Founding.

Marshall's opinion in *Marbury v. Madison* has overtones of this theory of government as well.)

Michael Zuckert argues very persuasively in his *The Natural Rights Republic* that Lockean political philosophy was the dominant element in early American political thought.[15] There were other important elements, it is true, including Old Whig constitutionalism, Puritan political theology, and the progressive realization of democracy understood as a variant of classical republicanism. But, while America was indeed an amalgam of these different views, "the natural rights philosophy remains America's deepest and so far most abiding commitment, and the others could enter the amalgam only so far as they were compatible, or could be made so, with natural rights."[16]

While the American founding, then, took its orientation primarily from modern natural rights philosophy, this point has to be qualified by two factors: (1) this does not mean that Locke and natural rights were understood by American citizens to be sharply contrasted to the natural law tradition; and (2) as Zuckert himself argues, if Lockean natural rights theory was the dominant element in the Founding, it was not the only one.

On the first point, there were enough points in common between various formulations of Lockean natural law and more classic approaches to natural law that it was possible for many Americans to ignore important differences between them. And, in this regard, it is as important to understand how Locke was received or understood by Americans as it is to understand Locke in himself.

For example, Locke's own presentation of modern "natural law" contained a natural theology that helped to provide continuity. And while there is considerable scholarly debate as to whether or not Locke took this seriously, there is no question, I think, that many "American Lockeans" did. Locke says in his *Second Treatise* that the Law of Nature (that "no one ought to harm another in his Life, Health, Liberty, or Possessions") is based on the principle that:

---

15. Michael Zuckert, *The Natural Rights Republic* (South Bend, Ind.: University of Notre Dame Press, 1996). For some quibbles with Zuckert, especially on issues regarding religion and on the centrality of Jefferson in the Founding, see my review of this book in *First Things* 15 (May 1998): 52–56.

16. Zuckert, *The Natural Rights Republic*, 95.

For Men being all the Workmanship of one Omnipotent, and infinitely wise Maker; All the Servants of one Sovereign Master, sent into the World by his order and about his business, they are his Property, whose Workmanship they are, made to last during his, not one anothers Pleasure.[17]

Second, the very language of Lockean philosophy, such as its employment of the term "laws of nature," and traditional distinctions such as the one between "liberty" and "license," helped to foster a sense of continuity.[18]

On the second point, no one would deny that others besides Locke influenced the Founding. The Founders drew on many sources, and if the Lockean strand was dominant, it was not exclusive. Lockean political philosophy was one element in a compound formed with elements from other traditions.[19]

First, there was the English common law. While Locke's influence was felt here, as can be seen in Blackstone's emphasis on the Lockean trinity of life, liberty, and property in his *Commentaries on the Laws of England,* there were other elements as well, as can be seen in Blackstone's more Aristotelian view of the genesis of government, in sharp contrast to Locke's discussion of a state of nature.

In this regard, a particularly interesting piece of writing is an unsigned article on "natural law" by the great common law jurist Justice Joseph Story, in the *Encyclopedia Americana* edited by Francis Lieber in 1832.[20] The overtones of traditional natural law elements in Story's version of natural law can be seen in the assumptions he sets out:

For the purposes of the present article, we shall assume, without undertaking to prove, that there is a God of infinite power, knowledge, wisdom, benevolence, justice, and mercy; that he has created man with suitable powers and faculties to pur-

17. John Locke, *Second Treatise of Government* Book II, chap. 2, #6.
18. For a recent argument that emphasizes those aspects of Locke that are consistent with the classical natural law, see Thomas West, "Vindicating John Locke: How a Seventeenth-Century 'Liberal' Was Really a 'Social Conservative,'" Family Research Council Witherspoon Lecture (23 February 2001).
19. Another survey of various elements that entered the blend that produced the American Constitution may be found in Forrest McDonald, *Novus Ordo Seculorum* (Lawrence: University Press of Kansas, 1985), esp. chaps. 1–3.
20. *Encyclopedia Americana,* ed. Francis Lieber, 9:150–58. This article is discussed in Eisgruber, "Justice Story, Slavery, and the Natural Law Foundations of American Constitutionalism," *University of Chicago Law Review* 55 (1988): 273–327.

sue and obtain happiness; that man is a moral, dependent and accountable being; that his soul is immortal; that his ultimate happiness or misery is dependent upon his own conduct; that there is a future state of retribution, according to supreme wisdom and goodness; that, by a right application of his powers and faculties, man may always discern and pursue his duty; that virtue, or doing good to mankind in obedience to the will of God, has attached to it the reward of everlasting happiness; and that vice, or doing wrong in disobedience to that will, is, by the very constitution of man's nature, necessarily connected with suffering and misery, directly or ultimately. In short, that man cannot be permanently happy by the practice of vice, and must be permanently happy by the practice of virtue.

While this set of assumptions may be read in quite different ways (so much turns on the substantive content of notions like "happiness" and "virtue" and "the will of God"), the focus on moral responsibility and duties, and on happiness and virtue, and on divine will and Providence suggests that this approach draws on much more than modern natural rights philosophy.

More particularly, one of the central features of Lockean philosophy was the importance of property rights. But England's well-developed common law dealt in great detail with these matters of justice—and the substance of this common law drew extensively on classical and medieval thought.[21]

In addition, the common law included important regulations of morality, including sexual or family-supporting morality. Divorce, for example, in English law at the time of the Founding, was very restricted; genuine divorce with the possibility of remarriage was largely restricted to those few who could obtain an act of Parliament.[22]

Second, the common law itself reflected another part of the blend of thought in the Founding, namely, Christianity. Justice Story pointed out that in the Founding "the general, if not the universal, sentiment in America was, that Christianity ought to receive encouragement from the state, so far as it is not incompatible with the private rights of conscience, and the freedom of religious worship."[23] And that famous foreign observer, Alexis

---

21. See James Gordley, *The Philosophical Origins of Modern Contract Doctrine* (Oxford, U.K.: Oxford University Press, 1991).

22. On divorce, see Sir William Blackstone, *Commentaries on the Laws of England*, Bk 1, chap. 15.

23. Joseph Story, *Commentaries on the Constitution of the United States* (Durham, N.C.: Carolina Academic Press, 1987), 700.

de Tocqueville, pointed out that Christianity helped to provide a common moral framework that made a healthy political liberty possible.[24]

Third, Americans were influenced by a group of writers on the law of nations, including figures such as Grotius,[25] Pufendorf,[26] Burlamaqui,[27] and Vattel.[28] The thought of these writers had different relations to classic natural law, and all except Grotius were firm "natural rights" theorists, but they added elements different in varying degrees from Locke's own natural rights theory.

Fourth, Americans took for granted elements of the heritage of classical and medieval philosophy whose importance has become recognized only as modern intellectual trends have assaulted them. For example, the whole political philosophy of rights seems to presuppose a realist epistemology, an assumption that human beings really are capable of grasping the laws of nature—an assumption largely at odds with some of the major trends in philosophy today (e.g., deconstructionism, historicism). (Again, whether or not Locke was an epistemological realist, many of those who followed his political works were.)

Nonproperty "Natural Law"

While property rights were the main area in which some variation of natural law thought had a significant impact in the late nineteenth and early twentieth century, there were also some cases involving the family. In particular, natural law makes an appearance in *Bradwell v. Illinois,* in which the Supreme Court upheld Illinois's refusal (pursuant to the common law) to grant a license to practice law to a woman, and in *Meyer v. Nebraska* and in *Pierce v. Society of Sisters,* in which the Court upheld parental rights.

In *Bradwell,* Justice Bradley wrote a concurring opinion (joined by Field and Swayne), arguing that the privileges and immunities of U.S. citizens did

---

24. Alexis de Tocqueville, *Democracy in America,* especially vol. 1, chap. 17.

25. Hugo Grotius, *The Law of War and Peace* (Roslyn, N.Y.: Walter J. Black, 1949).

26. Samuel Pufendorf, *On the Duty of Man and Citizen According to Natural Law* (Cambridge, U.K.: Cambridge University Press, 1991).

27. Jean Jacques Burlamaqui, *The Principles of Natural and Politic Law,* trans. Thomas Nugent (Philadelphia: Nicklin & Johnson, 1832).

28. Emerich Vattel, *The Law of Nations; or, Principles of the Law of Nature* (T. and W. J. Johnson, 1883).

not include the right of a woman to engage in any occupation whatsoever. He gave as the reason that:

> ... the civil law, as well as nature herself, has always recognized a wide difference in the respective spheres and destinies of man and woman. Man is, or should be, woman's protector and defender. The natural and proper timidity and delicacy which belongs to the female sex evidently unfits it for many of the occupations of civil life. The constitution of the family organization, which is founded in the divine ordinance, as well as in the nature of things, indicates the domestic sphere as that which properly belongs to the domain and functions of womanhood. The harmony, not to say identity, of interests and views which belong or should belong to the family institution, is repugnant to the idea of a woman adopting a distinct and independent career from that of her husband. . . .
>
> It is true that many women are unmarried and not affected by any of the duties, complications, and incapacities arising out of the married state but these are exceptions to the general rule. The paramount destiny and mission of woman are to fulfill the noble and benign offices of wife and mother. This is the law of the Creator. And the rules of civil society must be adapted to the general constitution of things, and cannot be based upon exceptional cases.[29]

This passage exemplifies one of the sources of criticism of natural law theory: starting from sound observations about natural law—for example, the importance of the institution of the family, and the relevance of sexual differences to that institution—the opinion moves to a conclusion that goes far beyond any justification offered, that is, that the maintenance of the family requires that married women—and unmarried women, as covered by the more general rule to which they are exceptions—not have careers. At the same time it may be doubted whether contemporary society can so easily justify looking down its nose at the shortcomings of this opinion. However wrongheaded it may be, contemporary American mores have not yet provided an alternative that successfully harmonizes fair opportunities for women with the maintenance of strong and stable families. While careers have, properly, been opened to women, married and unmarried, this has been done in ways that have, at least so far, coincided with great family instability. Egalitarian policies that simply ignore natural sexual differentiation as it relates to the well-being of the institution of the family may be as

---

29. 16 Wall. (83 U.S.) 130, 141–42 (1873) (Bradley, J., concurring).

socially harmful as older inegalitarian policies that unjustly curtailed employment opportunities for women.

In *Meyer v. Nebraska,* considering a Nebraska law that forbade teaching elementary school in any modern language other than English, the Court argued that:

> The American people have always regarded education and acquisition of knowledge as matters of supreme importance which should be diligently promoted. The Ordinance of 1787 declares, "Religion, morality, and knowledge being necessary to good government and the happiness of mankind, schools and the means of education shall forever be encouraged." Corresponding to the right of control, it is the natural duty of the parent to give his children education suitable to their station in life, and nearly all the States, including Nebraska, enforce this obligation by compulsory laws.[30]

Without directly invoking the natural law, the Court here relies on an understanding of the child and its relation to its parents that would seem to reflect a traditional natural law doctrine.

Pierce v. Society of Sisters is the only case I know of to be quoted in a papal encyclical (approvingly, in Pius XI's *Divini Illius Magistri* [*On Christian Education*]). Oregon had passed a law requiring all students to attend public schools. The Court said:

> Under the doctrine of *Meyer v. Nebraska,* we think it entirely plain that the Act of 1922 unreasonably interferes with the liberty of parents and guardians to direct the upbringing and education of children under their control: as often heretofore pointed out, rights guaranteed by the Constitution may not be abridged by legislation which has no reasonable relation to some purpose within the competency of the State. The fundamental theory of liberty upon which all governments in this Union repose excludes any general power of the State to standardize its children by forcing them to accept instruction from public teachers only. The child is not the mere creature of the State; those who nurture him and direct his destiny have the right, coupled with the high duty, to recognize and prepare him for additional obligations.[31]

Interestingly, in both cases, the nonproperty natural law argument is intertwined with a property rights argument: in *Meyer,* the right to engage in

---

30. 262 U.S. 390, at 400 (1923).
31. 268 U.S. 510, at 534–35 (1925) (internal citation omitted).

the occupation of teaching a foreign language, and in *Pierce,* the right of the school to teach. This is an example of the point that natural law and natural rights theories overlap at some points. The Supreme Court property rights jurisprudence of 1890 to 1937 was largely an outgrowth of a "natural law doctrine" rooted in natural rights political theory (rather than traditional natural law), but these cases show that it extended beyond property rights in some cases, to matters like the nature of the family that tend to be identified today with classic natural law doctrine. (Of course, as with the property rights cases, opinions like *Bradwell* also show how an extreme version of natural rights or natural law theory can bring odium on natural law arguments in general.)

The Confrontation with Totalitarianism

World War II involved a confrontation with a profoundly evil Nazi regime, and specifically it raised the question of responsibility for refusing to enforce an evil positive law command, such as the war crimes prosecuted at Nuremberg. Moreover, the confrontation with Soviet communist totalitarianism during the cold war reinforced questions about transpolitical standards of right and wrong. These circumstances naturally led to something of a revival of natural law. Two of the great representatives of this revival were Jacques Maritain and Yves Simon. These French thinkers had a considerable impact in America, for instance, through their books based on their Walgreen Foundation Lectures at the University of Chicago: Maritain's *Man and the State,* and Simon's *The Philosophy of Democratic Government.*[32]

Another thinker deeply influenced by the experience of totalitarianism was Walter Lippman, whose book *The Public Philosophy*[33] held forth as essential to the project of preventing the decline of the West a notion of natural law, albeit an eclectic version that collapsed natural law and natural rights into the same category, and looked forward to some new rearticulation of this tradition.

---

32. Jacques Maritain, *Man and the State* (Chicago: University of Chicago Press, 1951), and Yves Simon, *The Philosophy of Democratic Government* (Chicago: University of Chicago Press, 1951).

33. Walter Lippmann, *The Public Philosophy* (New York: Mentor, 1955).

John Courtney Murray also contributed to the post–World War II revival of natural law, in his *We Hold These Truths: Catholic Reflections on the American Proposition*.[34] Murray distinguished more sharply than Lippman between classic and Lockean natural law, but he contended that Locke was the bearer of more of the classic natural law tradition than he knew, and he argued for the superiority of that classic tradition over Lockean natural law.

This post–World War II revival never came close to making traditional natural law the dominant philosophy in American academia or political and social life. In fact, the general trend throughout the twentieth century has been strongly in other directions: the influence of various forms of progressive thought leading up to the New Deal (e.g., Woodrow Wilson, Charles Beard, Vernon Parrington, Herbert Croly), the rise of Deweyan pragmatism as the quintessential American philosophy, the victory of legal realism and sociological jurisprudence—the children of Holmes—in American legal thought, and the expanding power of scientific rationalism after World War II exemplified in behaviorism in the social sciences. In retrospect, the revival of natural law in the wake of the experience of such profound evil in the middle of the twentieth century appears to have been rather short-lived, having been overshadowed in the latter part of the century by new intellectual currents, especially the rise of antiperfectionist liberalism through the influence of John Rawls and the emergence as a major force of radical thought, beginning with the New Left in the 1960s, then achieving wide influence throughout the academy in the form of critical legal studies, feminism, and multiculturalism.

Natural Law in Contemporary American Life

In this last section of my paper, I would like to make some preliminary points about "finding" classical natural law in America and about the current status of natural law in Catholic theology and philosophy, which has historically been the major vehicle for the natural law tradition. Then I will examine trends in contemporary American intellectual and political life that bear most strongly on the status of natural law in our society.

---

34. John Courtney Murray, S.J., *We Hold These Truths: Catholic Reflections on the American Proposition* (New York: Sheed & Ward, 1960).

Preliminary Points
A Note of Caution

There are temptations and opportunities in the analysis of the role that "natural law" has played in American history. The temptation faced by natural law scholars and by their followers engaged in public life is to go back into American history and find a useful "handle" to grab on to—a way to show that "natural law" is really the "American" way, so that they come to their fellow citizens, not as "foreigners," but as fellow citizens who are heirs to the same heritage. At least in principle, however, this can cause the wish to be father to the thought. It may lead some to see in the past what they want to see there—especially a vibrant and powerful traditional natural law doctrine.

The fact of the matter is that the more influential forms of "natural law" in America have been forms of modern natural rights theory, and the influence of more traditional or Thomistic natural law theory has been quite limited.

And yet, even recognizing important differences between the classical/medieval and American natural law traditions, it may be possible to find in the American natural law tradition important sources of support for principles central to the older natural law theory that are under attack in contemporary America.

Today's culture wars involve especially issues of life and death, and of sexuality. It can be argued that these are precisely areas where there was the greatest apparent continuity between the classical/medieval and early modern traditions. Traditionally, American thought has emphasized the equality and dignity of all human beings. The source of human dignity—perhaps more taken for granted than really thought through—lies in our distinctive faculty of reason, which has generally been viewed by most Americans in a theological context: we are endowed with reason, and the rights and duties that come with it, by a Creative and Provident God, according to John Locke and the Declaration of Independence. Natural law, in both forms (classical/medieval and modern), emphasized reason, and rested on a natural theology (one that was widely accepted by mostly Protestant Christian Americans), and therefore seemed to provide a "natural" basis for American public philosophy for a long time. (It might even be said to have represented something like a Rawlsian "overlapping consensus," in which different sectors of society—e.g., Catholics, Calvinists, Anglicans, Baptists, Unitarians, and Deists—could join, finding common ground despite somewhat different understandings of its terms.) The core values of this traditional American liberalism included a common moral framework (noted especially by Tocqueville) that included defense of life and family. The history of the twentieth century, however, especially since the 1960s, has been the story of the unraveling of that American consensus, with intellectuals and other elites departing from it first, in the late nineteenth and early twentieth century, and with their influence on the rest of society accelerating dramatically after World War II, and especially in the 1960s.

Natural Law in Contemporary Catholic Teaching and Thought

The first observation about contemporary Catholic natural law teaching is the striking modification of the Thomistic natural law tradition in the Catholic Magisterium. First, the so-called social teachings of the Catholic Magisterium, which usually are considered to begin with Leo XIII in the late nineteenth century, have taken a form that is not entirely Thomistic, and there is considerable debate about the extent to which this marks a substantive change or merely a working out of implications of Thomistic natural law and a change in vocabulary—and, even if it is the latter, whether such a change is prudent.[35] Beginning with Leo XIII himself, and especially in the landmark encyclical *Rerum novarum,* these social teachings have used the language of "rights," which is noticeably absent in Thomas's natural law teaching. Moreover, that feature increased notably with the encyclicals of John XXIII and his successors, especially *Pacem in terris, Mater et magistra,* and *Populorum progressio.*[36]

Second, the current pope, John Paul II, has been the exponent of a brand of philosophy known as personalism.[37] I think that this personalism is not opposed to natural law; in fact, I think it demonstrably depends on natural law. For example, Karol Wojtyla's book on *Love and Responsibility* re-

---

35. See Ernest Fortin, *Ernest L. Fortin, Collected Essays,* Vol. 3, *Human Rights, Virtue, and the Common Good,* ed. Brian Benestad (Lanham, Md.: Rowman & Littlefield, 1996).

36. See Brian Benestad, *The Pursuit of a Just Social Order* (Washington, D.C.: Ethics and Public Policy Center, 1982).

37. An able exposition of the basics of John Paul II's philosophical background can be found in George Weigel's biography, *Witness to Hope* (New York: Cliff Street Books, 1999).

curs to traditional natural law teaching at key moments in the argument.[38] And when dealing specifically with current errors in moral theology in the encyclical *Veritatis splendor*, the pope refers extensively to natural law. Nonetheless, there is no question that personalist philosophy is somewhat different from natural law. Similarly, while the *Catechism of the Catholic Church* certainly is compatible with natural law theory—it even contains a brief, two-page description of natural law—the language of natural law is not prominent. (Interestingly, there is not even a separate major entry in the subject index for "natural law." It is included under "Law," and contains no entries outside the relatively brief, two-page description already referred to.[39])

Whatever the reasons for this deemphasis on natural law in Magisterial teachings (perhaps its rhetorical disutility in the contemporary world, perhaps a desire to reemphasize the scriptural and revelational basis of Catholic moral theology), it is worth noting.

In Catholic theology more generally, traditional natural law teaching has been under attack, in two ways. Some contemporary moral theologians simply reject it. Others maintain it, but effectively revise it to reach conclusions that have traditionally been at odds with it.[40] The most obvious example is the enormous disruption occasioned by the Church's reassertion of its teaching on contraception, in *Humanae vitae*.

Among those committed to traditional natural law theory, the most interesting development has been the ongoing debate between exponents of the "new natural law theory" of Germain Grisez, John Finnis, Robert George, et al.[41] and more traditional neo-Scholastic natural law theorists, for example, Ralph McInerny and Russell Hittinger.[42] Despite the deep

---

38. Karol Wojtyla, *Love and Responsibility*, trans. H. T. Willetts (New York: Farrar, Straus, Giroux, 1981).

39. *Catechism of the Catholic Church*, nos. 1954–60.

40. See Richard McBrien, *Catholicism*, 3d ed. (San Francisco: Harper, 1994).

41. See Germain Grisez, *The Way of the Lord Jesus*, Vol. 1 (Chicago: Franciscan Herald Press, 1983); John Finnis, *Natural Law and Natural Rights* (New York: Oxford University Press, 1980); and Robert George, "Recent Criticisms of Natural Law Theory," *University of Chicago Law Review* 55 (Fall 1988): 1371–1429.

42. See Ralph McInerny, *Ethica Thomistica* (Washington, D.C.: The Catholic University of America Press, 1997), and Russell Hittinger, *A Critique of the New Natural Law Theory* (South Bend, Ind.: University of Notre Dame Press, 1987).

personal commitment of both sides in this debate to the Catholic Magisterium—or, put another way, the fact that both sides seem to reach substantially the same conclusions on key moral issues—the tendency on both sides has been, I think, to view the other side not as allies with whom there are limited differences, but as proponents of views that are so deeply misguided as to be fundamentally incompatible with true natural law theory.

Confronting this division within natural law ranks, I find myself drawn toward two positions, which are, as scholars say politely, "in tension with each other." The more practical response is a concern that this perceived chasm undermines the unity and therefore the collective impact of natural law theorists on contemporary moral philosophy, a position that carries with it a predisposition to advocate a kind of "fusionism" (emphasis on the least common denominator between the two positions). The more theoretical response is an appreciation that this vigorous debate has pushed both sides to reexamine more deeply the traditional sources of natural law theory, especially the teaching of Thomas Aquinas, and a sense that the theoretical differences between the two sides in the debate may, in fact, be very substantial. This is one of the central questions facing today's natural law scholars (and those who take their orientation from them): Can the perceived gap between the positions be narrowed so as to present a coherent and defensible "united front," or is it necessary simply to make a choice between the rival positions?

Natural Law in Contemporary America
Public Discussion

The first thing that must be said about the status of natural law in contemporary America is that its influence is quite weak, and it remains, for the most part, at the margin of American intellectual and public life. Most obviously, the term is very rarely used in public discourse. But, more importantly, the one recent occasion on which it did become a major public issue suggests that it is even widely viewed as a political albatross.

This occasion for a significant public discussion of natural law and the Supreme Court was the 1991 nomination of Clarence Thomas. Natural law became an issue because Thomas had given speeches in which he appeared to argue that natural law was decidedly relevant to American constitutional law. In particular, he cited Justice Harlan's dissent in *Plessy v. Ferguson* as a good example of a judge rightly adverting to the higher law background to the Constitution (especially in the Declaration)—though Harlan did not *explicitly* cite natural law.

At the hearings on his nomination, however, Thomas backed off his earlier ringing endorsement of the relevance of natural law to constitutional interpretation. Not only did he deny that judges could strike down laws on the basis of natural law principles not embodied in the Constitution—a view clearly consistent with his earlier arguments—but he said that natural law was of merely "theoretical interest," without any practical impact on actual constitutional adjudication. Thomas was willing, later, in an exchange with committee chairman Joseph Biden, to respond affirmatively to Biden's statement: "I don't see how any reasonable person can conclude that natural law does not impact upon adjudication of a case, if you are a judge, if you acknowledge that you have to go back and look at what the Founders meant by natural law, and then at least in part have that play a part in . . . adjudication. . . ."[43] But even this was qualified substantially, on the grounds that "the provisions they [the Framers] chose were broad provisions, that adjudicating through our history and tradition, using our history and tradition evolve."[44]

This backing off of the issue—whether politically prudent or not—short-circuited any opportunity for a substantial public debate on the issue, which was an unfortunate missed opportunity to educate the American people. Such a debate could have helped to make the relevance and importance of natural law clear, while clarifying its limits as well. In the event, it turned out to be a nondebate. Thomas's flight from natural law suggested that even proponents of natural law saw it as politically dangerous baggage.

The Academy

In the intellectual world, the following anecdote is one example that bears out the observation of the current weakness of natural law thought. At a conference sponsored by the American Public Philosophy Institute in 1993, the distinguished Oxford legal philosopher Joseph Raz was giving a paper, and at one point began to say that "there is a consensus today . . ." and then hesitated, looked up at the audience (about half of whom were

---

43. Senate Judiciary Committee Confirmation Hearings on the Nomination of Clarence Thomas as Associate Justice of the Supreme Court of the United States, Part 1, 276–77.
44. Ibid., 277.

natural law–oriented scholars) and said "not here, of course"! That is, he had written about a "consensus," without adverting to the dissent of natural law theorists—because, it seems, they are not significant enough to detract from the fact of there being a "consensus."

The most important figure in current Anglo-American political and legal philosophy has been the neo-Kantian John Rawls, author of *A Theory of Justice* (1971) and *Political Liberalism* (1992). Arrayed against this antiperfectionist liberalism are the other major streams of contemporary thought: various forms of utilitarianism and of postmodern or multicultural thought (e.g., critical legal studies, feminism, critical race theory).[45] Natural rights theory, largely the provenance of certain libertarians, is, like natural law theory, a small backwater in contemporary intellectual life.[46] Even some of the very limited attention to natural law that there is demonstrates a defective understanding of it.[47]

Nor is it just current liberal and radical thought that is inhospitable to natural law theory. A good deal of contemporary conservative thought is tempted in the direction of positivism. Public figures such as Supreme Court justices William Rehnquist and Antonin Scalia, and Judge Robert Bork, are prominent in this regard.[48]

The general attitude toward natural law theory in this mainstream is that it is rigid, outdated, indeterminate, and even inimical to the well-being of individuals and communities. On this last note, it is particularly interesting to see the attitude toward natural law positions in Rawls and some of his

---

45. For an overview of contemporary political theory, see *Liberalism at the Crossroads*, eds. Christopher Wolfe and John Hittinger (Lanham, Md.: Rowman & Littlefield, 1994).

46. See, e.g., Randy Barnett, *The Structure of Liberty* (New York: Oxford University Press, 1998).

47. See, e.g., Lloyd Weinreb, *Natural Law and Justice* (Cambridge, Mass.: Harvard University Press, 1987), and the critique of this work in Robert George, "Recent Criticisms of Natural Law Theory."

48. Rehnquist is, I think, genuinely in the school of legal positivism, as his positive references to Oliver Wendell Holmes Jr. suggest. See William Rehnquist, "The Notion of a Living Constitution," *Texas Law Review* 54 (1976): 693–706. Bork and Scalia are not ultimately positivists, I think, but their language sometimes seems to suggest strongly that they are. See, e.g., Robert Bork, "Neutral Principles and Some First Amendment Problems," *Indiana Law Journal* 47 (1971): 1–35, and an address by Scalia at the Gregorian University, cited in Robert P. George, "The Tyrant State," *First Things* 67 (November 1996): 40.

followers, for example, Stephen Macedo. In *Political Liberalism,* Rawls originally indicated that his doctrine of "public reason" excluded such natural law positions as prohibition of abortion, at least in the first two trimesters. It was not just that such a natural law position was "wrong," but that it failed to meet the requirements for being a legitimate position to take in a modern liberal society. (Under criticism, Rawls withdrew this argument in the later paperback introduction to *Political Liberalism.*)

Macedo, who generally follows Rawls, has had a particularly interesting series of arguments about natural law and public reason, flip-flopping back and forth on the question of whether natural law arguments on issues like abortion and homosexuality (1) are simply wrong or (2) fail the test of public reason, and are therefore not legitimate kinds of arguments in a liberal society.[49]

The dominance of Rawls and liberalism in the academy is not confined there, since the academy has a disproportionate influence on American life, through its influence on judges, opinion makers, and the media elite. Two of the key developments in post–World War II America have been mass higher education and the expansion of leisure, entertainment, and the concomitant influence of media elites and others who shape popular culture. American intellectuals (like Western intellectuals generally) have been deeply influenced by philosophical movements away from "nature" for the entire century, but their influence on public life, while significant, was limited as long as it was confined to an academy that was relatively small. With the expansion of mass higher education after World War II many more Americans were taught by intellectual elites or those trained by them, and so their influence increased accordingly. At the same time, affluence led to a growth in leisure and entertainment, especially with the rise of television, and the media elites who shaped the entertainment industry also tended to share the cultural prejudices of the intelligentsia.[50]

---

49. See Robert George and Christopher Wolfe, "Natural Law and Public Reason," in *Natural Law and Public Reason,* eds. George and Wolfe (Washington, D.C.: Georgetown University Press, 2000).

50. Robert Lerner, Althea Nagai, and Stanley Rothman, *American Elites* (New Haven, Conn.: Yale University Press, 1996).

The Supreme Court and Natural Law

Outside the academy, in political and social life, natural law is also under broad assault. This is especially obvious in certain strands of Supreme Court decisions. First, as Michael Sandel has described in *Democracy's Discontent*,[51] the modern Court, at least since 1943 (though I think that 1938 is a defensible date as well), has frequently adopted a position of liberal "neutrality," resulting in what he calls the "procedural republic." This neutrality means that there must be no "orthodoxy" in American political life (other than the orthodoxy of no orthodoxy). Free speech cases gravitate toward relativism: obscenity standards broke down in a series of decisions during the 1960s,[52] prohibitions of public vulgarity were overturned in the 1970s,[53] flag burning and nude dancing came to fall under the rubric of free speech in the 1990s[54]—all in the name of preventing a public orthodoxy.[55]

Another form of liberal neutrality consisted of a fairly rigorous exclusion of religion from public life, though the Court waffled quite a bit in this area in the last third of the twentieth century. One area where it didn't waffle much, however, was the exclusion of religion in public education.[56]

But the most significant area in which the Court has led an assault on natural law doctrines has been in the so-called privacy area. Beginning with *Griswold v. Connecticut*[57] in 1965, a case dealing with an anti-contraception law, the Court has used the once-largely-discredited idea of substantive due process to erect a barrier to much public regulation of sexual morality. While *Griswold* retained the appearance of a certain deference to natural law thought, by rooting the newly created right in the institution of marriage, that foundation was soon after dismissed in *Eisenstadt v. Baird* (1972), which gave the right a thoroughly individualistic cast (in an opinion by the

---

51. Michael Sandel, *Democracy's Discontent* (Cambridge, Mass.: Harvard University Press, 1996).

52. See a trenchant account of the collapse of obscenity jurisprudence in Harry Clor, *Obscenity and Public Morality* (Chicago: University of Chicago Press, 1969), chaps. 1 and 2.

53. See, e.g., *Cohen v. California* 403 U.S. 15 (1971).

54. *Texas v. Johnson* 491 U.S. 397 (1989) and *Barnes v. Glen Theatre* 501 U.S. 560 (1991).

55. For a fuller discussion, see Christopher Wolfe, "Public Morality and the Modern Supreme Court," *American Journal of Jurisprudence* 45 (2000): 65–92.

56. See *Wallace v. Jaffree* 472 U.S. 38 (1985) and *Edwards v. Aguillard* 482 U.S. 578 (1987).

57. *Griswold v. Connecticut* 381 U.S. 479 (1965).

"Catholic" on the Court, William Brennan).[58] The Court then moved on to establish an extraordinarily broad and controversial right to abortion in *Roe v. Wade* (1973), reaffirming its central holding (in a plurality opinion by three Republican appointees) in *Planned Parenthood v. Casey* (1992).[59] Finally, the Court has capped its pro-abortion jurisprudence by striking down even state attempts to prohibit the gruesome "partial-birth abortion" procedure, in *Stenberg v. Carhart* (2000).[60]

The Court initially refused to extend the privacy right to homosexual acts, in *Bowers v. Hardwick* (1986)[61]—but the Court opinion simply cited the positive law (the people of Georgia have a right to legislate on the basis of their moral judgments), without making any effort to explain what the basis for that law (and moral judgment) might be, that is, why it might be reasonable. Not surprisingly, the Court eventually retreated. In *Romer v. Evans* (1996),[62] the Court struck down, on equal protection grounds, a Colorado state constitutional amendment essentially prohibiting gay rights ordinances, and in so doing characterized opposition to the legitimization of homosexuality—an unchallenged moral principle of Western law and of natural law theory for many centuries—as "mere animus." Then in *Lawrence v. Texas* (2003)[63] it explicitly overruled *Bowers* and struck down a state law prohibiting homosexual sodomy, this time specifically on right to privacy grounds.

And in the area of euthanasia, even when the Court refused to accept claims that the privacy right includes a broad constitutional right to physician-assisted suicide, in *Washington v. Glucksberg* and *Vacco v. Quill* (1997),[64] there was a cloud around that silver lining: five of the justices seemed to indicate that there might be a constitutionally protected right to obtain assistance in killing oneself, in some narrow circumstances.

One important feature of the debate on the Court in these cases is the general absence of any real debate between modern liberalism and natural law thought. Liberal political theory certainly is represented, but the oppo-

58. *Eisenstadt v. Baird* 405 U.S. 438 (1972).

59. *Roe v. Wade* 410 U.S. 113 (1973); *Planned Parenthood of Southeastern Pennsylvania v. Casey* 505 U.S. 833 (1992).

60. *Stenberg v. Carhart* 530 U.S. 914 (2000).

61. *Bowers v. Hardwick* 478 U.S. 186 (1986).

62. *Romer v. Evans* 517 U.S. 620 (1996).

63. *Lawrence v. Texas* 123 S. Ct. 2472 (2003).

64. *Washington v. Glucksberg* 521 U.S. 702 (1997) and *Vacco v. Quill* 521 U.S. 793 (1997).

sition to liberal autonomist thought is the "anti-judicial activism" position. There is no explanation of the reasons behind anti-contraception laws; there is no "pro-life" position opposed to the case for broad abortion rights; there is no view of the normativity of heterosexuality in cases regarding homosexuality. (There *is* something of an effort to defend traditional mores, I think, in the euthanasia cases—where the opinion, ironically, is written by Chief Justice Rehnquist, probably the most thoroughly positivist of the anti-judicial activists on the Court. And in *Stenberg v. Carhart,* Justice Scalia permits his personal revulsion for partial-birth abortion to show.) This "asymmetry" in the culture war debate on the Court—liberalism is defended, but natural law or "cultural conservatism" is not—may or may not be the correct judicial position. But it does, I think, have the effect of handicapping those in favor of traditional morality, whose views are not really represented (i.e., explained and defended) by any of the participants in these important debates.[65]

Elite or Popular Opinion?

An interesting and important question is whether this Supreme Court assault on natural law positions is the position of a minority intellectual elite, using its influence with judges to impose its position on the nation, or is the Supreme Court speaking for the nation as well as itself in this area? That question was an important aspect of the controversial *First Things* symposium on "The End of Democracy?: The Judicial Usurpation of Politics." The six authors (Robert Bork, Russell Hittinger, Hadley Arkes, Charles Colson, Robert George, and the editor, Richard John Neuhaus) raised serious questions about the legitimacy of the American regime,[66] on the basis of two overlapping considerations: first, the usurpation of legislative power by judges (especially those on the Supreme Court), and second,

---

65. Interestingly, there is another, quite different perspective, from which it is actually possible to characterize the main thrust of this modern Court jurisprudence as itself a form of natural law, as Russell Hittinger does in "Liberalism and the American Natural Law Tradition," *Wake Forest Law Review* 25 (1990): 429–99. Drawing on Hittinger, I discuss this matter in my "Natural Law and Judicial Review," in *Natural Law and Contemporary Public Policy,* ed. David Forte (Washington, D.C.: Georgetown University Press, 1998), 157–89.

66. The word "regime," in this context, means the comprehensive, fundamental "constitution" (small "c") of a given people or nation. The word, given currency by students of Leo Strauss, following his perceptive study of classical political philosophy, emphasizes the

the use of that power contrary to fundamental principles of natural law (e.g., with respect to abortion, euthanasia, and homosexual conduct). The symposium, which elicited some deep hostility even among some neoconservatives normally sympathetic to both *First Things* (several resigned from positions with the journal) and these authors, was a reminder of the permanent possibility of a tension or outright conflict between the prevailing principles of the American regime and natural law standards of political morality.[67] But, while the symposium was clearly correct in attacking both judicial usurpation and its employment contrary to natural law standards, lurking behind the discussion was the question of whether it is simply the Court that is hostile to those standards.

The answer to that question is clearly no, I think, though it is true that the Court pushes that hostility further than the nation. But the fact remains that there is ample evidence that the Court is not the only problem—the problem is much deeper, in the populace. This is clear in an area in which the Court has done relatively little of the damage: divorce. No-fault divorce laws swept the country in the late 1960s, and became pretty much the law of the land. And while there is much hand-wringing in some portions of the public, there has been very little practical effort to roll back these laws.

In the abortion area, the Court clearly went much further than the American people would have (as the Supreme Court decision in the partial-birth abortion case makes clear). But it is also true that, despite deep ambivalence regarding the abortion issue, and contradictory answers to various polling questions about it, Americans are not likely to support a broad rollback of abortion rights. Even apart from the fact that if the issue is returned to the states there will be some states—especially large ones like New York and California—that are likely to retain broad abortion rights, if the issue were decided nationally, it is hard to imagine any serious restrictions on first-trimester abortions (the large majority of abortions) being passed.

In the homosexuality area, the nation, again, is unwilling to go with intellectual elites the full distance of legitimizing homosexuality by acceptance of gay marriage, but it increasingly is disinclined to support anti-

---

integration of a nation's "form of government" and its "way of life," elements that modern political philosophy tends to separate.

67. See *The End of Democracy*, Vols. 1 and 2, ed. Mitchell Muncy (Dallas, Tex.: Spence, 1997, 1998).

sodomy laws, and seems likely to tolerate some form of domestic partnership laws or civil unions short of marriage.

These positions should not be surprising because they reflect popular attitudes regarding heterosexual morality. The dissent in *Bowers*—which the Court more or less ignored, perhaps because it could not respond to it—pointed out that the Georgia anti-sodomy law applied to heterosexuals as much as to homosexuals, and the dissenters were willing to support the proposition that there was clearly a privacy right to heterosexual sodomy. And in this regard, they are probably right that there would be majority popular support for rights to heterosexual oral sex, for example. And I say "heterosexual oral sex" rather than "oral sex between married heterosexuals" advisedly, in light of the extraordinarily widespread practice of and social acceptance of heterosexual cohabitation. (Even having to publicly discuss oral sex in a paper on American political and social life exemplifies the extent of the decline of American sexual mores.)

At the root of current social attitudes toward sexuality, I think, we can find the widespread heterosexual acceptance of masturbation, certain forms of fornication, and contraception. Once these practices are accepted, once sex is detached from marriage, family, and children, it is difficult to hold the line against a general right to adult consensual sexual activity. While there is no such general constitutional or political right of that sort yet, current trends are moving in that direction.

Intimately connected with the questions of sexual morality is the whole question of the role of women in society. Quite apart from the more radical forms of feminism, which exercise a disproportionate influence in academia and perhaps especially in legal scholarship, there is the widespread suspicion of older notions of sexual differentiation related to family life. Part of this suspicion is understandable, since those older notions often served as the basis for public policies unjustly restricting the freedom of women to work outside the home and participate in public life. Unfortunately, one form of response to these older notions has been an egalitarianism that exaggeratedly emphasizes specifically male criteria of power and prestige, achieving the "elevation" of women by making them more like men, implicitly reflecting a certain form of male disdain for feminine qualities and activities, and especially for "mere" family life (childrearing and homemaking). These forces tend to reinforce strongly attitudes toward sexuality that minimize its procreative dimension.

Nor is sexual morality the only area where traditional natural law teaching is weak today. Besides the life-and-death issues (abortion, euthanasia, and also artificial reproduction, which has widespread popular support), one can also point to issues of the use of nuclear weapons, regarding which many Americans (probably a large majority) accept frankly consequentialist arguments. (The fact that there are nonconsequentialist arguments, in my opinion, justifying the use of nuclear weapons in some ways, does not eliminate the significance of the fact that such arguments are not the ones most Americans find compelling.) Some natural law theorists would consider the death penalty a similar issue (though I would not).

And, more broadly, for all the ambivalence of Americans on many moral issues, and their frequent decrying of moral decay in society, there seems to be an unfortunate growing hostility to being "judgmental."[68] (This is reflected in the fact that, although the "religious right" has significant support in America, there is considerable hostility to it among "centrist" voters.) Nor should we find this surprising after several decades of moral education theory that is frankly utilitarian or consequentialist (e.g., "lifeboat" exercises in which students decide whether to chuck the lawyer, the minister, or the old man off an overloaded lifeboat).[69]

Bright Spots

In the midst of these many shadows, are there any bright spots regarding the status of natural law in American society? Well, there are some. First, in the account above, I have noted that Americans as a whole continue to resist the more radical tendencies of intellectual elites. For example, even California, not an overwhelmingly conservative state by any means, decisively passed a referendum confining legal marriage to a man and a woman only recently. And the partial-birth abortion debate really has had an effect on popular opinion, so that younger people, interestingly, are more likely to be opposed to abortion than some older segments of the population.

Second, there is a limited, but growing, respectability of certain forms of natural law theory in the academy and intellectual life. "Respectability"

---

68. While he overstates this argument dramatically, Alan Wolfe is at least partly right about this, I think, in his *One Nation, After All* (New York: Viking Press, 1998).

69. On contemporary moral education, see William Kirk Kilpatrick, *Why Johnny Can't Tell Right from Wrong* (New York: Simon & Schuster, 1992).

doesn't mean agreement—just a grudging respect of sorts. John Finnis's *Natural Law and Natural Rights* had a significant impact in this regard, and it is also reflected in Robert George's appointment to hold the McCormick Chair in Jurisprudence at Princeton University. Journals like *First Things* and the revivified *American Journal of Jurisprudence* and groups like the American Public Philosophy Institute also contribute to and reflect this revival.

Third, there is growing interest in natural law outside Catholic intellectual circles. In particular, evangelical Protestants are showing more interest and respect for it, as evidenced by the collection of essays in *A Preserving Grace: Protestants, Catholics, and Natural Law*.[70] The reason for this development—which is generally contrary to the main thrust of their intellectual tradition, rooted in the early Protestants' deep distrust of reason—can be found in the new political engagement of evangelicals. Prior to the 1960s, most evangelicals were not very politically active, but—as Nathan Glazer argued persuasively[71]—the Supreme Court's assault on religion and morality in public life mobilized them in the 1970s. The dynamics of this political engagement have included the fostering of a desire to find nonbiblical arguments to supplement traditional biblical ones, especially in dealing with the large segment of Americans who are either hostile to religion or (more frequently) uncomfortable with explicitly religious arguments in the public sphere.

Besides evangelical Protestants, some communitarians also express (usually cautious) interest in natural law reasoning. But the communitarian movement is a fairly loose accumulation of people who share some very general concerns, but also have relatively significant differences among themselves. If some of its representatives are more willing to accept natural law (or at least its substantive moral principles), the consensus usually breaks down if this is pushed too far. (It is notable, for example, that few communitarians are willing to tackle, or at least to emphasize, issues as controversial as abortion.[72])

---

70. *A Preserving Grace: Protestants, Catholics, and Natural Law*, ed. Michael Cromartie (Grand Rapids, Mich.: Eerdmans, 1997).

71. Nathan Glazer, "Toward A New Concordat," *This World* 2 (Summer 1982):109.

72. For examples of communitarian thought, see *New Communitarian Thinking*, ed. Amitai Etzioni (Charlottesville: University Press of Virginia, 1995). For a more critical assessment of communitarianism, see Bruce Frohnen, *The New Communitarians and the Crisis of Modern Liberalism* (Lawrence: University Press of Kansas, 1996).

Conclusion: Where Do We Go from Here?

There is no question that the only way to increase the impact of natural law theory in American life is the emergence of a whole new cohort of young natural law scholars and of political writers and activists who respect and draw on natural law thought. How to achieve this in an academy whose elite institutions strongly tend to "stack the deck" against natural law scholars and students, and in political and media worlds whose elites are similarly not very receptive to natural law thinking, is a question for which I have no satisfactory answer. The basic points are easy to list, difficult to achieve:

1. Natural law scholars must deepen their own study of the natural law tradition, often overcoming serious intellectual obstacles to a successful appropriation of the tradition, and identifying weaknesses in its formulation or defense, and developing persuasive and plausible applications of it to current realities.

2. They must work, separately and together, to demonstrate a sophisticated understanding of reigning intellectual paradigms and to develop compelling critiques—both internal and external—of them.

3. They must develop effective ways of explaining natural law theory to mainstream scholars who have either no knowledge of natural law or opinions that are largely caricatures of it.

4. They must anticipate and respond effectively to the arguments that are generally thought to have refuted natural law theory.

5. They must work to discover and educate younger people whose talents (intellectual and personal) are so clearly marked that they have a reasonable chance to advance in arenas where they will always be a suspect minority.

I will end this paper with two final questions for advocates of natural law thinking. The first involves effective rhetoric. Would natural law scholars benefit from finding another name for "natural law"? Does the "historical baggage" of this term and its association with Catholicism guarantee it "outsider" status in contemporary American academia and public life? If so, is there another term available? Second, can natural law scholars find better phrases to capture and describe their *substantive* vision, rather than relying on phrases like "traditional morality" that almost concede that their ideas are "old" ideas in a democratic society not known for its veneration of tradition?

❧ RESPONSE ❧

AQUINAS, LOCKE, AND LINCOLN IN THE AMERICAN REGIME

William Mathie

Several years ago I visited a seminar class on John Locke's *Second Treatise on Government* at a small Catholic college distinguished both for its devotion to the teaching of Thomas Aquinas and for its commitment to the seminar method of education. I had been hugely impressed by the enthusiasm students at the college had shown in discussing Dante, the Bible, and even Euclidean geometry. But Locke's treatise drew a very different response. The students I saw seemed unable, or perhaps unwilling, to find anything that excited their curiosity in this text. Reflecting upon what I saw in this class, I began to wonder if the difficulty created by Locke's work for the unusually devout and patriotic young Americans at this college might not be a test of their loyalties. For these students Locke had something like the stature of a Founding Father: he was in fact the teacher of those who had founded the American regime. But Thomas Aquinas was and is the teacher of the actual teachers of these young people. And so the difficulty emerges which I imagined responsible for the awkward tensions I observed in this seminar room. Either Locke says what Thomas says (as Locke seems occasionally prepared to let us believe) and there is not a lot to be said about what he says. Or he says something very different than, maybe contradictory to, Thomas's teaching. But is this a question a loyal Catholic citizen of the United States ought to pursue? For me as a Canadian it was, and is, easy enough to think this. After all, among the most illustrious of our ancestors as Canadians were those who had said "no" to the American Revolution. A few of them made explicit that what they objected to in the revolution was its Lockean character.[1]

---

1. The equation of what they feared and hated in the revolution with the teaching of

Professor Wolfe is forced to address the difficulty I suppose to have silenced the students I speak of, for he is a student of Thomistic natural law and of what he calls "the American natural law tradition," and his subject in this paper is the relationship between the two.[2] Unlike the students I have described, Wolfe is aware that his subject is important and controversial. Thomistic natural law is important because Thomistic natural law is "the best rational framework for understanding political and social life," and therefore also the best guide in advancing or obtaining the common good. Understanding how the American natural law tradition is related to Thomistic natural law is important because it helps Americans understand how they "have gotten to where [they] are today" and because it can help them bring their political life into line with the truth of Thomistic natural law. Perhaps more important—and speaking directly to the unspoken worry of the students I described—arriving at a clear account of the relationship between Thomistic natural law and the American natural law tradition will help Americans "determine . . . to what extent a good citizen [can] be a good person" (Wolfe, p. 198).

What, then, is the relationship between Thomistic natural law and the American natural law tradition for Wolfe? In one sense Wolfe's answer to this question is to be found in the details of his sober and penetrating analysis of those elements of what at least resembles Thomistic natural law as these are more or (usually) less prominent in, for example, decisions of the courts. But he is also willing to characterize that relationship in more general terms at various points in his discussion and to write, for example, of the relationship between the understanding of the Framers of the Constitution and the natural law tradition of which Thomas is, for Wolfe, the greatest exemplar. And this more general treatment of the relationship between the two traditions is of critical importance to Wolfe's inquiry for it must tell him how to read what he finds in the rulings of courts and actions of statesmen.

Locke is an occasional theme of some of the sermons and other statements developed by those who made up the inconsequential remnant William Nelson calls *The American Tory* (Boston: Beacon Press, 1964).

2. That Wolfe might accept or at least understand my account of his difficulty is suggested by his warning that proponents of Thomistic natural law will be tempted to grasp at whatever has the least resemblance to the American tradition in order to clear themselves of the charge that they adhere to something wholly foreign to it. See p. 243.

Thomistic natural law and the American natural law tradition are, Wolfe says, fundamentally different and yet "they have had enough in common to have made a significant difference in (i.e., a positive contribution to) the quality of the American polity, but . . . the overlap between them has been diminishing in modern America" (Wolfe, p. 198). Whether Wolfe means that the contribution he speaks of is derived from Thomistic natural law but made possible by the incorporation of some its elements into the American natural law tradition, or that the two "fundamentally different" notions have exercised some joint beneficial influence or even acted upon each other in some beneficial way is not entirely clear. In any case, Wolfe goes on to speak of the relationship between the two as constituting a consensus that has recently been unraveling (Wolfe, p. 215). Wolfe's metaphors of overlap and unraveling are surely suggestive, but what they suggest are not so much answers as new questions. We must proceed, as Wolfe proceeds, to consider the relationship between Thomistic natural law and the teaching of those like John Locke who were the teachers of the Framers of the American polity. And then if we find the differences between the two teachings great—even irreconcilable—we may be compelled to ask a further question, mentioned though not pursued by Wolfe: Is the overlap that is reduced, or the intertwining that is unraveling, constituted by those things about which Thomas and Locke actually agree or is it to be found in the minds of those first citizens and makers of the American regime who may have believed that Thomas and Locke were consistent when in fact they were not?

How ought we to understand the relationship between Thomistic natural law and what Wolfe and others label the natural rights teaching of Locke and take to be the "most important element in the philosophical framework of the American Constitution" (Wolfe, p. 205)? Wolfe says that the natural law tradition "ultimately transmogrified" into the new and different tradition of the natural rights doctrine (Wolfe, p. 202). Wolfe says that for Locke, as for Hobbes, the first or fundamental law of nature is self-preservation. What Hobbes says is that we have a right—not a duty—to preserve ourselves that is fundamental and inalienable. What makes this a right is that no one can be blamed for preserving himself. And the reason for this is that there is a natural impulse to do so that no one can be blamed for obeying. But neither the impulse nor the right are laws for Hobbes. And what Hobbes does sometimes call laws of nature are only conditional imperatives: If peace is possible, seek it! If you have made a covenant, keep it! They are in fact not laws at all properly speaking, as Hobbes acknowledges at the end of his discussion of them.[3] For Locke there is, as Wolfe says, a law of nature depending upon the fact that we are not our own but God's property—we are his workmanship put here to serve his ends. But, as Michael Zuckert has observed, the actual content of this law that claims to preserve mankind is a strange inference from the fact that we are not our own property, for it privileges our own self-preservation over the obligation to assist others, and only calls upon us to avoid the gratuitous harming of others.[4] Chiefly, it serves to empower each of us with what Locke calls the executive power to do harm to others in order to prevent what each of us might perceive as violations of the law of nature. Or one could say that it is Locke's way of denying what Aristotle and Aquinas both claim: that human beings are naturally political. Wolfe says we see here a reorientation of natural law from seeking the greatest good of fulfilling human capacities to avoiding the greatest evil—that is, violent death at the hands of others. While this is not incorrect, it seems to me that it would be more exact and revealing to say that we see the shift here from natural law to the right of self-preservation. Assuming, as Wolfe does, that the American tradition is shaped by Locke above all, the question then becomes: What is the relationship between a teaching that asserts the political priority of the right of self-preservation and one that speaks of natural law? Wolfe rightly—I think—rejects the claim that all that distinguishes natural rights from natural law "doctrines" is that the natural rights teaching is narrower than natural law and in fact says nothing about the full range of moral possibilities for human beings. If the American tradition, or at least what was understood by those who were the teachers of those who established the American tradition, speaks to the "full range of moral possibilities for human beings," is what it says compatible with what is said about those possibilities by Thomistic natural law?

Wolfe thinks we can find in the American natural law tradition "important sources of support for principles central to the older natural law theory" (Wolfe, p. 214) that are now under attack as a result of the contempo-

---

3. Hobbes, *Leviathan,* Part 1, chap. 15 [41].

4. See Michael Zuckert, *Natural Rights and the New Republicanism* (Princeton, N.J.: Princeton University Press, 1994), 218.

rary "culture wars." But the support for those principles Wolfe locates is found not in the teaching of Locke but in the perceptions or misperceptions of that teaching entertained by an earlier generation of Americans. And so Wolfe must speak of an "*apparent* continuity between the classical/medieval and early modern traditions (Wolfe, p. 214, emphasis added)," of an unarticulated identification of reason as the source of human dignity, of a widely accepted natural theology attributed by American Lockeans to Locke which Locke may well not have taken seriously (Wolfe, p. 214). Support for Thomistic natural law in the culture wars is found, it seems, not in what Locke thought but in what he is *thought* to have thought. When we probe below the surface of Locke's own teaching we find, I think, a far less benign account of those issues of human life and sexuality that have become central to the culture wars. Consider Locke's denial that generation as such is the basis of any rights or duties, his contractual account of all familial relationships including that of parents and children, not to mention his evident delight in linking the supposed natural instinct of all parents to love their offspring with the horrendous account he reports of Peruvian Indians who cannibalize their own children and, eventually, those women of conquered enemy tribes through whom they have bred these children.[5] Support in the culture wars is to be gotten out of Locke only on the assumption that "it is as important to understand how Locke was received or understood by Americans as it is to understand Locke in himself." (Wolfe, p. 206).

To be sure, we can say, as Wolfe does, that Locke is not the Framers' only teacher and what we see when we dig below the surface of Locke's writing may not be what the Framers saw. The American regime is not simply what Madison and those who shared his understanding intended, nor what their teacher Locke may have thought most deeply. It is also the work of those who allied themselves with Madison in framing the Constitution, of those who accepted the result of that work in Philadelphia for whatever reasons, of those who ratified that work, and even of subsequent generations who acted upon their own understanding of that work, whatever Madison himself may have supposed when he insisted that it is the reason and not the passions of the public that ought to rule.[6] And yet we may still wonder

---

5. Locke, *Two Treatises of Government*, 2.6, esp. §65; 1.6, §52, 57.
6. *Federalist Papers*, No. 49.

whether this is a satisfactory place to leave the issue Wolfe poses. Allan Bloom once addressed a similar difficulty: the tension between Locke's fundamental principles as we see them in his account of the state of nature and what Bloom took to be Locke's continued dependence upon the traditional family as a source of political loyalty. Bloom concluded that Locke's deeper and more radical view would ultimately prevail within political structures erected on his principles over whatever he may have hoped to preserve of the traditional understanding of the family. Why? Bloom replied: "[T]here are two contrary views of nature present here. And as the political philosophers have always taught, the one that is authoritative in the political regime will ultimately inform its parts."[7] And the students I have described were perhaps right after all to avoid a close discussion of Locke's *Treatise*.

Can we avoid this unhappy conclusion toward which, it seems to me, Wolfe's analysis finally points? I mentioned at the outset the smugness I had found in myself as a Canadian reflecting upon the unsatisfactory classroom discussion of Locke's teaching I had once observed. To conclude, I would like to substitute for the chauvinistic smugness that I have confessed something more nearly defensible. And so I would add that I came to that discussion and come now to the reading of Wolfe's paper not only as a Canadian but also as one who was first introduced to the issues posed by his paper through a great teacher and Canada's best known public philosopher, albeit a man almost unheard of in the United States. That teacher was George Grant and he was neither a Catholic nor a Thomist though his first work was a defense of the natural law tradition and the only works of his that have been published in America were published by the University of Notre Dame Press.[8] In the 1960s, Grant became the intellectual leader of Canadian nationalism through a book that identified America as the spearhead of a liberalism that was in the course of destroying all that was traditional and local.[9] A decade later he argued that what we see in the writings of John Rawls and in the reasoning of Harry Blackmun in *Roe v. Wade* is the moral

---

7. Allan Bloom, *The Closing of the American Mind* (New York: Simon & Schuster, 1987), 112.

8. George Parkin Grant, *Philosophy in the Mass Age* (1959; Toronto: University of Toronto Press, 1995).

9. George Parkin Grant, *Lament for a Nation* (Toronto: McLelland & Stewart, 1963).

death or self-destruction of liberalism—or the working out within liberalism of its own logic to the point that its own claim to bring about the justice of equal liberty must be abandoned.[10] Or the recognition that liberalism reaches its logical conclusion not in the equal liberty of the Declaration of Independence but in the analysis of Nietzsche. Where does Grant's analysis leave the issues posed by Wolfe's paper? The United States is, on the one hand, the country where the political, judicial, and academic arguments for abortion have been developed with the greatest theoretical clarity. While those arguments have been developed in more than one way—sometimes by denying personhood to some members of our species, sometimes by insisting that the rights of pregnant women include the right to abortion—always they have been developed in some kind of close theoretical relationship to the moral understanding of liberalism. And, indeed, in a series of decisions before and since *Roe v. Wade* those theoretical arguments have been given deadly authority. And yet America is also the country—very nearly the only country—where abortion remains an active political issue—perhaps even a fundamental one—and here too the arguments have been made by appeal to traditions within American political thought.

Do the arguments against the Supreme Court's abortion decisions or the theory of John Rawls have any foundation within the American tradition or are they remnants of an understanding foreign and hostile to it? The best prospect for a satisfactory answer to this question seems to me to begin with the recognition that the moral and political insufficiency of Locke's teaching has already manifested itself and been articulated within the American tradition—in an area in which Wolfe confesses a lacuna in his studies: he is unsure, he says, of the role played by natural law and Thomistic natural law in the debate surrounding American slavery. I conclude these remarks by asking whether we might not discover a foundation for the case against Justice Blackmun and his friends in Abraham Lincoln's critique of the repeal of the Missouri Compromise and the Dred Scot decision and

---

10. George Parkin Grant, *English Speaking Justice* (Toronto: Anansi, 1974). I have discussed Grant's argument and the answer to it furnished by Lincoln in "The Technological Regime: George Grant's Analysis of Modernity," in *George Grant in Process: Essays and Conversations,* ed. L. Schmidt (Toronto: Anansi, 1978), 157–66; "Reason, Revelation and Liberal Justice: Reflections on George Grant's Analysis of Roe v. Wade," *Canadian Journal of Political Science* 19 (September 1986): 443–66; and "Abortion and the Crisis of Liberal Justice," in *Life and Learning* 8, ed. Joseph Koterski (Washington, D.C.: University Faculty for Life, 1999), 59–70.

above all in those speeches of Lincoln in 1860 that acknowledge the failure of previous American statesmen to perceive the magnitude of the issue posed by the question of slavery.[11] At least as that critique has been interpreted by Harry Jaffa, we may find here an argument for the moral and political insufficiency of the Lockean or Jeffersonian understanding of the Declaration of Independence and American democracy.[12] Can we say that what we see within the reasoning of Lincoln—with increasing clarity and explicitness in his speeches over the twenty years culminating in the Second Inaugural Address—is that the defense of equal liberty and republican government requires that the soft and perhaps deceptive natural theology of Jefferson be replaced with the far sterner stuff of biblical revelation?

11. See, e.g., Lincoln's "Speech at New Haven, Connecticut," in *The Collected Works of Abraham Lincoln,* ed. Roy Basler (New Brunswick, N.J.: Rutgers University Press, 1953), 15–17.

12. Harry V. Jaffa, *The Crisis of the House Divided* (New York: Doubleday, 1959), 318–29.

8

KELSEN AND AQUINAS ON THE NATURAL LAW DOCTRINE

Robert P. George

Introduction

The[†] fiftieth anniversary of the publication of Hans Kelsen's influential essay "The Natural-Law Doctrine before the Tribunal of Science,"[1] provides an occasion to revisit a work in which the leading European legal theorist of the twentieth century outlined and strongly criticized the tradition of natural law theorizing. Contemporary scholars on the Continent and in the English-speaking world will, no doubt, examine Kelsen's essay from a variety of angles. I am struck, however, by the fact that it makes no reference whatsoever to the thought of the most famous and influential of all natural law theorists, namely, St. Thomas Aquinas. Kelsen refers frequently to the writings of Grotius, Pufendorf, Hobbes, Kant, Hegel, and classical

---

[†] A version of this paper appeared in the *Notre Dame Law Review*. The author gratefully acknowledges the generous support of the Earhart Foundation.

1. Hans Kelsen, "The Natural-Law Doctrine before the Tribunal of Science," originally published in the *Western Political Quarterly* 2 (December 1949): 481–513. Reprinted in *What Is Justice?: Justice, Law, and Politics in the Mirror of Science: Collected Essays by Hans Kelsen* (Berkeley and Los Angeles: University of California Press, 1957), 137–73.

Greek philosophers; but Aquinas's theory, or "doctrine," of natural law is left unaddressed. If, however, something called "the natural law doctrine" can be attributed to anyone, surely it can be attributed to Aquinas. I propose, therefore, to consider (1) the extent to which Kelsen's exposition of "the natural-law doctrine" captures or describes Aquinas's account of natural law, and (2) whether Kelsen's critique of natural law ethics and jurisprudence tells against the teachings of Aquinas.[2]

Natural Law, Moral Truth, and Religion

Let us begin by considering sentence by sentence the opening paragraph of Kelsen's essay.

Sentence One: "The natural-law doctrine undertakes to supply a definitive solution to the eternal problem of justice, to answer the question as to what is right and wrong in the mutual relations of men."[3]

Aquinas is concerned with "right and wrong" not only in "the mutual relations of men," but in human affairs generally. He famously argues that *all* acts of virtue, and not merely those ordained to the common good narrowly conceived, are the subject of natural law.[4] Questions of justice are, to be sure, central to his thought, but they are not the only questions. His prescriptions concern what we would call, though he did not, "self-regarding" as well as "other-regarding" conduct.[5] The principles and norms of natural law, as Aquinas understands them, would have relevance to the man permanently stranded alone on an island. Nevertheless, it is fair to say that Kelsen's statement is true, so far as it goes, when applied to Aquinas's conception of "the natural law doctrine."

Sentence Two: "The answer is based on the assumption that it is possible to distinguish between human behavior which is natural, that is to say which corresponds to nature because it is required by nature, and human

---

2. I shall, for the most part, refrain from commenting on the accuracy of Kelsen's attributions to other natural law thinkers of the various propositions he asserts to be constitutive of, or in some sense integral to, "the natural-law doctrine." For what it is worth, my view is that Kelsen's essay is on this score a "mixed bag."

3. Kelsen, "The Natural-Law Doctrine," 137.

4. *ST* I-II, q. 94, a. 3.

5. Aquinas is hardly oblivious to the distinction: see *ST* I-II, q. 91, a. 4, deploying the distinction in teaching that it is unwise for human law to prohibit every act of vice.

behavior which is unnatural, hence contrary to nature and forbidden by nature."[6]

Aquinas does, sometimes, employ the terms "natural" and "unnatural" in a morally normative sense. However, he makes abundantly clear that human choosing and acting is "natural" or "unnatural" in such a sense precisely insofar as it is reasonable or unreasonable.[7] Other natural law theorists have sought to infer the reasonableness or unreasonableness of a possible choice or action from judgments about its naturalness or unnaturalness.[8] And this approach is sometimes, though mistakenly, attributed to Aquinas.[9] The truth is, however, that for Aquinas things work precisely the other way round: it is the reasonableness or unreasonableness of a choice or action that controls judgment as to its naturalness or unnaturalness in any morally normative sense.[10]

Sentence Three: "This assumption implies that it is possible to deduce from nature, that is to say from the nature of man, from the nature of society, and even from the nature of things certain rules which provide an altogether adequate prescription for human behavior, that by a careful examination of the facts of nature we can find the just solution of our social problem."[11]

Aquinas certainly assumed no such thing. In his famous treatment of the question whether the natural law contains several precepts or only one, he says that the first principles of practical reason, which are the basic precepts of natural law, are self-evident *(per se nota)* and indemonstrable.[12] As such,

6. Kelsen, "The Natural-Law Doctrine," 137.

7. See *Scriptum super libros Sententiarum Petri Lombardiensis* IV, d. 2, q. 1, a. 4, sol. 1, ad 2 ("moral precepts are in accord with human nature because they are requirements of natural reason"), and *ST* I-II, q. 71, a. 2 ("virtues . . . are in accordance with human nature just insofar as they are in line with reason; vices are against human nature just insofar as they are against the order of reasonableness").

8. See, e.g., Thomas J. Higgins, *Man as Man: The Science and Art of Ethics* (Milwaukee, Wis.: Bruce, 1958), esp. 49–69, 88–100, 120–26.

9. Ibid. See also Lloyd L. Weinreb, *Natural Law and Justice* (Cambridge, Mass.: Harvard University Press, 1987), 33 ("natural law [according to Aquinas] directs us to fulfill our natural inclinations").

10. For a careful and amply documented explanation of this critical point, see John Finnis, *Aquinas: Moral, Political, and Legal Theory* (Oxford, U.K.: Oxford University Press, 1998), 90–94.

11. Kelsen, "The Natural-Law Doctrine," 137.

12. *ST* I-II, q. 94, a. 2. On the (much misunderstood) meaning of "self-evidence" in

they are not deduced from prior judgments about nature, human nature, the nature of society, or anything else.[13] On the contrary, practical reasoning proceeds from its own first principles. We needn't look to physics, metaphysics, anthropology, sociology, or any other speculative (or, to use the Aristotelian term, "theoretical") discipline to supply them.[14] Of course, information drawn from these disciplines, when considered in the light of practical principles, can be highly pertinent to moral inquiry.[15] Indeed, such information is often indispensable to sound judgments of right and wrong.[16] But, according to Aquinas, the primary principles of practical reason and basic precepts of natural law are not "deduce[d] from nature" (or anything else).

Sentence Four: "Nature is conceived of as a legislator, the supreme legislator."[17]

Not according to Aquinas. True, he allows that human goods, and the norms of morality directing choice and action with respect to these goods (and their privations), would be different if human nature were different, if, that is to say, human beings were fulfilled and perfected by activities and purposes ("goods") other than those that in fact fulfill and perfect us.[18] And in this sense morality and its content depends on (human) nature.[19] But precisely because we do not (and, indeed, cannot) deduce the "ought" of morality from the "is" of nature (or anything else—including God's will),[20] it is a mistake, or so Aquinas would say, to imagine that we could discover moral truth by inquiring into the intentions or purposes of nature conceived as some sort of lawgiver.

Thomistic ethical theory, see Robert P. George, "Recent Criticism of Natural Law Theory," *University of Chicago Law Review* 55 (1988): 1371–429, at 1387–89 and 1413.

13. See Germain Grisez, "The First Principle of Practical Reason: A Commentary on the *Summa Theologiae,* 1–2, Question 94, Article 2," *Natural Law Forum* 10 (1965): 168–201.

14. See Finnis, *Aquinas,* 90–94.

15. See George, "Recent Criticism of Natural Law Theory," 1412–14.

16. So, e.g., knowledge of the facts of human embryogenesis and intrauterine human development is critical to a proper application of moral principles to the question of abortion.

17. Kelsen, "The Natural-Law Doctrine," 137.

18. See John Finnis, *Natural Law and Natural Rights* (New York: Oxford University Press, 1980), 34.

19. See Robert P. George, "Natural Law and Human Nature," in Robert P. George, ed., *Natural Law Theory: Contemporary Essays* (Oxford, U.K.: Clarendon Press, 1992), 31–41.

20. See Finnis, *Aquinas,* 90.

Moving to the second paragraph of Kelsen's essay, we can see even more clearly that his account of "the natural-law doctrine" is at sharp variance with what Aquinas teaches about the natural law:

> This view presupposes that natural phenomena are directed toward an end or shaped by a purpose, that natural processes or nature conceived of as a whole are determined by final causes. It is a thoroughly teleological view, and as such does not differ from the idea that nature is endowed with will and intelligence. This implies that nature is a kind of superhuman personal being, an authority to which man owes obedience.[21]

Whatever views about final causes Aquinas retains from Aristotle's thought, he certainly would reject "the idea that nature is endowed with will and intelligence." Nature is not, in Aquinas's account, "a kind of superhuman personal being." Nor is the ground of our moral obligations a debt of obedience to the "will" of nature or, indeed, any other authority. Unlike many later theorists of natural law, Aquinas eschewed the voluntarism implied by this conception of moral obligation.[22] The force of practical—including moral—principles, according to Aquinas, is *rational;* these principles state *reasons* for action and restraint; to defy them is wrong inasmuch as it is *unreasonable.*[23] And, in this sense, the natural law is no extrinsic imposition of an alien will—whether the "will" of nature or anything (or anybody) else. It is, rather, intrinsic to human beings; its fundamental referents are the human goods that constitute human well-being and fulfillment and precisely as such are reasons for action.[24]

Moving now more deeply into Kelsen's second paragraph, we find him arguing as follows:

> At a higher stage of religious evolution, when animism is replaced by monotheism, nature is conceived of as having been created by God and is therefore regard-

---

21. Kelsen, "The Natural-Law Doctrine," 137.
22. On the impact of voluntarism on Christian moral theology after Aquinas, see Germain Grisez, *The Way of the Lord Jesus,* Vol. 1, *Christian Moral Principles* (Chicago: Franciscan Herald Press, 1983), 12–13. In the same work, Grisez provides a powerful critique of voluntarism and defense of the authentically Thomistic alternative account of moral obligation as a kind of rational necessity; see esp. 103–5. See also Finnis, *Natural Law and Natural Rights,* 42–48, 337–43.
23. See Finnis, *Aquinas,* 79–86.
24. Ibid.

ed as a revelation of his all powerful and just will. If the natural-law doctrine is consistent, it must assume a religious character. It can deduce from nature just rules of human behavior only because and so far as nature is conceived of as a revelation of God's will, so that examining nature amounts to exploring God's will. As a matter of fact, there is no natural-law doctrine of any importance which has not a more or less religious character.[25]

According to Aquinas, the natural law is a "participation of the eternal law in the rational creature."[26] And "the eternal law" is the supreme act of (practical) reason by which an omnipotent and omnibenevolent Creator freely orders the whole of his creation.[27] Thus, the natural law is a part of the rational plan by which God providentially governs the created order.[28] In this sense, Aquinas's natural law doctrine can be regarded as having a "religious character." Its religious character, however, has nothing to do with any putative deduction from nature, conceived as revelatory of the will of God or anyone (or anything) else, of moral norms or other "rules of human behavior." There is no sense, for Aquinas, in which one "reads off" from nature (or human nature) God's will regarding human conduct.[29]

It is worth pausing here to observe, moreover, that there is no sense in which the natural law, as the eternal law's participation in the rational creature, is incompatible with human freedom. The dependency of human choice and action on divine power and causality does not vitiate the human power of creative free choice. Indeed, Aquinas interprets the biblical teaching that man is an *imago dei*[30] precisely as meaning that human beings are endowed with the God-like attributes of practical rationality and freedom.

25. Kelsen, "The Natural-Law Doctrine," 138.
26. *ST* I-II, q. 91, a. 2.
27. *ST* I-II, q. 91, a. 1.
28. Finnis sums up Aquinas's teaching on "the eternal law" as follows: "God envisages and freely chooses the whole order of things, prescribing (so to speak) that order by impressing its principles (the 'laws of physics,' the 'laws of logic,' and so forth) onto or into the various orders of created entity and process. And this act is to the common benefit of the whole (and thus of its parts). So we can think of this supreme act of government as legislative, and its rational content as a law which, like its author, is timeless (even though that content is freely chosen, not necessary, and regulates creatures which are all within time)"; see *Aquinas,* 307 (notes omitted).
29. Ibid., 309.
30. Gn 1:27.

Man is said to be made in God's image, insofar as the image *implies an intelligent being endowed with free will and self-movement:* now that we have treated of the exemplar, i.e., God, and of those things which come forth from the power of God in accordance with his will, it remains for us to treat of His image, i.e., man, inasmuch as he too is the principle of his actions, as having free will and control of his actions.[31]

Thus it is that, though God directs the brute animals to their proper ends by instinct or "natural appetite," human beings he directs to their proper ends by the God-like power of practical reason, namely, the power to understand what is humanly (including morally) good and bad and freely to choose to act in light of the reasons thus provided.[32]

According to Aquinas, the whole of the created order is suffused with meaning and value inasmuch as it is the product of God's free and intelligent action. At the same time, part—though not all—of the created order also has meaning and value by virtue of the contributions of human freedom and reason (which human capacities are themselves, as parts of the created order, suffused with meaning and value by virtue of divine wisdom and free choice).[33] This part of the created order is governed by the principles of natural law by which free and intelligent creatures order their lives according to the directives of practical reason. In precisely this sense, the natural law is "a participation of the eternal law in the rational creature."

Does Aquinas's natural law theory presuppose religious premises? Can it be accepted only by those who presuppose God's existence and believe that he has revealed something of his will for human beings? I have said enough already to indicate that the answer to these questions must be "no." At the same time, one may not infer from the fact that principles of natural law, according to Aquinas's account, can be understood and acted upon without appeal to religious premises that God does not exist, or that God's existence is simply irrelevant to natural law theory.

---

31. *ST* I-II, Prologue.

32. *ST* I-II, q. 91, a. 2.

33. These points are explained more fully in George, "Recent Criticism of Natural Law Theory," 1384–85. Unfortunately, a key line on page 1384 was omitted by the printer in the version of this essay that appeared in the *University of Chicago Law Review*. It would be better, therefore, for readers to consult the revised version appearing as chap. 2 of Robert P. George, *In Defense of Natural Law* (Oxford, U.K.: Clarendon Press, 1999), sec. C.

[J]ust as the fact that a good explanation of molecular motion can be provided, without adverting to the existence of an uncreated creator of the whole state of affairs in which molecules and the laws of their motion obtain, does not of itself entail either (i) that no further explanation of that state of affairs is required or (ii) that no such further explanation is available, or (iii) that the existence of an uncreated creator is not that explanation, so too the fact that natural law can be understood, assented to, applied, and reflectively analysed without adverting to the question of the existence of God does not of itself entail either (i) that no further explanation is required for the fact that there are objective standards of good and bad and principles of reasonableness (right and wrong) or (ii) that no such further explanation is available, or (iii) that the existence of God is not that explanation.[34]

Let us now move beyond the opening paragraph of Kelsen's essay to his critique of "the natural-law doctrine." His principal objection to natural law theory is that it "obliterates the essential difference which exists between scientific laws of nature, the rules by which the science of nature describes its object, and the rules by which ethics and jurisprudence describe their objects, which are morality and law."[35] This objection boils down to the proposition that "it does not follow from the fact that something is, that it ought to be or to be done, or that it ought not to be or not to be done . . . there is no logical inference from the 'is' to the 'ought,' from natural reality to moral or legal value."[36]

That certain natural law theorists (including some who have claimed the patronage of Aquinas) have proposed to derive the "ought" of morality from the "is" of (human) nature is true.[37] It is equally true, however, that Aquinas is not among them, nor are his leading contemporary followers.[38]

---

34. Finnis, *Natural Law and Natural Rights*, 49.

35. Kelsen, "The Natural-Law Doctrine," 139.

36. Ibid., 140.

37. The origins of this approach to natural law theory are not in Aquinas, but, rather, in later writings such as those of the early-seventeenth-century Spanish Jesuit moral and political thinker Francisco Suarez. See esp. his *De Legibus ac de Deo Legislator* (1612), Bk I, chap. 5, and Book II, chap. 6. For a useful account of Suarez's influence, and a valuable critique of his approach to natural law theory, see Finnis, *Natural Law and Natural Rights*, 43–47, 54–57, 337–43, and 347–50.

38. Germain Grisez and John Finnis, e.g., among other leading contemporary moral philosophers and theologians working broadly within the Thomistic tradition, explicitly reject as logically illicit any proposal to derive "ought" from "is." See Grisez, *The Way of the Lord Jesus*, Vol. 1, *Christian Moral Principles*, 105; and Finnis, *Natural Law and Natural Rights*, 33–36.

Although Hume is widely credited with discovering the logical fallacy inherent in any attempt at such a derivation,[39] Aquinas, among other premodern thinkers, was quite well aware of the fallacy and sought more scrupulously than did Hume himself to avoid committing it.[40] Accepting Aristotle's distinction between "theoretical" (or "speculative") and "practical" reasoning, Aquinas insisted, as we have seen, that practical reasoning proceeds from its own first principles. He did not treat practical principles as theoretical principles that are given normative force by an act of the will. He did not treat theoretical knowledge of human nature as providing a sufficient premise for practical knowledge, let alone for practical knowledge of moral obligation.[41] He did not suppose that having first discovered the "facts" about human nature by way of nonpractical inquiry, we then identify ethical obligations by applying a norm such as "follow nature."[42]

Hume and his followers, perhaps including Kelsen,[43] suppose that if "values" cannot be derived from "facts," then they cannot be objective (or "true"), but must, rather, be mere projections of feeling, emotion, or other subrational factors capable of motivating human behavior. They deny that practical reasons, as such, can motivate people. So they conclude that, unless

---

39. For what is often taken to be Hume's statement of discovery of the logical fallacy, see *A Treatise of Human Nature* (1740), Bk 3, part 1, sec. 1.

40. On Hume's lack of care in this regard, see Finnis, *Natural Law and Natural Rights*, 37–38, n. 43.

41. Indeed, something very much like the reverse is true. A complete (theoretical) account of human nature presupposes practical knowledge (a set of "value judgments") which provides data for theoretical inquiry, understanding, and judgment. Aquinas adheres to the Aristotelian methodological (and epistemological) principle according to which we come to know human nature by knowing human potentialities; these we know by knowing human acts; and these we know by knowing their objects, viz., the more-than-merely instrumental goods *(bona)* to which the self-evident and indemonstrable first principles of practical reason direct human choice and action. See Finnis, *Aquinas*, 90–91.

42. All of this is made abundantly clear in Germain Grisez's "The First Principle of Practical Reason: A Commentary on the *Summa Theologiae*, 1–2, Question 94, Article 2." This unsurpassed textual study corrects many common misunderstandings of Aquinas's theory of natural law, including, notably, the idea that Thomistic ethical theory purports to deduce the "ought" of morality from the "is" of (human) nature. See also Grisez's later treatment of the matter in *The Way of the Lord Jesus,* Vol. 1, *Christian Moral Principles,* 103–5, and, at 112, observing that "St. Thomas was careful to explain that practical conclusions always must be resolved into practical principles which are distinct from and irreducible to theoretical ones."

43. See Kelsen, "The Natural-Law Doctrine," 141.

natural law theorists commit "the naturalistic fallacy" of purporting to derive "ought" from "is," their doctrine collapses into a form of ethical noncognitivism.[44] But this simply begs the question against Thomists and others who claim that we can understand, and thereby be motivated to act for the sake of, more-than-merely-instrumental practical reasons.[45] It does a poor job of accounting for the experience of most people who, after all, often suppose that they are moved to do things (or to avoid doing things that they might otherwise do) not as a matter of brute desire, but, rather, because they perceive the worth or value, and thus the practical point, of doing (or avoiding doing) them.[46] Moreover, it flies in the face of powerful retorsive arguments that show that any truly knowledge-seeking defense of Humean moral skepticism, or other forms of noncognitivism, will be self-refuting inasmuch as it contradicts in practice the very claims it seeks to defend in theory.[47]

Kelsen's claim that "from the point of view of science the natural-law doctrine is based on the logical fallacy of an inference from the 'is' to the 'ought'"[48] simply has no force whatsoever against the natural law doctrine as it is understood by Aquinas. For Aquinas's theory of natural law proposes no such inference. When Kelsen goes on to say that "[t]he norms allegedly deduced from nature are—in truth—tacitly presupposed, and are based on subjective values, which are presented as the intentions of nature as a legislator,"[49] again his critique has no applicability to Aquinas. To be sure, the critique itself, it seems, tacitly presupposes the Humean idea that all "values" are subjective, namely, that people cannot be aware of and act on more-than-merely-instrumental reasons as such, and this is in direct contradiction to Aquinas's view. But insofar as the truth of the Humean idea is not obvious—indeed, that idea is, at best, highly problematic—Kelsen's

---

44. See Jeffrey Goldsworthy, "Fact and Value in the New Natural Law Theory," *American Journal of Jurisprudence* 41 (1996): 21–46.

45. See Robert P. George, "A Defense of the New Natural Law Theory," *American Journal of Jurisprudence* 41 (1996): 47–61. A revised version of this essay, free of multiple printer's errors that make it difficult for readers to grasp the sense of several sentences in the original, appears as chap. 1 of George, *In Defense of Natural Law*.

46. Ibid.

47. See Finnis, *Aquinas*, 58–61.

48. Kelsen, "The Natural-Law Doctrine," 141.

49. Ibid.

marshaling of the idea in his critique of "the natural-law doctrine" need trouble no one interested in defending Aquinas or his natural law doctrine. If the idea is to be marshaled effectively against Aquinas and his contemporary followers, then its proponents must, among other things, provide a plausible account of common moral experience with which it is apparently incompatible, and they must come to terms with the problems of retorsion that appear, at least, to render any intellectually serious defense of the idea self-refuting.

Natural Law and Positive Law

In the second section of his essay, Kelsen focuses on the natural law doctrine of the relationship between natural and positive law. His central claim against the doctrine here is that it renders the positive law "superfluous."[50]

> Faced by the existence of a just ordering of society, intelligible in nature, the activity of positive-law makers is tantamount to a foolish effort to supply artificial illumination in bright sunshine.[51]

Yet, he insists:

> [N]one of the followers of this doctrine had the courage to be consistent. None of them has declared that the existence of natural law makes the establishment of positive law superfluous. On the contrary. All of them insist upon the necessity of positive law. In fact, one of the most essential functions of all natural-law doctrines is to justify the establishment of positive law or the existence of the state competent to establish positive law. In performing this function most of the doctrines entangle themselves in a highly characteristic contradiction. On the one hand they maintain that human nature is the source of natural law, which implies that human nature must be basically good. On the other hand they can justify the necessity of positive law with its coercive machinery only by the badness of man.[52]

Here, I believe, Kelsen offers a spectacularly poor argument (or a pair of muddled-together arguments). It likely tells against no historically important natural law theorist. It certainly casts no doubt on Aquinas's theory. We have already seen that Kelsen's particular account of human nature as the "source of natural law" in natural law doctrines has no applicability to

---

50. Ibid., 142.   51. Ibid.
52. Ibid. (notes omitted).

Aquinas's teaching. Again, though it is true that, for Aquinas, human goods are what they are because human nature is constituted as it is, there is no sense in which Aquinas proposes to deduce knowledge of human goods—practical knowledge—from methodologically antecedent—theoretical—knowledge of human nature. The first principles of practical reason and the basic precepts of natural law, which direct choice and action to the goods of knowledge, friendship, and other more-than-merely instrumental reasons for action, far from being inferred from anthropological, historical, metaphysical, theological, or any other theoretical premises, are grasped in non-inferential acts of understanding whereby "the practical intellect"—one's single intelligence directed toward answering the question of what is to be chosen and done—grasps the intelligible point of a possible action in its promise to instantiate a human benefit, namely, something (e.g., knowledge, friendship) humanly fulfilling and, as such, worthwhile for its own sake.[53]

Now, the fact that there are goods for human beings that, as such, provide reasons for action, does not entail that there are no bads; on the contrary, the privations of human goods (e.g., ignorance, muddleheadedness, misunderstanding, animosity) are bads that provide reasons (which may or may not in any particular case be conclusive) for people to avoid them, where possible.[54] Nor does the ability of human beings to understand certain ends or purposes as humanly fulfilling, and, as such, good entail that human beings cannot choose in ways that are incompatible with the integral directiveness of the human goods, namely, immorally. Indeed, one can, for the sake of a certain good or the instantiation of goods in certain persons, choose in ways that unreasonably damage or shortchange other goods or treat other persons unfairly.[55] Any such choice will be unreasonable inasmuch as one's reason for it was in truth defeated by a conclusive (moral)

---

53. *ST* I-II, q. 94, a. 2.

54. See *ST* I-II, q. 94, a. 2, where Aquinas formulates the first and most general principle of practical reason as "good is to be done and pursued *and bad is to be avoided*" (emphasis supplied). On the proper interpretation of this principle and, particularly, the meaning of "good" and "bad" as including what is worthwhile and the privation of the worthwhile generally, and not (merely) what is morally right and wrong, see Grisez, "The First Principle of Practical Reason: A Commentary on the *Summa Theologiae*, 1–2, Question 94, Article 2."

55. See Germain Grisez, John Finnis, and Joseph Boyle, "Practical Principles, Moral Truth, and Ultimate Ends," *American Journal of Jurisprudence* 32 (1987): 99–151, at 123–25.

reason against it. But a defeated reason remains a reason—for unreasonable choices are not necessarily utterly irrational—albeit one that can be acted for by a person who, at some level, at least, understands the wrongfulness of his deed, only on the basis of emotional motives that compete with and cut back upon or fetter reason.[56]

One need not suppose that people are inherently "bad" in order to acknowledge the evident truth that human emotions, when inadequately integrated in the human personality, can motivate people to perform immoral acts. This is by no means to suggest that emotions are themselves inherently bad or ought somehow to be gotten rid of. (Indeed, in the properly integrated personality emotions support morally upright choosing.) It is only to say that people can be emotionally motivated to do things that are contrary to the integral directiveness of human goods—sometimes for the sake of genuine, albeit partial, human goods to which they are deeply committed or attached.[57] And this fact about human beings is, in part, what calls for and justifies "the establishment of positive law" and "the existence of the state competent to establish positive law."[58]

At the same time, it is important to see that in Aquinas's account of the matter, positive law would remain necessary even in a human society in which people could always be counted upon to do the morally right thing. This is because any society—even a "society of saints"—needs law, and a system of lawmaking, to provide authoritative stipulations for the coordination of actions for the sake of the common good.[59] Of course, in such a society laws against murder, rape, theft and other morally wrongful acts

---

56. Ibid.

57. Ibid.

58. This is plainly Aquinas's view as set forth in *ST* I-II, q. 95, a. 1 (addressing the question "Was it useful for laws to be framed by men?"); see also *ST* I-II, q. 96, a. 5.

59. See Finnis's explanation of Aquinas's position in *Natural Law and Natural Rights*, 28, and *Aquinas*, 35–37. Consistently with Aquinas's legal theory (and Aristotle's thought; see *Nicomachean Ethics* V, 7), contemporary analytical jurisprudence has emphasized and valuably explored the importance of law in providing authoritative, and thus binding, solutions to problems of coordinating human behavior for the sake of the common good. See esp. Edna Ullman-Margalit, *The Emergence of Norms* (Oxford, U.K.: Clarendon Press, 1977). For a summary of some important contemporary work in this area, with particular attention to the question of a prima facie (defeasible) moral obligation to obey law, see John Finnis, "Law as Co-ordination," *Ratio Juris* 2 (1989): 97–104.

would be unnecessary, and punishment and other coercive features of real-life legal systems would have no place since, *ex hypothesi,* no one would willfully fail to abide by the law's just and authoritative stipulations. But the vast majority of laws by which people—particularly in complex modern societies—are governed in their daily lives as citizens would remain pertinent.

Thus, Aquinas holds that positive law is necessary *both* because actual human beings sometimes need the threat of punishment to deter them from doing what the natural law already proscribes (or require them to do what it prescribes) as a matter of basic justice *and* because authoritative stipulations are frequently needed to coordinate action for sake of the common good.[60] And he further holds that *all* just positive laws—including laws that are purely norms of coordination—are derived, in some sense, from the natural law.[61] The task of the legislator, he suggests, is to give effect to relevant principles of natural law in the shape of principles and norms of positive law for the governance of human society.

This work of giving effect to the principles of natural law is accomplished in two distinct ways, two forms of "derivation." Some laws, such as those prohibiting murder, rape, theft, and other grave injustices that are straightforwardly contrary to natural law, are derived from the natural law by a process akin to the deduction of demonstrable conclusions from general premises in the sciences.[62] Other positive laws, however, cannot be derived from the natural law in so direct and straightforward a fashion. Where law is required to resolve a coordination problem, it is often the case that a variety of possible solutions, all having certain incommensurable advantages and disadvantages, are rationally available as options. One solution, however, must be authoritatively chosen by the legislator if the problem is to be solved. Consider, for example, the regulation of highway traffic. From the basic principle of natural law that identifies human health and safety as goods to be preserved, together with the empirical fact that unregulated driving, even among motorists of impeccable goodwill, places these human goods in jeopardy, it follows that *a* scheme of regulation (coordination) is necessary for the common good. Yet, typically, various reasonable, but in-

---

60. *ST* I-II, q. 96, a. 4; Finnis, *Aquinas,* 248 at n. 148, and 265 at n. 66.
61. *ST* I-II, q. 95, a. 2.
62. *ST* I-II, q. 95, a. 2.

compatible, schemes are possible. For the sake of the common good, then, the relevant lawmaking authority must stipulate that *one* from among the *various* possible schemes shall be given the force of law. In selecting a scheme, the lawmakers operate not by any process analogous to the deduction of demonstrable conclusions from premises, but, rather, by a process of choosing between reasonable, yet incompatible, options—a process that Aquinas refers to as *determinatio*.[63]

Laws that come into being as *determinationes*, according to Aquinas, have their binding force "not from reason alone," but also from "having been laid down" by valid lawmaking authority.[64] Although it is the case that but for the law's enactment no one would be under any general moral duty to behave as it requires, and despite the fact that the lawmaker(s) could, compatibly with the requirements of natural law, have stipulated a different requirement or set of requirements, "its directiveness derives not only from the fact of its creation by some recognized source of law (legislation, judicial decision, custom, etc.), but also from its rational connection with some principle or precept of morality."[65]

It is entirely clear, then, that the existence of natural law, as Aquinas conceives it, does not render positive law otiose. On the contrary, Aquinas quite reasonably views positive law, and the institutions of government that enjoy the power of lawmaking, to be indispensable to the common good of any society—even a hypothetical society of saints. They are themselves, as it were, requirements of natural law.[66] Although the binding force of (just) positive law always depends in part on its derivation from principles of nat-

---

63. *ST* I-II, q. 95, a. 2. On Aquinas's theory of *determinatio*, see Robert P. George, "Natural Law and Positive Law," in *The Autonomy of Law: Essays on Legal Positivism*, ed. Robert P. George (Oxford, U.K.: Clarendon Press, 1996), 321–34, at 327–30; and Finnis, *Natural Law and Natural Rights*, 281–90 and 294–96, and *Aquinas*, 266–74.

64. *ST* I-II, q. 104, a. 1.

65. Finnis, *Aquinas*, 267 (note omitted).

66. I have had occasion elsewhere to explain the point as follows: "It is meaningful and correct to say that the legislator (including the judge to the extent that the judge in the jurisdiction in question exercises a measure of law-creating power) makes the natural law effective for his community by deriving the positive law from the natural law. The natural law itself requires that such a derivation be accomplished and that someone (or a group or institution) be authorized to accomplish it"; see George, "Natural Law and Positive Law," 329–30.

ural law, the positive law, in Aquinas's account of it, is no mere emanation or simple reflection of those principles. Indeed, insofar as human law is a matter of *determinatio,* lawmakers enjoy a measure of rational creative freedom that Aquinas himself analogizes to that of "the craftsman [or, as we might say, the architect] [who] needs to determine the general form of a house to some particular shape,"[67] yet who may design the structure, compatibly with the purposes it is meant to serve, to any of a vast number of possible shapes. The existence of this freedom in no way entails the utter independence of positive law from natural law (any more than the creative freedom of the architect entails the complete independence of his *determinationes* from the general principles of architecture that must be observed if a house is to be structurally sound and otherwise suitable for purposes of habitation, or from the governing terms of his commission). But it also marks the reasons of principle that Aquinas has for completely rejecting, as he does, the notions ascribed by Kelsen to "natural law doctrine"—that, given the reality of natural law, positive law is "superfluous."

Natural Law, Unjust Law, and Resistance to Tyranny

The third section of "The Natural-Law Doctrine"[68] introduces Kelsen's version of a familiar charge against natural law theory, namely, its alleged merging of the categories of "moral" and "legal" such that either (1) all positive laws are morally good, or (2) morally bad laws are in no meaningful sense truly laws. The section opens with the following sally against theorists of natural law:

If the positive law is, as all followers of the natural-law doctrine assert, valid only so far as it corresponds to the natural law, any norm created by custom or stipulat-

67. *ST* I-II, q. 95, a. 2. Also see Finnis, *Aquinas,* 309 at n. 69, citing *SCG* III, c. 97.
68. The remaining sections (4 through 6) of Kelsen's essay focus mainly on problems of state power and private property. He is particularly concerned with post-Grotian thought, especially that of Locke, Comte, Spencer, Hegel, and Marx. He claims that "the most outstanding champions of natural law, from Grotius to Kant, have done their best to prove that private property is a sacred right conferred by divine nature upon man" (153). While some of the issues he raises could fruitfully be explored in light of Aquinas's teachings, I shall not conduct that exploration in the present paper. For a sound exposition of the Thomistic natural law doctrine of property, see Joseph M. Boyle Jr., "Natural Law, Ownership, and the World's Resources," *Journal of Value Inquiry* 23 (1989): 191–207.

ed by a human legislator which is contrary to the law of nature must be considered null and void. This is the inevitable consequence of the theory which admits the possibility of positive law as a normative system inferior to natural law. The extent to which a writer abides by this consequence is a test of his sincerity. Very few stand this test.[69]

Those who fail the test—the vast majority—are driven inexorably, Kelsen suggests, into the opposite position, namely, that "conflict between positive and natural law, although theoretically possible, is practically excluded."[70] Indeed, Kelsen goes so far as to allege that "the natural-law doctrine has no other function than to justify the positive law—any positive law established by an effective government."[71] So, in effect, natural law theory, which begins by opening up *in theory* the possibility of the radical moral critique of regimes of positive law and government, ends by functioning *in practice* as an ideological apologetic for existing regimes—whatever they happen to be.

Kelsen's principal targets here are Hobbes and Pufendorf, who, he alleges, despite their differences in other important respects, and notwithstanding Pufendorf's critique of Hobbes's straightforward identification of positive with natural law, hold in common the view that the natural law must serve in the end to justify virtually any extant regime of positive law. Kelsen argues, moreover, that "there is a principle advocated by *all* leading representatives of the natural-law doctrine, by which a conflict between the natural and the positive—if at all admitted as possible—is deprived of any effect that could be dangerous to the established legal authority: it is the dogma that under the law of nature there is no or only a restricted right of resistance."[72] Is such an inherently "conservative" view justly attributable to Aquinas?

A commonplace criticism of Aquinas is that his evident endorsement of Augustine's statement that "an unjust law seems not to be a law"[73] shows that he is guilty of merging the categories of "legal" and "moral" in such a way as to render it analytically impossible for positive law and natural law

---

69. Kelsen, "The Natural-Law Doctrine," 144.
70. Ibid., 145.
71. Ibid.
72. Ibid., 148; emphasis added.
73. *ST* I-II, q. 96, a. 4, quoting Augustine, *De libero arbitrio* I, c. 11.

to be in conflict.[74] (Of course, Kelsen himself does not consider Aquinas's specific treatment of the relationship of natural to positive law in the essay here under review; Kelsen could not plausibly deny, however, that Aquinas's treatment falls within what he says "all followers of the natural-law doctrine assert.") We have already seen that Aquinas's account of the derivation of positive law from natural law is complex and, in certain respects, quite subtle. Still further complexities and subtleties can be brought into focus if we consider the context of Aquinas's endorsement of Augustine's statement. It will become clear that Aquinas's conception of "law" and "legality" is every bit as rich and highly nuanced as the conceptions advanced by modern analytical legal philosophers. To be sure, Aquinas does not go very far in carrying out the analytical work of explicitly identifying the respects in which concrete instances of the phenomenon of human law can deviate from "law" in a social-theoretical "focal" or "paradigmatic" sense (a sense in part built up out of consideration of concrete instances, albeit from an "internal" viewpoint that itself requires the application of critical-practical intelligence[75]) while still retaining constitutive features of the concept of law. But he deploys the term "law" in an appropriately flexible way to take into account the differences between the demands of (1) intrasystemic legal analysis or argumentation (e.g., in the context of professional legal advocacy or judging); (2) what we would call "descriptive" social theory (e.g., "sociology of law"); and (3) fully critical (i.e., "normative," "moral," conscience-informing) discourse.

That Aquinas believed that laws could be, and indeed sometimes were, unjust is evident both from his many explicit references to unjust laws and from the very considerable attention he devoted to the problem of legal injustice. Central to his reflections was precisely the question whether, and if so how, unjust laws bind in conscience those subject to them to obey.[76] It is clear that Aquinas believed that human positive law creates a moral duty of

---

74. So, e.g., Arthur C. Danto flatly ascribes to "the Thomistic defenders of natural law" the belief that "there cannot be an unjust law." See his "Human Nature and Natural Law," in *Law and Philosophy*, ed. Sidney Hook (New York: New York University Press, 1964), 187. To similar effect, see H. L. A. Hart, *The Concept of Law* (Oxford, U.K.: Clarendon Press, 1961), 205, 206.

75. See Hart, *The Concept of Law*, 59–60, 86–88, 95–96, 113, 197, 226; Joseph Raz, *Practical Reason and Norms*, 2d ed. (Princeton, N.J.: Princeton University Press, 1990), 171, 177; and Finnis, *Natural Law and Natural Rights*, 11–19.

76. *ST* I-II, q. 96, a. 4.

obedience even where the conduct it commands (or prohibits) would, in the absence of the law, that is, morally, as a matter of natural law, be optional. This critical-moral belief in the power of positive law to create (or, where moral obligation already exists, reinforce) moral obligation naturally suggests the question whether this power (and the duties that are imposed by its exercise on those subject to it) is absolute or defeasible. If defeasible, under what conditions is it defeated?

To answer this question, it is necessary to press the critical-moral analysis. What is the source of the power in the first place? Plainly it is the capacity of law to serve the cause of justice and the common good by, for example, coordinating behavior to make possible the fuller and/or fairer realization of human goods by the community as a whole. But, then, *from the critical-moral viewpoint,* laws that, due to their injustice, damage, rather than serve, the common good, lack the central justifying quality of law. Their law-creating power (and the duties they purport to impose) is thus weakened or defeated. Unjust laws are, Aquinas says, "not so much laws as acts of violence."[77] As violations of justice and the common good, they lack the moral force of law; they bind in conscience, if at all, only to the extent that one is under an obligation not to bring about bad side effects that would, in the particular circumstances, likely result from one's defiance of the law (e.g., causing "demoralization or disorder,"[78] as by undermining respect for law in a basically just legal system, or unfairly shifting the burdens of a certain unjust law onto the shoulders of innocent fellow citizens[79]). That is to say, unjust laws bind in conscience, if at all, not *per se,* but only *per accidens.* They are laws, not "simpliciter," or, as we might say, in the "focal" or "paradigmatic" sense, but only in a derivative or secondary sense ("secundum quid").

Nothing in Aquinas's legal theory suggests that the injustice of a law renders it something other than a law (or "legally binding") for purposes of intrasystemic juristic analysis and argumentation. True, he counsels judges,

---

77. *ST* I-II, q. 96, a. 4.

78. *ST* I-II, q. 96, a. 4. Note, however, that, according to Aquinas, one may never obey a law requiring one to do something unjust or otherwise morally wrong. And sometimes *disobedience* is required to avoid causing (or contributing to) "demoralization or disorder." (On issues relevant to the translation of Aquinas's phrase "scandalum vel turbatio," see Finnis, *Aquinas,* 223 at n. 23, 273 at n. 112, and 274 at n. d.)

79. See *ST* II-II, q. 60, a. 5.

where possible, to interpret and apply laws in such a way as to avoid unjust results where, as best they can tell, the lawmakers did not foresee circumstances in which a strict application of the rule they laid down would result in injustice, and where they would, had they foreseen such circumstances, have crafted the rule differently.[80] But even here he does not appeal to the proposition that the injustice likely to result from an application of the rule strictly according to its terms nullifies those terms from the legal point of view.

Nor does Aquinas say or imply anything that would suggest treating Augustine's comment that "an unjust law seems not to be a law" as relevant to social-theoretical (or historical) investigations of what is (or was) treated as law and legally binding in the legal system of any given culture (however admirable or otherwise from the critical-moral viewpoint). So, for example, though H. L. A. Hart was among those who misunderstood Aquinas and his stream of the natural law tradition on precisely this point, no follower of Aquinas should suppose that Hart's "descriptive sociology" of law errs by treating as laws (and *legal* systems) various social norms (and social norm-generating institutions) that fulfill the criteria or conditions for legality or legal validity of Hart's concept of law, despite the fact that his social-theoretical enterprise (reasonably!) prescinds to a considerable extent (indeed, it seeks to prescind as far as possible) from critical-moral evaluation of laws and legal systems. The criticism Hart's work invites from a natural law perspective has nothing to do with his willingness to treat unjust laws as laws; it has rather to do with his unwillingness to follow through on the logic of his own method and his insight into the necessity of adopting or reproducing an *internal* point of view—a method that, if followed through, will identify the focal or paradigmatic case of law as *just* law—law that serves the common good—and the focal or paradigmatic case of the internal (or "legal") point of view as the viewpoint of someone who understands law and the legal system as valuable (and legal rules as, ordinarily, binding in conscience) because (or insofar as) they are just—and, qua just, serve the common good.[81]

---

80. *ST* II-II, q. 60, a. 5.

81. This criticism of Hart (and Raz) is carefully developed by Finnis; see *Natural Law and Natural Rights,* 12–18. On Hart's misinterpretation of Aquinas on these matters, see Finnis, chap. 12.

With this background in mind, let us address directly the question whether Aquinas ("like all followers of the natural-law doctrine") embraces some principle that excludes or effectively restricts the right of people to resist tyranny or gravely unjust regimes of law. Throughout his writings, Aquinas grapples with the problem of tyranny, and indeed with the question of the legitimacy of tyrannicide. In his early work, as well in his most mature writings, he defends the proposition, not only that the unjust acts of tyrants are devoid of moral authority, but that they constitute a kind of criminality that can justify revolutionary violence for the sake of the common good and even tyrannicide as a kind of resistance to, and/or just punishment of, the tyrant.

It is true that one work, *De regno ad regem Cypri,* a theological treatise from Aquinas's middle period written to inform the conscience of a Christian king, suggests disapproval of tyrannicide. This work is probably authentic, or, at least, substantially so, though some responsible commentators have doubted Aquinas's authorship. However, that may be, even Finnis, who treats the work as probably authentic, warns that it is "never a fully reliable and satisfactory source for the opinion of Aquinas."[82] The warning seems particularly apt with respect to the question of tyrannicide in view of the inconsistency of the teaching of *De regno* both with earlier and later works of unquestioned authenticity and great clarity.

Tyranny, for Aquinas, is paradigmatically rule (whether by the one, the few, or the many) in the private interests, or for the private ends, of the ruler or rulers at the expense of the common (i.e., public) good.[83] The tyrant, in effect, uses, rather than serves, those over whom he exercises power and for whose sake (from the critical-moral viewpoint) public authority exists.[84] Aquinas's earlier writings distinguish between two types of tyranny: (1) the tyranny of those who abuse authority they legitimately acquired and hold; and (2) the tyranny of those who obtained and hold power by usurpation. He suggests that usurping tyrants—as, in effect, parties making war against the political community—may legitimately be resisted and even killed by anyone who has the effective power to do so.[85] By con-

---

82. See Finnis, *Aquinas,* 288; also see 228 and 254 at n. d.

83. *ST* II-II, q. 42, a. 2.

84. *ST* I-II, q. 105, a. 1. Note Aquinas's claim (at ad 5) that tyrants "prey on their subjects" and rule them "as though they were . . . slaves."

85. See *Scriptum super libros Sententiarum Petri Lombardiensis* II, d. 44, q. 2, a. 2.

trast, where legitimate rule has degenerated into tyranny, the tyrant(s) are entitled to something like what we might call "due process of law." It is up to other public officials, operating as such, and not (ordinarily) to private citizens, to overthrow their regimes and, if necessary, bring them personally to trial and punishment (including, where appropriate, capital punishment).[86]

It is noteworthy that in his most mature writings Aquinas, as Finnis observes, "seems to have lost interest in the contrast between usurpers and other kinds of tyrant."[87] In the *Summa theologiae,* he treats tyranny *of any kind* as an essentially criminal type of rule—indeed, a form of sedition—that can justify the revolutionary action of the people and the punishment of the tyrant(s).[88] (I say "can" justify since, as always for Aquinas, a final moral judgment as to the justice of resort to force must take into account the impact of likely unintended bad side effects. Otherwise morally permissible revolutionary action might, in any particular case, be unjust to innocent third parties who would, in the circumstances, be made unfairly to bear the burdens of such side effects.)

Aquinas's "natural-law doctrine," then, does not subscribe to the principle (advocated, according to Kelsen, by *all* leading representatives of the natural law doctrine) that "deprives of any effect" conflicts between positive and natural law "which could be dangerous to the established legal authority." Although Aquinas does not treat the right of revolution in the face of tyranny as absolute, he plainly does not embrace Kelsen's alleged "dogma that under the law of nature there is no or only a restricted right of resistance." Tyrants—not least those who came to power by legal means and govern by issuing and enforcing laws *(lex tyrannica)*[89]—must look elsewhere than to Aquinas for moral arguments designed to insulate them from insurrection and punishment for their misrule. Nothing in his thought merges natural and positive law in such a way as to confer upon positive law an automatic conformity to the requirements of natural law. On the contrary, according to Aquinas, the positive law of any regime, and those rulers who create and enforce it, stand under the judgment of natural law. Tyrannical

---

86. On the distinction between usurping tyrants and legitimate rulers who degenerate into tyranny, see Finnis, *Aquinas,* 289–90 and the sources cited therein.

87. Ibid., 290, citing *ST* II-II, q. 42, a. 2 and q. 104, a. 6.

88. *ST* II-II, q. 42, a. 2.

89. *ST* I-II, q. 92, a. 1.

rule is a "perversion" of law,[90] and, as such, far from creating a duty of obedience, gives rise to a (prima facie) right of resistance to the uttermost.

Conclusion

Despite his sometimes sweeping statements about its substance, and what "all" of its principal exponents have held, we have seen that Kelsen's exposition of "the natural-law doctrine" has virtually no points of contact with Aquinas's thought. Hence, Kelsen's critique of the doctrine has little or no applicability to Thomistic natural law theory. Neither Aquinas's theory of the identification of natural law principles, nor his account of their relation to divine power and to positive law, nor his views regarding their implications for the problems of legal injustice and tyranny, are captured in Kelsen's exposition and critique. Kelsen did well, one might conclude, to avoid mentioning Aquinas if he was to insist on describing "the natural-law doctrine" as he did. Still, it is odd, to say the least, for the "tribunal of science" to have left unheard and unmentioned the thought of so central an exponent of the natural law tradition.

90. *ST* I-II, q. 92, a. 1.

9

THOMAS AQUINAS ON NATURAL LAW AND THE COMPETENCE TO JUDGE

Russell Hittinger

Introduction

In† the only question of the *Summa theologiae* devoted solely to the virtue of judgment, Thomas observes that the word judgment *(iudicium)* originally meant a decision about what is just, but was extended to "signify a right decision in any matter whether speculative or practical."[1] In its broadest sense, *iudicium* is the act whereby "a cognitive power judges of its proper object."[2] Given the natural capacity of the intellect to apprehend and to particularize universal forms,[3] everyone has some competence to render judgment: to say that such and such is the case, or ought to be the case.[4] Thus Aristotle's dictum that "everyone judges well of what he knows."[5]

---

† A version of this paper appears as chap. 4 of Russell Hittinger, *The First Grace: Rediscovering the Natural Law in a Post-Christian World* (Wilmington, Del.: ISI Books, 2003).

1. *ST* II-II, q. 60, a. 1 ad 1.

2. *ST* I-II, q. 93, a. 2 ad 3. The word mind *(mens)* itself is taken from judging and measuring *(iudicare vel mensurare)*, *ST* I, q. 79, a. 9 ad 4.

3. *SCG* II, c. 48.

4. Thomas explains that free action depends upon this endowment of the intellect. See *Commentary on Aristotle's De Anima,* Bk III, lectio 16.

5. And with the acquired virtues, speculative and practical, this competence is enhanced,

Iudicium can also mean "a superior judging of a subordinate by a kind of practical judgment, as to whether he should be such and such or not."⁶ *Iudicium* in this sense of the term is an inherent feature of authority, wherever it might be found, with or without a further capacity to make or impose laws. For example, we can think of an abbot judging that a brother ought to be a bell-ringer, or perhaps a father judging that his son ought to play sports. Though lawful, the command *(imperium)* that issues from the judgment of a private person does not count as a law *(lex)* or as the sentence of a law *(sententia legis)*. Unlike the commands that issue from the judgments of a *legislator* or a *iudex*, the judgments of a private person lack authority to command the obedience of the commonwealth.

Finally, there is a proper meaning of the word. Thomas contends that *iudicium* "properly denotes the act of a judge as such [*iudicis inquantum est iudex*]." For the judge, he notes, asserts the right *(ius dicens)* and the right is the object of justice.⁷ By rendering or binding others to render to each what is his due *(ius)*, the judge is said to be the "personification of justice."⁸ This judgment and the directive command that issues from it necessarily imply obligation and coercive power.⁹ And, because the sentence is like a "particular law," the judge is not only a superior in the broad sense of the term, but a superior who has public authority.¹⁰ The judge has authority to take cognizance of a fault or obligation, and to issue a sentence that binds or looses, condemns or absolves. With the exception of Christ, who has judicial powers vested in his own person, and who exercises them as a matter of natural right, no human being naturally has judicial power *(potestas iudiciaria)* in the proper sense of the term.¹¹ He can receive it like Daniel, who

---

extensively as to the range of objects and intensively with regard to the surety and ease of judgment.

6. *ST* I-II, q. 93, a. 2 ad 3.

7. *ST* II-II, q. 60, a. 1.

8. *ST* II-II, q. 58, a. 1 ad 5.

9. *ST* II-II, q. 60, a. 6 ad 1 *(Sed iudicium importat quandam impulsionem)*; II-II, q. 67, a. 1 *(debet habere vim coactivam)*.

10. *ST* II-II, q. 67, a. 1.

11. *SCG* IV, c. 72. "To judge belongs to God in virtue of His own power: wherefore His judgment is based on the truth which He Himself knows, and not on knowledge imparted by others: the same is to be said of Christ, Who is true God and true man: whereas other judges do not judge in virtue of their own power, so that there is no comparison [*Alii autem indices non iudicant secundum propriam potestatem*]"; see *ST* II-II, q. 67, a. 2 ad 2.

exercised judgment by divine instinct[12]; he can receive it as a power implicitly vested in the power to rule, and in this way the supreme legislative authority has the *potestas iudiciaria* in the fashion of an ordinary; or he can receive it by delegation from the sovereign, which, for Thomas, is the usual way a *iudex* receives his office to judge.

With this brief summary of definitions and terms, we can move to the disputed question of this paper. The *iudex* is said to be the "personification of justice," who not only judges what is the *ius* but also commands that it be given. What is the obligation of the *iudex* with respect to the natural law, and how does it differ from that of the *legislator*? Does a judge qua judge have authority to ignore or change laws, or to remit sentences required by laws, on the basis of his judgment of what is required by natural law?

The title of my paper suggests a set of polemics that are well known and much discussed in our polity. Insofar as possible, however, I wish to avoid anachronism by not forcing Thomas's mind into the well-worn grooves of our perplexities and debates over activist courts.[13] My goal is to provide an accurate exposition of what Thomas has to say about judges and the natural law. To that end, I shall also put aside any treatment of the topic in secondary literature. I do so in order to keep my exposition as clean as possible, and because in my judgment the secondary literature tends to be misleading on this subject.

My investigation has four parts. First, I need to make some general remarks about law and natural law. Since this is itself an enormous subject I shall focus upon aspects of Thomas's natural law doctrine that are useful for answering the question about judges. In particular, we need to understand the difference between a natural and a delegated power to judge according to the natural law. Second, I shall discuss how jurisprudence differs from other modes of prudence. Third, I will try to answer the question at hand: namely, how the *legislator* and the *iudex* stand respectively within the orbit of natural law and human jurisprudence. Finally, I will turn to three cases discussed by Thomas in which the judge seems to be in an awkward position vis-à-vis the legislator with respect to laws that seem contrary to natural law, either on their face or as applied.

---

12. *ST* II-II, q. 67, a. 1 ad 1.

13. For such matters, see Russell Hittinger, "Natural Law in the Positive Laws: A Legislative or Adjudicative Issue?," *Review of Politics* 55 (January 1993): 5–34.

What Is Law "In"?

Thomas's *definitio legis* is well known. Law is a binding ordinance of reason for the political common good, actually promulgated by a competent authority.[14] Our first question is, "What is law *in?*" Although it might seem an odd question, especially for legal theorists chiefly interested in legal epistemology, it is one that Thomas took pains to answer. In Thomas's intellectual world, the recurrent questions are embarrassingly realistic: What is the definition of a thing?; What is it "in"?; In what sense is the thing a cause or an effect?; What kind of cause is it?; What kind of effect is it?; Does it move or doesn't it move? In my view, clarity about the question "What is law *in?*" is crucial for understanding the relationship between a legislator and a judge.

In the *Summa theologiae,* Thomas takes his first stab at the question in answer to the objection that St. Paul speaks in Romans 7 of "another law in my members"—the so-called *lex membrorum*.[15] This seems to imply that law is "in" a man in a physical sense. If this is so, how can we say that law is a command of reason? Thomas replies:

> ... [I]t should be said that since law is a kind of rule and measure, it may be in something in two ways. First, as in that which measures and rules [*modo in mensurante et regulante; et quia hoc est proprium rationis*]. Since this is proper to reason, it follows that, in this way, law is in the reason alone. Second, as in that which is measured and ruled [*modo in regulato et mensurato*]. In this way, law is in all those things that are inclined to something by reason of some law, so that any inclination arising from a law may be called a law, not essentially but by participation as it were.[16]

---

14. *ST* I-II, q. 90, aa. 1–4. Notably, Thomas does not include coercion *(vis coactiva)* in the definition. Of its essence, law is a binding directive of reason *(vis directiva)* intended to move a multitude of free and intelligent agents to a common good. The multitude is not moved by physical but by moral necessity. Eliminate any one of the four principles of law (command of reason, authority, common good, promulgation) and we have coactive rather than directive force. Coercion is an act of law, *actus legis*. See *ST* I-II, q. 92, a. 2. Coaction is said to be lawful if it flows from the four principles that constitute direction; but none of the four traits of law depend essentially upon coercion.

15. *ST* I-II, q. 90, a. 1, obj. 1.

16. *ST* I-II, q. 90, a. 1 ad 1.

As a measure and a rule of human acts, law is "in" the intellect that actually performs the act of measuring and ruling; in a derivative sense, law can be said to be "in" whatever is measured and ruled. Properly speaking, law is always "in" the active principle,[17] which is to say, in a mind; and when two coordinate powers combine to produce the effect in the passive principle, the formal notion is taken from the superior active principle.[18]

For example, we observe an ordered or a law-abiding pattern of traffic. If we ask where the law abides properly and essentially *(modo proprie et essentialiter)*, we would answer, in the mind of the legislator who imposed the rules and measures: "all traffic to the right," "stop on red," and so on. Derivatively, *modo in regulato*, it is in the minds of motorists who partake of the rules and measures. What causes the traffic to stop at the red light? The law that resides in the mind of the legislator and in the minds of the motorists who stop their cars; chiefly, however, it is in the legislator in whose mind the measure is framed, and who, by promulgation, makes it to be known. In a very extended sense of the term *(per similitudine)* law is "in" things: the law books, the red light, the physical flow of traffic itself.[19] As we will see, the proposition that law is predicated properly of the active principle is the ground for Thomas's doctrine of original intent, as well as for his insistence that the judge must sometimes favor the intent rather than the written words of the legislator.

This distinction between a regulating principle and the thing regulated applies no less to natural law. In answer to the question whether there is a natural law *in nobis*, Thomas immediately answers that it depends upon what is meant by "in."[20] Since law is properly and essentially in the intellect of the legislator, natural law is "in" the divine mind. Hence, in answer to the further issue of the immutability of natural law, Thomas points out the obvious. The human mind is changeable and imperfect. Natural law, therefore, "endures without change owing to the unchangeableness of the divine reason, the author of nature."[21]

Does this mean that natural law is "in" man merely in the extended sense that a traffic law is "in" the law books or "in" the red light? No. Thomas contends that the human mind participates, or has a share in, the active

17. *ST* I-II, q. 91, a. 1 ad 3.
19. *ST* I-II, q. 91, a. 2 ad 3.
21. *ST* I-II, q. 97, a. 1 ad 1.
18. *ST* I-II, q. 13, a. 1.
20. *ST* I-II, q. 91, a. 2.

principle of the eternal law. The human mind is a measured-measure *(mensura-mensurata)*, not a measuring-measure *(mensura-mensurans)*.²² Having received a law, the human mind can go on to judge and command according to that law. And the fullest participation in the active principle of law (and that which exhibits most profoundly the *imitatio dei*) is man's ability to appropriate the natural law and to make more laws; that is to say, not just to use the natural law to govern oneself, but also to govern others.

Thomas is very careful not to say that nature is a law, or to say that law is "in" nature in a proper sense of the term. Rather, the word "natural" is predicated of our share in the eternal law for two reasons. First, it is by the natural power of reason that we partake of the law; second, by mode of promulgation the law is instilled or indicted in us so as to be known naturally *(naturaliter)*.²³ Even so, natural law is not law because it is "in" us. This is why Thomas, in answer to the objection that positing an eternal law and a natural law is a needless reduplication of laws, answers that natural law is not diverse from the eternal law, and that there are not two laws.²⁴ There is rather one law, the eternal law, which *modo in mensurante et regulante* is God; by participation, *modo in regulato et mensurato*, it is in the creature.

In the case of natural law, the law is denominated "natural" according to the mode of reception, not according to the pedigree of legislation. If we focus upon the mode of promulgation, there are as many species of law as there are ways to communicate it. But if we are interested in proper definitions, there are only two kinds of law that correspond to two kinds of minds. There is law that proceeds from the mind of God, and there is law

---

22. "[I]t should be said that human reason is not itself the rule of things, but rather the principles naturally instilled in it are general rules and measures of things to be done; concerning these, the natural reason is the rule and measure, not of things that are from nature" (*ST* I-II, q. 91, a. 3 ad 2). And see *ST* I-II, q. 93, a. 1 ad 3; q. 93, a. 4.

23. *ST* I-II, q. 90, a. 4 ad 1. *Quod promulgatio legis naturae est ex hoc ipso quod Deus eam mentibus hominum inseruit naturaliter cognoscendam.* It is worth recalling that, for Thomas, law is an extrinsic principle of action; see *ST* I-II, q. 90, prol. But in saying that law is a *principium extrinsecum* he does not mean something exterior in the psychological sense of the term. As we have said, law properly exists in a mind. Law is an extrinsic principle because it is not a predicate of human nature. Man is a rational animal, but he is not a law. Therefore, the use of the word nature *(natura, naturalis, naturale, naturaliter)* in connection with law is meant to highlight how the intrinsic principles of human nature receive or hold the legal measure.

24. *ST* I-II, q. 91, a. 2 ad 1.

that proceeds from the mind of man who partakes of the eternal law.[25] As Augustine said, one is eternal, the other temporal.[26]

For Thomas, all human judgment is set within a legal order—although to be sure not every human judgment is a legal judgment. This is the heart and soul of Thomas's doctrine of natural law, which is very attractive to some and repellent to others. Thomas is saying that every human person has a share in the active principle of law, which means that there is a natural competence to render judgment according to (natural) law. Thus we find in *ST* I-II, q. 94, a. 2, the proposition that the habit of *synderesis* holds the "first precept of law" *(primum praeceptum legis)*: "the good is to be done and pursued and evil resisted." This is the impression of created light by which God makes the creature share in the eternal law.[27] Whatever else we might know about human goods, whether naturally or by investigation, we never know them in the absence of this primordial grasp of law. To separate the grasp of human goods from the *primum praeceptum legis* inevitably results in (1) positing a legal principle that must then go in search of goods, or (2) positing human goods bereft of law. The first is legally observant but axiologically dumb, the latter is axiologically contentful but legally dumb. Within these two poles we will find most of the perplexities and dead-ends of modern moral philosophy.

In any event, the radical implications of Thomas's teaching should be evident. Every created intelligence not only has competence to make judgments, but to make judgments according to law. The legal order of things does not begin or end either with the excellence of virtue, possessed by a few, or with the offices and statutes of human positive law. Divine providence, he observes, gives rules to men not merely as individual members of

---

25. Angels too are under the natural law; see *ST* I, q. 60, a. 5. Thomas differed from other medieval theologians in holding that angels are not a source of law. "It is for the sovereign alone to make a law by his own authority; but sometimes after making a law, he promulgates it through others. Thus God made the Law by His own authority, but He promulgated it through the angels" (*ST* I-II, q. 98, a. 3 ad 3).

26. *ST* I-II, q. 91, a. 3, *sed contra*. Hence, the *De legibus* (*ST* I-II, qq. 90–108) can be delineated: law *in sapientia dei* (qq. 91, 93); *in cognitione* (qq. 94–97); *in gentibus* (qq. 98–105); and *per gratiam* (qq. 106–8). See Stephen Louis Brock, *The Legal Character of Natural Law According to St. Thomas Aquinas*, Ph.D. dissertation, University of Toronto (1988), chap. 2-C.

27. See Matthew Cuddeback, *Light and Form in St. Thomas Aquinas's Metaphysics of the Knower*, Ph.D. dissertation, The Catholic University of America (1998).

a species, but "inasmuch as they are personal acts" *(secundum quod sunt actus personales)*.[28] Thomas's philosophy has been used by Dominican Scholastics to defend the liberties of *naturales* in the New World, by Jesuits to defend rights of resistance to tyrants, and famously in our own time by Martin Luther King. Thomas, of course, does not hold that conscience is a law unto itself,[29] for conscience is not a law but rather an act that judges according to law.[30] Even so, one does not need a political or an ecclesiastical office to judge according to the natural law. Therefore, we must ask what delimits the natural competence to judge, and whether the limits are merely arbitrary.

Judgment and *Prudentia Regnativa*

All human judgment depends upon the intellect receiving the first measures of action, which Thomas calls the natural law. The primary precepts of natural law are never the object of judgment—they are not subject, as it were, to judicial review, for they are the principles according to which any judgment has the note of rectitude and authority. At least at a rudimentary level, everyone grasps the precepts of natural law. "The right ends of human life are fixed," Thomas explains, and therefore there is a "naturally right judgment about such ends."[31] Thomas groups these under the triad of *to be, to live,* and *to know*—effects of God that are desirable and lovable to all.[32]

---

28. *SCG* III, c. 129. See also *SCG* III, c. 114.

29. "Man does not make the law for himself, but through the act of his knowledge, by which he knows a law made by someone else, he is bound to fulfill the law" (*De Veritate,* q. 17, a. 3 ad 1).

30. *ST* I, q. 79, a. 13. Thus, the passage in *Gaudium et spes:* "Deep within his conscience man discovers a law which he has not laid upon himself but which he must obey. Its voice, ever calling him to love and to do what is good and to avoid evil, tells him inwardly at the right moment: do this, shun that. For man has in his heart a law inscribed by God. His dignity lies in observing this law, and by it he will be judged. His conscience is man's most secret core, and his sanctuary. There he is alone with God whose voice echoes in his depths" (*Gaudium et spes,* no. 16).

31. *ST* I-II, q. 47, a. 15.

32. The triadic structure of first precepts in *ST* I-II, q. 94, a. 2 follow this pattern. See also *ST* I-II, q. 19, a. 4.

Much more, of course, is necessary for human action. First, with respect to the precepts of the natural law, there is more to be known about the law, by way of drawing *conclusiones* from the first precepts. Second, with respect to the application of precepts to facts, one needs considerable experience in order to take counsel and to judge of what one has discovered. In addition to a norm *(praeceptum)*, a discovery *(consilium)*, and a judgment *(iudicium)*, right reason in action also requires a command *(imperium)* that actually applies judgment to action. And since command is an act of the intellect presupposing the will, right action requires acquired virtues. Unless and until there is a command, Thomas teaches, nothing has happened in the practical order.[33] For counsel and judgment are chiefly acts of the speculative intellect. Thus Thomas concludes that "a natural appetite for good would not suffice for man, nor a natural judgement, to enable him to act correctly, unless it were more fully determined and perfected."[34]

This is not the place to rehearse the full complement of knowledge and virtue necessary for right judgment. It will suffice for our present purposes to imagine an agent whose natural capacity to judge is reasonably well perfected. What is he entitled to judge and command? It is necessary to include both the *iudicium* and the *imperium* in the question because without the latter there is no practical issue at stake. Henceforth, I will use the expression "ordering judgment" to signify the conjunction of judgment and command. For Thomas, practical reason differs from the speculative in seeking to cause something (in oneself, in others, or in things).[35] And it

---

33. "Prudence is "right reason applied to action," as stated above (a. 2). Hence that which is the chief act of reason in regard to action must needs be the chief act of prudence. Now there are three such acts. The first is "to take counsel," which belongs to discovery, for counsel is an act of inquiry, as stated above (I-II, q. 14, a. 1). The second act is "to judge of what one has discovered," and this is an act of the speculative reason. But the practical reason, which is directed to action, goes further, and its third act is "to command," which act consists in applying to action the things counseled and judged. And since this act approaches nearer to the end of the practical reason, it follows that it is the chief act of the practical reason, and consequently of prudence" (*ST* II-II, q. 47, a. 8).

34. *On Virtues in General*, a. 6.

35. Hence the notion of the speculative reason becoming practical by extension, *quod intellectus speculativus per extensionem fit practicus* (*ST* I, q. 79, a. 11, *sed contra*). It is not intention, counsel, or judgment that marks the entry into the practical deployment of the intellect, but *imperium*.

does so either by a judgment and a command that dispose something to bring about an effect in the real world, or by necessitating that effect.[36] In either case, without the notion of motion there is no practical reason, and that this notion of ordering motion makes its appearance in the act of *imperium*.[37]

Since *imperium* is the chief act of practical reason, and hence of prudence, we can outline authority to judge in terms of the subjective parts or species of prudence. Properly divided, they are the prudence whereby a man rules himself and a prudence whereby he rules a multitude.[38] I shall not belabor the first, which is sometimes called "monastic prudence" *(prudentia monastica seu regitiva unius)*. Given the first share in the natural law—and supposing that the agent has developed some of the complements of knowledge and virtue—an individual is competent to render an ordering judgment about his own acts. The perfection of such acts consists in this:

---

36. "Now the speculative and practical reason differ in this, that the speculative merely apprehends its object, whereas the practical reason not only apprehends but causes. Now one thing is the cause of another in two ways: first perfectly, when it necessitates its effect, and this happens when the effect is wholly subject to the power of the cause; secondly imperfectly, by merely disposing to the effect, for the reason that the effect is not wholly subject to the power of the cause. Accordingly in this way the reason is cause of certain things in two ways: first, by imposing necessity; and in this way it belongs to reason, to command not only the lower powers and the members of the body, but also human subjects, which indeed is done by commanding; secondly, by leading up to the effect, and, in a way, disposing to it, and in this sense the reason asks for something to be done by things not subject to it, whether they be its equals or its superiors. Now both of these, namely, to command and to ask or beseech [*imperare et petere sive deprecari*], imply a certain ordering, seeing that man proposes something to be effected by something else, wherefore they pertain to the reason to which it belongs to set in order" (*ST* II-II, q. 83, a. 1).

37. "Now the reason can intimate or declare something in two ways. First, absolutely: and this intimation is expressed by a verb in the indicative mood, as when one person says to another: 'This is what you should do.' Sometimes, however, the reason intimates something to a man by moving him thereto [*movendo ipsum ad hoc*]; and this intimation is expressed by a verb in the imperative mood; as when it is said to someone: 'Do this.' Now the first mover, among the powers of the soul, to the doing of an act is the will.... Since therefore the second mover does not move, save in virtue of the first mover, it follows that the very fact that the reason moves by commanding, is due to the power of the will. Consequently it follows that command is an act of the reason, presupposing an act of the will, in virtue of which the reason, by its command, moves (the power) to the execution of the act" (*ST* I-II, q. 17, a. 1).

38. *ST* II-II, q. 48, a. 1.

the individual is able to make the precepts of natural law efficacious in his own acts, amid all of the details and variations that need to be considered in order to act rightly. Individual prudence proceeds from law, but issues in something that looks like the opposite of a legal statute, namely, adequacy of action to singular, contingent facts.[39]

Thomas also speaks of domestic prudence *(prudentia oeconomica)*, which is skill in delivering ordering judgments for a family. The title to make such judgments is usually derived from a fundament of nature—the fact that one is the natural *pater familias* or *mater familias*. Like individual prudence, this too proceeds from law, but unlike the former its end term is a command that moves others. Thomas is prepared to call these commands ordinances or statutes *(facere aliqua praecepta vel statuta)*, but they lack the ratio of law.[40] When one commands one's children to go to bed, one has not issued a curfew.[41] In certain codes of ancient law, the *paterfamilias* receives from the city delegated power to make and enforce legal judgments, even those of criminal law. In that case, however, we are not speaking simply of domestic prudence.

The kind of prudence that proceeds from law to law is regnative prudence *(prudential regnativa)*. The word is taken from *regnum,* or kingdom, because it is the "best of all governments." But it comprehends "all other rightful forms of government."[42] Here, we are speaking of legislative prudence, the capacity to make and impose laws *(leges ponere)*.[43] The chief act of a *principatus regalis* is directing by law a multitude to a political end. Through the act of *determinatio,* the legislator makes determinate what is left indeterminate by natural law. What makes his judgment unique is that it remains totally within the genus of law. Having received law he makes

---

39. As Yves Simon has remarked, "the final prudential judgment in this mode is in a certain sense incommunicable. Incommunicable, that is, not in the sense that it cannot be discussed, but rather incommunicable in the sense that the term of action is not available for retail distribution to other agents. The incommunicability of the last practical judgment results from the affective and non-logical character of the act that determines this judgment" (see *Practical Knowledge* [New York: Fordham University Press, 1991], 24).

40. *ST* I-II, q. 90, a. 3 ad 3.

41. Moreover, admonition rather than punishment is naturally suitable to the relations of a domestic society.

42. *ST* II-II, q. 50, a. 1 ad 2.

43. *ST* II-II, q. 50, a. 1 ad 3.

more law. For Thomas, while the authority to issue binding judgments in the form of *leges* has a natural ground and a natural end, such power does not belong to any person as a natural endowment. Thomas thinks that the authority is implicitly vested in the community.[44] Unlike modern theorists, who are fascinated with the regime-founding moment, where by legislative fiat the offices of government come into being, Thomas is not very interested in precisely how that authority gets delegated—with one notable exception. He treats in considerable detail the pedigree and distribution of authority in the Church. For here, Christ immediately confers the keys to the kingdom: the discerning key, or the power to judge, and the key of command, or the power to bind or loose.[45] The reason Thomas paid more attention to the ecclesiastical regime is not difficult to surmise. He lived in the immediate wake of the Investiture Controversy as well as the claims made for the papal monarchy by Pope Innocent III.

In those subject to the law, the corresponding prudence is called political prudence *(prudentia politica)*. Thomas explains:

> ... [M]en who are *servi* or *subditi* in any sense, are moved by the commands of others in such a way that they move themselves by their free-will; wherefore some kind of rectitude of government is required in them, so that they may direct themselves in obeying their superiors; and to this belongs that species of prudence which is called political.[46]

Both the human legislator and the judge need this virtue with respect to the *principatus regalis* of the natural commonwealth. Because every human legal official first receives a natural law before he makes or adjudicates a human law, every human authority is a *subitus* or a *servus* to the author of the natural law (not in the first place a servant of the people, but of God). Beyond this primal virtue of obedience, the human *principatus regalis* is a *principatus politicus* in another way. Wherever there is a political constitution, the human legislator also obeys the judgments of the body politic.[47]

---

44. *ST* I-II, q. 90, a. 3.   45. *SCG* IV, c. 72.
46. *ST* II-II, q. 50, a. 2.

47. "When a man has sole and absolute power over everything, his rule is said to be regal. When, on the other hand, he rules in accord with the disciplined instructions [*sermones disciplinales*], that is, in accordance with laws laid down by the discipline of politics, his rule is political. It is as though he were part ruler, namely, as regards the things that come under his power, and part subject, as regards the things in which he is subject to the law" (*In I Pol.*, lect.

In the case of the legislator, *iudicium* is Janus-faced. The legislator receives a law, and on that pattern makes more law. Accordingly, this is jurisprudence in its purest form. Where do we place the *iudicium* of the *iudex?* He is not the mediatrix of natural and human law, for the judge always presupposes that such mediation has been done by a legislator and there is at hand a human law to be applied to the facts of the case. Thus, we cannot say that law is "in" the judge as it is "in" the mind of the legislator. The legislator imitates God by moving a multitude of men. The *iudex,* however, must exercise a twofold obedience before he can render judgment: first, he must dispose himself to obey the natural law (such is the case for every human being) *and* then he must dispose himself to obey the law made by the human legislator. He is, as it were, twice moved before he can move others. Until the human legislator speaks, there is quite literally nothing for the *iudex* to do (though, to be sure, there is plenty for him to do as a private person: namely, to use the natural law to make judgments about his own action, or perhaps the action of a household). And for this reason, among others, the judge qua judge has a quite imperfect share in regnative prudence. It would seem, then, that the virtue of the judge is not jurisprudence in the purest sense of the term, but rather *prudentia politica*—the virtue of a *servus* or of a *subditus* who has a partial share in the power of the legislator, and whose judgments are guided by the virtue of obedience.

Subordination of the Judge to Inanimate Law

Medieval theorists routinely spoke of animated justice: *iustum animatum, lex animata, lex viva.* Thomas's disciple, Aedgidius Romanus, asserted in the *Mirror of Princes* that "it is better to be ruled by a good king than by good law."[48] The idea seems self-recommending. If there are to be ordering judgments, it is better that such judgments flow from a soul attuned to the higher law and to the precepts needed by the people. Thomas does not disagree, so far as it goes. Indeed, he frequently uses personified justice language in reference to legal officials, including judges.[49] And beyond that, he

---

1, #13). St. Augustine said: "Only God can be happy by his own power with no one ruling" (*De Genesi contra Manichaeos,* II, cap 15 §22).

48. Ernst H. Kantorowicz, *The King's Two Bodies: A Study in Mediaeval Political Theology* (Princeton, N.J.: Princeton University Press, 1957), 135.

49. *ST* III, q. 59, a. 2 ad 1; II-II, q. 58, a. 1 ad 5; II-II, q. 60, a. 1.

argued that good habits of judging are obligatory for anyone who would take the job: "[T]he authority to judge, which is the key of knowledge, cannot be accepted without sin by one who lacks knowledge; whereas knowledge void of authority can be possessed without sin."[50]

The important point for our purposes is where Thomas disagreed with the rubric of animated justice, emphasizing instead the usefulness of *iustum inanimatum,* especially as it applies to the *iudex.* In response to the objection that recourse to a judge is more useful than statutes, Thomas replies:

> As the Philosopher says (Rhet. i, 1), "it is better that all things be regulated by law, than left to be decided by judges": and this for three reasons. First, because it is easier to find a few wise men competent to frame right laws, than to find the many who would be necessary to judge aright of each single case. Secondly, because those who make laws consider long beforehand what laws to make; whereas judgment on each single case has to be pronounced as soon as it arises: and it is easier for man to see what is right, by taking many instances into consideration, than by considering one solitary fact. Thirdly, because lawgivers judge in the abstract and of future events; whereas those who sit in judgment of things present, towards which they are affected by love, hatred, or some kind of cupidity; wherefore their judgment is perverted.

He concludes: "Since then the animated justice of the judge is not found in every man, and since it can be deflected, therefore it was necessary, whenever possible, *for the law to determine how to judge,* and for very few matters to be left to the decision of men."[51]

Thomas's argument against a system of animated justice is prudential; he is trying to establish in the order of utility *(utile)* that inanimate justice is better *(melius)* wherever possible *(in quibuscumque possibile).* Every polity needs a fresh supply of binding directives drawn from the natural law by way of *determinationes.*[52] According to the dictum of the ancient jurists, justice may be defined: *ius suum cuique tribuere,* to give to each what is his *ius.* Human laws determine the *iura* left indeterminate by natural law: in legal justice, the *ius* to be given by the individual to the polity; in distributive justice, the *ius* to be given by the community to the individual; and in commutative justice, the *ius* to be given by one private party to another. Until

---

50. *ST* Suppl., q. 17, a. 3 ad 2.
51. *ST* I-II, q. 95, a. 1 ad 2; emphasis added.
52. In the very next article, *ST* I-II, q. 95, a. 2.

or unless someone can rightfully claim "this is owed to me [him, or them]," there is no issue of justice, or what's worse, the issue of justice is in doubt.⁵³

Thomas is saying that animated justice is not suitable for achieving this end, at least not in a systematic fashion with respect to legal and distributive justice. Judgment in the individual case does not yield general standing laws: rules that have adequate generality and prospectivity.⁵⁴ Judicial judgment embodies the kind of prudence that gravitates to the particular facts of a singular case rather than to the prudence that considers the prospective well-being of a multitude; were we to find a judge considering the merit or demerit of policy decisions that affect the body politic, we might wonder whether he is attending to the litigation at hand.⁵⁵

Yet another thing to consider is the problem of having the *iudex* wear the two hats of judge and legislator. Interestingly, Thomas does not seem to think that this is a problem in the case of the *legislator*. The *principes* holds plenary authority in the republic.⁵⁶ In virtue of the fact that he makes the law, he retains ultimate authority to interpret and judge it.⁵⁷ For Thomas,

---

53. For a useful analysis of the traditional dictum, see Javier Hervada, *Natural Right and Natural Law: A Critical Introduction* (Pamplona: Servicio de Publicaciones de la Universidad de Navarra, 1990), 19–45.

54. Note the similarity of Thomas's position to Lon Fuller's discussion of the hapless Rex in *The Morality of Law*, rev. ed. (New Haven, Conn.: Yale University Press, 1969), chap. 2.

55. "The principle of government by law," Simon notes, "is subject to such precarious conditions that, if it were not constantly reasserted, it soon would be destroyed by the opposite and complementary principle, viz., that of adequacy to contingent, changing, and unique circumstances" (see his *The Tradition of Natural Law*, 84).

56. *ST* II-II, q. 67, a. 4.

57. *ST* II-II, q. 60, a. 6. For Thomas's discussion of why God as supreme legislator has authority over all particular judgments, see *SCG* III, c. 76. "The higher providence gives rules to the lower providence: even as the politician gives rules and laws to the commander in chief; who gives rules and laws to the captains and generals. Consequently if there be other providences subordinate to the highest providence of the supreme God: it follows that God gives the second and third governors the rules of their office. Either, therefore, He gives general rules and laws or particular.—If He gives them general rules, since general rules are not always applicable to particular cases, especially in matters that are subject to movement and change, it would be necessary for these governors of the second or third rank to go beyond the rules given them in deciding about matters confided to their care. Consequently they would exercise judgement on the rules given to them, as to when to act according to them, and when it would be necessary to disregard them: which is impossible, because such a

the *iudex*—in our usual sense of the term—is a *iudex inferior,* a judge who enjoys delegated authority, and whose proximate rule for judging is the law that abides in the mind of the legislator.⁵⁸

So, once again, we find that there is a limit on the scope of judicial judgment. If the judge does not apply a known law to particular facts, he fails as a judge. But Thomas suggests that if he were to shape his ruling to affect the entire body politic he would also fail as a legislator; his sentence resolving the disputes of litigants is not apt to have sufficient generality to move a multitude toward a common good. Hence, the judge will not govern men politically, for to govern men politically one must supply ordering judgments of adequate generality. (We must remember that Thomas is not thinking within the framework of American constitutional law where the powers of government are separated rather than merely distinguished, and where the sovereign (the people) reigns but does not rule.⁵⁹

In sum, unless he is the supreme judge, the judge has no authority to render judgment except according to the rule in the mind of the legislator. If, on the basis of his estimation of the natural law, he should choose to ignore the *leges legales* of the legislator, or even to judge them wrongful, the judge usurps authority and inflicts an injury upon the commonwealth. The natural law forbids such an act on three grounds. First, usurpation *(iudicium usurpatum)* is an offense against natural justice because one takes more than one's fair share of authority; second, the judge disobeys properly constituted authority in the legislator; and third, the judge deflects that part of the natural law that the legislator was trying to make effective in the positive law.⁶⁰ "Hence it is necessary to judge according to the written law," Thomas insists, "else judgment would fall short either of the natural or of the positive right."⁶¹

But what is the judge to do if he has reason to believe that the law

---

judgement belongs to the superior, since the interpretation of laws and dispensation from their observance belong to Him who made the law [*quod esse non potest, quia hoc iudicium ad superiorem pertinet; nam eius est interpretari leges et dispensare in eis, cuius est eas condere*]."

58. Pontius Pilate, e.g., is a *iudex inferior* under the authority of Caesar. Thus, Thomas reasons, he had no authority to lawfully remit punishment (*ST* II-II, q. 60, a. 4).

59. Certainly, there is nothing in Thomas corresponding to Alexander Hamilton's *Federalist* 78, where the legislative power is characterized as "will" and the judicial as "judgment."

60. *ST* II-II, q. 60, a. 2.

61. *ST* II-II, q. 60, a. 5.

somehow falls short of the *ius naturale?* Let us turn to three cases mentioned by Thomas. I shall take them in the order of difficulty, beginning with the easiest.

Three Cases

In the question devoted to homicide, Thomas asks whether it is ever lawful to kill the innocent. As we would expect, he answers that it is in no way lawful to slay the innocent.[62] But what about the case of a judge who knows that a defendant in a capital case is the victim of false testimony? The *ius naturale* would seem to require that he be exonerated rather than punished. Yet the human law requires the judge to pronounce sentence according to the evidence acquired in a public judicial procedure. Thomas writes:

> If the judge knows that man who has been convicted by false witnesses, is innocent he must, like Daniel, examine the witnesses with great care, so as to find a motive for acquitting the innocent: but if he cannot do this he should remit him for judgment by a higher tribunal. If even this is impossible, he does not sin if he pronounce sentence in accordance with the evidence, for it is not he that puts the innocent man to death, but they who stated him to be guilty. He that carries out the sentence of the judge who has condemned an innocent man, if the sentence contains an inexcusable error, he should not obey, else there would be an excuse for the executions of the martyrs: if however it contain no manifest injustice, he does not sin by carrying out the sentence, because he has no right to discuss the judgment of his superior; nor is it he who slays the innocent man, but the judge whose minister he is.[63]

We might be reminded of Pontius Pilate, who, as Thomas notes elsewhere, properly fulfilled his office as a *iudex inferior* under Caesar.[64] According to the Roman procedure of *cognitio extra ordinem,* the imperial authority is at liberty to receive a free formulation of charges and penalties (in this case from the Sanhedrin). After a formal accusation, the *imperium* may proceed according to the principle *arbitrium iudicantis,* that is to say, he is at liberty to take the *consilium* of his cabinet or friends, and go on to issue the verdict and assign a punishment. The Gospels, especially John's, report a re-

62. *ST* II-II, q. 64, a. 6.   63. *ST* II-II, q. 64, a. 6 ad 3.
64. See note 58 above.

luctance on the part of Pilate to issue the sentence, and even more to execute it. Some scholars doubt that Pilate fulfilled Roman law.[65] It is more likely that he rendered the judgment *extra ordinem* according to the authority vested in the imperial governor.[66] From this point of view, the trial of Jesus is a spectacular instance of the problem of animated justice. For the Roman practice of *cognitio extra ordinem* is nothing more nor less than the animated justice of the Roman *imperium,* free to proceed with almost no artificial constraints of law, and entirely vulnerable to the passions of the moment.

Thomas's case is much simpler. Here we have an inferior judge with no authority to proceed *extra ordinem*. He has no power to introduce evidence or to fashion sentences on his own recognizance. But what makes the hypothetical case especially easy to resolve is that there is no flaw in the law. The law is not contrary to the *ius naturale*. Nor is there reason to believe either that the instruments and procedures of the law are inherently flawed or that the judge neglected to use the procedures available to his office. Provided that appeals to a higher tribunal have been exhausted, the conclusion is clear: the judge must pronounce sentence according to the law. In so doing, Thomas says, the judge commits no injustice. He would, however, act unjustly were he to introduce private evidence or fashion a sentence contrary to what the law demands.[67] "In matters touching his own person," Thomas writes, "a man must form his conscience from his own knowledge, but in matters concerning the public authority, he must form his conscience in accordance with the knowledge attainable in the public judicial procedure."[68]

The second case concerns judgment rendered *praeter verba legis,* outside the letter of the law. Thomas gives different examples: (1) In order to protect the city during a siege, an ordinance prescribes that the gates be shut: May they be opened to save the lives of citizens pursued by the enemy?[69]; (2) The law requires that deposits be restored: Is one obligated to command that the

65. See Ann Wroe, *Pilate* (London: Random House, 2000).

66. A. N. Sherwin-White, *Roman Law and Roman Society in the New Testament* (Reprint, Grand Rapids, Mich.: Baker Book House, 1978), lectures 1–2.

67. He may judge only according to what he "knows as a public person" (*ST* II-II, q. 67, a. 2).

68. *ST* II-II, q. 67, a. 2 ad 4.

69. *ST* I-II, q. 96, a. 6.

ius be given in the case of a madman who wants his weapon returned?[70] In these discussions, Thomas does not supply a tapestry of detail that would interest lawyers. But his delineation of the principles is interesting.

While the success of individual prudence is measured by adequacy of judgment to the particular, jurisprudence succeeds only if the lawmaker can frame general standing statutes. But he can never legislate so successfully as to eliminate a certain material (not a moral) deficiency, namely, unusual events or facts that render the scope of the statute problematic or doubtful. Thus, the perfection of judgment called *gnome* renders a verdict on the basis of the "natural law in those cases where the common law fails to apply."[71] In such cases, the judge follows the principle of *epikeia,* and gives equity *(aequitas).* Indeed, Thomas contends that it would be sinful not to give equity.[72] The question is whether this obligation authorizes the judge to put aside the positive law and revert to his estimation of what natural law requires in the case at hand.

The answer to that question is No. Thomas's treatment of *gnome* and *epikeia* do not open the door to a judicial consideration of facts only in the light of natural law. To explain why this is so, we should begin with the obvious. Notice, in the first place, that Thomas does not ask whether it is permissible to judge *contra legem,* but rather to judge *praeter verba legis*—not judging contrary to the positive law, but outside of its letter(s). In the second place, in none of the examples discussed by Thomas do we have reason to worry that the law is unjust. *Gnome* and *epikeia* presuppose (1) that there is a valid law inherited from the legislator, and (2) that the law is not contrary to natural justice. Should the law fail in either of these two respects, it is no law at all, and thus all questions of giving equity or judging *praeter verba legis* are moot. In the third place, we need to take note of why Thomas says it is sinful not to give equity: "Without doubt he transgresses the law who by adhering to the letter of the law strives to defeat the intention of the lawgiver."[73] In other words, the moral fault does not consist merely in

70. *ST* II-II, q. 120, a. 1.

71. *ST* I-II, q. 57, a. 6 ad 3. Here, Thomas uses the expression *lex communis,* indicating the exercise of *gnome* within a legal framework; elsewhere he speaks of *communes regulas agendorum,* common rules of action (*ST* II-II, q. 51, a. 4), indicating a broader scope of *gnome* in reaching a verdict about unusual facts.

72. *ST* II-II, q. 120, a. 1 ad 1.

73. *ST* II-II, q. 120, a. 1 ad 1.

the fact that the litigant or defendant doesn't receive his *ius,* but in the fact that the judge disobeys the law that is in the mind of the legislator.

Legitimate judgments of equity require the judge to "follow the intention of the lawgiver" *(sequitur intentionem legislatoris)*.[74] When the judge gives equity he gives the equity that the lawgiver has in view.[75] Thomas is quite insistent that the judge may not pass judgment on the law itself, or even declare that "it was not well made."[76] And when the interpretation of the legislator's intent is doubtful, the judge's first responsibility is to remit the question to the sovereign.[77]

Therefore, Thomas's understanding of equity does not permit the judge to prefer natural law to the law of the human legislator. The judge can bring natural law into the picture only on the assumption that this or that precept of natural law is what the legislator had in mind, and which is contained in a materially defective (but not morally defective) way in the written statute.

The third case is the more difficult. Consider a human ordinance that requires acts contrary to the natural law—Thomas mentions idolatry, but it could be any act that is *malum in se,* for example, murder, theft, or adultery. Unlike the first two cases, the judge cannot take refuge in procedures or repair to the legislator's original intent. Concerning such ordinances, Thomas answers straightaway: "judgment should not be delivered according to them [*eas non est iudicandum*]."[78] And by judgment here I take him to mean the entire spectrum of *iudicium* whether it be a subordinate legal official or a citizen.

Two things make this case interesting and a bit complicated. First, Thomas says that no judgment should be rendered according to the flawed measure; he does not say that one is entitled to make a new rule and measure, for that would imply legislative authority. A corrupt law does not give the judge a license to legislate. Second, Thomas delineates several ways that a law is corrupt, and depending upon the mode of corruption the prohibition against delivering a judgment might be more or less strict.

Laws, he explains, may be unjust in two ways[79]:

---

74. *ST* I-II, q. 96, a. 6 ad 2.
75. *ST* II-II, q. 60, a. 5 ad 2.
76. *ST* II-II, q. 120, a. 1 ad 2.
77. *ST* I-II, q. 96, a. 6 ad 2; II-II, q. 120, a. 1 ad 2.
78. *ST* II-II, q. 60, a. 5 ad 1.
79. *ST* I-II, q. 96, a. 4.

First, by being contrary to human good, through being opposed to the things mentioned above—either in respect of the end, as when an authority imposes on his subjects burdensome laws conducive not to the common good, but rather to his own cupidity or vainglory—or in respect of the author, as when a man makes a law that goes beyond the power committed to him—or in respect of the form, as when burdens are imposed unequally on the community, although with a view to the common good. The like are acts of violence rather than laws; because, as Augustine says (De Lib. Arb. i, 5), "a law that is not just, seems to be no law at all." Wherefore such laws do not bind in conscience, except perhaps in order to avoid scandal or disturbance, for which cause a man should even yield his right, according to Mt 5:40, 41: "If a man . . . take away thy coat, let go thy cloak also unto him; and whosoever will force thee one mile, go with him other two."

Secondly, laws may be unjust through being opposed to the Divine good: such are the laws of tyrants inducing to idolatry, or to anything else contrary to the Divine law: and laws of this kind must nowise be observed, because, as stated in Acts 5:29, "we ought to obey God rather than man."

Under the first heading, a human ordinance can be unjust in three ways: *ex fine,* "laws" ordained to a private good; *ex auctore,* "laws" enacted by one who has usurped authority; and *ex forma,* "laws" that unjustly distribute benefits and burdens. Thomas contends that on any of these three counts the ordinance does not bind. One might be obligated to comply with the command, but on grounds other than the *ratio* of the ordinance itself—for instance, to avoid greater harm to the community. Thus put, when one complies one does not judge according to the ordinance, but according to the natural law, which teaches one how to deal with the corrupt law.

But what about the act of the *iudex?* It is relatively easy to understand how a private person could comply with, rather than obey, an unjust law. The *iudex,* however, performs an essentially public act of speaking the law and authoritatively applying it to the case. He cannot sincerely say, "This is no law at all but I will issue a binding judgment having it enforced." If the legislator cannot make unjust laws bind in conscience neither can the *iudex.* And if the sentence of a judge is not binding, it is no sentence at all. That is to say, he has not judged as a judge.

Moreover, the three ways an ordinance can go wrong are rather different. Take an ordinance that fails *ex fine.* Let's say that a sovereign makes himself the chief beneficiary of the profits drawn from the nation's industries, but at the same time he pays everyone a decent wage. If a dispute over the ordinance should come into his court, must a judge refuse to render judgment according to the "law"? Suppose on the next count that a junta illegally, even immorally, seizes power and then promptly enacts a "law" changing the date on which income taxes are to be paid. Again, it is easy to see how a citizen would feel morally obligated to comply with the unjust ordinance. But can the judge render judgment according to that ordinance? Finally, with respect to ordinances flawed *ex forma,* how seriously must be the deformation to put the judge into a situation where he must not render judgment? Thomas allows that this kind of deformation can satisfy the other two criteria: it can be made for the common good by a proper authority. So let us imagine that a Washington think-tank persuades Congress to tax only the poor and the lower middle class. It is a far-fetched example for our own polity, but it is exactly what Thomas means by unjust *ex forma.* When we pause to consider the fact that human polities are frequently afflicted with ordinances that are unjust *ex forma,* we might suspect that the answer, no judgment should be rendered, is too rigorist. Even so, I think that this is the conclusion to be drawn from Thomas's understanding of the principles.

A constitutional court might enjoy authority to invalidate laws that are unjust in any of these three modes; especially, one would think, laws that are unjust *ex auctore*—provided, of course, that this court has access to some other law that is not corrupt, for example, a constitution. Thomas, however, would not allow a freewheeling appeal to natural law, even for a constitutional court; in any event, I find no evidence in his writings of such a principle or practice on which judges can invalidate unjust positive law for no other reason than the natural law.

The second way that a human ordinance is unjust is the case of a law that commands something directly contrary to divine law. The term *lex divina* can mean different things in Thomas, usually one or another mode of divine positive law. We can think, for example, of an emperor who, usurping the authority given to the apostles, makes laws on the number and administration of the sacraments. Clearly, in this case judgment should not be rendered.

By the divine law he also means the Decalogue, which is nothing less than the *conclusiones* of the natural law promulgated by divine positive law.[80]

---

80. *ST* I-II, q. 100.

Here, we have the human legislator commanding his subjects to worship idols, to slaughter the innocent, to commit adultery, and so forth. He commands the people in the moral order of things to do what they must not do, and not to do what they must do. Whereas in the three earlier modes the principle of the common good permits some room, even obligation, for compliance, there is none here. For no appeal to the common good can defeat the truth that these actions can never be ordered to the common good. In the face of such ordinances the *iudex* must do the same thing as any private person: render no judgment according to the "law." All citizens must imitate the Egyptian midwives, obeying God rather than men.

The tricky part of this scheme is how we formulate the various aspects of injustice. Martin Luther King, for example, seemed to think that the segregation laws were not merely corrupt *ex forma*, but contrary to divine law. And we ourselves might wonder where to place abortion law. That law is certainly corrupt *ex forma,* and probably corrupt *ex auctore*. Although the law does not directly command a violation of the Fifth Commandment, it certainly forbids legal officials and by extension ordinary citizens from doing what they must otherwise do: namely, to protect the lives of the innocent. Indeed, it makes not merely difficult, but impossible, the legal protection of those innocents who are most vulnerable to attack. This is not the place to untangle the knots of legal abortion in our polity; it does seem however that Thomistic principles would not permit subordinate legal officials—trial judges, executives, legislators, police—to issue an ordering judgment according to that law.

Conclusion

Human judgment in any of its modes always proceeds from law. The nucleus of Thomas's doctrine of natural law is that in human action we find law all the way down, as it were; but it is not a matter of law all the way out. Every person may judge according to the natural law. Capacity to judge according to the natural law, moreover, is found wherever there is authority to judge other persons. In either case, the natural law must be preferred to any human ordinance that directly contradicts the divine law.

Only properly constituted political authorities may use the natural law to make more laws. The judge uses natural law only in conjunction with the legislator, and here specifically in cases where the written law, which is said to contain the natural right, needs assistance in reaching a certain set of facts. The judge's loyalty and obedience to the natural law require him to consider the law in the mind of the *principatus regalis*. Therefore, the *iudex* is not torn between two jurisdictions. The human law is derived from the natural law. Moreover, the precepts of justice that forbid usurpation are themselves precepts of natural justice. Judicial preference for natural law over positive law is a contradiction in terms.

Loyalty to the higher law might obligate the judge not to render judgment; he may lawfully refuse to be moved by a corrupt ordinance. In this case, however, the judge does not prefer the natural law to human law. Rather, he obeys the natural law in the face of commands that are no law at all. Yet even in the extreme case of refusing to render judgment, the judge, insofar as he is a judge, is not entitled to plough ahead and substitute his own law for that of the legislator.

CONTRIBUTORS

Benedict M. Ashley, O.P., is emeritus professor of moral theology at Aquinas Institute of Theology, St. Louis, and adjunct professor at the Center for Health Care Ethics, Medical School of St. Louis University.

Father Ashley was born May 3, 1915. He solemnly professed as a member of the Dominican Order, Chicago Province, in 1942, and was ordained a priest in 1948. Father Ashley is a graduate of the University of Chicago and the University of Notre Dame and has doctorates in philosophy and political science, and the postdoctoral degree of master of sacred theology conferred by an international committee of the Order of Preachers.

He was formerly president of Aquinas Institute of Theology, St. Louis; professor of theology at the Institute of Religion and Human Development in Houston; professor of theology at the John Paul II Institute for Studies in Marriage and Family in Washington, D.C.; and a visiting lecturer in humanities at the University of Chicago, the Institute for Psychological Sciences, Arlington, Va., and the Center for Thomistic Studies, the University of St. Thomas, Houston, Texas; and a fellow of the John Paul II Cultural Center, Washington, D.C.

Father Ashley has been honored with the medal *Pro Ecclesia et Pontifice* conferred by John Paul II, and the Thomas Linacre Award from the National Federation of Catholic Physicians' Guilds and has received a doctor of divinity degree, *honoris causa,* from Aquinas Institute of Theology, St. Louis.

Among his publications are (with Kevin O'Rourke, O.P.) *Health Care Ethics,* now in its fourth English edition, and *Ethics of Health Care.* He has also published *Justice in the Church, Living the Truth in Love, Theologies of the Body,* and *Choosing a World View and Value System.*

Romanus Cessario, O.P., priest of the Eastern Province of the Dominicans, currently serves as professor of systematic theology at St. John's Seminary, Brighton, Mass. His doctoral thesis, *Christian Satisfaction in Aquinas*, was directed by the late Colman O'Neill, O.P., and published in 1982; a revised version, *The Godly Image* (St. Bede's Press/Fordham University Press), appeared in 1990.

Father Cessario has published articles on dogmatic and moral theology as well as on the history of Thomism. Among his books are *The Moral Virtues and Theological Ethics* (University of Notre Dame Press, 1991); *Perpetual Angelus: As the Saints Pray the Rosary* (Alba House, 1995); a short history of Thomism, *Le thomisme et les thomistes* (Les Éditions du Cerf, 1999); *Christian Faith and the Theological Life* (The Catholic University of America Press, 1996); *The Virtues, or the Examined Life* (Continuum, 2002); and, in collaboration with Kevin White, a translation of the fifteenth-century Dominican theologian John Capreolus's *Treatise on the Virtues* (The Catholic University of America Press, 2001). His *Introduction to Moral Theology* (2001) inaugurated the multivolume Catholic Moral Thought series at The Catholic University of America Press. Father Cessario serves on the editorial boards of several journals and is senior editor of the monthly worship aid *Magnificat*. For the last decade and a half he has lectured extensively in both the United States and Europe.

Robert Fastiggi is an associate professor of systematic theology at Sacred Heart Major Seminary in Detroit. He received an A.B. in religion from Dartmouth College, and an M.A. and a Ph.D. in historical theology from Fordham University. From 1985 to 1999, he taught in the Department of Religious Studies at St. Edward's University in Austin, Texas.

Dr. Fastiggi's is the author of *The Natural Theology of Yves de Paris* (Scholars Press, 1991) and has published articles in a number of journals, including *Crisis, The Thomist, Homiletic and Pastoral Review*, and the *Josephinum Journal of Theology*. He is a contributor to the *New Catholic Encyclopedia* (2nd ed.) and is the general editor of new English edition of Denzinger's *Enchiridion* (to be published by Ignatius Press).

Robert P. George is McCormick Professor of Jurisprudence and director of the James Madison Program in American Ideals and Institutions at Princeton University. He is a member of the President's Council on

Bioethics, is a former presidential appointee to the United States Commission on Civil Rights, and has served as a judicial fellow at the Supreme Court of the United States, where he received the 1990 Justice Tom D. Clark Award.

Professor George is a Phi Beta Kappa graduate of Swarthmore College and holds graduate degrees in law and theology from Harvard University. He earned his D.Phil. in legal philosophy from Oxford University, where his work was supervised by John Finnis and Joseph Raz.

He is the author of *In Defense of Natural Law* and *Making Men Moral: Civil Liberties and Public Morality*, and the editor of *The Autonomy of Law: Essays on Legal Positivism*, *Natural Law, Liberalism and Morality*, and *Natural Law Theory: Contemporary Essays*. His articles and review essays have appeared in such journals as the *Harvard Law Review*, the *Yale Law Journal*, the *Columbia Law Review*, the *Review of Politics*, and the *Review of Metaphysics*. He serves on editorial boards of the *American Journal of Jurisprudence*, *First Things*, and *Academic Questions*. He is a member of the board of governors of the Ave Maria School of Law and the boards of directors of the Ethics and Public Policy Center, the Institute for American Values, and the National Association of Scholars.

Professor George is also a practicing constitutional lawyer. In 1994, he represented Mother Teresa of Calcutta as counsel of record on an *amicus curiae* brief asking the Supreme Court to reverse its decision in *Roe v. Wade* and "declare the inalienable rights of the unborn child." In 1989 he helped to revise the Constitution of the Principality of Liechtenstein. He is a member of the Council on Foreign Relations.

John Goyette is a tutor at Thomas Aquinas College, Santa Paula, Calif. He received a Ph.D. in philosophy from The Catholic University of America in 1998. He has taught philosophy at The Catholic University of America and at Sacred Heart Major Seminary in Detroit, Mich. Dr. Goyette has published essays on Newman's *Idea of a University*, Augustine's notion of Christian education in *De doctrina christiana*, and on Aristotelian/Thomistic natural philosophy. His articles, essays, and reviews have appeared in The Catholic University of America Press, St. Augustine's Press, *The Thomist*, *Maritain Studies*, and the *Review of Metaphysics*.

Contributors

Russell Hittinger holds the Warren Chair of Catholic Studies at the University of Tulsa where he is also a research professor in the School of Law. He specializes in issues of theology and law. Since August 2002 he has been chair of the Department of Philosophy and Religion. From 1991 to 1996, he was a research scholar at the American Enterprise Institute for Public Policy Research, in Washington, D.C., where he worked on issues of law and religion. From 1991 to 1996, he was an associate professor in the School of Philosophy, The Catholic University of America, where he taught political philosophy and philosophy of law. From 1990 to 1991 he was a visiting professor at Princeton University, where he taught U.S. constitutional law and church-state issues. He has also taught at Fordham University and at New York University, where he taught medieval political and legal theory.

His books and articles have appeared in such places as the University of Notre Dame Press, Oxford University Press, the *Review of Metaphysics,* the *Review of Politics,* and the *International Philosophical Quarterly,* as well as in several law journals. His book *The First Grace: Re-Discovering Natural Law in a Post-Christian Age* was published in November 2002. He is on the editorial boards of *First Things* and the *American Journal of Jurisprudence.*

His article "Privacy and Liberal Legal Culture" was part of a 1990 *World and I* symposium that won the Silver Gavel Award of the American Bar Association in 1991. In May 1997 the John Templeton Foundation put him on the Templeton Honor Roll for Teaching in the Liberal Arts. He received the Josephine Yalch Zekan Award, Best Scholarly Article in Faith and Law, College of Law, University of Tulsa, in both 1997 and 2003. In 2000, he was a senior research fellow at the Notre Dame Center for Ethics and Culture, where he is finishing a book called *The Popes and the Desacralized Caesar: Roman Theories of the Modern State 1800–1989.* In 2001, he was appointed to the Pontificia Academia Sancti Thomae Aquinatis, a pontifical council founded by Pope Leo XIII. He was also a visiting professor at the Pontifical Università Regina Apostolorum, Rome, in Spring 2001.

Mark S. Latkovic is professor of moral and systematic theology at Sacred Heart Major Seminary in Detroit, Mich., where he has taught since 1990. Dr. Latkovic received an M.A. in theology from The Catholic University of America in Washington, D.C., and a license in sacred theology and a doctorate in sacred theology from the John Paul II Institute for Studies on Marriage and Family, Washington, D.C., where he was a McGivney Fellow.

During his tenure at the seminary, Dr. Latkovic has taught numerous courses, including Catholic social teaching, bioethics and sexuality, marriage and law, and principles of Christian morality. His articles, essays, and reviews have appeared in such publications as the *Linacre Quarterly, Crisis, Catholic Faith, Homiletic and Pastoral Review, Ethics and Medics, Markets and Morality, Fellowship of Catholic Scholars Quarterly, Josephinum Journal of Theology, National Catholic Bioethics Quarterly,* and *Logos: A Journal of Catholic Thought and Culture.* Dr. Latkovic was the vice-chair of Adam Cardinal Maida's Medical-Moral Committee and he is a frequent speaker and lecturer. He is also the book review editor for the *Linacre Quarterly.*

Steven A. Long received his undergraduate degree from the University of Toledo and his M.A. in philosophy from the University of Toledo. He pursued postgraduate study at the Institute for Philosophy at the University of Leuven in Belgium. While in Belgium he also undertook private studies with Fr. Jan Walgrave, O.P., the renowned Newman scholar and Thomist. He pursued further studies at The Catholic University of America in Washington, D.C., where he received his pontifical Ph.D. in philosophy in 1993. He has published in *Revue thomiste, The Thomist,* the English language edition of *Nova et vetera,* the *International Philosophical Quarterly, Communio, Louvain Studies,* and other journals. He lectures in the United States and Europe, and is an associate editor of the English language edition of *Nova et vetera.* Dr. Long currently teaches at the University of St. Thomas in St. Paul, Minn.

William Mathie, a Canadian, teaches political philosophy in the Political Science Department at Brock University. He was a student of George Grant at McMaster University and has written about Grant's understanding of our technological society and of the crisis for justice posed by the decisions in Canadian and U.S. courts that have eliminated most American and all Canadian legal restrictions upon abortion. Dr. Mathie pursued the study of political philosophy at the University of Chicago in the 1960s where Leo Strauss was then engaged in a radical rethinking of the issues at the heart of our political and moral life, of the quarrel between the inventors of the modern understanding of politics and their predecessors, and of the tension between biblical revelation and philosophy.

Dr. Mathie has published studies of the ancient and modern understanding of justice as exemplified by Aristotle and Thomas Hobbes and has written about federalism and conflicting accounts of community. He has also written on Alexis de Tocqueville's understanding of the role of women as the makers of morals in modern democracy. He hopes soon to complete two projects: the first is an interpretation of Hobbes's *Leviathan,* and the second a book on the conflict between philosophers and fathers of families as a central but often ignored theme of Plato's *Republic.*

Dr. Mathie was the founder, and has been the director, of the Great Books/Liberal Studies Program at Brock University in Canada. The program is an attempt to restore the idea of liberal education as a training for freedom through reading together and discussing the great works of reason and imagination that have animated Western civilization. He has also written on what we might learn about liberal education from Tocqueville, Adam Smith, Leo Strauss, Allan Bloom, and John Henry Newman.

William E. May is the Michael J. McGivney Professor of Moral Theology at the John Paul II Institute for Studies on Marriage and Family at The Catholic University of America in Washington, D.C., where he has been teaching since 1991. From 1971 through 1991, he taught moral theology at The Catholic University of America.

Dr. May received his Ph.D. in philosophy from Marquette University in 1968 with a study of the metaphysics of Henri Bergson. Among the more than twelve books written by Dr. May are *An Introduction to Moral Theology, Marriage: The Rock on Which the Family Is Built,* and (with Ronald Lawler, O.F.M. Cap., and Joseph Boyle) *Catholic Sexual Ethics.* Dr. May has authored more than two hundred essays, which have appeared in such journals as the *American Journal of Jurisprudence,* the *New Scholasticism, The Thomist, Anthropotes, Scripta Theologica, Faith and Reason,* the *Linacre Quarterly,* and the *National Catholic Bioethics Quarterly.* His most recent book is *Catholic Bioethics and the Gift of Human Life* (Our Sunday Visitor, 2000). He is also the editor and translator of numerous works.

Dr. May, at the appointment of Pope John Paul II, served on the International Theological Commission from 1986 to 1997. Pope John Paul also appointed him a "peritus" for the 1987 Synod of Bishops on the vocation and mission of the lay faithful in the Church and in the world. In 1991 he received the *Pro Ecclesia et Pontifice* medal. He has also received the Cardinal Wright Award from the Fellowship of Catholic Scholars, the Thomas

Linacre Award from the National Federation of Catholic Physicians' Guilds, and the St. Dominic Medal from the Dominican House of Studies in Washington, D.C.

Ralph McInerny is the Michael P. Grace Professor of Medieval Philosophy and director of the Jacques Maritain Center at the University of Notre Dame, where he has taught since 1955. He is a fellow of the Pontifical Academy of Thomas Aquinas and delivered the Gifford Lectures at the University of Glasgow in 1999–2000. He is the cofounder, with Michael Novak, of *Crisis,* and the founder and editor of *Catholic Dossier.* For many years he was the editor of *New Scholasticism.* He served as president of the American Catholic Philosophical Association, the Metaphysical Society of America, and the Fellowship of Catholic Scholars, whose quarterly he edited. Under his direction, the Maritain Center is publishing twenty volumes of Maritain's works in English.

Among his scholarly writings are *Aquinas and Analogy, Aquinas on Human Action, Ethica Thomistica, A Student's Guide to Philosophy, A First Glance at Thomas Aquinas: A Handbook for Peeping Thomists, Characters in Search of Their Author* (the Gifford Lectures), and *The Defamation of Pius XII.* His life of Jacques Maritain, *The Very Rich Hours of Jacques Maritain,* as well as his life of Aquinas are in the press. Professor McInerny is also the author of many novels and mysteries, among them the Father Dowling Mysteries, the Sister Mary Teresa Dempsey Mysteries (as Monica Quill), the Andrew Broom mysteries, and a new series of mysteries set at Notre Dame, the most recent of which is *Celt and Pepper.*

Earl Muller, S.J., is professor of theology at Sacred Heart Major Seminary in Detroit. He was born in 1947 in Columbia, S.C. In 1965, he entered the Society of Jesus in New Orleans. He received a B.S. in physics and philosophy from Spring Hill College in Mobile, Ala., in 1974 and an M. Div. from Regis College in Toronto in 1977. He was ordained to the Roman Catholic priesthood the same year. Subsequently, he pursued doctoral studies at Marquette University in Milwaukee, graduating in 1987. His dissertation, under the direction of Donald J. Keefe, S.J., was entitled *Trinity and Marriage in Paul: Theological Shape as Ground for a Scriptural Warrant for a Communitarian Analogy of the Trinity.*

From 1971 to 1974, he taught science and mathematics at Jesuit High

School in Tampa, Fla. From 1983 to 1986, Father Muller was an instructor of theology at Spring Hill College. He was assistant professor of theology at Marquette University from 1987 to 1995, and from 1995 to 1999 was a *professore aggiunto* in theology at the Pontifical Gregorian University in Rome. In addition to the publication of his dissertation, he has coedited two volumes: *Augustine: Presbyter factus sum* in Collectanea Augustiniana, vol. 2, Augustinian Historical Institute of Villanova University and *Theological Education in the Catholic Tradition: Contemporary Challenges*.

Richard S. Myers is professor of law at Ave Maria School of Law. He is a Phi Beta Kappa graduate of Kenyon College. He earned his law degree at Notre Dame. He began his legal career by clerking for Judge John F. Kilkenny of the U.S. Court of Appeals for the Ninth Circuit. Professor Myers also worked for Jones, Day, Reavis & Pogue in Washington, D.C., from 1981 to 1985. His law practice focused on antitrust law and appellate litigation, including work on several cases before the U.S. Supreme Court. He began his law-teaching career at Case Western Reserve University School of Law, where he taught from 1986 to 1992. He then taught at the University of Detroit Mercy School of Law from 1992 until 1998. Since 2000, he has taught at Ave Maria School of Law.

His courses have focused on antitrust, civil procedure, conflict of laws, constitutional law, federal jurisdiction, and First Amendment issues. He has published extensively on constitutional law in the law reviews of The Catholic University of America, Case Western Reserve University, Notre Dame University, and Washington and Lee University.

David Novak has held the J. Richard and Dorothy Shiff Chair of Jewish Studies as Professor of the Study of Religion and Professor of Philosophy at the University of Toronto since 1997. He is a member of University College and the Joint Centre for Bioethics. From 1997 to 2002 he also was director of the Jewish Studies Programme there. From 1989 to 1997 he was the Edgar M. Bronfman Professor of Modern Judaic Studies at the University of Virginia. Previously he taught at Oklahoma City University, Old Dominion University, the New School for Social Research, the Jewish Theological Seminary of America, and Baruch College of the City University of New York. From 1966 to 1969 he was Jewish chaplain to St. Elizabeth's Hospital, National Institute of Mental Health, in Washington, D.C.

From 1966 to 1989 he served as a pulpit rabbi in several communities in the United States.

David Novak was born in Chicago in 1941. He received his A.B. from the University of Chicago in 1961, his M.H.L. (master of Hebrew literature) in 1964, and his rabbinical diploma in 1966 from the Jewish Theological Seminary of America. He received his Ph.D. in philosophy from Georgetown University in 1971.

David Novak is a founder, vice-president, and coordinator of the Jewish Law Panel of the Union for Traditional Judaism, and is a faculty member of the Institute of Traditional Judaism in Teaneck, N.J. He serves as secretary-treasurer of the Institute on Religion and Public Life in New York City and is on the editorial board of its journal *First Things*. He is a fellow of the American Academy for Jewish Research and the Academy for Jewish Philosophy, and a member of the Board of Consulting Scholars of the James Madison Program in American Ideals and Institutions at Princeton University. In 1992–1993 he was a fellow at the Woodrow Wilson International Center for Scholars in Washington, D.C. In 1995 he was Distinguished Visiting Professor of Religion and Business Ethics at Drew University. In 1996 he delivered the Lancaster/Yarnton Lectures at Oxford University and at Lancaster University. He has lectured throughout North America, Europe, Israel, and South Africa.

David Novak is the author of eleven books, the latest being *Covenantal Rights: A Study in Jewish Political Theory* (Princeton University Press, 2000), which won the award of the American Academy of Religion for "best book in constructive religious thought in 2000." He has edited four books, and is the author of over two hundred articles in scholarly and intellectual journals.

Janet E. Smith holds the Father Michael J. McGivney Chair of Life Issues at Sacred Heart Major Seminary in Detroit. She received her B.A. in classics from Grinnell College, her M.A. in classical languages from the University of North Carolina, and her Ph.D. in classical languages from the University of Toronto. She is the author of *Humanae Vitae: A Generation Later* and edited *Why Humanae Vitae Was Right: A Reader*. Dr. Smith has published on natural law, virtue, Aquinas's ethics, abortion, contraception, various bioethical issues, *Veritatis splendor,* the *Catechism of the Catholic Church,* and Plato and myth.

Dr. Smith has received numerous honors and awards such as the Pro-Life Person of the Year, Diocese of Dallas, 1995; Haggar Award for Excellence in Teaching, University of Dallas, 1994; Cardinal Wright Award from the Fellowship of Catholic Scholars, 1993; and Consultor for the Pontifical Council of the Family, 1995–2000. Dr. Smith is a frequent lecturer on the Church's teaching on sexuality, nationally and internationally.

Christopher Wolfe is professor of political science at Marquette University. He graduated with a B.A. from Notre Dame in 1971 and went on to earn a Ph.D. in political philosophy at Boston College. He taught American political thought and constitutional law at Assumption College from 1975 to 1978, and has been at Marquette since 1978, where he currently chairs the Department of Political Science.

Dr. Wolfe's books include *The Rise of Modern Judicial Review, Judicial Activism: Bulwark of Liberty or Precarious Security?, How to Read the Constitution,* and *Essays on Faith and Liberal Democracy.* His articles have appeared in such journals as the *American Journal of Jurisprudence,* the *Review of Politics,* the *Texas Law Review,* and the *Marquette Law Review.* He is currently at work on a long-term project on liberalism, natural law, and American public philosophy. Dr. Wolfe is a founder and president of the American Public Philosophy Institute. The Institute, which was founded in 1989, is a group of scholars from various disciplines that seeks to bring natural law theory to bear on contemporary scholarly and public discussions.

Martin D. Yaffe is professor of philosophy and religion studies at the University of North Texas, where he has taught since 1968. Dr. Yaffe earned a B.A. from the University of Toronto, graduating in 1963. He did graduate studies in philosophy at the University of Toronto and at the Claremont Graduate School, where he earned his Ph.D.

Dr. Yaffe wrote the interpretive essay and notes for St. Thomas Aquinas's *The Literal Exposition on the Book of Job: A Scriptural Commentary Concerning Providence* (1270), which was translated by Anthony Damico. He wrote *Shylock and the Jewish Question,* which in 1998 was nominated for an Award for Excellence in the Study of Religion, American Academy of Religion. He is editor of *Judaism and Environmental Ethics: A Reader,* and translator of Benedict Spinoza's *Theologico-Political Treatise* (1670). He is also the author of numerous articles and scholarly reviews.

WORKS CITED

Other items, including Supreme Court cases, the documents of ecumenical councils, pontifical and ecclesiastical documents, and citations from classical authors, including St. Thomas Aquinas, are cited fully in the appropriate notes. Quoted translations of classical authors, however, appear below.

Aertsen, Jan. *Nature and Creature: Thomas Aquinas's Way of Thought*. Translated by H. D. Morton. Leiden: E. J. Brill, 1988.

Anastaplo, George. *The Constitution of 1787: A Commentary*. Baltimore: Johns Hopkins University Press, 1997.

Aquinas, St. Thomas. *Commentary on Aristotle's Nicomachean Ethics*. Translated by C. I. Litzinger. South Bend, Ind.: Dumb Ox Books, 1993.

———. *The Summa Theologica*. Translated by the Fathers of the English Dominican Province. New York: Benziger, 1948.

———. *Summa theologiae*. Translated by Thomas Gilby et al. Cambridge, U.K.: Blackfriars, 1964–1974.

Aristotle. *Metaphysics*. Translated by W. D. Ross. In *The Basic Works of Aristotle*. New York: Random House, 1941.

———. *Nicomachean Ethics*. Translated by W. D. Ross. In *The Basic Works of Aristotle*. New York: Random House, 1941.

Arnhart, Larry. *Aristotle on Political Reasoning: A Commentary on the "Rhetoric."* DeKalb: Northern Illinois University Press, 1981.

———. *Darwinian Natural Right: The Biological Ethics of Human Nature*. Albany: State University of New York Press, 1998.

Ashley, Benedict. "Aristotle's Sluggish Earth, Part 1: Problematics of the *De Caelo*." *New Scholasticism* 32 (January 1958): 1–31.

———. "Aristotle's Sluggish Earth, Part 2: Media of Demonstration." *New Scholasticism* 32 (April 1958): 202–34.

———. "Dominion or Stewardship?: Theological Reflections." In *Birth, Suffering, and Death: Catholic Perspectives at the Edges of Life*, edited by Kevin M. Wildes et al., 85–106. Boston: Kluwer Academic, 1992.

———. *Justice in the Church: Gender and Participation.* Washington, D.C.: The Catholic University of America Press, 1996.

———. *Living the Truth in Love: A Biblical Introduction to Moral Theology.* Staten Island, N.Y.: Alba House, 1996.

———. "Scriptural Grounds for Concrete Moral Norms." *The Thomist* 52 (January 1988): 1–22.

———. *Theologies of the Body: Humanist and Christian.* 2d ed. St. Louis: Pope John Center, 1995.

———. "What Is the End of the Human Person?: The Vision of God and Integral Human Fulfillment." In *Moral Truth and Moral Tradition: Essays in Honor of Peter Geach and Elizabeth Anscombe,* edited by Luke Gormally, 68–96. Dublin: Four Courts Press, 1994.

———. "What Is the Natural Law?" *Ethics and Medics* 12 (June 1987): 1–2.

Ashley, Benedict, and Kevin O'Rourke. *Health Care Ethics: A Theological Analysis.* 4th ed. Washington, D.C.: Georgetown University Press, 1997.

Barnett, Randy. *The Structure of Liberty.* New York: Oxford University Press, 1998.

Basler, Roy, ed. *The Collected Works of Abraham Lincoln.* New Brunswick, N.J.: Rutgers University Press, 1953.

Benardete, Seth. *The Bow and the Lyre: A Platonic Reading of the Odyssey.* Lanham, Md.: Rowman & Littlefield, 1997.

Benestad, Brian. *The Pursuit of a Just Social Order.* Washington, D.C.: Ethics and Public Policy Center, 1982.

Bloom, Allan. *The Closing of the American Mind.* New York: Simon & Schuster, 1987.

Bork, Robert. "Neutral Principles and Some First Amendment Problems." *Indiana Law Journal* 47 (1971): 1–35.

Boyle, Joseph M. Jr. "Natural Law, Ownership, and the World's Resources." *Journal of Value Inquiry* 23 (1989): 191–207.

Bradley, Denis J. M. *Aquinas on the Twofold Human Good.* Washington, D.C.: The Catholic University of America Press, 1997.

Bradley, Gerard V., and Robert P. George. "The New Natural Law Theory: A Reply to Jean Porter." *American Journal of Jurisprudence* 38 (1994): 303–15.

Brock, Stephen Louis. *The Legal Character of Natural Law According to St. Thomas Aquinas.* Ph.D. dissertation, University of Toronto, 1988.

Brown, Oscar J. *Natural Rectitude and Divine Law in Aquinas.* Toronto: Pontifical Institute of Medieval Studies, 1981.

Burlamaqui, Jean Jacques. *The Principles of Natural and Politic Law.* Translated by Thomas Nugent. Philadelphia: Nicklin & Johnson, 1832.

Burrell, David B. *Knowing the Unknowable God.* South Bend, Ind.: University of Notre Dame Press, 1986.

Cessario, Romanus. *Introduction to Moral Theology.* Washington, D.C.: The Catholic University of America Press, 2001.

Cessario, Romanus, Guy Bedouelle, and Kevin White, eds. *Jean Capreolus en son temps, 1380–1444*. Mémoire Dominicaine, numéro spécial, 1. Paris: Les Editions du Cerf, 1997.

Chenu, Marie-Dominique. *Introduction à l'étude de Saint Thomas d'Aquin.* 1950; reprint, Paris:Vrin, 1954. English translation by A. M. Landry and D. Hughes. *Toward Understanding Saint Thomas Aquinas.* Chicago: Henry Regnery, 1964.

———. "Le plan de la Somme théologique de Saint Thomas." *Revue thomiste* 47 (1939): 93–107.

———. Review of *Saint Thomas d'Aquin et la vie de l'Eglise* by André Hayen (Louvain/Paris: Publications universitaires, 1952). *Bulletin thomiste* 8 (1947–1953): 771–72.

Clor, Harry. *Obscenity and Public Morality.* Chicago: University of Chicago Press, 1969.

Corbin, Michel. *Le chemin de la théologie chez Thomas d'Aquin.* Bibliothéque des Archives de Philosophie, n.s., vol. 16. Paris: Beauchesne, 1974.

Cromartie, Michael, ed. *A Preserving Grace: Protestants, Catholics, and Natural Law.* Grand Rapids, Mich.: Eerdmans, 1997.

Cuddeback, Matthew. *Light and Form in St. Thomas Aquinas's Metaphysics of the Knower.* Ph.D. dissertation, The Catholic University of America, 1998.

Damich, Edward. "The Essence of Law According to Thomas Aquinas." *American Journal of Jurisprudence* 30 (1985): 79–96.

Danto, Arthur C. "Human Nature and Natural Law." In *Law and Philosophy,* edited by Sidney Hook, 187–99. New York: New York University Press, 1964.

de Laplace, Pierre Simon. *Philosophical Essay on Probabilities.* Translated by F. W. Truscott and F. L. Emory. New York: Dover, 1951.

de Lubac, Henri. *Augustinianism and Modern Theology.* Translated by Lancelot Sheppard. New York: Herder & Herder, 1969.

de Scorraile, Raoul. *Francois Suarez de Le Compagnie de Jesus.* Vol. 2. Paris: Lethielleux, 1912.

Dewan, Lawrence. "St. Thomas, Our Natural Lights, and the Moral Order." *Angelicum* 67 (1990): 283–307.

Dienstag, J. I., ed. *Studies in Maimonides and St. Thomas Aquinas.* New York: KTAV, 1975.

Dobbs-Weinstein, Idit. *Maimonides and St. Thomas on the Limits of Reason.* Albany: State University of New York Press, 1995.

Donohoo, Lawrence J. "The Nature and Grace of *Sacra Doctrina* in St. Thomas's *Super Boetium de Trinitate*." *The Thomist* 63 (July 1999): 343–401.

Eisgruber, Christopher L. "Justice Story, Slavery, and the Natural Law Foundations of American Constitutionalism." *University of Chicago Law Review* 55 (1988): 273–327.

Eldredge, Niles. *Reinventing Darwin: The Great Debate at the High Table of Evolutionary Theory.* New York: John Wiley & Sons, 1995.

Etzioni, Amitai, ed. *New Communitarian Thinking*. Charlottesville: University Press of Virginia, 1995.
Festugière, André-Jean. "Appendice." In *Mémorial André-Jean Festugière. Antiquité paienne et chrétienne*. Vingt-cinq études publiées et réunies par E. Lucchesi et H.-D. Saffrey. *Cahiers d'orientalisme 10*. Geneva: Editions P. Cramer, 1984.
Finnis, John. *Aquinas: Moral, Political, and Legal Theory*. New York: Oxford University Press, 1998.
———. *Fundamentals of Ethics*. Washington, D.C.: Georgetown University Press, 1983.
———. "Law as Co-ordination." *Ratio Juris* 2 (1989): 97–104.
———. *Moral Absolutes: Tradition, Revision, and Truth*. Washington, D.C.: The Catholic University of America Press, 1991.
———. "Natural Inclinations and Natural Rights: Deriving 'Ought' from 'Is'" According to Aquinas." In *Lex et Libertas: Freedom and Law According to St. Thomas Aquinas*, Studi Tomistici, Vol. 30, edited by L. J. Elders and K. Hedwig, 43–55. Vatican City: Libreria Editrice Vaticana, 1987.
———. *Natural Law and Natural Rights*. New York: Oxford University Press, 1980.
———. "Natural Law and the 'Is'-'Ought' Question: An Invitation to Professor Veatch." *Catholic Lawyer* 26 (1981): 266–77. Reprinted in *Natural Law*, edited by John Finnis, 1:313–24. New York: New York University Press, 1991.
Finnis, John, Joseph Boyle, and Germain Grisez. *Nuclear Deterrence, Morality and Realism*. New York: Oxford University Press, 1987.
Fortin, Ernest. "Augustine, Aquinas, and the Problem of Natural Law." *Mediaevalia* 4 (1978): 183–86.
———. *Collected Essays*, Vol. 3, *Human Rights, Virtue, and the Common Good: Untimely Meditations on Religion and Politics*, edited by Brian Benestad. Lanham, Md.: Rowman & Littlefield, 1996.
———. "On the Presumed Medieval Origin of Individual Rights." In Ernest L. Fortin, *Collected Essays*, Vol. 2, *Classical Christianity and the Political Order: Reflections on the Theologico-Political Problem*, edited by Brian Benestad, 243–64. Lanham, Md.: Rowman & Littlefield, 1996.
Fox, Marvin. *Interpreting Maimonides*. Chicago: University of Chicago Press, 1990.
Franck, Isaac. "Maimonides and Aquinas on Man's Knowledge of God: A Twentieth-Century Perspective." *Review of Metaphysics* 38 (1985): 591–615.
Frohnen, Bruce. *The New Communitarians and the Crisis of Modern Liberalism*. Lawrence: University Press of Kansas, 1996.
Fuller, Lon. *The Morality of Law*. Rev. ed. New Haven, Conn.: Yale University Press, 1969.
Gaboriau, Florent. *Entrer en théologie avec saint Thomas d'Aquin*. Paris: FAC, 1993.
———. *Thomas d'Aquin en dialogue*. Paris: FAC, 1993.
———. *Thomas d'Aquin, penseur dan l'Eglise*. Paris: FAC, 1992.

Gell-Mann, Murray. *The Quark and the Jaguar: Adventures in the Simple and the Complex.* New York: W. H. Freeman and Co., 1994.
George, Robert P. "A Defense of the New Natural Law Theory." *American Journal of Jurisprudence* 41 (1996): 47–61.
———. *In Defense of Natural Law.* Oxford, U.K.: Clarendon Press, 1999.
———. "Natural Law and Human Nature." In *Natural Law Theory: Contemporary Essays,* edited by Robert P. George, 31–41. Oxford, U.K.: Clarendon Press, 1992.
———, ed. *Natural Law and Moral Inquiry: Ethics, Metaphysics, and Politics in the Work of Germain Grisez.* Washington, D.C.: Georgetown University Press, 1998.
———. "Natural Law and Positive Law." In *The Autonomy of Law: Essays on Legal Positivism,* edited by Robert P. George, 321–34. Oxford, U.K.: Clarendon Press, 1996.
———. "Recent Criticisms of Natural Law Theory." *University of Chicago Law Review* 55 (1988): 1371–1429.
———. "The Tyrant State." *First Things* 67 (November 1996): 39–42.
George, Robert P., and Christopher Wolfe, "Natural Law and Public Reason." In *Natural Law and Public Reason,* edited by Robert P. George and Christopher Wolfe, 51–74. Washington, D.C.: Georgetown University Press, 2000.
Gilby, Thomas. "Appendix 5: Sacra Doctrina." In St. Thomas Aquinas, *Summa Theologiae,* 1:58–66. Cambridge, U.K.: Blackfriars, 1964.
———. "Appendix 2: The Theological Classification of Law." In St. Thomas Aquinas, *Summa theologiae,* 28:162–64. Cambridge, U.K.: Blackfriars, 1966.
Gilson, Etienne. "Cajetan et l'existence." *Tijdschrift voor Philosophie* 15 (1953): 267–86.
———. *Letters of Etienne Gilson to Henri de Lubac.* Annotated by Henri de Lubac. Translated by Mary Emily Hamilton. San Francisco: Ignatius Press, 1988.
———. "Maimonide et la philosophie de l'Exode." *Medieval Studies* 8 (1951): 223–25.
———. Review of *Introduction à l'étude de Saint Thomas d'Aquin* by M. D. Chenu (Paris: Vrin, 1950). *Bulletin Thomiste* 8 (1951): 5–10.
———. *The Spirit of Medieval Philosophy.* Translated by A. H. C. Downes. New York: Charles Scribner's Sons, 1936.
———. *The Unity of Philosophical Experience.* New York: Charles Scribner's Sons, 1965.
Glazer, Nathan. "Toward a New Concordat." *This World* 2 (Summer 1982): 109–18.
Gleick, James. *Chaos: Making a New Science.* New York: Penguin Books, 1988.
Goldsworthy, Jeffrey. "Fact and Value in the New Natural Law Theory." *American Journal of Jurisprudence* 41 (1996): 21–46.
Gordley, James. *The Philosophical Origins of Modern Contract Doctrine.* New York: Oxford University Press, 1991.
Grant, George Parkin. *English Speaking Justice.* Toronto: Anansi, 1974.

———. *Lament for a Nation.* Toronto: McLelland and Stewart, 1963.

———. *Philosophy in the Mass Age.* Toronto: University of Toronto Press, 1995.

Grisez, Germain. *Abortion: The Myths, the Realities, and the Arguments.* New York: Corpus Books, 1970.

———. "A Critique of Russell Hittinger's Book, *A Critique of the New Natural Law Theory.*" *New Scholasticism* 62 (1988): 62–74.

———. *Contraception and the Natural Law.* Milwaukee, Wis.: Bruce, 1964.

———. "Dualism and the New Morality." In *L'Agire Morale,* Vol. 5, *Atti del Congresso sul Settimo Centenario di Santo Tomasso d'Aquino,* 323–30. Naples: Edizioni Domenicane, 1975.

———. "The First Principle of Practical Reason: A Commentary on the *Summa Theologiae*, 1–2, Question 94, Article 2." *Natural Law Forum* 10 (1965): 168–201.

———. "Natural Law and Natural Inclinations." *New Scholasticism* 61 (1987): 307–20.

———. "Natural Law, God, Religion, and Human Fulfillment." *American Journal of Jurisprudence* 46 (2002): 3–35.

———. *The Way of the Lord Jesus,* Vol. 1, *Christian Moral Principles.* Chicago: Franciscan Herald Press, 1983.

———. *The Way of the Lord Jesus,* Vol. 2, *Living a Christian Life.* Quincy, Ill.: Franciscan Press, 1993.

Grisez, Germain, and John Finnis. "The Basic Principles of Natural Law: A Reply to Ralph McInerny." *American Journal of Jurisprudence* 26 (1981): 21–31; reprinted in *Natural Law,* edited by John Finnis, 1:341–52. New York: New York University Press, 1991.

Grisez, Germain, John Finnis, and Joseph Boyle. "Practical Principles, Moral Truth, and Ultimate Ends." *American Journal of Jurisprudence* 32 (1987): 99–151; reprinted with table of contents in *Natural Law,* edited by John Finnis, 1:236–89. New York: New York University Press, 1991.

Grisez, Germain, and Joseph Boyle. *Life and Death with Liberty and Justice: A Contribution to the Euthanasia Debate.* South Bend, Ind.: University of Notre Dame Press, 1979.

Guttmann, Jakob. *Das Verhältnis des Thomas von Aquino zum Judenthum und zur jüdischen Litteratur.* Gottingen: Vandenhock und Ruprecht's Verlag, 1891.

Guttmann, M. "Maimonide sur l'universalite de la morale religieuse." *Revue d'etudes juives* 99 (1935): 33–43.

Hall, Pamela M. *Narrative and the Natural Law: An Interpretation of Thomistic Ethics.* South Bend, Ind.: University of Notre Dame Press, 1994.

Hart, H. L. A. *The Concept of Law.* Oxford, U.K.: Clarendon Press, 1961.

Hartman, David. *Maimonides: Torah and Philosophic Quest.* Philadelphia: Jewish Publication Society of America, 1976.

Hayen, André. "La structure de la Somme théologique et Jésus," *Sciences ecclésiastiques* 12 (1960): 59-82.

———. *Saint Thomas d'Aquin et la vie de l'Eglise*. Louvain: Publications universitaires, 1952.

Hervada, Javier. *Natural Right and Natural Law: A Critical Introduction*. Pamplona, Spain: Servicio de Publicationes de la Universidad de Navarra, 1990.

Higgins, Thomas J. *Man as Man: The Science and Art of Ethics*. Milwaukee, Wis.: Bruce, 1958.

Hill, William J. "Bañez and Bañezianism." In *The New Catholic Encylopedia*, 2:48–50. Washington, D.C.: The Catholic University of America Press, 1967.

———. *The Triune God*. Washington, D.C.: The Catholic University of America Press, 1982.

Hittinger, Russell. *A Critique of the New Natural Law Theory*. South Bend, Ind.: University of Notre Dame Press, 1987.

———. *The First Grace: Rediscovering the Natural Law in a Post-Christian World*. Wilmington, Del.: ISI Books, 2003.

———. "Liberalism and the American Natural Law Tradition." *Wake Forest Law Review* 25 (1990): 429–99.

———. "Natural Law and Catholic Moral Theology." In *A Preserving Grace: Protestants, Catholics, and Natural Law*, edited by Michael Cromartie, 1–30. Grand Rapids, Mich.: Eerdmans, 1997.

———. "Natural Law in the Positive Laws: A Legislative or Adjudicative Issue?" *Review of Politics* 55 (January 1993): 5–34.

———. "The Recovery of Natural Law and the Common Morality." *This World* 18 (Summer 1987): 62–74.

———. "Theology and Natural Law Theory." *Communio* 17 (Fall 1990): 402–8.

Hood, John. *Aquinas and the Jews*. Philadelphia: University of Pennsylvania Press, 1995.

Jaffa, Harry V. *The Crisis of the House Divided*. New York: Doubleday, 1959.

———. *Thomism and Aristotelianism: A Study of the Commentary by Thomas Aquinas on the Nicomachean Ethics*. Chicago: University of Chicago Press, 1952.

John Paul II. "Let Us Offer the World New Signs of Hope." *L'Osservatore Romano*, No. 8 (23 February 2000): 4.

———. "Message to Pontifical Academy of Sciences on Evolution." *Origins* 26, no. 25 (5 December 1996): 414–16.

Kant, Immanuel. *Critique of Pure Reason*. Translated by N. Kemp Smith. New York: Macmillan, 1929.

———. *Grounding for the Metaphysics of Morals*. Translated by James W. Ellington. Indianapolis, Ind.: Hackett, 1993.

———. *Religion within the Limits of Reason Alone*. Translated by T. H. Greene and H. H. Hudson. New York: Harper & Brothers, 1960.

Kantorowicz, Ernst H. *The King's Two Bodies: A Study in Mediaeval Political Theology.* Princeton, N.J.: Princeton University Press, 1957.
Kass, Leon R. *Toward a More Natural Science: Biology and Human Affairs.* New York: Free Press, 1985.
Kass, Leon R., and James Q. Wilson. *The Ethics of Human Cloning.* Washington, D.C.: AEI Press, 1998.
Kellner, Menachem. *Dogma in Medieval Jewish Thought.* Oxford, U.K.: Oxford University Press, 1986.
Kelsen, Hans. "The Natural-Law Doctrine before the Tribunal of Science." *Western Political Quarterly* 2 (December 1949): 481–513. Reprinted in *What Is Justice?: Justice, Law, and Politics in the Mirror of Science: Collected Essays by Hans Kelsen,* 137–73. Berkeley and Los Angeles: University of California Press, 1957.
Kendall, Willmoore, and George Carey. *Basic Symbols of the American Political Tradition.* Baton Rouge: Louisiana State University Press, 1970.
Kilpatrick, William Kirk. *Why Johnny Can't Tell Right from Wrong.* New York: Simon & Schuster, 1992.
Kristeller, Paul Oskar. *Le thomisme et la pensee italienne de renaissance.* Montreal: Vrin, 1967.
Lafont, Ghislain. *Structures et méthode dans la Somme théologique de Saint Thomas d'Aquin.* Reprinted with new preface. Paris: Les Editions du Cerf, 1996.
Latkovic, Mark S. *The Fundamental Moral Theology of Benedict Ashley, O.P.: A Critical Study. Toward a Response to the Second Vatican Council's Call for Renewal in Moral Theology.* Ann Arbor, Mich.: University Microfilms, 1998.
———. "Natural Law in the Moral Thought of Benedict Ashley, O.P." *Fellowship of Catholic Scholars Quarterly* 22 (Fall 1999): 2–5.
Lerner, Robert, Althea Nagai, and Stanley Rothman. *American Elites.* New Haven, Conn.: Yale University Press, 1996.
Levering, Matthew. "Israel and the Shape of Thomas Aquinas's Soteriology." *The Thomist* 63 (1999): 65–82.
Lippmann, Walter. *The Public Philosophy.* New York: Mentor, 1955.
Lisska, Anthony. *Aquinas's Theory of Natural Law.* Oxford, U.K.: Clarendon Press, 1996.
Lonergan, Bernard. *Insight.* New York: Harper & Row, 1978.
Long, Steven A. "Man's Natural End." *The Thomist* 64 (April 2000): 211–37.
———. "Providence, liberté et loi naturelle." *Revue thomiste* 102 (December 2002): 355–406.
———. "Reproductive Technology and the Natural Law." *National Catholic Bioethics Quarterly* 2 (Summer 2002): 221–28.
———. "St. Thomas Aquinas through the Analytic Looking-Glass." *The Thomist* 65 (April 2001): 259–300.
Luther, Martin. *De servo arbitrio.* In *Erasmus-Luther: Discourse on Free Will.* Translated by Ernst Winter. New York: Frederick Ungar, 1961.

MacIntyre, Alasdair. *After Virtue*. 2d ed. South Bend, Ind.: University of Notre Dame Press, 1984.
Maimonides, Moses. *The Guide of the Perplexed*. Translated by Shlomo Pines. Chicago: University of Chicago Press, 1963.
———. Introduction to Pirqei Avot. In *Ethical Writings of Maimonides,* edited by Raymond L. Weiss and Charles Butterworth, chap. 6, 59–95. New York: Dover, 1975.
Maimonides, Moses. *Mishneh Torah*. Translated in the Yale Judaica Series. New Haven, Conn.: Yale University Press, 1949–1972.
Maritain, Jacques. *An Essay on Christian Philosophy*. New York: Philosophical Library, 1955.
———. *Man and the State*. Chicago: University of Chicago Press, 1951.
———. *Science and Wisdom*. New York: Charles Scribner's Sons, 1940.
———. *The Sin of the Angels*. Westminster, Md.: Newman Press, 1959.
Marshner, William. "A Tale of Two Beatitudes." *Faith and Reason* 16, no. 2 (1990): 177–99.
Mathie, William. "Abortion and the Crisis of Liberal Justice." In *Life and Learning VIII,* edited by Joseph Koterski, 59–70. Washington, D.C.: University Faculty for Life, 1999.
———. "Reason, Revelation and Liberal Justice: Reflections on George Grant's Analysis of *Roe v. Wade.*" *Canadian Journal of Political Science* 19 (September 1986): 443–66.
———. "The Technological Regime: George Grant's Analysis of Modernity." In *George Grant in Process: Essays and Conversations,* edited by L. Schmidt, 157–66. Toronto: Anansi, 1978.
May, William. *An Introduction to Moral Theology*. Rev. ed. Huntington, Ind.: Our Sunday Visitor, 1994 [newly revised 2003].
———. "The Natural Law Doctrine of Suarez." *New Scholasticism* 58 (Autumn 1984): 409–23.
McBrien, Richard. *Catholicism*. 3d ed. San Francisco: Harper, 1994.
McDonald, Forrest. *Novus Ordo Seculorum*. Lawrence: University Press of Kansas, 1985.
McInerny, Ralph. *Aquinas on Human Action: A Theory of Practice*. Washington, D.C.: The Catholic University of America Press, 1992.
———. *Ethica Thomistica: The Moral Philosophy of Thomas Aquinas*. Washington, D.C.: The Catholic University of America Press, 1982; rev. ed., 1997.
———. "Portia's Lament: Reflections on Practical Reason." In *Natural Law and Moral Inquiry: Ethics, Metaphysics, and Politics in the Work of Germain Grisez,* edited by Robert P. George, 82–103. Washington, D.C.: Georgetown University Press, 1998.
———. "The Principles of Natural Law," *American Journal of Jurisprudence* 25 (1980): 1–15; reprinted in *Natural Law,* edited by John Finnis, 1:325–39. New York: New York University Press, 1991.

———. *The Question of Christian Ethics.* Washington, D.C.: The Catholic University of America Press, 1993.
Merriell, D. Juvenal. *To the Image of the Trinity: A Study in the Development of Aquinas's Teaching.* Toronto: Pontifical Institute of Mediaeval Studies, 1990.
Muncy, Mitchell, ed. *The End of Democracy I and II.* Dallas, Tex.: Spence, 1997, 1998.
Murray, John Courtney. *We Hold These Truths: Catholic Reflections on the American Proposition.* New York: Sheed & Ward, 1960.
Nelson, William. *The American Tory.* Boston: Beacon Press, 1964.
Neuhaus, Richard John, ed. *The End of Democracy?* Dallas, Tex.: Spence, 1997.
Nicolas, Jean-Hervé. *Synthèse dogmatique.* Fribourg: Editions Universitaires, 1986.
Novak, David. *Covenantal Rights.* Princeton, N.J.: Princeton University Press, 2000.
———. "Does Maimonides Have a Philosophy of History?" In *Studies in Jewish Philosophy,* edited by N. M. Samuelson, 397–420. Lanham, Md.: University Press of America, 1987.
———. *The Image of the Non-Jew in Judaism.* New York: Edwin Mellen Press, 1983.
———. *Jewish-Christian Dialogue.* New York: Oxford University Press, 1989.
———. *Maimonides on Judaism and Other Religions.* Cincinnati: Hebrew Union College Press, 1997.
———. *Natural Law in Judaism.* Cambridge, U.K.: Cambridge University Press, 1998.
———. "The Treatment of Muslims and Islam in the Legal Writings of Maimonides." In *Studies in Islamic and Jewish Traditions,* edited by W. M. Brinner and S. D. Ricks, 233–50. Chico, Calif.: Scholars Press, 1986.
———. *The Theology of Nahmanides Systematically Presented.* Atlanta, Ga.: Scholars Press, 1992.
Oberman, Heiko. *The Harvest of Medieval Theology: Gabriel Biel and Late Medieval Nominalism.* Cambridge, Mass.: Harvard University Press, 1963.
O'Callaghan, John, and Thomas J. Hibbs, eds. *Recovering Nature: Essays in Natural Philosophy, Ethics, and Metaphysics in Honor of Ralph McInerny.* South Bend, Ind.: University of Notre Dame Press, 1999.
O'Donoghue, D. "The Thomist Concept of the Natural Law." *Irish Theological Quarterly* 22 (1955): 89–109.
Penrose, Roger. *The Emperor's New Mind: Concerning Computers, Minds, and the Laws of Physics.* New York: Viking-Penguin, 1990.
Pines, Shlomo. "Translators Introduction: The Philosophic Sources of *The Guide of the Perplexed.*" In Moses Maimonides, *The Guide of the Perplexed.* Translated by Shlomo Pines, lvii–cxxxiv. Chicago: University of Chicago Press, 1963.
Porter, Jean. "Basic Goods and the Human Good in Recent Catholic Moral Theology." *The Thomist* 47 (1993): 27–41.
Prouvost, Géry, ed. *Etienne Gilson-Jacques Maritain: Correspondence 1923–1971.* Paris: Vrin, 1991.

Ratzinger, Joseph Cardinal. *Salt of the Earth.* San Francisco: Ignatius Press, 1997.
Rawls, John. *Political Liberalism.* New York: Columbia University Press, 1996.
———. *A Theory of Justice.* Rev. ed. Cambridge, Mass.: Harvard University Press, 1999.
Raz, Joseph. *Practical Reason and Norms.* 2d ed. Princeton, N.J.: Princeton University Press, 1990.
Reed, John J. "Natural Law, Theology and the Church." *Theological Studies* 26 (1965): 40–64.
Rehnquist, William. "The Notion of a Living Constitution" *Texas Law Review* 54 (1976): 693–706.
Rhonheimer, Martin. *Natur als Grundlage der Moral: Eine Auseinandersetzung mit autonomer und teleologisher Ethik.* Tyrolia: Verlag, 1987. English translation by Gerald Malsbary, *Natural Law and Practical Reason: A Thomist View of Moral Autonomy.* New York: Fordham University Press, 2000.
Rogers, Eugene F. Jr. *Thomas Aquinas and Karl Barth.* South Bend, Ind.: University of Notre Dame Press, 1995.
Rondet, Henri. "Bulletin de théologie historique: Etudes médiévales." *Recherches de science religieuse* 38 (1951): 138–60.
Sandel, Michael. *Democracy's Discontent.* Cambridge, Mass.: Harvard University Press, 1996.
Sarachek, J. *The Conflict over the Rationalism of Maimonides.* New York: Hermon Press, 1970.
Segerstrale, Ullica. *Defenders of the Truth: The Battle for Science in the Sociobiology Debate and Beyond.* New York: Oxford University Press, 2000.
Sheerin, F. L. "Molinism." In *The New Catholic Encylopedia,* 9:1011–13. Washington, D.C.: The Catholic University of America Press, 1967.
Sherwin-White, A. N. *Roman Law and Roman Society in the New Testament.* Oxford, U.K.: Oxford University Press, 1969. Reprint, Grand Rapids, Mich.: Baker Book House, 1978.
Simon, Yves. *The Philosophy of Democratic Government.* Chicago: University of Chicago Press, 1951.
———. *Practical Knowledge.* New York: Fordham University Press, 1991.
———. *The Tradition of Natural Law.* Edited by Vukan Kuic. New York: Fordham University Press, 1992.
Story, Joseph. *Commentaries on the Constitution of the United States.* Durham, N.C.: Carolina Academic Press, 1987.
———. "Natural Law." In *Encyclopedia Americana,* ed. Francis Lieber, 9:150–58.
Strauss, Leo. *Natural Right and History.* Chicago: University of Chicago Press, 1953.
———. "On Natural Law." In *Studies in Platonic Political Philosophy,* 137–46. Chicago: University of Chicago Press, 1983.
———. *Persecution and the Art of Writing.* Chicago: University of Chicago Press, 1988.

Tattersall, Ian. *Becoming Human: Evolution and Human Uniqueness*. New York: Harcourt Brace, 1998.
Twersky, I. *The Code of Maimonides*. New Haven, Conn.: Yale University Press, 1980.
Ullman-Margalit, Edna. *The Emergence of Norms*. Oxford, U.K.: Clarendon Press, 1977.
Vattel, Emerich. *The Law of Nations; or, Principles of the Law of Nature*. T and W. J. Johnson, 1883.
Veatch, Henry. *For an Ontology of Morals: A Critique of Contemporary Ethical Theory*. Evanston: Northwestern University Press, 1971.
von Balthasar, Hans Urs. "Nine Theses in Christian Ethics." In *International Theological Commission: Texts and Documents 1969–1985*, edited by Michael Sharkey, 105–28. San Francisco: Ignatius Press, 1989.
Weigel, George. *Witness to Hope*. New York: Cliff Street Books, 1999.
Weinreb, Lloyd L. *Natural Law and Justice*. Cambridge, Mass.: Harvard University Press, 1987.
Weiss, Raymond L. *Maimonides' Ethics: The Encounter of Philosophic and Religious Morality*. Chicago: University of Chicago Press, 1991.
West, Thomas. "Vindicating John Locke: How a Seventeenth-Century 'Liberal' Was Really a 'Social Conservative'" *Family Research Council Witherspoon Lecture* (23 February 2001).
Westberg, Daniel. *Right Practical Reason*. Oxford, U.K.: Clarendon Press, 1994.
———. "Thomistic Law and the Moral Theory of Richard Hooker." *American Catholic Philosophical Quarterly* 68 (1994): 203–14.
Wojtyla, Karol. *Love and Responsibility*. Translated by H. T. Willetts. New York: Farrar, Straus, Giroux, 1981.
Wolfe, Alan. *One Nation, After All*. New York: Viking Press, 1998.
Wolfe, Christopher. "Issues Facing Contemporary American Public Philosophy." In *Public Morality, Civic Virtue, and the Problem of Modern Liberalism*, edited by T. William Boxx and Gary M. Quinlivan, 171–214. Grand Rapids, Mich.: Eerdmans, 2000.
———. "Natural Law and Judicial Review." In *Natural Law and Contemporary Public Policy*, edited by David Forte, 157–89. Washington, D.C.: Georgetown University Press, 1998.
———. "Public Morality and the Modern Supreme Court." *American Journal of Jurisprudence* 45 (2000): 65–92.
———. Review of *The Natural Rights Republic*, by Michael Zuckert (South Bend, Ind.: University of Notre Dame Press, 1996). *First Things* 83 (May 1998): 52–56.
Wolfe, Christopher, and John Hittinger, eds. *Liberalism at the Crossroads*. Lanham, Md.: Rowman & Littlefield, 1994.
Wolfson, Harry A. *Spinoza*. Cambridge, Mass.: Harvard University Press, 1934.
Wroe, Ann. *Pilate*. London: Random House, 2000.

Yaffe, Martin D. "Interpretive Essay." In Thomas Aquinas, *The Literal Exposition on Job: A Scriptural Commentary Concerning Providence,* 1–65. Translated by A. Damico. Atlanta, Ga.: Scholars Press, 1989.

———. "Myth and 'Science' in Aristotle's Theology." *Man and World* 12 (1979): 70–88.

———. Review of *Aquinas and the Jews* by John Hood (Philadelphia: University of Pennsylvania Press, 1995). *Association for Jewish Studies Review* 22 (1997): 122–25.

Zuckert, Michael. *Natural Rights and the New Republicanism.* Princeton, N.J.: Princeton University Press, 1994.

———. *The Natural Rights Republic.* South Bend, Ind.: University of Notre Dame Press, 1996.

INDEX

Abortion, 21, 89, 89n, 114, 127, 220, 222–24, 226–27, 235 240n, 283
American natural law tradition, xx–xxi, 197–98, 205–12, 214, 223n, 230–233
Aristotle, xi–xiii, 8, 10, 18, 19–22, 25–39, 44, 46, 47n, 57, 60n, 67, 68–72, 148, 186, 198, 232, 241, 245, 29n, 261
Ashley, Benedict, x–xi, xviii, 17, 20, 22, 113–14, 121–129, 135, 142, 150–52, 157–60, 162
Assisted suicide, 114, 160, 222
Augustine, 59, 81n, 90, 91, 193, 199, 253–54, 256, 267, 281
Autonomy, xix, 86–87, 88–89, 108, 132n, 167, 177n, 178n, 192. *See also* Freedom

Basic human goods, xviii–xix, 143–50, 163; hierarchy of, xix, 116, 125–26, 128, 130, 135–39, 141–42, 150, 159, 174, 185–86, 188, 191; incommensurability of, 150, 152, 166, 174, 185–86, 190
Boyle, Joseph, xviii, 113, 142–56, 252n

Cajetan, Cardinal, 27, 29–30
Chenu, Marie-Dominique, xvii, 102–7
Christ, 32, 45, 51, 59–60, 62, 262, 272; as concrete norm, xv–xvii, 90–93, 106–7; divine wisdom and, xv–xvii, 80–87, 96–97, 102–4; divinity of, xv, xvii, 80, 81, 104–6; humanity of, xvii, 104, 106–7; preeminence of, xvi, 96–97
Christian philosophy, 27–28
Common good, xxii, 89, 98, 126, 134, 166, 189n, 197–98, 230, 238, 249–51, 255, 257, 264, 276, 281–83
Conscience, xxii, 127n, 143, 150, 153, 208, 254–55, 257, 268, 278, 281

Constitution of the United States, xx, 73, 205–7, 211, 217–18, 219n, 221–23, 230–33, 276
Contraception, 23, 142, 216, 221, 223, 225

Decalogue, 21, 59, 77, 99, 118, 136–37, 141, 146, 160, 162, 282
Declaration of Independence, 66, 73, 205, 214, 235, 236
de Lubac, Henri, 29–30, 187
de Tocqueville, Alexis, 209, 215
Divine positive law, 61, 63, 99, 199, 282–83
Divorce, 23, 208, 224

Ends: hierarchy of, xviii, xix, 13, 89, 116, 126–28, 130, 135, 139–42, 148, 150, 159, 167, 174, 188, 191; natural order of, 173–74, 185–91. *See also* Ultimate end
English common law, 207–9
Eternal law, xv–xvi, 45, 80–85, 93, 94, 184–85, 199–200, 266–67; natural law as participation in, xiii, xviii–xx, 35, 74, 89, 108, 114, 116, 119, 122, 132–33, 166, 167n, 177n, 179, 185, 189, 191, 200, 242–43, 265–66; passive participation in, 119, 178n, 188–90

Fact-value, 148–50
Final end. *See* Ultimate end
Finnis, John, ix, x, xviii, xix, 79, 113, 142–56, 157, 160–61, 165n, 167n, 168, 175, 177n, 191n, 216, 227, 241n, 242n, 244n, 249n, 257, 258
Freedom: as indifference to divine causality, xix, 176–77, 178n, 181, 184; as indifference to finite goods, 181–83; subject to divine providence, xix, 74, 86–87, 167, 178–82, 184, 191. *See also* Autonomy

George, Robert, 79, 113, 143n, 171n, 216, 223, 227
Gilson, Ettiene, xviii, 27–30, 103–4, 192
Grace as perfection of nature, xiv, 37, 47, 58n, 77, 85, 95, 99–100, 173n, 189n
Grisez, Germain, x, xviii–xx, 45, 113–14, 138, 142–56, 157–63, 165, 216, 239, 244n

Hall, Pamela, xviii, 113–21, 127–29, 133, 135, 142, 146–47, 157–59, 162
Happiness, xi–xii, xiv, 12–16, 22, 33, 68, 75, 91, 122. *See also* Integral human fulfillment
Hegel, Georg Wilheml Friedrich, 38, 237, 252n
Hittinger, Russell, xviii, 79, 142, 216, 219, 223
Hobbes, Thomas, 202–4, 231–32, 237, 253
Homosexual rights, 17, 71n, 220, 222–25
Human law, xxiii, 45, 61, 89n, 108, 199, 238n, 252, 254, 272–74, 277, 284
Human nature, xi, xv, 4–6, 7–11, 12–15, 20, 46, 53–54, 56, 65, 74, 83, 85, 104, 108, 123–25, 134, 147–49, 151, 158, 168, 171, 175, 186, 202–3, 239–40, 243–45, 247–48, 266n
Hume, David, 245–46

Imago Dei, 83n, 88, 90n, 242
Incarnation, xvi, 81–83, 94, 96–97, 101n, 103–4, 106
Integral human fulfillment, 144–46, 150, 153, 162. *See also* Happiness
Is-ought, 148–50

John Paul II, ix, 9, 15n, 37, 81n, 89n, 93, 185, 215
Judge and/or judging, xx, xxii–xxiii, 217–19, 221–22, 223–24, 251n, 254, 255–56, 261–84
Justice, xxii, 20, 22, 61, 68, 86, 89, 98, 114, 143, 154, 161, 177n, 205, 208, 235, 238, 250, 254, 255–56, 258, 262–63, 273–76, 278, 284

Kabbalists, xiv, 64–65
Kant, Immanuel, xxii, xx, 47, 60, 67, 109, 131n, 166, 177n, 186–87, 190, 192–93, 202, 204, 219, 237, 252n
Kelsen, Hans, 237–50

Latkovic, Mark, 121–25
Legislator and/or legislation, xxiii, 63, 240, 246, 250, 251n, 252, 262–65, 271, 272–73, 275–76, 280, 283–84
Leo XIII, 27, 37, 215

Liberalism, 204, 213, 215, 219–20, 222–23, 234–35
Lincoln, Abraham, xxi, 235–36
Locke, John, xxi, 73, 203–9, 213, 229, 231–34

Maimonides, Moses, xiii–xv; and Mosaic law, 51, 52–53, 57, 63; and natural law teaching, 48–56, 62–71, 74–75; and Noahide law, 50–52, 56–57; rationalistic tendencies, xiv, 49, 75
Maritain, Jacques, xii, 27–29, 157, 167n, 212
Marriage, 17, 23, 70, 114, 123, 137, 141–42, 208, 221, 225–26
Modes of responsibility, 144, 146, 153, 162–63
Molina, Luis de, 91, 100, 179–80
Murder, 21, 71, 74, 117–18, 121, 137, 204, 249–50, 280

Natural inclinations, 115–17, 120–21, 133–35, 138–40, 158, 165, 171, 175, 184, 186, 200, 239n
Natural law: and divine law, xiv, 43–65, 108, 296; and divine providence, ix, xii, xx, 74, 84, 88, 167; first principles of, xi–xii, xviii, 75, 122, 126, 130, 136–38, 157–63; knowledge of, xix, 76–77, 117, 123–25, 167, 228; metaphysical ground of, ix, xiii–xv, xix–xx, 55–56, 70, 74–77, 165–66, 178n, 185–87, 192–93; and the Old Law, 45–46, 58n, 77, 117, 119, 201n; as participation in eternal law, xiv, xviii–xx, 35, 74, 108, 116, 166, 167n, 177n, 179, 191, 242–43; precepts of, xi, 14, 35, 61, 116–18, 121, 126, 130, 133–41, 159–63, 166, 201n, 239, 268; specific moral norms and, 136–37; theonomic conceptions of, xix, 167, 184, 192
Natural right tradition, xx–xxi, 46, 153–54, 199, 202–6, 208–9, 212, 219, 231
New Law, xiv, 45, 57–58, 63, 72, 90–91, 108, 165–67
New natural law theory, x, xviii–xix, 142–44, 147–50, 152, 154, 166–67, 170, 172, 174, 177, 185–87, 190–91, 193, 217, 246n

Old Law, xiv, 45–46, 57–60, 63, 72, 76–77, 90, 117–19, 201n

Plato, xiv, 8, 13, 47, 55, 67–69, 72, 103, 105–6, 193, 199
Practical reason, xviii–xix, 35, 37, 44, 52, 84n, 117, 119–20, 130, 135n, 143, 151–54,